the bloomsbury reader in the study of myth

Also available from Bloomsbury:

A Beginner's Guide to the Study of Religion, Bradley L. Herling

The Bloomsbury Reader in Cultural Approaches to the Study of Religion, edited by Sarah J. Bloesch and Meredith Minister

The Bloomsbury Reader in Religion, Sexuality, and Gender, edited by Donald L. Boisvert and Carly Daniel-Hughes

the bloomsbury reader in the study of myth

Edited by Jonathan Miles-Watson and Vivian Asimos

BLOOMSBURY ACADEMIC
LONDON · NEW YORK · OXFORD · NEW DELHI · SYDNEY

BLOOMSBURY ACADEMIC
Bloomsbury Publishing Plc
50 Bedford Square, London, WC1B 3DP, UK
1385 Broadway, New York, NY 10018, USA

BLOOMSBURY, BLOOMSBURY ACADEMIC and the Diana logo are trademarks of
Bloomsbury Publishing Plc

First published in Great Britain 2019

Cover design by Maria Rajka
Cover image: Jain Purushkara Yantra, circa 1780 © Universal Art Archive / Alamy Stock Photo

A catalogue record for this book is available from the British Library.

A catalog record for this book is available from the Library of Congress.

ISBN: HB: 978-1-3500-8224-3
        PB: 978-1-3500-8225-0
        ePDF: 978-1-3500-8226-7
        eBook: 978-1-3500-8227-4

Typeset by Integra Software Services Pvt. Ltd.
Printed and bound in Great Britain

To find out more about our authors and books visit www.bloomsbury.com
and sign up for our newsletters.

Contents

Copyright acknowledgements

We are grateful to the following sources for permission to reproduce in this book material previously published elsewhere. We have made every effort to secure the permission of relevant parties, but if we have inadvertently missed any relevant permissions then we will move to rectify this at the earliest opportunity.

Part 1

Section A

1) Excerpt from C. Scott Littleton (1965), 'A Two-Dimensional Scheme for the Classification of Narratives.' *Journal of American Folklore* 78 (307): pp. 21–27. Reprinted with the permission of the American Folklore Society. doi:10.2307/538100.

2) Excerpt from Daniel Ben-Amos (1983), 'The Idea of Folklore: An Essay.' *In Fields of Offerings: Studies in Honor of Raphael Patai*, ed. Vincent Sanua. Madison: Fairleigh Dickinson University Press, pp. 57–63. Reprinted with permission from Associated University Presses.

3) Excerpt from Bronislaw Malinowski (2011), *Myth in Primitive Psychology*. New York: W.W. Norton & Company, Inc, pp. 100–146.

Part 2

Section A

1) Excerpt from James George Frazer (1990), *The Golden Bough*. London: Palgrave Macmillan, pp. 658–667.

2) Excerpt from Otto Rank (2004), translated by Gregory C. Richter and E. James Liberman. *The Myth of the Birth of the Hero: A Psychological Exploration of Myth*. Baltimore: Johns Hopkins University Press, pp. 47–92. Reprinted with permission of Johns Hopkins University Press.

3) Excerpt from Joseph Campbell (1959), 'The Historical Development of Mythology.' *Daedalus 88* (2): pp. 232–254. Reprinted with permission from MIT Press Journals.

Section B

1) Excerpt from Carl Gustav Jung (1978), 'UFOs as Rumours.' In *Flying Saucers: A Modern Myth of Things Seen in the Skies*. Princeton: Princeton University Press, pp. 8–23. Reprinted with permission from Princeton University Press and Taylor & Francis Group.

2) Excerpt from Alan Dundes (1998), 'The Vampire as Bloodthirsty Revenant: A Psychoanalytic Post Mortem.' In *The Vampire: A Casebook*, ed. Alan Dundes. Madison: Board of Regents of the University of Wisconsin System. Reprinted by permission of The University of Wisconsin Press.

3) Excerpt from Amba J. Sepie (2017), 'More than Stories, More than Myths: Animal/Human/Nature(s) in Traditional Ecological Worldviews.' *Humanities* 6 (4): p. 78. Reprinted under Creative Commons Licence 4.0.

Section C

1) Excerpt from Mircea Eliade (1968), 'The Structure of Myths.' In *Myth and Reality*, New York: Harper & Row, pp. 1–20. Reprinted with permission by Harper Collins.

2) Excerpt from Friedrich Max Müller (1856), *Comparative Mythology*. Routledge, pp. 103–116.

3) Excerpt from Nick Allen (2000), 'Cúchulainn's Women and Some Indo-European Comparisons.' *Emania* 18: pp. 57–64. Reprinted with permission by Nick Allen.

Part 3

Section A

1) Excerpt from Claude Lévi-Strauss (1995), 'Jewels and Wounds.' In *The Story of the Lynx*. University of Chicago Press, pp. 95–106. Reprinted with permission of author's estate.

2) Excerpt from Edmund Leach (1962), 'Pulleyar and the Lord Buddha: An Aspect of Religious Syncretism in Ceylon.' *The Psychoanalytic Review* 49 (2): pp. 81–103. Reprinted with permission of Guilford Publications Inc.

3) Excerpt from Manuel Aguirre (2011), 'An Outline of Propp's Model for the Study of Wondertales,' *Northanger Library Project*. Reprinted with permission of Manuel Aguirre.

Section B

1) Excerpt from Seth Kunin (2004), *We Think What We Eat*, London: Bloomsbury. Reprinted with permission of Bloomsbury.

2) Excerpt from Stephen Hugh-Jones (1988), 'The Gun and the Bow: Myths of White Men and Indians.' *L'Homme* 28 (106/107), pp. 138–155. Reprinted with permission of Stephen Hugh-Jones.

3) Excerpt from Mary Douglas (1967), 'The Meaning of Myth, with Special Reference to "La Geste d'Asdiwal".' In *The Structural Study of Myth and Totemism*, ed. Edmund Leach. Edinburgh: Association of Social Anthropologists of the Commonwealth, pp. 49–70. Reprinted with permission by Association of Social Anthropologists of the Commonwealth.

Section C

1) Excerpt from Frances Harwood (1976), 'Myth, Memory, and the Oral Tradition: Cicero in the Trobiands.' *American Anthropologist,* New Series 78 (4), pp. 783–796. Reprinted with permission from the American Anthropological Association.

2) Excerpt from Jonathan Miles-Watson (2012), 'The Cathedral on the Ridge and the Implicit Mythology of the Shimla Hills.' *Suomen Antropologi: Journal of the Finnish Anthropological Society* 37 (4), pp. 30–46. Reprinted with permission from Jonathan Miles-Watson.

3) Excerpts from Miriam Kahn (1990), 'Stone-faced Ancestors: The Spatial Anchoring of Myth in Wamira, Papua New Guinea.' *Ethnology* 29 (1), pp. 51–66. Reprinted with permission from Ethnology at the University of Pittsburgh.

Part 4

Section A

1) Excerpt from Ika Willis (2016), 'Amateur Mythographies: Fan Fiction and the Myth of Myth.' In 'The Classical Canon and/as Transformative Work,' edited by Ika Willis, special issue, *Transformative Works and Cultures*, no. 21. doi: 0.3983/twc.2016.0692. Reprinted with permission of Transformative Works and Cultures.

2) Excerpt from Lauren Dundes, Madeline Streiff and Zachary Streiff (2018), 'Storm Power, an Icy Tower and Elsa's Bower: The Winds of Change in Disney's Frozen.' *Social Science* 7 (6): p. 86. Reprinted under Creative Commons License 4.0.

3) Excerpt from Marilyn Sutton and Thomas Sutton (1969), 'Science Fiction as Mythology,' *Western Folklore* 28 (4): pp. 230–237. Reprinted with permission Western Folklore.

Section B

1) Excerpt from Robert Segal (1996), 'Does Myth Have a Future?' In *Myth and Method*, eds. Laurie L. Patton and Wendy Doniger. Charlottesville: University Press of Virginia, pp. 82–106.

Acknowledgements

We would like to thank the successive classes of students in our *Myth and Meaning* modules at Durham University (UK) and Luther College (USA), who have helped to refine the selection of this material through their comments on (and engagement with) the wide range of mythographers that we have presented them with over the years. We are particularly grateful to Sarah Eitrheim who during her time as a John Jay Research Fellow was involved in early conversations about this Reader. Thanks are also due to the many publishing agents who have helped to facilitate the publication of this book, but especially Lalle and Lucy (at Bloomsbury) who have guided us surefootedly through this process. We are extremely grateful to the five anonymous reviewers, who both encouraged the publication of this work and whose guidance helped further sharpen the shape and content of the volume. Finally, we would like to thank our friends and family for their support and patience throughout this project.

In search of mythology: Introduction

The readings that we have collected together in this book demonstrate both the depth of tradition and the extent of recent innovation that exists in the study of mythology. The academic exploration of mythology has been a cornerstone of a range of nested disciplines (anthropology, classics, literary studies and religious studies) since their foundation. These disciplines continue to produce important reflections on (and analyses of) mythology. However, they have been joined in recent years by insightful work coming from the newer disciplines of cultural studies and media studies. Despite the centrality of mythology to all these disciplines, the study of mythology remains divisive, with little agreement about either the substance of mythology or its function. In this book we aim to introduce the reader to these lively, interdisciplinary debates, and we have deliberately chosen to showcase a range of established and emerging voices. It is hoped that through direct engagement with the full range of insight that these diverse thinkers represent the reader will be given a firm foundation for further exploration, reflection and analysis.

Outline of the book

This Reader is organized thematically and follows the track for understanding mythology that we have found most successful as a way of introducing this material to undergraduate students. Therefore, while it is not necessary to follow the readings in the order that they are presented here, the Reader has been deliberately constructed to give the material a sense of development and flow. This book is organized into four main parts, which cluster readings around the central questions of the origin, form, function and future of mythology. These large sections of the book are further divided into groups of three readings, which all cluster around a unifying topic (such as dreams, history or place), often providing competing approaches or interpretations to a single issue. It is hoped that by placing these readings in conversation with each other, the book will provide a rich, textured introduction to these topics. To help facilitate this, the Reader provides section introductions that frame the debate and link it to wider ideas or issues that are found both elsewhere in the book and beyond its pages. It is, however, possible to either engage with the readings in isolation or to profitably compare material across sections. To aid in these processes, we have provided both a brief introductory note to each individual reading and (in this general introduction) an outline of the overall themes, topics and concerns of this Reader.

The first part of the Reader explores the important area of definitions. As such it flows naturally from this introduction's attempt to locate mythology, both clearing the way for the subsequent sections and consolidating an understanding of the difference between an academic approach to mythology and popular conceptions. The first chapter in this section contains a sample of Littleton's (now-classic) classification of myth, legend and folklore. This chapter is followed by Ben-Amos's essay 'The Idea of Folklore', which calls into question the distinctions made in the previous chapter and provides an important alternative source of definitions for students to engage with. The final chapter of this first section is Malinowski's often-parodied definition of myth, which takes the discussion in a radically different direction and raises the important question of the relationship between myth and society. This reading is far richer than textbook summaries would allow and provides a good foundation for the later sections of this Reader. The first section therefore begins with classic typologies and ends with questions that will help students think critically about the readings that follow.

The second part of the Reader groups together theorists who try to locate an origin for myth that, in part, explains the apparent similarity of geographically and temporally distant material. The first section of this part explores theories that either find the origin of myth's repeating patterns in sacred actions, sacralized profane action or some combination of the two. It presents selections from the classic, global, theories of myth that are found in the writings of James Frazer, Otto Rank and (in a rather different form) Joseph Campbell. Here the two heroes' journeys unite with the sacrificial priest to initiate the reader into the cultic milieu of universalist thought. Section B of Part Two moves to explore further the way that myth bridges inner and outer worlds, collective experience and individual psyche, through a focus on the relation between myth and dreams. Jung's contribution on UFOs retains its relevance, despite its age, and this pairs well with Sepie's article, which both demonstrates the truly excellent material that is currently produced at the cutting edge of mythography and interrogates many of the core conceits of the earlier material. The second part ends with a section that explores theorists who either understand history as the antithesis, or the seed of myth. These include Mircea Eliade, Max Müller and Nicholas Allen. The arguments presented here centre around broader issues (truth and falsehood, identity and cultural heritage) and are of the utmost relevance to today's students, despite the apparent generation gap.

The third part of the book switches the debate to explore structuralism, neostructuralism and those spatial theories that are largely built upon the former work. It opens with an important and concise demonstration of the structuralist technique by Lévi-Strauss, which is followed by an example of how structuralism can be adopted to engage with functionalist and Freudian theories, provided by Edmund Leach, before the section is rounded out with a wonderfully concise summary, by Aguirre, of Proppian Structuralism. Section B of this part complicates the Straussian approach further; Stephen Hugh-Jones develops significantly the concepts of implicit mythology, the relevance of ritual to structuralism and the importance of participant observation for structuralist analysis. Mary Douglas's essay questions Lévi-Strauss's approach, while also pointing out some of its more positive aspects. Finally, the work that we have selected by Seth Kunin operates to both integrate the material that surrounds it and clearly outline the scope (and process) of the neostructuralist project.

The last section of Part Three focuses on the often-overlooked spatial theories of myth, starting with Frances Harwood's detailed exploration of the spatial elements of myth in the Trobriands, which also serves to return us to Malinowski. The next reading presents Jonathan Miles-Watson's spatial analysis of Himalayan mythology as a way of demonstrating how Lévi-Strauss's theory of implicit mythology can be used to build a powerful technique for the analysis of postcolonial, urban societies. The section ends with Miriam Khan's work on the importance of paying attention to stones for the interpretation of mythology in Papua New Guinea. Collectively, these works develop the nascent spatial elements of the previous contributions and explore the importance of myth for understanding how we make ourselves at home in the world.

The fourth and final part of the Reader asks the important question of where myths are going. The first section focuses on myths and popular culture, and helps demonstrate how myth is used, as well as how mythography can be applied, to familiar aspects of the modern world. In this section we explore the relation of mythology (and myth analysis) to Disney princesses (Dundes et al.), science fiction (Suttons) and fan fiction (Willes). The last section of the Reader gives the editors the opportunity to outline their understanding on the future of mythology before concluding with Robert Segal's highly informed exploration of the likely outcome for the future of mythology, which is based upon the theoretical presuppositions of several of the key thinkers that are found in earlier sections of this work. This final section therefore returns us back to the core themes that began (and run throughout) this book – themes that are built upon the tensions that bind together different understandings of mythology's form, function and veracity.

Myth and truth?

The problems surrounding the general interpretation of myth are encapsulated by the way, at a recent Sociology conference, a highly respected (and well-known) academic casually defined myth as any widely held delusional belief. This definition has the merit of being relatively open ended; however, this Western, commonsense, understanding of mythology runs counter to many academic definitions and is a highly problematic approach to the term. It is, nevertheless, part of a persistent tradition of ethnocentric classificatory systems, which famously found articulation in the writings of Tylor (1871: 286–287) and can still be found in twenty-first-century academic explorations of myth (cf Cunliffe 2001: 7). Tylor's approach to myth was a reaction against the trend of his time, which was to view myths as primarily relating events that are intended to be allegorical (Segal 1999: 10). He was therefore keen to argue that for certain people, myths were as real as science was for his audience. He suggested that myth is, in fact, a kind of precursor to science, a sort of imperfect logic, which seeks to explain events that occur in the physical world (Tylor 1871: 286–287). The Tylorian definition of myth, as a faulty form of science, slides easily into the colloquial understanding of myth as falsehood, and both are problematic because of their ethnocentric assumption of a qualitative difference between the interpreter and the interpretation, which in turn creates a category of a human (the native and/or the child) whose engagement with the world is somehow lacking.

The understanding that mythology is other people's science is regularly bound up with the suggestion of it as other people's history. By which, it is usually implied that myth is a more limited way of understanding the past than history. It is common to find newspaper articles, shows and conversations that revolve around discovering if a well-known event actually occurred in history, if it is merely myth or some combination of the two. This approach is, in turn, tied to the appealing, if limiting, suggestion that myth may lead us towards true historical discoveries. A good example of this is the now-notorious, yet widely digested television shows and publications of Graham Hancock (see, for example, Hancock 2012).

Although it is possible to find the crude myth/history division of popular speech in academic publications, the relationship between myth and history has tended to be more carefully considered in the academic arena than it is in the popularist material that we have explored so far. We see this in the phenomenological thought of Eliade, who brings the categories of myth and history into his famous sacred/ profane opposition (cf Eliade, Part Two, Section B, Chapter 1). For Eliade, myth 'narrates a sacred history, an event that took place in primordial time ... [It contains] Supernatural Beings who do not belong to the everyday world ... [and] is always an account of creation of one sort or another' (1963: 5–6). Encapsulated in this sentence is Eliade's concept of (and subsequent approach to) myth, which is opposed to more linear, profane, views of history. This idea of myth as a sacred and participative act of collective remembrance has resonances with Lévi-Strauss's understanding of Amazonian myth's ability to ameliorate the traumas of history through an emphasis on continuity (Lévi-Strauss and Charbonnier 1969: 33–39). In contrast, Western mythology (read history) celebrates historical rupture as a series of linear steps in a process of cultural evolution (cf Lévi-Strauss, Part Three, Section A, Chapter 1 and Hugh-Jones, Part Three, Section B, Chapter 2).

An alternative approach has been taken by a number of comparative mythographers (Müller 1897; Dumézil 1988; MacCana 1997; et al.), who have viewed recorded mythology as source material in the quest to recover a forgotten history. In the famous Indo-European approach, extant mythology from across India and Europe is employed as a gateway to understanding, or (re)constructing, the now lost culture of a postulated ancient race (known as the Aryans). The existence of a single proto Indo-European culture is far from certain and based primarily on linguistic similarities that spread throughout India and Europe, which can be taken as a purely linguistic relationship (cf Allen, Part Two, Section C, Chapter 3) but can also be viewed as the result of a historical relationship. From here, it is but a small step to the suggestion that just as traces of Aryan language survive in modern languages, so too traces of their mythology survive in modern myth and ritual (cf Müller, Part Two, Section C, Chapter 1). Scanning through mythology, across huge expanses of space and time, these mythographers were able to find affinities in the material (sometimes with the benefit of considerable reinterpretation of the source material). However, there are significant problems with this fundamental model, foremost of which is that, with a data pool so large and a little ingenuity, it is possible to find any pattern desired if you look hard enough. More worryingly, the preoccupation with reconstructing a system of a hypothetical lost people, at times, blinds these analysts to a subtle understanding of the mythology's host culture. While in its later incarnations, the comparative approach is made into a strength, in the vast majority of Indo-European analyses, it is a clear weakness.

For all its ingenuity, Frazer's understanding of myth (cf Frazer, Part Two, Section A, Chapter 1), as a form of ritual explanation, is liable to the same 'cherry-picking' allegations as Müller. Indeed, Frazer's attempt to solve the mystery of the murder of the priest at Lake Nemi prompts him to range freely through space and time, in an effort to reconstruct a lost central pattern of purportedly (almost) universal significance. Similarly, Campbell's suggestion that myth speaks to a universal pattern of loss, gain and return rests on a reductionist technique (cf Campbell, Part Two, Section A, Chapter 3). For Campbell, myth is a metaphorical/poetical insight into the ultimate truth (Campbell and Moyers 2011). This is an extreme version of the classical psychiatric approach to mythology that sees it as a reflection of inner processes (cf Jung, Part Two, Section B, Chapter 1 and Dundes, Part Two, Section B, Chapter 2). The psychiatric argument is based upon the belief that myth is a form of psychological therapy, which allows for the public outworking of universal, personal, psychological problems. This notion is encapsulated by Jung in the *Psychology of Child Archetype*, where he writes that 'myths are original revelations of the preconscious psyche, involuntary statements about unconscious psychic happenings, and anything but allegories of physical processes' (2002: 87). Jung here implies that the analysis techniques of both Tylor and Frazer have made the mistake of taking the content of myth far too literally and have consequently missed the symbolic relation of myth to the preconscious.

The definition of myth is seemingly more open ended than Tylor's definition, for, in this understanding, myth relates to a broader range of material (not simply nature), without the need for a violent reconstruction, such as that which Frazer and Müller impose on the material. As Kunin (2003: 15) has pointed out, if the psychological approaches were content to suggest that myth is an outward expression of psychological issues, the model would be at least plausible; however, in stating that there is a common content of those unconscious or preconscious issues, the approaches fall into the same trap of universalism that Frazer does. Indeed, we would want to push this concern even further than Kunin does to suggest that the Cartesian notion of inward and outward worlds, which lies behind the psychological model, is not only ethnocentric but also inaccurate (see, for example, Ingold 2000: 157–172).

Myth and society

Myth is tied more concretely back to the social societies that it is drawn from by Malinowski (Part One, Section A, Chapter 3). Malinowski shares Eliade's notion that myth 'is a narrative resurrection of a primeval reality, told in satisfaction of deep religious wants, [and] moral cravings' (2003: 177). However, Malinowski then goes on to suggest that myth also fulfils several other roles, which increasingly distance his position from Eliade's understanding. Malinowski ultimately ends with a statement that is more reminiscent of Tylor's position: myth acts to enhance and codify 'social submissions, assertions, [and] even practical requirements' (2003: 177). Thus Malinowski's definition of myth is quite open ended and allows myth a wide range of social functions. This emphasis on the social function of myth requires significant attention be given to the context of myth recital.

Malinowski's imperative to contextualize myth stands in contrast to the global comparative theories discussed above. For Malinowski, like Tylor, believes that myth is something which cannot be stripped away from its context and is best understood by careful observation of how it is used. Furthermore, he discounts the notion of historical reconstruction of a myth's use, let alone its content. In particular Malinowski develops his argument with regard to a Trobriand origin myth, which he claims must be interpreted neither as faulty history nor as symbolic expressions of deep psychological needs. Instead, Malinowski argues that 'the personage and beings that we find in them [that is to say myths] are what they appear to be on the surface, and not symbols of hidden realities' (2003: 184).

Malinowski's highlighting of the need for cultural contextualization of myth and the use of myth is vital if we are to understand what myths mean to anyone other than ourselves. However, in limiting myth to a surface-level interpretation, Malinowski seems to be swinging too far in the opposite direction. Indeed, it is hard to understand why Malinowski's analysis precludes the existence of a more fundamental level of meaning. Malinowski, however, is useful for shifting the debate from what myth might be towards a discussion of what myth might do; in so doing, he opens the possibility of myth operating at more fundamental levels, whilst remaining tied to the social contexts in which it arose.

In Mary Douglas's highly influential analysis of taboo in the Hebrew Bible (2003), she demonstrates powerfully both the categorizing tendencies of humans and the way that myth reflects those structuring systems. It follows therefore that myth can be a gateway to an appreciation of these underlying categorizing systems and as such the key to helping us understand how various societies carve up the world. This idea comes through strongly in the work of Lévi-Strauss (Part Three, Section A, Chapter 1), which was to completely revolutionize the field of mythography. Lévi-Strauss's technique operates on the assumption that myth raises problems, or contradictions, that are inherent in the world and works towards their resolution. Myth, however, raises these problems neither in a literal way (as the functionalists claim) nor in a socially unmoored way (as psychoanalysts would have), but through a series of (often-dialectical) relations (Lévi-Strauss 1955). Myth, for Lévi-Strauss, is therefore something that must be interpreted both symbolically and contextually.

It is important to stress that for Lévi-Strauss elements in one mythic system that seem to resemble another are no more necessarily related than words in different languages that seem to resemble each other (1955). Therefore, the Indo-Europeanists were right to build on a linguistic analogy; however, they erred in not applying to myth the linguistic principle that what matters is the similarity in relation between words, not the words themselves (cf De Saussure 2011). Similarly, it is the relations between elements of myth (called mythemes) that reveal the underlying classificatory systems of the culture and unlock the keys to understanding both cultural systems and (at a more profound level) the human condition (Lévi-Strauss 1955).

Lévi-Straus's work on mythology is extensive and developed over a protracted period. It is therefore not surprising that his thought shifts over time and collectively contains some ambiguity. One key area of ambiguity relates to the issue of whether myth shapes structure or is shaped by it. This issue is highlighted in the neostructuralist period by scholars, such as Derrida, who argue against an authoritative reading of the structure of a myth and instead posit a process of deconstruction that undermines the hegemonic structures, while leaving open the possibility of replacing them through alternative readings, or mythic constructions (Derrida 1993). This idea is echoed in feminist mythopoetic readings of myth (see Dundes et al Part Four, Section A, Chapter 2) that highlight (often using psychiatric symbol analysis) the underlying patriarchal structures of received myths and seek to replace them with narratives that contain disruptive, equalizing structures (Fiorenza 2015).

At a certain point this process becomes true mythopoiesis – moving beyond myth analysis into myth creation. In truth, many of the theories of myth that have been outlined above can be seen as forms of myth creation: Müller is labelled a Solar Myth, by Littledale (1906: 279), and Eliade, in his memoirs, confesses that his analysis stems from the 'pleasure of inventing, of dreaming, of thinking at all, relieved of the strictures of systematic thought' (Rennie 1996: 3). From this perspective myth creation is tied to the creative act, including that of academic analysis, and as such an ongoing and unavoidable part of life today, as several of the chapters in the later stages of the book suggest. It is hoped that this book will help to inform that process by placing into debate with each other the contrasting and lively attempts to grapple with the issue of myth and, in so doing, add to the continuing development of our understanding of this at once widely known and yet seldom understood category of human expression.

References

Campbell, J. and Moyers, B. (2011). *The Power of Myth*. New York: Anchor.

Cunliffe, Barry (2001). *Facing the Ocean: The Atlantic and Its Peoples, 8000 BC–AD 1500*. Oxford: Oxford University Press.

Derrida, J. (1993). 'Structure, Sign, and Play in the Discourse of the Human Sciences'. In *A Postmodern Reader*. Edited by J. Natoli and L. Hutcheon, 223–242. New York: SUNY Press.

De Saussure, F. (2011). *Course in General Linguistics*. New York: Columbia University Press.

Douglas, M. (2003). *Purity and Danger: An Analysis of Concepts of Pollution and Taboo*. London: Routledge.

Dumézil, Georges (1988). *The Destiny of a King*. Chicago: University of Chicago Press.

Eliade, Mircea (1963). *Myth and Reality*. New York: Harper & Row.

Fiorenza, E. S. (2015). *Wisdom Ways: Introducing Feminist Biblical Interpretation*. New York: Orbis books.

Hancock, G. (2012). *Fingerprints of the Gods: The Evidence of Earth's Lost Civilization*. New York: Three Rivers Press.

Ingold, T. (2000). *The Perception of the Environment: Essays in Livelihood, Dwelling and Skill*. London & New York: Routledge.

Jung, Carl Gustav (2002). 'The Psychology of the Child Archetype'. In *Science of Mythology: Essays on the Myth of the Divine Child and the Mysteries of Eleusis*. Edited by C. G. Jung and K. Kerényi, 83–116. London: Routledge.

Kunin, S. D. (2003). *Religion: The Modern Theories*. Edinburgh: Edinburgh University Press.

Lévi-Strauss, C. (1955). The Structural Study of Myth. *The Journal of American Folklore* 68 (270): 428–444.

Lévi-Strauss, C., and Charbonnier, G. (1969). *Conversations with Claude Lévi-Strauss*. London: Jonathan Cape.

Littledale, R. F. (1906). 'The Oxford Solar Myth'. In *Echoes from Kottabos*. Edited by R. Y. Tyrrell and E. Sullivan. 279–290. London: EG Richards.

MacCana, Proinsias (1997). *Celtic Mythology*. London: Chancellor.

Malinowski, B. (2003). 'Myth in Primitive Psychology'. In *A Reader in the Anthropology of Religion*. Edited by Lambek. Oxford: Blackwell.

Müller, F. Max (1897). *Contributions to the Science of Mythology*. London: Longmans, Green, and Co.

Rennie, B. S. (1996). *Reconstructing Eliade: Making Sense of Religion*. State University of New York Press.

Segal, Robert Alan (1999). *Theorizing about Myth*. Amherst: University of Massachusetts Press.

Tylor, Edward Burnett (1871). *Primitive Culture: Researches into the Development of Mythology, Philosophy, Religion, Art, and Custom*. 2 Volumes. London: John Murray, Albemarle Street.

part one

What is myth?

Section A: What is myth?

Locating the field

It is necessary for a systematic exploration of the various approaches that constitute the academic study of myth to begin with a clear sense of the scope and limits of the category of mythology. What may seem like a simple (and even) trivial task is both highly challenging and rewarding, not least because of the vast array of definitions and understandings that exist. Myth is clearly a story of some sort, but most people would not be happy with the idea that all stories are myths. What is more, when we ask the question of myth's nature, we inevitably come to the consideration of how myth relates to other types of narratives, such as legend and the folktale. One possible dividing line between myth and other narratives is that of truth. While for many myth is a story that is false, others have taken the opposing view, defining myth as a story that is true, venerable and (even) sacred (cf Bascom 1965: 9). This, in turn, leads to the question of what is meant by truth, in particular the nature of the truth that is to be conveyed (natural, social or psychological). The texts in this section all grapple with this question in their own way, and they each move towards the development of a distinct (yet clear) concept of myth.

C. Scott Littleton's 'A Two-Dimensional Scheme for the Classification of Narratives' differentiates myth from other material on precisely the grounds of its veracity and its secularity (true/false: sacred/secular). Our second reading for this section, which is a piece by Ben-Amos, complicates this sketch. Here, Daniel Ben-Amos draws on his background as a folklorist to offer a strongly argued conception of mythology in relation to folklore. This centres on the universality of folklore and its existence as a broad-based, yet distinct form of narrative. Finally, Malinowski's *Myth in Primitive Psychology* utilizes his understanding of myth as it is contextually employed to reveal the relationship of myth to social systems. He neatly demonstrates how myth's truth can be found in the way that it relates to the ideal social order of those who tell the narrative. Malinowski also opens the exploration of the contingency of myth's truth, which is shown to rest upon both who tells the myth and the context of the telling. Collectively, these readings introduce distinct, yet equally influential, ways of delimiting the field of study. In so doing, they provide a firm foundation for the later sections of this Reader, where we will often find ourselves drawn back to these core definitions.

Reference

Bascom, W. (1965). 'The Forms of Folklore: Prose Narratives'. *The Journal of American Folklore* 78 (307): 3–20.

A two-dimensional scheme for the classification of narratives

C. Scott Littleton

1

Covington Scott Littleton (1933–2010) was an American anthropologist. He was born in Los Angeles and spent most of his life in and around the city. He obtained BA, MA and PhD degrees from the University of California, Los Angeles, before working at Occidental College, United States. At Occidental, he was Professor of Anthropology and served as the chairman of first the combined sociology and anthropology department and then the (newly independent) anthropology department. Littleton's research, throughout his career, focussed primarily on the exploration of mythology and folklore, especially the King Arthur legends. Later in his career, he turned increasingly towards exploring the occult and UFO phenomenon, spurred by an increasing desire to understand a strange personal sighting of a UFO. In this chapter, Littleton develops his famous two-dimensional scheme for the classification of narratives (including folklore, legend and myth). This leads Littleton to seek a universal classification for mythology that helps to distinguish it from other forms of narrative. In so doing, Littleton taps into wider concerns about both the veracity and the sacrality of narrative.

Even the most cursory examination of the wide and diverse range of terms that have been used by anthropologists, folklorists, mythologists, and others to refer to various categories of folk literature will reveal a terminological confusion second to none in the social sciences. One man's myth is all too often another man's legend; what to one scholar is manifestly an example of 'lower mythology' is to another simply a folk tale or *Märchen*. Rarely indeed does one find a clear-cut statement as to the key differences between the terms utilized.

Yet closer inspection of the many definitions of myth, folktale, *Märchen*, legend, saga, epic, and the rest of the sometimes bewildering array of terms which since the days of Euhemerus have been coined to refer to various types of folk narratives does in fact reveal some common denominators. If one analyzes the classic nineteenth- and twentieth-century definitions and usages of the terms in question, from Max Müller to Malinowski, from Hartland and Lang to Thompson and Bidney, it becomes clear that two basic criteria are almost always applied, more often than not implicitly, in the categorization of narratives or tales – regardless of the specific terms or labels used. These are (1) the extent to which a narrative is or is not based upon objectively determinable facts or scientifically acceptable hypotheses, and (2) the extent to which it does or does not express ideas that are central to the magico-religious beliefs and ideology of the people who tell it. It is the purpose of this paper to bring these fundamental criteria to light and to suggest in terms of them a tentative two-dimensional classificatory scheme.

The first criterion, that which relates to the relative degree to which a narrative is grounded in fact or fancy, has perhaps best been expressed by Bidney in his assertion that 'Myth originates wherever thought and imagination are employed uncritically or deliberately used to promote social delusion.'[1] In this use of the term myth Bidney thus implicitly distinguishes between two broad categories of narratives: those that are grounded in fact or rationality and those that are not (such as myths, folk tales). The second criterion, that which relates to what I may term, following Durkheim, Radcliffe-Brown, Redfield, Warner, and others, the relative sacredness or secularity of a narrative, is implicit in almost all modern social anthropological attempts to distinguish between myths and folk tales. Lessa and Vogt, for example, define myths simply as 'sacred stories.'[2]

But neither of these two criteria – no matter how rigorously applied – is alone sufficient for the purpose at hand, which is to arrive at meaningful categories of narratives. For it seems to me that such categories can be arrived at only if both are applied, only if each criterion is translated into a dichotomy between two polarities or ideal types: the first criterion, thus, is translated into a dichotomy between absolutely factual (or scientific) and absolutely fabulous (or non-scientific), and the second appears as a dichotomy between absolutely secular and absolutely sacred.[3] The result is a two-dimensional scheme which can be expressed graphically (see Graph I).

At this point, however, one fundamental theoretical assumption should be made clear. The dichotomies suggested here are necessarily asymptotic and therefore must be phrased in terms of continua.[4] No given narrative will ever completely approximate any one of these several poles or ideal types;[5] there is no such thing as a wholly or absolutely sacred or fabulous narrative, nor is there one that is wholly factual or secular. All must fall somewhere in between. A narrative is located on each continuum (or axis) in terms of the degree to which it more closely approximates one or the other of the poles in question – that is, in terms of the degree to which it is more sacred than secular, more fabulous than factual, or vice versa.

It is, of course, difficult to quantify the degree of sacredness or secularity of a narrative, let alone the degree to which it is factual or fabulous; and the rating system is at present still largely based upon rule of thumb. Nevertheless, in order to facilitate comparisons, I have devised a 20-point scale, wherein a score of one is applied to those narratives which seem most closely to approximate, respectively, the factual and secular poles, and a score of 20 is applied to those which most closely approximate, respectively, the fabulous and sacred poles.

As I see it, the scheme yields five major categories. Using traditional labels wherever possible, these are (1) *myth*, composed of narratives which are extremely sacred and patently fabulous (those narratives which score above 10 on the sacred-secular axis and above 15 on the factual-fabulous axis, or vice versa); (2) *legend* (or *saga*), composed of narratives which are relatively sacred and fabulous (those which score between 5 and 15 on both axes); (3) *folktale* (or *Märchen*), composed of relatively secular albeit fabulous narratives (those which score below 10 on the sacred-secular axis and between 15 and 20 on the factual-fabulous axis, or below 5 on the sacred-secular axis and above 10 on the factual-fabulous axis); (4) *history*, composed of relatively secular and factual narratives (those which score below 10 on the sacred-secular axis and below 5 on the factual-fabulous axis, or vice versa); and (5) *sacred history*, composed of narratives which are relatively (or extremely) sacred yet firmly grounded in fact (those which score above 10 on the sacred-secular axis and below 5 on the factual-fabulous axis, or above 15 on the sacred-secular axis and between 5 and 10 on the factual-fabulous axis). The distribution of these five categories, the boundaries between which necessarily overlap to some extent, can be seen in Graph I.

The first category, that of myth, necessarily includes all of those narratives which purport to explain the creation of the universe, of the supernatural beings who direct it, and of the human beings who populate it. It will also include perhaps the majority of those narratives which in an oral tradition function to explain the basic facts of human existence, such as birth, death, storms, floods, fire, and earthquakes. Here, for example, would be located such narrative phenomena as the Greek theogony, Genesis I, the ancient Irish account of the *Tuatha de Danann*, much of the *Elder Edda*, especially the *Voluspa*, the Hawaiian and other Polynesian creation stories, the Babylonian *Gilgamesh* cycle, and the Rig Vedic account of how Indra released the waters from captivity and thereby permitted the cosmos to assume its present shape.[6] In short, the category here labeled myth includes all of those narratives which in the eyes of the tellers are extremely sacred and in the judgement of the investigator are unrelated to historical or scientific facts.

The second category, that of legend or saga, includes those narratives which cluster around the mid-point of the graph: those which have at least a marginal relationship to historic or scientific fact and which are generally more open to rational interpretation by those who tell them. The range here runs from narratives which border on myth or

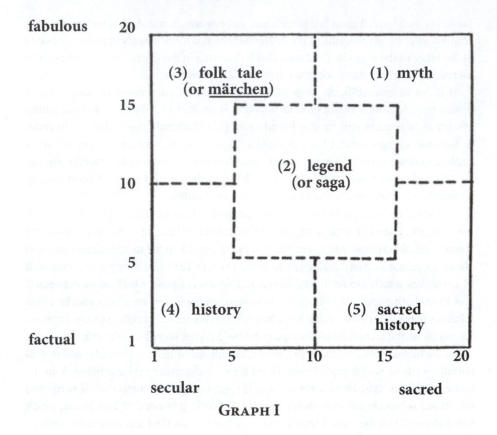

GRAPH I

folktale to those which border on history or sacred history. Perhaps the best examples of narratives that fit this category can be found in the ancient epic literatures of the Old World, especially those which concern heroic rather than divine beings. Much (but by no means all) of the *Iliad, Mahābhārata,* and *Volsung-asaga* might be located here, as might the Russian tales of the hero Igor and the Irish accounts of Finn and the *fianna*.[7]

The third category, that of folktale or *Märchen*, includes those narratives which are told primarily for entertainment – though they may well reflect themes also expressed in myths and legends and thus serve to reinforce the didactic functions served by the latter, especially as far as children are concerned – and are indeed open to rational interpretation. Their factual content, however, may be as minimal as that of the most fabulous of myths. It is this sort of 'popular tales and traditions' that William Thoms sought to distinguish when he coined the term 'folk-lore' in 1846. Examples here are legion in any tradition, in large measure, it would seem, because the relatively secular character of such narratives permits a range of variation and adaptation far wider than that generally present among myths and, to a lesser extent, legends. The folktale, as Stith Thompson[8] and others have long since amply demonstrated, is certainly the most easily diffusible category of folk narrative; this again is a reflection of secularity.

The fourth category, history, includes narratives that generally conform to the basic definition of history: a factual and objective record of past events. That such a category of narratives, no matter how minimal, is inevitably present in all folk or oral traditions seems obvious, Lord Raglan and his supporters to the contrary notwithstanding.[9] Yet history, whether oral or literate, is never wholly factual or objective (that is, secular), and this is taken into account here. For as I see it, there is no sharp line between history and either myth, folktale, or legend; and a given narrative is here classed as history only if it is indeed more secular than sacred and more factual (in the judgment of the investigator) than fabulous. It is suggested, however, that when applied to an oral tradition this category will probably contain fewer items than any other and that with the passing of a few generations most narratives initially classifiable as history will have moved into the categories of myth, legend, or folktale.

The fifth and last category, that of sacred history, comes close to approximating what a number of theologians and Old Testament scholars have labeled *Heilsgeschichte*,[10] or the idea that in the Old Testament there can be found more or less factual accounts which have nevertheless become fundamental in the development of Judaism. Here again, this is a logical category which will, it seems to me, be present in all traditions, at least to some extent. It includes narratives that are grounded in fact yet at the same time relatively closed to interpretation or analysis on the part of the culture concerned. The lives of Saul, David, and Solomon, as well as those of the later prophets, are examples of sacred history. To a much lesser degree, the American Revolution, the life of Washington, and the careers of Lincoln and Robert E. Lee (at least in Virginia) also fit into this category. Inevitably, only a fraction of what begins as history passes into the category of sacred history. Indeed, the latter category often seems to serve as a halfway house, as it were, between history and myth or legend.

It remains to suggest some of the scheme's possible applications. In the first place, of course, it could prove useful to one who is concerned with the synchronic analysis of a given narrative tradition, if only as a taxonomic device. A second application would be to comparative studies of two or more contemporary traditions. Each could be plotted and the lie of the points might well yield patterns not otherwise readily apparent. A third and in my opinion even more interesting application would be to the historical analysis of specific narratives or sets of narratives, to the study of what happens to them as they pass from generation to generation. By means of a series of overlays, each representing a given point in time, one could plot shifts from one category to another.

A simple example of this use is seen in Graph II, wherein the movement of what might be termed the 'Alexander narrative' is plotted from the centuries immediately following the Macedonian conqueror's death to the beginning of the modern era. In Julius Caesar's day the narrative is clearly classifiable as history. But by A.D. 1000 it has become, in Europe and elsewhere, a legend. In the medieval Alexandrian romances the subject of the narrative becomes a Christian knight bent upon the conversion of the East; historicity has dropped off sharply and sacred connotations have been added. By A.D. 1600, however, historical scholarship has fairly well restored the historical Alexander and thus the narrative – at least in Europe – shifted once again into the category of history, where it has remained. Utilizing the scale mentioned earlier, this oscillation of the 'Alexander narrative' between the categories of history and legend can be plotted in terms of a series of co-ordinates. Beginning approximately at the intersection of two on both the sacred-secular and factual-fabulous axes, it moves to the vicinity of eight on both axes and then returns to approximately its initial position (see Graph II).

This is not to suggest that all myths begin as history. It is equally conceivable that a narrative may begin its career as a myth, originating in a dream or hallucination, perhaps, and later shift into the realm of legend or folk tale. The point here is simply that the scheme in question provides a device for plotting these shifts.

As far as the shift from myth to legend is concerned, perhaps the best single examples come from the Indic and Norse traditions. Some years ago the eminent Swedish mythologist Stig Wikander[11] was able to demonstrate the specific links between the major divinities of the *Rig Veda* (Varuna, Mitra, Indra, the Nāsatya, and others) and the heroic protagonists of the *Mahābhārata* – the five *Pāṇḍava* or 'Sons of Paṇḍu.' Yudhiṣṭhira, eldest of the five, is a projection of the sovereign Vedic god Mitra (Paṇḍu himself is a projection of Varuṇa); Arjuna and Bhīma are both projections of the warrior god Indra; and Nakula and Sahadeva are projections of the twin Nāsatya. Here, of course, Wikander draws heavily upon

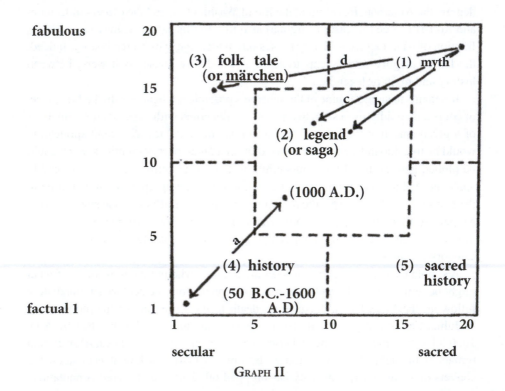

GRAPH II

Georges Dumézil's thesis as to the nature of Vedic myth and the extent to which it reflected an inherited Indo-European ideology;[12] that both the *Rig Veda* and *Mahābhārata* reflect this ideology is certainly of the highest significance. But for my purposes, however, the important thing here is that a transposition from the divine to the human plane has taken place; figures that originally were clearly mythic have been transposed into the human, quasi-historical realm. This indeed is a shift from the category of myth into the category of legend. The *Pāṇḍava*, though by no means historical or secular figures, are nevertheless delineated as human beings and are, like the heroes of the *Iliad*, certainly more open to interpretation than their mythical prototypes.

Wikander has also demonstrated the mythic roots of much of the narrative material contained in Snorri's *Edda* and *Heimskringla* and the *Gesta Danorum* of Saxo Grammaticus.[13] Here, Othinn, Thorr, and others appear as culture heroes – as bringers of civilization and its blessings to the primitive inhabitants of Scandinavia. Once again a transposition – this time a euhemeristic one – has occurred between the divine and human planes and is necessarily accompanied by an increase in secularity.

In terms of the scale these two shifts from myth to epic or legend begin at approximately the intersection of 17 or 18 on both axes and end at roughly 10 or 12 (the Norse shift may perhaps be seen as moving even farther to the left, ending up possibly at 7 or 8 on the sacred-secular axis; see Graph II).

It is interesting to note that in both these latter examples the development or introduction of a new religion seems to have been of prime importance in precipitating this shift. In the case of the *Mahābhārata* it seems fairly certain that it was not composed until after a synthesis had been achieved between the relatively simple polytheism introduced by the Aryan invaders in the fifteenth century B.C., and the religious system of the indigenous population.[14] By the time the epic was composed, the great Vedic gods had already begun to fall into disrepute and had largely been replaced by those of classical Hinduism: Brahma, Vishnu, etc. Thus, in effect, a new religion had evolved and a reinterpretation of the former divinities became necessary. In Scandinavia the new religion was, of course, Christianity, and the effect of its introduction upon the Norse narrative tradition was broadly analogous to what happened in India.

That the introduction or development of a new religion can also precipitate a shift in the direction of the folk tale is equally evident. Indeed, a fair amount of contemporary Irish, Germanic, and even American folklore seems to bear witness to such a shift. Gerschel, for example, has ably demonstrated the extent to which an important aspect of ancient Germanic theology has carried over into a family of modern German and Swiss folk tales.[15] Chase has emphasized the extent to which the figure of Woden is implicit in a large proportion of the so-called 'Jack tales,' numerous variants of which have been collected in the Southern Appalachians.[16] As far as the scale is concerned, these shifts from myth to folk tale begin at approximately 17 or 18 on both axes and end somewhere in the vicinity of 4 or 5 on the sacred-secular axis and 15 to 17 on the factual-fabulous axis (see Graph II).

Finally, a word or two is in order concerning the difference between fabulousness and falsity. When I suggest that myths are by definition fabulous narratives, I do not mean to imply that they are necessarily untrue. For no social anthropologist today would deny that myths, as sacred narratives, inevitably reflect important social and cultural realities and are thus 'true' in the broadest sense of the word. What I do mean to imply is that it is possible to arrive at meaningful categories of narratives simply by classifying them according to whether their manifest content is or is not derived from historical fact or congruent with acceptable scientific hypotheses. The dichotomy between truth and falsity is wholly another matter.

Graph I represents the axes formed by the intersection of the continua from sacred to secular and from factual to fabulous and includes the five major categories of narratives which can be described in terms of these axes.

Graph II represents the application of the two axes to a description of narrative shifts: *vector a* represents the oscillation of the 'Alexander narrative' between history and legend; *vectors b* and *c* represent, respectively, the shifts in Indic and Norse narratives from myth to legend; *vector d* represents the shift from Germanic myth to modern German, Swiss, and American folklore.

Notes

1   David Bidney, 'Myth, Symbolism, and Truth,' in *Myth: A Symposium*, ed. Thomas A. Sebeok, Bibliographic and Special Series of the American Folklore Society, V (Philadelphia, PA, 1955), p. 13.

2   William A. Lessa and Evon Z. Vogt, *Reader in Comparative Religion* (New York, 1958), p. 134.

3   For a discussion of the extent to which the sacred implies a deeply rooted resistance to change or to rational interpretation, see Howard A. Becker and R. J. Myers, 'Sacred and Secular Aspects of Human Sociation,' *Sociometry*, V (1942) 207ff.

4   I am indebted here to Professor Robert M. Rennick, of the Department of Sociology, State University College, Cortland, New York, for access to the manuscript of his excellent paper, 'The Asymptotic Dichotomy,' a portion of which was read before the American Sociological Association, New York, 1960.

5   For a brief discussion of the use of ideal types in sociological analysis see William J. Goode, 'A Note on the Ideal Type,' *American Sociological Review* XII (1947): 473–475; see also Becker, *Through Values to Social Interpretation* (Durham, 1950), especially 47, who discusses in some detail the asymptotic and other dichotomies regularly employed by social scientists.

6   For the Hawaiian creation story see Martha W. Beckwith, *The Kumulipo: A Hawaiian Creation Chant* (Chicago, 1951); for an analysis of Vedic cosmogony see W. Norman Brown, 'The Creation Myth of the Rig Veda,' *Journal of the American Oriental Society*, LXII (1942): 85–97.

7   For a summary account of the Igor tales, see Norma Lorre Goodrich, *The Medieval Myths* (New York, 1961), pp. 155–172; for an analysis of the Finn cycle, see Alwyn and Brinley Rees, *Celtic Heritage: Ancient Tradition in Ireland and Wales* (London, 1961).

8   Cf. Stith Thompson, *The Folk Tale* (New York, 1961).

9   Cf. Lord Raglan, *The Hero: A Study in Tradition, Myth, and Drama* (London, 1936); Stanley Edgar Hyman, 'The Ritual View of Myth and the Mythic,' in *Myth: A Symposium*, Thomas A. Sebeok, ed., Bibliographic and Special Series of the American Folklore Society, V (Philadelphia, PA, 1955), 84–94. For a refutation of the ritualist thesis see William Bascom, 'The Myth Ritual Theory,' *Journal of American Folklore*, LXX (1957): 103–114.

10 Cf., for example, G. Ernest Wright, *God Who Acts* (London, 1952), p. 115.

11 See Stig Wikander, 'Pāndava-sagan och Mahābhāratas mytiska förutsättningar,' *Religion och bibel* VI (1947): 27–39; 'Nakula et Sahadeva,' *Orientalia Suecana* VI (1957), 66–69.

12 Dumézil has suggested that the ancient Indo-European-speaking peoples, among whom the authors of the *Rig Veda* and *Mahābhārata* must be ranked, characteristically divided their pantheons into three functionally differentiated, hierarchically ranked strata. The highest of these, in Vedic India represented by the gods Varuna and Mitra, was charged with the maintenance of correct religious beliefs and attitudes and with insuring the sanctity of contracts; the second level, represented by Indra, was charged with maintaining the military posture of the society and thus with ensuring its physical survival; the third and lowest level, represented by the Nasatya, was concerned with the maintenance of physical well-being, with the provision of sustenance. The archaic social order of India, and to a lesser extent those characteristic of the earliest phases of most other Indo-European speaking societies, reflected this divine division of labor; cf. the classic division of Aryan society into *Brahman, Kshatriya*, and *Vaisya* (the *Shudra*, or lowest level, originally seems to have comprised the conquered indigenous population). For a general introduction to Dumézil's thesis see his *L'idéologie tripartie des Indo-Européens*, Collection Latomus, XXXI (Brussels, 1958).

13 See Wikander, 'Germanische und indo-iranische Eschatologie,' *Kairos* (1960), 83–88.

14 There is good reason to believe that many elements of Hinduism (as opposed to the religion of the *Vedas*) are ultimately derived from the Indus Valley civilization. For example, the horned figure surrounded by beasts who so often appears upon stamp seals found at Harappa and Mohenjo-daro is probably a prototype of Shiva. Also, the prominent position of the humped cow in Indus Valley iconography is significant. Cf. Stuart Piggott, *Prehistoric India* (Harmondsworth, 1950), 201–203, who observes (303) that ' … it is even possible that early historic Hindu society owed more to Harappa than it did to the Sanskrit-speaking invaders.'

15 I.e., the extent to which these tales perpetuate the Indo-European penchant for tripartition (see Note 13), which is as clearly evident in ancient Germanic mythology as it is in that of the ancient Indians; Gerschel, like Wikander, is a devout disciple of Professor Dumézil. See Lucien Gerschel, 'Sur un schéme trifonctionnel dans une famille de légendes germaniques,' *Revue de l'Histoire des Religions*, CL (1956): 55–92; see also Dumézil, *Les dieux des Germains* (Paris, 1959).

16 Richard Chase, *The Jack Tales* (Boston, 1943); *American Folk Tales and Songs* (New York, 1956), p. 63.

References

Bascom, W. (1957). The Myth Ritual Theory. *Journal of American Folklore* LXX: 103–114.

Becker, H. (1950). *Through Values to Social Interpretation: Essays on Social Contexts, Actions, Types, and Prospects.* Durham, NC: Duke University Press.

Becker, H. A., and R. J. Myers (1942). Sacred and Secular Aspects of Human Sociation. *Sociometry* V: 207ff.

Beckwith, M. W. (1951). *The Kumulipo: A Hawaiian Creation Chant.* Chicago: Chigaco University Press.

Bidney, D. (1955). 'Myth, Symbolism, and Truth'. In *Myth: A Symposium.* Edited by Thomas A. Sebeok, Bibliographic and Special Series of the American Folklore Society, V. Philadelphia, PA.

Brown, W. N. (1942). The Creation Myth of the Rig Veda. *Journal of the American Oriental Society* LXII: 85–97.

Chase, R. (1943). *The Jack Tales.* Boston, MA: Houghton Miffin.

Chase, R. (1956). *American Folk Tales and Songs.* New York: New American Library.

Dumezil, G. (1958). L'ideologie tripartie des Indo-Europeens. *Collection Latomus* 31.

Dumezil, G. (1959). *Les dieux des Germains.* Paris: Presses universitaires de France.

Gerschel, L. (1956). Sur un scheme trifonctionnel dans une famille de legendes germaniques. *Revue de l'Histoire des Religions* CL: 55–92.

Goode, W. J. (1947). A Note on the Ideal Type. *American Sociological Review* XII: 473–475.

Goodrich, N. L. (1961). *The Medieval Myths.* New York: New American Library.

Hyman, S. E. (1955). 'The Ritual View of Myth and the Mythic'. In *Myth: A Symposium.* Edited by Thomas A. Sebeok, Bibliographic and Special Series of the American Folklore Society, V. Philadelphia, PA.

Piggott, S. (1950). Prehistoric India. *Revue Philosophique de la France Et de l'Etranger* 147: 372–374.

Raglan, F. R. S. S. (1936). *The Hero: A Study in Tradition, Myth, and Drama.* London: Watts.

Rees, B., and Rees, A. (1961). *Celtic Heritage: Ancient Tradition in Ireland and Wales.* London: Thames and Hudson.

Thompson, S. (1961). *The Folktale.* Dryden: New York.

Wikander, S. (1947). Pandava-sagan och Mahabharatas mytiska forutsattningar. *Religion och bibel* VI: 27–39.

Wikander, S. (1957). Nakula et Sahadeva. *Orientalia Suecana* VI: 66–69.

Wikander, S. (1960). Germanische und indo-iranische Eschatologie. *Kairos*: 83–88.

William, L., and Vogt, E. Z. (1958). *Reader in Comparative Religion: An Anthropological Approach.* New York: Pearson.

Wright, G. E. (1952). *God Who Acts.* London: SCM Press.

The idea of folklore: An essay

Dan Ben-Amos

2

Dan Ben-Amos is a leading figure in the study of folklore, which is closely allied to the exploration of mythology. He studied Hebrew Literature (with an interest in folklore) at Hebrew University of Jerusalem, before undertaking graduate studies at Indiana University, USA. In the 1960s, when Ben-Amos was a student, Indiana was the major centre for the study of folklore in the United States, and several of that era's doctoral candidates went on to establish careers as highly influential folklorists (including Alan Dundes). Today, Ben-Amos is Professor of Jewish and African folklore at University of Pennsylvania, in Philadelphia, USA. He is the author of many influential publications that explore mythology and folklore. We have here chosen to include a section of his essay, 'The Idea of Folklore', which attempts to define the limits of folklore through a detailed exploration of common misconceptions of specialized narratives (including myth).

The concept of folklore emerged in Europe midway in the nineteenth century. Originally it connoted tradition, ancient customs and surviving festivals, old ditties and dateless ballads, archaic myths, legends and fables, and timeless tales, and proverbs. As these narratives rarely stood the tests of common sense and experience, folklore also implied irrationality: beliefs in ghosts and demons, fairies and goblins, sprites and spirits; it referred to credence in omens, amulets, and talismans. From the perspective of the *urbane literati,* who conceived the idea of folklore, these two attributes of traditionalism and irrationality could pertain only to peasant or primitive societies. Hence they attributed to folklore a third quality: rurality. The countryside and the open space of wilderness were the proper breeding grounds for folklore. Man's close contact with nature in villages and hunting bands was considered the ultimate source of his myth and poetry. As outgrowth of human experience with nature, folklore itself was thought to be a natural expression of man, before city, commerce, civilization, and culture contaminated the purity of his life.

The triad of attributes – traditionalism, irrationality and rurality – was to dominate the concept of folklore for many years to come; often it still does. It provided standards for inclusion or exclusion of stories, songs, and sayings within the domain of folklore proper. Those which possessed at least one of these qualities were christened folkstories, folksongs, riddles and folk sayings; those which did not were reprovingly rejected.

In their turn, these three terms of meaning generated additional attributes, which together constituted the sense of the concept of folklore in common use, in print and in speech. The cloak of tradition concealed the identity of those who authored folktales, ballads, and proverbs. Compounding matters, the transmission from generation to generation obscured their origin. Thus by default and not by merit, anonymity became an earmark of folklore. Indigenous prose or poetry became part of folklore only after the memory of their creator had been erased. Then the seal of anonymity sanctioned tradition as genuine. It legitimized songs and tales as integral parts of the cultural heritage of society.

Yet the anonymity of folk narratives, rhymes, and riddles hardly solved the enigma of origin. The responsibility for authorship had to be placed in the hands of some creator, be he divine or human. So in the absence of any individual who could justifiably and willingly claim paternity of myths and legends, the entire community was held accountable for them. After all, the existing evidence appeared to support such an allegation. Narrators and singers often attribute their tales and songs not to a single individual, but to the collective tradition of the community. Even in the exceptional cases in which they indeed claimed authorship, scholarship succeeded in unveiling analogues in their own and other traditions. Such parallels cast doubt upon any contentions for originality and sustained the assertion of the communality of folklore.

In fact, communality has become a central attribute, rivalled only by 'tradition' in the formation of the concept of folklore. There was no room in folklore for private tales and poems. Any expression had to pass through the sieve of communal approval before it could be considered folklore. But the identification of the processes that would justify the attribution of communality to any story or song proved to be rather complex, even logically thorny. Were folktales and folksongs only in the communal domain, free to all to speak and sing? Or should these property rights have been limited to the moment of origin, thus regarding folk expressions as a communal creation, and solving along the way the question of authorship? Furthermore, how does the community foster its bond between people and their folklore, and exactly which of its aspects relate to the society at large; the themes, the language, the forms, or the particular tales, songs and proverbs? These and other issues are the whetstones that sharpened debates that were crucial to the idea of folklore. From various viewpoints the attribute of communality implies communal creation, re-creation, or, simply, expression.

Communal creation involves some anachronistic reasoning: the tales, songs, and sayings that the community shared together, were also created together. Such an explanation might have solved the problem of authorship, but inferring origins from results might be valid only biologically, not logically. In the cultural and social spheres, the mode of existence cannot necessarily attest to the genesis of forms. Historical processes such as diffusion of themes, dissemination of ideas, and imitation of manners do affect the state and nature of folklore. Consequently, collective knowledge of tales and songs could not be an unequivocal indicator of creation. The notion of communal recreation countered this dilemma. It prolonged the moment of origin over historical periods, and conceived of the formation of songs, for example, not in a single exhilarating burst of poetic creativity, but through repetitive recitations of singers on communal occasions. Each improvised and embellished the text, yet conformed to the communal aesthetic and ethical standards. Such an interpretation of the communality of folklore also allows the viewing of folk prose and poetry as expressions of social fears and wishes, ideals and values. Folklore reflected the collective experience of society and was the mirror that the community constantly faced.

Paradoxically, intertwined with the attribute of communality is the idea that folklore is universal. While folksongs and tales might be forged within a particular community and express its unique experience, they also transcend the boundaries that language and space impose, and emerge in diverse groups and remote countries, still maintaining sameness to a large extent. The attribute of universality appeared to be both formal and thematic. All peoples distinguish poetry from prose, pithy sayings from epic poems; all construct narratives, fictional or historical, stringing events in sequences; and all can combine music and movement with words, and can sing and dance to their hearts' content. These are inherent abilities of humanity.

In that sense, folklore withstood the test that language failed. While modern discoveries about animals clearly demonstrate that some master the rudiments of language communication (whales sing), so far neither monkeys nor rats have been caught telling legends to their infants. But the universality of folklore was not confined to the formal basis alone. The themes, the metaphors, and the subjects of stories, songs, and sayings of peoples who live in countries remote from each other and who speak completely unrelated languages, exhibited a high degree of similarity that history could not explain. Migrations and contacts in war and peace could not account for the common features that the tales and poems of native Australians, Africans, and Americans shared. All include stories of gods, of creation and of destruction; all tell about marvelous events, beings and places; and all dwell upon the supernatural, the extraordinary, the absolute, and the incongruous. Their metaphors relate to nature, beliefs, and societies, and their songs celebrate victories and lament failures in the struggle for survival. Often, similarities are even more striking as the same narrative episodes and verbal or visual images appear in the expressions of unrelated peoples.

The dual attributes of universality and communality were locked together and created an apparent paradox in the idea of folklore, converging the general and the particular into a single concept. Evidence supported both. The themes and forms of folklore appeared to be universal, yet no other expression is so imbued with regional, local, and cultural references, meanings, and symbols. There are two ways to resolve this contradiction. First, universality and communality can be viewed not as contradictory but as complimentary attributes. The relations that govern folklore are universal; the references to culture and history are specific. The principles of distinctiveness in form and in theme – the unusual, incongruous, and, conversely, the absolutely harmonious are universal – but the languages, the social and historical experiences, the religious systems, and the moral values that make up the substance of folklore of respective societies are communal. Second, these two attributes could be historically related, one preceding the other. If folklore was communal at first, later its properties achieved universality by historical processes, such as diffusion of themes and population contacts through migration, trade, or warfare. Such an assumption would imply a single source, or place and time of origin, from which folklore features were universally diffused. But if folklore were universal first, then its basic forms and themes should have been formulated prior to any historical and evolutionary developments. In such case, folklore embodies the original homogeneity of the culture of man before diversity arose, following the Tower of Babel struck. Consequently, folklore also possesses the attribute of primariness, an attribute that made the impact of folklore on modern thought and art so powerful.

The mythology of all nations does not only tell about, but *is*, the dawn of humanity. It incarnates the commonality in all communities and voices the primordial expression of man. In its fundamental forms folklore emerged before human diversity developed and thus it embodies the most rudimentary forms of verbal and visual symbols. The primariness of folklore had historical and evolutionary aspects. Historically, folklore allegedly dated back to time immemorial, and hence, at its original stage, preceded any known recorded history. When man hunted and gathered his food, or even when he began to farm the land and to herd his cattle, but had not as yet quite mastering writing, he was already narrating tales and singing songs. The folklore of the world, it was hence assumed, abounds with symbols, themes, and metaphors that pertain to the beginning of human civilization, and could shed light on the dark corners of history that no other document could illuminate. The forms of folklore were regarded as the cores at the heart of artistic forms. They were the primitive, crude expressions out of which the literary, visual, and musical cultural heritage of the peoples of the world has emerged. Folklore comprised the symbolic forms at the base of the complex expressions of literate societies.

Naturally, folklore in its primary stage could not have been accessible to modern man, and would have been completely lost had it not been for the attempt to recapture tales and songs as they existed in nonliterate societies, that is, as they were told and sung orally without recourse to any written devices to aid in memorization and transmission of texts. No one claims that the current prose and poetry of peasants and nonliterate culture reflect human expression in its archaic, primordial form. Repeated recitations, loss of memorization, creative improvisation, and more general historical processes of cultural contacts and technical evolution contributed to alterations in both the particular themes and the general tenor of folklore. However, in spite of the recognition of such historical factors, a basic assumption in folklore is that those stories, songs, and sayings continued to exist in the same way their ancient predecessors did, that is, in oral performance, and that they were transmitted from generation to generation only orally, as they were before the advance of literacy. Hence the oral nature of folklore became one of its crucial attributes, the touchstone of authenticity and originality. As long as stories, songs, and proverbs conformed with the principle of oral circulation and transmission, they qualified as 'pure' folklore, but when, alas, somewhere along the line they came in contact with written texts, they were branded contaminated. No longer could they represent the primary expression of man.

These attributes of traditionalism, irrationality, and rurality; anonymity, communality, and universality; primacy and oral circulation became consolidated in the idea of folklore. They cluster, implying one another, and suggesting the existence of intrinsic relations between them. The occurrence of one quality in a song or tale often implies most of the others. A peasant song, for example, is considered as having long-standing tradition in the community. The possibility that it might be a recent composition, or one borrowed from some external source such as an urban center, would have denied the song its folkloric nature and contradicted the basic assumptions held about it. Being rural, other attributes similarly follow: the author is anonymous, and the song belongs to the cultural heritage of the entire community. Most likely, as poetry, it would express deep-seated emotions or uncontrolled desires, which in turn project universal primary human qualities, unaffected by civilization. Thus, combined in a hypothetical song, these attributes convey the meaning of the concept of folklore.

Consequently, these attributes, which are only descriptive and interpretive terms at best, acquired a normative status, setting the standards and boundaries for the substance of folklore proper. They become defining terms, bound by an a *priori* notion of what folklore should have been but only occasionally was, transforming the desired into necessary conditions and injecting interpretations into alleged observations. They have become terms of value with which to state the worth of songs and sayings and to rate their import in the light of ideals only implicitly understood.

In the process of research and interpretation, desired goals could often turn into a *priori* assumptions and serve as initial premises rather than the final results. This, in fact, had often happened with qualities attributed to stories, songs, and sayings, which have become the basic premises upon which research was designed and theory constructed. Naturally, there have been sufficient examples that supported these contentions. Stories have circulated orally, existing in the traditions of rural communities for many years; their authors, if there were any, were long forgotten, and their analogues recovered in distant lands. But even if there were texts that measured up to all the criteria of folklore, these standards should not have been the defining terms for the substance of folklore.

The penalty for transferring norms into premises and ideal goals into a *priori* conditions is a limited range for research and theory. Past folklore scholarship paid its dues twice over. The diversity and richness that folklore is, were confined by the constraints that the notions about it imposed. The study of traditions in villages flourished, but the equivalent manifestations in cities went unnoticed. Anonymous tales and songs were avidly recorded; stored, and dissected, but equally entertaining songs and stories whose authors were alive and known were ignored as irrelevant. Other attributes became frames for interpretation. The relationship between expressions and the community was, and is, a major paradigm for analysis. The implicit irrationality of ideas found in tales and metaphors has been the only basis for their explanation, and has opened the gate to a host of psychological interpretations. Significant as they are, these notions blocked the way for alternate modes of explanation, directions of research, and construction of theories. They have predefined and identified the substance and the problems of study, silencing the expressions and the people themselves. In recent years the clouds of a *priori* premises began to disperse. Still, with a sense of innovation and intellectual rebellion Hermann Bausinger (1961) expounded upon folk culture in a technical world, (*Volkskund in des technische Welt*), and American folklorists gathered to discuss *The Urban Experience and Folk Tradition* (Paredes and Stekert, 1971). Even more recently Alan Dundes and Carl R. Pagter published a collection of written materials as urban folklore in their book *Urban Folklore from the Paperwork Empire* (Austin, Texas: American Folklore Society, 1975), and with a similar sense of innovation Richard M. Dorson convened a conference on the subject of modern folklore, and published its papers in the volume *Folklore in the Modern World*, in the series *World Anthropology* (The Hague: Mouton, 1978). But these are recent developments when scholarly traditions yield to the demands of reality. Throughout the formative years of folklore study, and in many years that followed, the attributes of the idea of folklore dictated the conception of its substance and the limits of its research. They became unchallenged premises and assumptions that were taken for granted.

Regardless of the validity of these attributes, they contributed to the popularity of the idea of folklore. At the same time, however, these very qualities impeded the transformation of folklore from an idea into a field of scholarship. These attributes burdened folklore research with unproven assumptions, untested beliefs, and a projection of popular attitudes toward the substance that makes up the subject of folklore inquiry. In order to progress with research in the field of folklore, it is necessary, as some have already done, to unload the attributes of the past and to observe folklore freshly, as it exists in social reality. Within this context folklore is a culturally unique mode of communication, and its distinctiveness is formal, thematic, and performative. There is a correlation between these three levels of expression, by which the speakers of folklore set it apart from any other communication in society.

As a distinct mode of communication folklore exists in any society; it is the sole property of neither peasants nor primitives. No doubt folklore could be traditional, but it is not so by definition; it could be anonymous, but it is not essentially so. Any of the qualities that were, and still are, attributed to folklore might be inherent in some forms, in some cultures, and any time they are, it is up to the folklorists to demonstrate it anew.

References

Bausinger, H. (2005). *Volkskultur in der technischen* Welt. Campus Verlag.

Dorson, R. M. (1978). *Folklore in the modern world*. The Hague: Mouton.

Dundes, A., & Pagter, C. R. (1992). *Work hard and you shall be rewarded: Urban folklore from the paperwork empire*. Detroit: Wayne State University Press.

Stekert, E. J., & Paredes, A. (1971). *The urban experience and folk tradition*. Austin: University of Texas Press.

Myth in primitive society

Bronislaw Malinowski

3

Bronislaw Malinowski (1894–1942) was raised in the shadow of the Jagiellonian University in Kraków, where his father worked as a Professor of philology (with an interest in folklore). He was awarded a PhD from Jagiellonian in 1908, for his work on physics and mathematics. A chance encounter with Frazer's *The Golden Bough* is credited as the trigger for Malinowski to explore anthropology and the related issues of myth, religion and society at the London School of Economics (LSE), UK. After undertaking four years of fieldwork in Oceania (and spending several more consolidating his ideas), Malinowski was finally awarded a PhD from the LSE in 1916. After graduation, he worked at LSE, initially as a Lecturer and then as the university's first Professor of Social Anthropology; Malinowski's final years saw him become a visiting professor at Yale University, which is located in the United States.

Malinowski is widely considered the architect of British anthropology's emphasis on prolonged periods of engaged fieldwork (known as participant observation). It was during Malinowski's own, foundational, fieldwork that he is said to have come to the realization that to understand how locals behaved, you had to live as they did. However, he was also a considerable theorist, and he is credited with inventing a highly influential practical approach to the interpretation of society, known as Functionalism. Malinowski's work on myth specifically focuses on its social function and is typified by his now-famous definition of myth as a 'social charter'. In the material that we have chosen to include here, Malinowski puts forward a compelling case for the secret to achieving an understanding of mythology lying in observing its social use.

The anthropologist is not bound to the scanty remnants of culture, broken tablets, tarnished texts, or fragmentary inscriptions. He need not fill out immense gaps with voluminous, but conjectural, comments. The anthropologist has the myth-maker at his elbow. Not only can he take down as full a text as exists, with all its variations, and control it over and over; he has also a host of authentic commentators to draw upon; still more he has the fullness of life itself from which the myth has been born. And as we shall see, in this live context there is as much to be learned about the myth as in the narrative itself.

Myth as it exists in a savage community, that is, in its living primitive form, is not merely a story told but a reality lived. It is not of the nature of fiction, such as we read today in a novel, but it is a living reality, believed to have once happened in primeval times, and continuing ever since to influence the world and human destinies. This myth is to the savage what, to a fully believing Christian, is the Biblical story of Creation, of the Fall, of the Redemption by Christ's Sacrifice on the Cross. As our sacred story lives in our ritual, in our morality, as it governs our faith and controls our conduct, even so does his myth for the savage.

The limitation of the study of myth to the mere examination of texts has been fatal to a proper understanding of its nature. The forms of myth which come to us from classical antiquity and from the ancient sacred books of the East and other similar sources have come down to us without the context of living faith, without the possibility of obtaining comments from true believers, without the concomitant knowledge of their social organization, their practiced morals, and their popular customs – at least without the full information which the modern fieldworker can easily obtain. Moreover, there is no doubt that in their present literary form these tales have suffered a very considerable transformation at the hands of scribes, commentators, learned priests, and theologians. It is necessary to go back to primitive mythology in order to learn the secret of its life in the study of a myth which is still alive – before, mummified in priestly wisdom, it has been enshrined in the indestructible but lifeless repository of dead religions.

Studied alive, myth, as we shall see, is not symbolic, but a direct expression of its subject matter; it is not an explanation in satisfaction of a scientific interest, but a narrative resurrection of a primeval reality, told in satisfaction of deep religious wants, moral cravings, social submissions, assertions, even practical requirements. Myth fulfills in primitive culture an indispensable function: it expresses, enhances, and codifies belief; it safeguards and enforces morality; it vouches for the efficiency of ritual and contains practical rules for the guidance of man. Myth is thus a vital ingredient of human civilization; it is not an idle tale, but a hard-worked active force; it is not an intellectual explanation or an artistic imagery, but a pragmatic charter of primitive faith and moral wisdom.

[…]

We will examine a number of myths [from Trobriand] in detail, but for the moment let us glance at the subjects of some typical myths. Take, for instance, the annual feast of the return of the dead. Elaborate arrangements are made for it, especially an enormous display of food. When this feast approaches, tales are told of how death began to chastise man, and how the power of eternal rejuvenation was lost. It is told why the spirits have to leave the village and do not remain at the fireside, finally why they return once in a year. Again, at certain seasons in preparation for an overseas expedition, canoes are overhauled and new ones built to the accompaniment of a special magic. In this there are mythological allusions in the spells, and even the sacred acts contain elements which are only comprehensible when the story of the flying canoe, its ritual, and its magic are told. In connection with ceremonial trading, the rules, the magic, even the geographical routes are associated with corresponding mythology. There is no important magic, no ceremony, no ritual without belief; and the belief is spun out into accounts of concrete precedent. The union is very intimate, for myth is not only looked upon as a commentary of additional information, but it is a warrant, a charter, and often even a practical guide to the activities with which it is connected. On the other hand the rituals, ceremonies, customs, and social organization contain at times direct references to myth, and they are regarded as the results of mythical event. The cultural fact is a monument in which the myth; is embodied; while the myth is believed to be the real cause which has brought about the moral rule, the social grouping, the rite, or the custom. Thus these stories form an integral part of culture. Their existence and influence not merely transcend the act of telling the narrative, not only do they draw their substance from life and its interests – they govern and control many cultural features, [and] they form the dogmatic backbone of primitive civilization.

This is perhaps the most important point of the thesis which I am urging; I maintain that there exists a special class of stories, regarded as sacred, embodied in ritual, morals, and social organization, and which form an integral and active part of primitive culture. These stories live not by idle interest, not as fictitious or even as true narratives; but are to the natives a statement of a primeval, greater, and more relevant reality, by which the present life, fates, and activities of mankind are determined, the knowledge of which supplies man with the motive for ritual and moral actions, as well as with indications as to how to perform them.

[...]

We may best start with the beginning of things, and examine some of the myths of origin. The world, say the natives, was originally peopled from underground. Humanity had there led an existence similar in all respects to the present life on earth. Underground, men were organized in villages, clans, districts; they had distinctions of rank, they knew privileges and had claims, they owned property, and were versed in magic lore. Endowed with all this, they emerged, establishing by this very act certain rights in land and citizenship, in economic prerogative and magical pursuit. They brought with them all their culture to continue it upon this earth.

There are a number of special spots – grottoes, clumps of trees, stone heaps, coral outcrops, springs, heads of creeks – called 'holes' or 'houses' by the natives. From such 'holes' the first couples (a sister as the head of the family and the brother as her guardian) came and took possession of the lands, and gave the totemic, industrial, magical, and sociological character to the communities thus begun.

The problem of rank which plays a great role in their sociology was settled by the emergence from one special hole, called Obukula, near the village of Laba'i. This event was notable in that, contrary to the usual course (which is: one original 'hole,' one lineage), from this hole of Laba'i there emerged representatives of the four main clans one after the other. Their arrival, moreover, was followed by an apparently trivial but, in mythical reality, a most important event. First there came the *Kaylavasi* (iguana), the animal of the Lukulabuta clan, which scratched its way through the earth as iguanas do, then climbed a tree, and remained there as a mere onlooker, following subsequent events. Soon there came out the Dog, totem of the Lukuba clan, who originally had the highest rank. As a third came the Pig, representative of the Malasi clan, which now holds the highest rank. Last came the Lukwasisiga totem, represented in some versions by the Crocodile, in others by the Snake, in others by the Opossum, and sometimes completely ignored. The Dog and Pig ran round, and the Dog, seeing the fruit of the *noku* plant, nosed it, then ate it. Said the Pig: 'Thou eatest *noku*, thou eatest dirt; thou art a low-bred, a commoner; the chief, the *guya'u*, shall be I.' And ever since, the highest subclan of the Malasi clan, the Tabalu, have been the real chiefs.

In order to understand this myth, it is not enough to follow the dialogue between the Dog and the Pig which might appear pointless or even trivial. Once you know the native sociology, the extreme importance of rank, the fact that food and its limitations (the taboos of rank and clan) are the main index of man's social nature, and finally the psychology of totemic identification – you begin to understand how this incident, happening as it did when humanity was *in statu nascendi*, settled once for all the relation between the two rival clans. To understand this myth you must have a good knowledge of their sociology, religion, customs, and outlook. Then, and only then, can you appreciate what this story means to the natives and how it can live in their life. If you stayed among them and learned the language you would constantly find it active in discussion and squabbles in reference to the relative superiority of the various clans, and in the discussions about the various food taboos which frequently raise fine questions of casuistry. Above all, if you were brought into contact with communities where the historical process of the spread of influence of the Malasi clan is still in evolution, you would be brought face to face with this myth as an active force.

Remarkably enough the first and last animals to come out, the iguana and the Lukwasisiga totem, have been from the beginning left in the cold: thus the numerical principle and the logic of events is not very strictly observed in the reasoning of the myth.

If the main myth of Laba'i about the relative superiority of the four clans is very often alluded to throughout the tribe, the minor local myths are not less alive and active, each in its own community. When a party arrives at some distant village they will be told not only the legendary historical tales, but above all the mythological charter of that community, its magical proficiencies, its occupational character, its rank and place in totemic organization. Should there arise land quarrels, encroachment in magical matters, fishing rights, or other privileges the testimony of myth would be referred to.

Let me show concretely the way in which a typical myth of local origins would be retailed in the normal run of native life. Let us watch a party of visitors arriving in one or the other of the Trobriand villages. They would seat themselves in front of the headman's house, in the central place of the locality. As likely as not the spot of origins is nearby, marked by a coral outcrop or a heap of stones.

This spot would be pointed out, the names of the brother and sister ancestors mentioned, and perhaps it would be said that the man built his house on the spot of the present headman's dwelling. The native listeners would know, of course, that the sister lived in a different house nearby, for she could never reside within the same walls as her brother.

As additional information, the visitors might be told that the ancestors had brought with them the substances and paraphernalia and methods of local industry. In the village of Yalaka, for instance, it would be the processes for burning lime from shells. In Okobobo, Obweria, and Obowada the ancestors brought the knowledge and the implements for polishing hard stone. In Bwoytalu the carver's tool, the hatted shark tooth, and the knowledge of the art came out from underground with the original ancestors. In most places the economic monopolies are thus traced to the autochthonous emergence. In villages of higher rank the insignia of hereditary dignity were brought; in others some animal associated with the local subclan came out. Some communities started on their political career of standing hostility to one another from the very beginning. The most important gift to this world carried from the one below is always magic; but this will have to be treated later on and more fully.

If a European bystander were there and heard nothing but the information given from one native to the other, it would mean very little to him. In fact, it might lead him into serious misunderstandings. Thus the simultaneous emergence of brother and sister might make him suspicious either of a mythological allusion to incest, or else would make him look for the original matrimonial pair and inquire about the sister's husband. The first suspicion would be entirely erroneous, and would shed a false light over the specific relation between brother and sister, in which the former is the indispensable guardian, and the second, equally indispensable, is responsible for the transmission of the line. Only a full knowledge of the matrilineal ideas and institutions gives body and meaning to the bare mention of the two ancestral names, so significant to a native listener. If the European were to inquire who was the sister's husband and how she came to have children, he would soon find himself once more confronted by an entirely foreign set of ideas – the sociological irrelevance of the father, the absence of any ideas about physiological procreation, and the strange and complicated system of marriage, matrilineal and patrilocal at the same time.[1]

The sociological relevance of these accounts of origins would become clear only to a European inquirer who had grasped the native legal ideas about local citizenship and the hereditary rights to territory, fishing grounds, and local pursuits.

For according to the legal principles of the tribe all such rights are the monopolies of the local community, and only people descendent in the female line from the original ancestress are entitled to them. If the European were told further that, besides the first place of emergence, there are several other 'holes' in the same village, he would become still more baffled until, by a careful study of concrete details and the principles of native sociology, he became acquainted with the idea of compound village communities, i.e., communities in which several subclans have merged.

It is clear, then, that the myth conveys much more to the native than is contained in the mere story; that the story gives only the really relevant concrete local differences; that the real meaning, in fact the full account, is contained in the traditional foundations of social organization; and that this the native learns, not by listening to the fragmentary mythical stories, but by living within the social texture of his tribe. In other words, it is the context of social life, it is the gradual realization by the native of how everything which he is told to do has its precedent and pattern in bygone times, which brings home to him the full account and the full meaning of his myths of origin.

For an observer, therefore, it is necessary to become fully acquainted with the social organization of the natives if he wants really to grasp its traditional aspect. The short accounts, such as those which are given about local origins, will then become perfectly plain to him. He will also clearly see that each of them is only a part, and a rather insignificant one, of a much bigger story, which cannot be read except from native life. What really matters about such a story is its social function. It conveys, expresses, and strengthens the fundamental fact of the local unity and of the kinship unity of the group of people descendent from a common ancestress. Combined with the conviction that only common descent and emergence from the soil give full rights to it, the story of origin literally contains the legal charter of the community. Thus, even when the people of a vanquished community were driven from their grounds by a hostile neighbor their territory always remained intact for them; and they were always, after a lapse of time and when their peace ceremony had been concluded, allowed to return to the original site, rebuild their village, and cultivate their gardens once more.[2] The traditional feeling of a real and intimate connection with the land; the concrete reality of seeing the actual spot of emergence in the middle of the scenes of daily life; the historical continuity of privileges, occupations, and distinctive characters running back into the mythological first beginnings – all this obviously makes for cohesion, for local patriotism, for a feeling of union and kinship in the community. But although the narrative of original emergence integrates and welds together the historical tradition, the legal principles, and the various customs, it must also be clearly kept in mind that the original myth is but a small part of the whole complex of traditional ideas. Thus on the one hand the reality of myth lies in its social function; on the other hand, once we begin to study the social function of myth, and so to reconstruct its full meaning, we are gradually led to build up the full theory of native social organization.

One of the most interesting phenomena connected with traditional precedent and charter is the adjustment of myth and mythological principle to cases in which the very foundation of such mythology is flagrantly violated. This violation always takes place when the local claims of an autochthonous clan, i.e., a clan which has emerged on the spot, are overridden by an immigrant clan. Then a conflict of principles is created, for obviously the principle that land and authority belong to those who are literally born out of it does not leave room for any newcomers. On the other hand, members of a subclan of high rank who choose to settle down in a new locality cannot very well be resisted by the autochthons – using this word again in the literal native mythological sense. The result is that there come into existence a special class of mythological stories which justify and account for the anomalous state of affairs. The strength of the various mythological and legal principles is manifested in that the myths of justification still contain the antagonistic and logically irreconcilable facts and points of view, and only try to cover them by facile reconciliatory incident, obviously manufactured *ad hoc*. The study of such stories is extremely interesting, both because it gives us a deep insight into the native psychology of tradition, and because it tempts us to reconstruct the past history of the tribe, though we must yield to the temptation with due caution and scepticism.

[...]

As far as the sociological theory of these legends goes the historical reconstruction is irrelevant. Whatever the hidden reality of their unrecorded past may be, myths serve to cover certain inconsistencies created by historical events, rather than to record these events exactly. The myths associated with the spread of the powerful subclans show on certain points a fidelity to life in that they record facts inconsistent with one another. The incidents by which this inconsistency is obliterated, if not hidden, are most likely fictitious; we have seen certain myths vary according to the locality in which they are told. In other cases the incidents bolster up non-existent claims and rights.

The historical consideration of myth is interesting, therefore, in that it shows that myth, taken as a whole, cannot be sober dispassionate history, since it is always made *ad hoc* to fulfill a certain sociological function, to glorify a certain group, or to justify an anomalous status. These considerations shows us also that to the native mind immediate history, semi-historic legend, and unmixed myth flow into one another, form a continuous sequence, and fulfill really the same sociological function.

And this brings us once more to our original contention that the really important thing about the myth is its character of a retrospective, ever-present, live actuality. It is to native neither a fictitious story, nor an account of a dead past; it is statement of a bigger reality still partially alive. It is alive. It is alive in that its precedent, its law, its moral, still rule the social life of the natives, It is clear that myth functions especially where there is a sociological strain, such as in matters of great difference in rank and power, matters of precedence and subordinations, and unquestionably where profound historical changes have taken place. So much can be asserted as a fact, though it must always remain doubtful how far we can carry out historical reconstruction from the myth.

We can certainly discard all explanatory as well as all symbolic interpretations of these myths of origin. The personages and beings which we find in them are what they appear to be on the surface, and not symbols of hidden realities. As to any explanatory function of these myths, there is no problem which they cover, no curiosity which they satisfy, no theory which they contain.

[...]

The science of myth in living higher cultures, such as the present civilization of India, Japan, China, and last but not least, our own, might well be inspired by the comparative study of primitive folklore; and in its turn civilized culture could furnish important additions and explanations to savage mythology. This subject is very much beyond the scope of the present study. I do, however, want to emphasize the fact that anthropology should be not only the study of savage custom in the light of our mentality and our culture, but also the study of our own mentality in the distant perspective borrowed from Stone Age man. By dwelling mentally for some time among people of much simpler culture than our own, we may be able to see ourselves from a distance, [and] we may be able to gain a new sense of proportion with regard to our own institutions, beliefs, and customs. If anthropology could thus inspire us with some sense of proportion, and supply us with finer sense of humor, it might justify claim to be a very great science.

I have now completed the survey of fact and the range of conclusions; it only remains to summarize them briefly. I have tried to show that folklore, these stories handed on in a native community, live[s] in the culture context of tribal life and not merely in narrative. By this I mean that the ideas, emotions, and desires associated with a given story are experienced not only when the story is told, but also when in certain customs, moral rules, or ritual proceedings, the counterpart of the story is enacted. And here a considerable difference is discovered between the several types of story. While in the mere fireside *tale* the sociological context is narrow, the *legend* enters much more deeply into the tribal life of the community, and the *myth* plays a most important function. Myth, as a statement of primeval reality which still lives in present-day life and as a justification by precedent, supplies a retrospective pattern of moral values, sociological order, and magical belief. It is, therefore, neither a mere narrative, nor a form of science, nor a branch of art or history, nor an explanatory tale. It fulfills a function *sui generis* closely connected with the nature of tradition, and the continuity of culture, with the relation between age and youth, and with the human attitude towards the past. The function of myth, briefly, is to strengthen tradition and endow it with a greater value and prestige by tracing it back to a higher, better, more supernatural reality of initial events.

Myth is, therefore, an indispensable ingredient of all culture. It is, as we have seen, constantly regenerated; every historical change creates its mythology, which is, however, but indirectly related to historical fact. Myth is a constant by-product of living faith, which is in need of miracles; of sociological status, which demands precedent; of moral rule, which requires sanction.

Notes

1   For a full statement of the psychology and sociology of kinship and descent see articles
on 'The Psychology of Sex and the Foundations of Kinship in Primitive Societies',
'Psycho-analysis and Anthropology', 'Complex and Myth in Mother Right', all three in
the psychological journal, *Psyche*, October 1923, April 1924, and January 1925. The first
article is included in *The Father in Primitive Psychology* (Psyche Miniature, 1926).

2   *Cf.* The account given of these facts is in the article on 'War and Weapons among the
Trobriand Islanders', *Man*, January 1918; and in Professor Seligman's *Melanesians*, pp.
663–668.

References

Malinowski, B. (1920). War and Weapons among the Natives of the Trobriand Islands. *Man*
20: 10–12.

Malinowski, B. (1923). Psycho-analysis and Anthropology. *Nature* 112 (2818): 650.

Malinowski, B. (1923). The Psychology of Sex and the Foundations of Kinship in Primitive
Societies. *Psyche* 4 (98): 128.

Malinowski, B. (1925). Complex and Myth in Mother-Right. *Psyche* 5: 194–216.

Malinowski, B. (1927). *The Father in Primitive Psychology*. London: Kegan Paul, Trench,
Trubner & Co.

Seligman, C. G., Barton, F. R., and Giblin, E. L. (1900). *The Melanesians of British New
Guinea*. Cambridge: University Press.

part two

Why do myths exist?

Section A: Global theories of myth

Are all myths the same?

Professor Joseph Campbell was teaching an introductory class on mythology, at Sarah Lawrence College, in the United States, when he began to see patterns in the different myths that he was teaching. This understanding culminated in his now-famous book *The Hero with a Thousand Faces*, which argues that fundamentally all hero myths are variants of the same story. The feeling that myths, seemingly separated by great expanses of time and space, are somehow connected is a common one, and Campbell was far from the first academic to comment on this. Otto Rank, also featured in this section (Part Two, Section A, Chapter 2), had developed and published an alternative hero's journey long before Campbell and Sir James George Frazer's *The Golden Bough*, which traced patterns of mythic communication and ritual action around the world, captured the public imagination before Campbell was born (see Part Two, Section A, Chapter 1).

The texts in this section are therefore united in their perception of widespread, if not universal, repeating patterns of action and themes. For Frazer, the origin of these themes is human beings' shared (ritual) connection to the cycles of nature, whereas both Campbell and Rank trace this origin to more inward forms of the human condition. In simplistic terms, Rank can be seen to be following a psychoanalytical, Freudian view, which places the origin of myths in childhood trauma, whereas Campbell can be positioned as a Jungian, who sees myths as expression of universal archetypes. This is, of course, an overgeneralization that does not do justice to the subtleties of either position or the proclaimed source material, but the Freud/Jung binary can provide a useful lens for the beginning of engagement with Rank and Campbell's theories.

The quest for universal patterns is a tantalizing one that combines the thrill of the detective's trail with the satisfaction of the sense of wisdom that comes from the final, grand reveal, after which it all seems so obvious. However, for all its allure, this approach also is susceptible to serious errors, the chief of which is that the quest for similarity can lead to an overlooking of important differences. The reduction of complex myths and societies to a handful of pertinent elements does not allow for a full understanding of the mythology in its own terms. What is more, the decontextualization of mythic elements can lead to misinterpretation, especially when the analysts are stretched to cover societies and languages that they have only a surface-level understanding of. Finally, it is worth remembering that humans are pattern-making creatures, and when presented with (even chaotic) data, it is our habit to sort it into recognizable patterns.

In all three of the texts that we have included in this section, the inevitable errors, which the tendencies listed above cause to creep into the analysis, are well documented. Nevertheless, it is our view that the texts in this section still reward the informed and critically aware reader, who takes the time to engage with this material directly. Despite their flaws, all these theorists do have something valuable to offer: they resonate with popular understanding and have collectively had a dramatic impact on common conceptions of global mythology.

Balder and the mistletoe

James Frazer

1

Sir James George Frazer (1854–1941) the Scottish anthropologist, folklorist and classicist is most well known for his work *The Golden Bough* (first pub. 1890), which has influenced generations of scholars in the fields of anthropology, classical studies and literature. The text, which was greatly expanded in later editions, has never been out of print. Frazer studied at Glasgow University before moving to Trinity College, Cambridge University, where he sat his Classics Tripos examinations in 1878. He was offered a college fellowship in 1879, after which he remained in Cambridge for most of his life, apart from a year at the University of Liverpool, where he was Professor of social anthropology. He was elected member of the British Academy in 1902 and was Knighted in 1914.

Frazer's primary work lies in the exploration of religion, where he was heavily influenced by both E. B. Tylor's *Primitive Culture* and the thought of William Robertson Smith, a fellow Scotsman who he met during his time at Cambridge. Robertson Smith was the co-editor of *Encyclopaedia Britannica, 9th edition*, and he asked Frazer to contribute articles on 'totemism' and 'taboo', which sparked his interest in comparative myths and anthropology. Frazer's view of myth is often classified as part of the myth-ritual school, which demonstrates that the origins of myth lie in ritual, and in *The Golden Bough*, he aims to establish precisely those links through a wide-ranging exploration of mythology. The material that follows is taken from *The Golden Bough* and demonstrates how, in an attempt to explain a particular Norse myth, Frazer leads us through a vast range of myths and rituals from other times and places. The section is also notable as one of the most commonly critiqued elements of Frazer's work, which has been the subject of sustained, largely justified criticism in the decades since its first publication.

The reader may remember that the preceding account of the popular fire-festivals of Europe was suggested by the myth of the Norse god Balder, who is said to have been slain by a branch of mistletoe and burnt in a great fire. We have now to enquire how far the customs which have been passed in review help to shed light on the myth. In this enquiry it may be convenient to begin with the mistletoe, the instrument of Balder's death.

From time immemorial the mistletoe has been the object of superstitious veneration in Europe. It was worshipped by the Druids, as we learn from a famous passage of Pliny. After enumerating the different kinds of mistletoe, he proceeds: 'In treating of this subject, the admiration in which the mistletoe is held throughout Gaul ought not to pass unnoticed. The Druids, for so they call their wizards, esteem nothing more sacred than the mistletoe and the tree on which it grows, provided only that the tree is an oak. But apart from this they choose oak-woods for their sacred groves and perform no sacred rites without oak-leaves; so that the very name of Druids may be regarded as a Greek appellation derived from their worship of the oak. For they believe that whatever grows on these trees is sent from heaven, and is a sign that the tree has been chosen by the god himself. The mistletoe is very rarely to be met with; but when it is found, they gather it with solemn ceremony. This they do above all on the sixth day of the moon, from whence they date the beginnings of their months, of their years, and of their thirty years' cycle, because by the sixth day the moon has plenty of vigour and has not run half its course. After due preparations have been made for a sacrifice and a feast under the tree, they hail it as the universal healer and bring to the spot two white bulls, whose horns have never been bound before. A priest clad in a white robe climbs the tree and with a golden sickle cuts the mistletoe, which is caught in a white cloth. Then they sacrifice the victims, praying that God may make his own gift to prosper with those upon whom he has bestowed it. They believe that a potion prepared from mistletoe will make barren animals to bring forth, and that the plant is a remedy against all poison.'

[...]

[...] both [Italians and Druids] deemed it an effectual remedy for a number of ailments, and both of them ascribed to it a quickening virtue, the Druids believing that a potion prepared from mistletoe would fertilise barren cattle, and the Italians holding that a piece of mistletoe carried about by a woman would help her to conceive a child. Further, both peoples thought that if the plant were to exert its medicinal properties it must be gathered in a certain way and at a certain time. It might not be cut with iron, hence the Druids cut it with gold; and it might not touch the earth, hence the Druids caught it in a white cloth. In choosing the time for gathering the plant, both peoples were determined by observation of the moon; only they differed as to the particular day of the moon, the Italians preferring the first, and the Druids the sixth.

With these beliefs of the ancient Gauls and Italians as to the wonderful medicinal properties of mistletoe we may compare the similar beliefs of the modern Aino of

Japan. We read that they, 'like many nations of the Northern origin, hold the mistletoe in peculiar veneration. They look upon it as a medicine, good in almost every disease, and it is sometimes taken in food and at others separately as a decoction. The leaves are used in preference to the berries, the latter being of too sticky a nature for general purposes. ... But many, too, suppose this plant to have the power of making the gardens bear plentifully. When used for this purpose, the leaves are cut up into fine pieces, and, after having been prayed over, are sown with the millet and other seeds, a little also being eaten with the food. Barren women have also been known to eat the mistletoe, in order to be made to bear children. That mistletoe which grows upon the willow is supposed to have the greatest efficacy. This is because the willow is looked upon by them as being an especially sacred tree.'

Thus the Aino agree with the Druids in regarding mistletoe as a cure for almost every disease, and they agree with the ancient Italians that applied to women it helps them to bear children. Again, the Druidical notion that the mistletoe was an 'all-healer' or panacea may be compared with a notion entertained by the Walos of Senegambia. These people 'have much veneration for a sort of mistletoe, which they call tob; they carry leaves of it on their persons when they go to war as a preservative against wounds, just as if the leaves were real talismans (gris-gris).' The French writer who records this practice adds: 'Is it not very curious that the mistletoe should be in this part of Africa what it was in the superstitions of the Gauls? This prejudice, common to the two countries, may have the same origin; blacks and whites will doubtless have seen, each of them for themselves, something supernatural in a plant which grows and flourishes without having roots in the earth. May they not have believed, in fact, that it was a plant fallen from the sky, a gift of the divinity?'

This suggestion as to the origin of the superstition is strongly confirmed by the Druidical belief, reported by Pliny, that whatever grew on an oak was sent from heaven and was a sign that the tree had been chosen by the god himself. Such a belief explains why the Druids cut the mistletoe, not with a common knife, but with a golden sickle, and why, when cut, it was not suffered to touch the earth; probably they thought that the celestial plant would have been profaned and its marvellous virtue lost by contact with the ground. With the ritual observed by the Druids in cutting the mistletoe we may compare the ritual which in Cambodia is prescribed in a similar case. They say that when you see an orchid growing as a parasite on a tamarind tree, you should dress in white, take a new earthenware pot, then climb the tree at noon, break off the plant, put it in the pot and let the pot fall to the ground. After that you make in the pot a decoction which confers the gift of invulnerability. Thus just as in Africa the leaves of one parasitic plant are supposed to render the wearer invulnerable, so in Cambodia a decoction made from another parasitic plant is considered to render the same service to such as make use of it, whether by drinking or washing. We may conjecture that in both places the notion of invulnerability is suggested by the position of the plant, which, occupying a place of comparative security above the ground, appears to promise to its fortunate possessor a similar security from some of the ills that beset the life of man on earth.

We have already met with examples of the store which the primitive mind sets on such vantage grounds.

Whatever may be the origin of these beliefs and practices concerning the mistletoe, certain it is that some of them have their analogies in the folk-lore of modern European peasants. For example, it is laid down as a rule in various parts of Europe that mistletoe may not be cut in the ordinary way but must be shot or knocked down with stones from the tree on which it is growing. Thus, in the Swiss canton of Aargau 'all parasitic plants are esteemed in a certain sense holy by the country folk, but most particularly so the mistletoe growing on an oak. They ascribe great powers to it, but shrink from cutting it off in the usual manner. Instead of that they procure it in the following manner. When the sun is in Sagittarius and the moon is on the wane, on the first, third, or fourth day before the new moon, one ought to shoot down with an arrow the mistletoe of an oak and to catch it with the left hand as it falls. Such mistletoe is a remedy for every ailment of children.'

Here among the Swiss peasants, as among the Druids of old, special virtue is ascribed to mistletoe which grows on an oak: it may not be cut in the usual way: it must be caught as it falls to the ground; and it is esteemed a panacea for all diseases, at least of children. In Sweden, also, it is a popular superstition that if mistletoe is to possess its peculiar virtue, it must either be shot down out of the oak or knocked down with stones. Similarly, 'so late as the early part of the nineteenth century, people in Wales believed that for the mistletoe to have any power, it must be shot or struck down with stones off the tree where it grew.'

[...]

Again the ancient Italian opinion that mistletoe extinguishes fire appears to be shared by Swedish peasants, who hang up bunches of oak-mistletoe on the ceilings of their rooms as a protection against harm in general and conflagration in particular. A hint as to the way in which mistletoe comes to be possessed of this property is furnished by the epithet 'thunder-bosom,' which people of the Aargau canton in Switzerland apply to the plant. For a thunder-besom is a shaggy, bushy excrescence on branches of trees, which is popularly believed to be produced by a flash of lightning; hence in Bohemia a thunder-besom burnt in the fire protects the house against being struck by a thunder-bolt. Being itself a product of lightning it naturally serves, on homoeopathic principles, as a protection against lightning, in fact as a kind of lightning-conductor. Hence the fire which mistletoe in Sweden is designed especially to avert from houses may be fire kindled by lightning; though no doubt the plant is equally effective against conflagration in general.

Again, mistletoe acts as a master-key as well as a lightning-conductor; for it is said to open all locks. But perhaps the most precious of all the virtues of mistletoe is that it affords efficient protection against sorcery and witchcraft. That, no doubt, is the reason why in Austria a twig of mistletoe is laid on the threshold as a preventive of nightmare; and it may be the reason why in the north of England they say that if you wish your dairy to thrive you should give your bunch of mistletoe to the first cow that calves after New Year's Day, for it is well known that nothing is so fatal to milk and butter as witchcraft. Similarly in Wales, for the sake of ensuring good luck to the dairy, people used to give a branch of mistletoe to the first cow that gave birth to a calf after the first hour of the New Year; and in rural districts of Wales, where mistletoe abounded, there was always a profusion of it in the farmhouses. When mistletoe was scarce, Welsh farmers used to say, 'No mistletoe, no luck'; but if there was a fine crop of mistletoe, they expected a fine crop of corn. In Sweden mistletoe is diligently sought after on St. John's Eve, the people 'believing it to be, in a high degree, possessed of mystic qualities; and that if a sprig of it be attached to the ceiling of the dwelling-house, the horse's stall, or the cow's crib, the Troll will then be powerless to injure either man or beast.'

[...]

Be that as it may, certain it is that the mistletoe, the instrument of Balder's death, has been regularly gathered for the sake of its mystic qualities on Midsummer Eve in Scandinavia, Balder's home. The plant is found commonly growing on pear-trees, oaks, and other trees in thick damp woods throughout the more temperate parts of Sweden. Thus one of the two main incidents of Balder's myth is reproduced in the great midsummer festival of Scandinavia. But the other main incident of the myth, the burning of Balder's body on a pyre, has also its counterpart in the bonfires which still blaze, or blazed till lately, in Denmark, Norway, and Sweden on Midsummer Eve. It does not appear, indeed, that any effigy is burned in these bonfires; but the burning of an effigy is a feature which might easily drop out after its meaning was forgotten. And the name of Balder's balefires (Balder's Balar), by which these midsummer fires were formerly known in Sweden, puts their connexion with Balder beyond the reach of doubt, and makes it probable that in former times either a living representative or an effigy of Balder was annually burned in them. Midsummer was the season sacred to Balder, and the Swedish poet Tegner, in placing the burning of Balder at midsummer, may very well have followed an old tradition that the summer solstice was the time when the good god came to his untimely end.

Thus it has been shown that the leading incidents of the Balder myth have their counterparts in those fire-festivals of our European peasantry which undoubtedly date from a time long prior to the introduction of Christianity. The pretence of throwing the victim chosen by lot into the Beltane fire, and the similar treatment of the man, the future Green Wolf, at the midsummer bonfire in Normandy, may naturally be interpreted as traces of an older custom of actually burning human beings on these occasions; and the green dress of the Green Wolf, coupled with the leafy envelope of the young fellow who trod out the midsummer fire at Moosheim, seems to hint that the persons who perished at these festivals did so in the character of tree-spirits or deities of vegetation. From all this we may reasonably infer that in the Balder myth on the one hand, and the fire-festivals and custom of gathering mistletoe on the other hand, we have, as it were, the two broken and dissevered halves of an original whole. In other words, we may assume with some degree of probability that the myth of

Balder's death was not merely a myth, that is, a description of physical phenomena in imagery borrowed from human life, but that it was at the same time the story which people told to explain why they annually burned a human representative of the god and cut the mistletoe with solemn ceremony. If I am right, the story of Balder's tragic end formed, so to say, the text of the sacred drama which was acted year by year as a magical rite to cause the sun to shine, trees to grow, crops to thrive, and to guard man and beast from the baleful arts of fairies and trolls, of witches and warlocks. The tale belonged, in short, to that class of nature myths which are meant to be supplemented by ritual; here, as so often, myth stood to magic in the relation of theory to practice.

But if the victims – the human Balders – who died by fire, whether in spring or at midsummer, were put to death as living embodiments of tree-spirits or deities of vegetation, it would seem that Balder himself must have been a tree-spirit or deity of vegetation. It becomes desirable, therefore, to determine, if we can, the particular kind of tree or trees, of which a personal representative was burned at the fire-festivals. For we may be quite sure that it was not as a representative of vegetation in general that the victim suffered death. The idea of vegetation in general is too abstract to be primitive. Most probably the victim at first represented a particular kind of sacred tree. But of all European trees none has such claims as the oak to be considered as pre-eminently the sacred tree of the Aryans. We have seen that its worship is attested for all the great branches of the Aryan stock in Europe; hence we may certainly conclude that the tree was venerated by the Aryans in common before the dispersion, and that their primitive home must have lain in a land which was clothed with forests of oak.

Now, considering the primitive character and remarkable similarity of the fire-festivals observed by all the branches of the Aryan race in Europe, we may infer that these festivals form part of the common stock of religious observances which the various peoples carried with them in their wanderings from their old home. But, if I am right, an essential feature of those primitive fire-festivals was the burning of a man who represented the tree-spirit. In view, then, of the place occupied by the oak in the religion of the Aryans, the presumption is that the tree so represented at the fire-festivals must originally have been the oak. So far as the Celts and Lithuanians are concerned, this conclusion will perhaps hardly be contested. But both for them and for the Germans it is confirmed by a remarkable piece of religious conservatism. The most primitive method known to man of producing fire is by rubbing two pieces of wood against each other till they ignite; and we have seen that this method is still used in Europe for kindling sacred fires such as the need-fire, and that most probably it was formerly resorted to at all the fire-festivals under discussion. Now it is sometimes required that the needfire, or other sacred fire, should be made by the friction of a particular kind of wood; and when the kind of wood is prescribed, whether among Celts, Germans, or Slavs, that wood appears to be generally the oak. But if the sacred fire was regularly kindled by the friction of oak-wood, we may infer that originally the fire was also fed with the same material. In point of fact, it appears that the perpetual fire of Vesta at Rome was fed with oak-wood, and that oak-wood was the fuel consumed in the perpetual fire which burned under the sacred oak at the great Lithuanian sanctuary of Romove. Further, that oak-wood was formerly the fuel burned in the midsummer fires may perhaps be inferred from the custom, said to be still observed by peasants in many mountain districts of Germany, of making up the cottage fire on Midsummer Day with a heavy block of oak-wood. The block is so arranged that it smoulders slowly and is not finally reduced to charcoal till the expiry of a year. Then upon next Midsummer Day the charred embers of the old log are removed to make room for the new one, and are mixed with the seed-corn or scattered about the garden. This is believed to guard the food cooked on the hearth from witchcraft, to preserve the luck of the house, to promote the growth of the crops, and to keep them from blight and vermin. Thus the custom is almost exactly parallel to that of the Yule-log, which in parts of Germany, France, England, Serbia, and other Slavonic lands was commonly of oak-wood. The general conclusion is, that at those periodic or occasional ceremonies the ancient Aryans both kindled and fed the fire with the sacred oak-wood.

But if at these solemn rites the fire was regularly made of oak-wood, it follows that any man who was burned in it as a personification of the tree-spirit could have represented no tree but the oak. The sacred oak was thus burned in duplicate; the wood of the tree was consumed in the fire, and along with it was consumed a living man as a personification of the oak-spirit. The conclusion thus drawn for the European Aryans in general is confirmed in its special application to the Scandinavians by the relation in which amongst them the mistletoe appears to have stood to the burning of the victim in the midsummer fire. We have seen that among Scandinavians it has been customary to gather the mistletoe at midsummer. But so far as appears on the face of this custom, there is nothing to connect it with the midsummer fires in which human victims or effigies of them were burned. Even if the fire, as seems probable, was originally always made with oak-wood, why should it have been necessary to pull the mistletoe? The last link between the midsummer customs of gathering the mistletoe and lighting the bonfires is supplied by Balder's myth, which can hardly be disjoined from the customs in question. The myth suggests that a vital connexion may once have been believed to subsist between the mistletoe and the human representative of the oak who was burned in the fire. According to the myth, Balder could be killed by nothing in heaven or earth except the mistletoe; and so long as the mistletoe remained on the oak, he was not only immortal but invulnerable. Now, if we suppose that Balder was the oak, the origin of the myth becomes intelligible. The mistletoe was viewed as the seat of life of the oak, and so long as it was uninjured nothing could kill or even wound the oak. The conception of the mistletoe as the seat of life of the oak would naturally be suggested to primitive people by the observation that while the oak is deciduous, the mistletoe which grows on it is evergreen. In winter the sight of its fresh foliage among the bare branches must have been hailed by the worshippers of the tree as a sign that the divine life which had ceased to animate the branches yet survived in the mistletoe, as the heart of a sleeper still beats when his body is motionless. Hence when the god had to be killed – when the sacred tree had to be burnt – it was necessary to begin by breaking off the mistletoe. For so long as the mistletoe remained intact, the oak (so people might think) was invulnerable; all the blows of their knives and axes would glance harmless from its surface. But once tear from the oak its sacred heart – the mistletoe – and the tree nodded to its fall. And when in later times the spirit of the oak came to be represented by a living man, it was logically necessary to suppose that, like the tree he personated, he could neither be killed nor wounded so long as the mistletoe remained uninjured. The pulling of the mistletoe was thus at once the signal and the cause of his death.

On this view the invulnerable Balder is neither more nor less than a personification of a mistletoe-bearing oak. The interpretation is confirmed by what seems to have been an ancient Italian belief, that the mistletoe can be destroyed neither by fire nor water; for if the parasite is thus deemed indestructible, it might easily be supposed to communicate its own indestructibility to the tree on which it grows, so long as the two remain in conjunction. Or, to put the same idea in mythical form, we might tell how the kindly god of the oak had his life securely deposited in the imperishable mistletoe which grew among the branches; how accordingly so long as the mistletoe kept its place there, the deity himself remained invulnerable; and how at last a cunning foe, let into the secret of the god's invulnerability, tore the mistletoe from the oak, thereby killing the oak-god and afterwards burning his body in a fire which could have made no impression on him so long as the incombustible parasite retained its seat among the boughs.

The myth of the birth of the hero

Otto Rank

2

Otto Rank (1884–1939) was an Austrian psychoanalyst, who is commonly viewed as the natural successor to Freud's legacy. Rank trained as a locksmith, before encountering Freud's work through independent study. His application of Freud's techniques came to the attention of Freud, who was so impressed by the quality of the work that he recruited him into the Vienna Psychoanalytic Society. Over a period of twenty years, Rank was to work closely with Freud, editing books journals as well as advising on issues of the psychoanalytic approach to mythology and literature. During this time, Rank was awarded a PhD from the University of Vienna, for a thesis exploring the Lohengrin legend.

In 1924 Rank published *The Trauma of Birth*, which placed the child's relation to the mother before that of the father. This was seen by many, including eventually Freud, as a step away from Freud's core propositions, and Rank's latter years were spent in conflict with the main Freudian camp. The reading that we have chosen to include here predates Rank's split with Freud and may be seen as typical of Rank's Freudian analysis of mythology. As such, it focuses on the relationship of the child to the father and myth to neurosis. It is an approach to mythology that (for all its problems) has proved highly influential; as an attempt to map the life of a hero, this analysis provides a useful counterpoint to Campbell's much later, now-famous, hero's journey.

A cursory review of these variegated hero myths forcibly brings out a series of uniformly common features, with a typical ground work, from which a standard saga, as it were, may be constructed. This schedule corresponds approximately to the ideal human skeleton which is constantly seen, with minor deviations, on trans-illumination of figures which outwardly differ from one another. The individual traits of the several myths, and especially apparently crude variations from the prototype, can only be entirely elucidated by the myth-interpretation. The standard saga itself may be formulated according to the following scheme:

The hero is the child of most distinguished parents; usually the son of a king. His origin is preceded by difficulties, such as continence, or prolonged barrenness, or secret intercourse of the parents, due to external prohibition or obstacles. During the pregnancy, or antedating the same, there is a prophecy, in form of a dream or oracle, cautioning against his birth, and usually threatening danger to the father, or his representative. As a rule, he is surrendered to the water, in a box. He is then saved by animals, or by lowly people (shepherds) and is suckled by a female animal, or by a humble woman. After he has grown up, he finds his distinguished parents, in a highly versatile fashion; takes his revenge on his father, on the one hand, is acknowledged on the other, and finally achieves rank and honors.[1]

The normal relations of the hero towards his father and his mother regularly appearing impaired in all these myths, as shown by the schedule, there is reason to assume that something in the nature of the hero must account for such a disturbance, and motives of this kind are not very difficult to discover. It is readily understood – and may be noted in the modern epigones of the heroic age – that for the hero who is exposed to envy, jealousy and calumny to a much higher degree than all others, the descent from his parents often becomes the source of the greatest distress and embarrassment The old saying that 'A prophet is not without honor save in his own country and in his father's house,' has no other meaning but this, that he whose parents, brothers and sisters, or playmates, are known to us, is not so readily conceded to be a prophet (Gospel of St. Mark, VI, 4). There seems to be a certain necessity for the prophet to deny his parents; also, the well-known opera of Meyerbeer is based upon the avowal that the prophetic hero is allowed, in favor of his mission, to abandon and repudiate even his tenderly beloved mother.

A number of difficulties arise, however, as we proceed to a deeper enquiry into the motives which oblige the hero to sever his family relations. Numerous investigators have emphasized that the understanding of myth formation requires our going back to their ultimate source, namely the individual faculty of imagination.[2] The fact has also been pointed out that this imaginative faculty is found in its active and unchecked exuberance only in childhood. Therefore, the imaginative life of the child should first be studied, in order to facilitate the understanding of the far more complex and also more handicapped mythical and artistic imagination in general.

[…]

As we proceed to fit the above features into our scheme, we feel justified in analogizing the ego of the child with the hero of the myth, in view of the unanimous tendency of family romances and hero myths; keeping in mind that the myth throughout reveals an endeavor to get rid of the parents, and that the same wish arises in the phantasies of the individual child at the time when it is trying to establish its personal independence. The ego of the child behaves in this respect like the hero of the myth, and as a matter of fact, the hero should always be interpreted merely as a collective ego, which is equipped with all the excellences. In a similar manner, the hero in personal poetic fiction usually represents the poet himself, or at least one side of his character.

Summarizing the essentials of the hero myth, we find the descent from noble parents, the exposure in a river, and in a box, and the raising by lowly parents; followed in the further evolution of the story by the hero's return to his first parents, with or without punishment meted out to them. It is very evident that the two parent couples of the myth correspond to the real and the imaginary parent couple of the romantic phantasy. Closer inspection reveals the psychological identity of the humble and the noble parents, precisely as in the infantile and neurotic phantasies.

In conformity with the overvaluation of the parents in early childhood, the myth begins with the noble parents, exactly like the romantic phantasy, whereas in reality adults soon adapt themselves to the actual conditions. Thus the phantasy of the family romance is simply realized in the myth, with a bold reversal to the actual conditions. The hostility of the father, and the resulting exposure, accentuate the motive which has caused the ego to indulge in the entire fiction. The fictitious romance is the excuse, as it were, for the hostile feelings which the child harbors against his father, and which in this fiction are projected against the father. The exposure in the myth, therefore, is equivalent to the repudiation or non-recognition in the romantic phantasy. The child simply gets rid of the father in the neurotic romance, while in the myth the father endeavors to lose the child. Rescue and revenge are the natural terminations, as demanded by the essence of the phantasy.

[...]

Another attempt at a reversal to a more original type consists in the following trait: The return to the lowly father, which has been brought about through the separation of the father's role from that of the king, is again nullified through the lowly father's secondary elevation to the rank of a god, as in Perseus and the other sons of virgin mothers; Karna, Ion, Romulus, Jesus. The secondary character of this godly paternity is especially evident in those myths where the virgin who has been impregnated by divine conception, later on marries a mortal (Jesus, Karna, Ion) who then appears as the real father, while the god as the father represents merely the most exalted childish idea of the magnitude, power and perfection of the father.[3] At the same time, these myths strictly insist upon the motive of the virginity of the mother, which elsewhere is merely hinted at. The first impetus is perhaps supplied by the transcendental tendency, necessitated through the introduction of the god. At the same time, the birth from the virgin is the most abrupt repudiation of the father, the consummation of the entire myth, as illustrated by the Sargon legend, which does not admit any father, besides the vestal mother.

The last stage of this progressive attenuation of the hostile relation to the father is represented by that form of the myth in which the person of the royal persecutor not only appears entirely detached from that of the father, but has even lost the remotest kinship with the hero's family, which he opposes in the most hostile manner, as its enemy (in Feridun, Abraham, King Herod against Jesus, and others). Although of his original threefold character as the father, the king, and the persecutor, he retains only the part of the royal persecutor or the tyrant, the entire plan of the myth conveys the impression as if nothing had been changed, but as if the designation as 'father' had been simply replaced by the term of 'tyrant'. This interpretation of the father as a 'tyrant' which is typical of the infantile ideation,[4] will be found later on to possess the greatest importance for the interpretation of certain abnormal constellations of this complex.

The prototype of this identification of the king with the father, which regularly recurs also in the dreams of adults, presumably is the origin of royalty from the patriarchate in the family, which is still attested by the use of identical words for king and father, in the Hindoo-Germanic languages[5] (compare the German 'Landesvater,' father of his country, = king). The reversal of the family romance to actual conditions is almost entirely accomplished in this type of myth. The lowly parents are acknowledged with a frankness which seems to be directly contradictory to the tendency of the entire myth.

Precisely this revelation of the real conditions, which hitherto had to be left to the interpretation, enables us to prove the accuracy of the latter from the material itself. The biblical Moses-legend has been selected, as especially well adapted to this purpose.

Briefly summarizing the outcome of the previous interpretation-mechanism, to make matters plainer, we find the two parent-couples to be identical, after their splitting into the personalities of the father and the tyrannical persecutor has been connected; the high born parents being the echo, as it were, of the exaggerated notions which the child originally harbored concerning its parents. The Moses-legend actually shows the parents of the hero divested of all prominent attributes; they are simple people, devotedly attached to the child, and incapable of harming it. Meanwhile, the assertion of tender feelings for the child is a confirmation, here as well as everywhere, of the bodily parentage (compare Akki, the gardener, in the Gilgamos-legend; the teamster, in the story of Karna; the fisher, in the Perseus myth, etc.). The amicable utilization of the exposure motive, which occurs in this type of myth, is referable to such a relationship. The child is surrendered in a basket to the water, but not with the object of killing it (as for example the hostile exposure of Œdipus and many other heroes), but for the purpose of saving it (compare also Abraham's early history, p. 15). The danger fraught warning to the exalted father becomes a hopeful prophecy for the lowly father (compare, in the birth story of Jesus, the oracle for Herod and Joseph's dream), entirely corresponding to the expectations placed by most parents in the career of their offspring.

Retaining from the original tendency of the romance, the fact that Bitiah, Pharaoh's daughter, drew the child from the water, *i.e.*, gave it birth, the outcome is the familiar theme (grandfather type) of the king, whose daughter is to bear a son, but who on being warned by the ill-omened interpretation of a dream, resolves to kill his forthcoming grandson. The handmaiden of his daughter (who in the biblical story draws the box from the water, at the behest of the princess), is charged by the king with the exposure of the newborn child in a box, in the waters of the river Nile, that it may perish (the exposure motive, from the viewpoint of the highborn parents, here appearing in its original disastrous significance). The box with the child is then found by lowly people, and the poor woman raises the child (as his wet nurse), and when he is grown up he is recognized by the princess as her son (just as in the prototype the phantasy concludes with the recognition by the highborn parents).

If the Moses-legend were placed before us in this more original form, as we have reconstructed it from the existing material,[6] the sum of this interpretation-mechanism would be approximately what is told in the myth as it is actually transmitted; namely that his true mother was not a princess, but the poor woman who was introduced as his nurse, her husband being his father.

This interpretation is offered as the tradition, in the re-converted myth; and the fact that this tracing of the progressive mutation furnishes the familiar type of hero myth, is the proof for the correctness of our interpretation.

It has thus been our good fortune to show the full accuracy of our interpretative technique upon the material itself, and it is now time to demonstrate the tenability of the general viewpoint upon which this entire technique is founded. Hitherto, the results of our interpretation have created the appearance of the entire myth formation as starting from the hero himself, namely from the youthful hero. At the start we took this attitude in analogizing the hero of the myth with the ego of the child. Now we find ourselves confronted with the obligation to harmonize these assumptions and conclusions with the other conceptions of myth formation, which they seem to directly contradict.

The myths are certainly not constructed by the hero, least of all by the child hero, but they have long been known to be the product of a people of adults. The impetus is evidently supplied by the popular amazement at the apparition of the hero, whose extraordinary life history the people can only imagine as ushered in by a wonderful infancy. This extraordinary childhood of the hero, however, is constructed by the individual myth-makers – to whom the indefinite idea of the folk-mind must be ultimately traced – from the consciousness of their own infancy. In investing the hero with their own infantile history, they identify themselves with him, as it were, claiming to have been similar heroes in their own personality. The true hero of the romance is, therefore, the ego, which finds itself in the hero, by reverting to the time when the ego was itself a hero, through its first heroic act, *i.e.*, the revolt against the father. The ego can only find its own heroism in the days of infancy, and it is therefore obliged to invest the hero with its own revolt, crediting him with the features which made the ego a hero. This object is achieved with infantile motives and materials, in reverting to the infantile romance and transferring it to the hero. Myths are, therefore, created by adults, by means of retrograde childhood fantasies,[7] the hero being credited with the myth-maker's personal infantile history. Meanwhile the tendency of this entire process is the excuse of the individual units of the people for their own infantile revolt against the father.

Besides the excuse of the hero for his rebellious revolt, the myth therefore contains also the excuse of the individual for his revolt against the father. This revolt had burdened him since his childhood, as he had failed to become a hero. He is now enabled to excuse himself by emphasizing that the father has given him grounds for his hostility. The affectionate feeling for the father is also manifested in the same fiction, as has been shown above. These myths have therefore sprung from two opposite motives, both of which are subordinate to the motive of vindication of the individual through the hero: on the one hand the motive of affection and gratitude towards the parents; and on the other hand, the motive of the revolt against the father. It is not stated outright in these myths, however, that the conflict with the father arises from the sexual rivalry for the mother, but is apparently suggested that this conflict dates back primarily to the concealment of the sexual processes (at childbirth), which in this way became an enigma for the child. This enigma finds its temporary and symbolical solution in the infantile sexual theory of the basket and the water.[8]

[...]

This explanation of the psychological significance of the myth of the birth of the hero would not be complete without emphasizing its relations to certain mental diseases. Also readers without psychiatric training – or these perhaps more than any others, must have been struck with these relations. As a matter of fact, the hero myths are equivalent in many essential features to the delusional ideas of certain psychotic individuals, who suffer from delusions of persecution and grandeur, – the so called paranoiacs. Their system of delusions is constructed very much like the hero myth, and therefore indicates the same psychogenic motives as the neurotic family romance, which is analysable, whereas the system of delusions is inaccessible even for psychoanalytical approaches. For example, the paranoiac is apt to claim that the people whose name he bears are not his real parents, but that he is actually the son of a princely personage; he was to be removed for some mysterious reason, and was therefore surrendered to his 'parents' as a foster child. His enemies, however, wish to maintain the fiction that he is of lowly descent, in order to suppress his legitimate pretensions to the crown or to enormous riches.[9] Cases of this kind often occupy alienists or tribunals.[10]

This intimate relationship between the hero myth and the delusional structure of paranoiacs has already been definitely established through the characterization of the myth as a paranoid structure, which is here confirmed by its contents. The remarkable fact that paranoiacs will frankly reveal their entire romance has ceased to be puzzling, since the profound investigations of Freud have shown that the contents of hysterical fantasies, which can often be made conscious through analysis, are identical up to the minutest details with the complaints of persecuted paranoiacs; moreover, the identical contents are also encountered as a reality, in the arrangements of perverts for the gratification of their desires.[11]

The egotistical character of the entire system is distinctly revealed by the paranoiac, for whom the exaltation of the parents, as brought about by him, is merely the means for his own exaltation. As a rule the pivot for his entire system is simply the culmination of the family romance, in the apodictic statement: I am the emperor (or god). Reasoning in the symbolism of dreams and myths, which is also the symbolism of all fancies, including the 'morbid' power of imagination – all he accomplishes thereby is to put himself in the place of the father, just as the hero terminates his revolt against the father. This can be done in both instances, because the conflict with the father – which dates back to the concealment of the sexual processes, as suggested by the latest discoveries – is nullified at the instant when the grown boy himself becomes a father. The persistence with which the paranoiac puts himself in the father's place, i.e., becomes a father himself, appears like an illustration to the common answer of little boys to a scolding or a putting off of their inquisitive curiosity: You just wait until I am a papa myself, and I'll know all about it!

Besides the paranoiac, his equally a-social counterpart must also be emphasized. In the expression of the identical fantasy contents, the hysterical individual who has suppressed them, is offset by the pervert, who realizes them, and even so the diseased and passive paranoiac – who needs his delusion for the correction of the actuality, which to him is intolerable – is offset by the active criminal, who endeavors to change the actuality according to his mind. In this special sense, this type is represented by the anarchist. The hero himself, as shown by his detachment from the parents, begins his career in opposition to the older generation; he is at once a rebel, a renovator, and a revolutionary. However, every revolutionary is originally a disobedient son, a rebel against the father.[12] (Compare the suggestion of Freud, in connection with the interpretation of a ' revolutionary dream'. Traurndeutung, II edition, p. 153. See English translation by Brill. Macmillan. Annotation.)

But whereas the paranoiac, in conformity with his passive character, has to suffer persecutions and wrongs which ultimately proceed from the father, and which he endeavors to escape by putting himself in the place of the father or the emperor –the anarchist complies more faithfully with the heroic character, by promptly himself becoming the persecutor of kings, and finally killing the king, precisely like the hero. The remarkable similarity between the career of certain anarchistic criminals and the family romance of hero and child has been illustrated by the author, through special instances (Belege zur Rettungsphantasie, *Zentralblatt f. Psychoanalyse*, I, 1911, p. 331, and Die Rolle des Familienromans in der Psychologie des Attentäters, Internationale Zeitschrift für aerztliche Psychoanalyse, I, 1913). The truly heroic element then consists only in the real justice or even necessity of the act, which is therefore generally endorsed and admired;[13] while the morbid trait, also in criminal cases, is the pathologic transference of the hatred from the father to the real king, or several kings, when more general and still more distorted.

As the hero is commended for the same deed, without asking for its psychic motivation, so the anarchist might claim indulgence from the severest penalties, for the reason that he has killed an entirely different person from the one he really intended to destroy, in spite of an apparently excellent perhaps political motivation of his act.[14]

For the present let us stop at the narrow boundary line where the contents of innocent infantile imaginings, suppressed and unconscious neurotic fantasies, poetical myth structures, and certain forms of mental disease and crime lie close together, although far apart as to their causes and dynamic forces. We resist the temptation to follow one of these divergent paths which lead to altogether different realms, but which are as yet unblazed trails in the wilderness.

Notes

1   The possibility of further specification of separate items of this schedule will be seen from the compilation as given by H. Lessmann, at the conclusion of his work on 'The Kyros Saga in Europe'.

2   See also Wundt, who psychologically interprets the hero as a projection of human desires and aspirations (loc. cit., p. 48).

3   A similar identification of the father with God (heavenly father, etc.) occurs, according to Freud, with the same regularity in the fantasies of normal and pathological psychic activity as the identification of the emperor with the father. It is also noteworthy in this connection that almost all peoples derive their origin from their god (Abraham, 'Dream and Myth,' Monograph Series, No. 15).

4   An amusing example of unconscious humor in children recently ran through the daily press: A politician had explained to his little son that a tyrant is a man who forces others to do what he commands, without heeding their wishes in the matter. 'Well,' said the child, 'then you and mamma are also tyrants!'

5   See Max Müller, 'Essais,' vol. II (Leipzig, 1869), p. 20 et seq. Concerning the various psychological contingencies of this setting, compare p. 83 et al. of the author's 'Incest Book.'

6   Compare E. Meyer (*Bericht d. Kgl. preuss. Akad. d. Wiss.*, XXXI, 1905, p. 640). The Moses legends and the Levites: 'Presumably Moses was originally the son of the tyrant's daughter (who is now his foster mother), and probably of divine origin.' The subsequent elaboration into the present form is probably referable to national motives.

7   This idea which is derived from the knowledge of the neurotic fantasy and symptom construction, was applied by Professor Freud to the interpretation of the romantic and mythical work of poetic imagination, in a lecture entitled: 'Der Dichter und das Phantasieren' (Poets and Imaginings) (Reprint, 2d series of Collected Short Articles), p. 1970.

8   For ethno-psychologic parallels and other infantile sexual theories which throw some light upon the supplementary myth of the hero's procreation compare the author's treatise in *Zentralblatt für Psychoanalyse*, II, 1911, pp. 392–425.

9   Abraham, 'Dream and Myth', p. 40; Fraz Riklin, *Wunscherfüllung und Symbolik im Märchen* (Zurich: Fraz Deutiche, 1908), p. 74.

10 Brief mention is made of a case concerning a Mrs. v. Hervay, because of a few subtle psychological comments upon the same, by A. Berger (Feuilleton der Neue Freie Presse, November 6, 1904, No. 14,441) which in part touch upon our interpretation of the hero myth. Berger writes as follows: 'I am convinced that she seriously believes herself to be the illegitimate daughter of an aristocratic Russian lady. The desire to belong through birth to more distinguished and brilliant circles than her own surroundings probably dates back to her early years; and her wish to be a princess gave rise to the delusion that she was not the daughter of her parents, but the child of a noblewoman who had concealed her illegitimate offspring from the world by letting her grow up as the daughter of a sleight-of-hand man. Having once become entangled in these fancies, it was natural for her to interpret any harsh word that offended her, or any accidental ambiguous remark that she happened to hear, but especially her reluctance to be the daughter of this couple, as a confirmation of her romantic delusion. She therefore made it the task of her life to regain the social position of which she felt herself to have been defrauded. Her biography manifests the strenuous insistence upon this idea, with a tragic outcome.'

The female type of the family romance, as it confronts us in this case from the a-social side, has also been transmitted as a hero myth in isolated instances. The story goes of the later Queen Semiramis (in Diodos. II, 4) that her mother, the goddess Derketo, being ashamed of her, exposed the child in a barren and rocky land, where she was fed by doves and found by shepherds, who gave the infant to the overseer of the royal flocks, the childless Simmas, who raised her as his own daughter. He named her Semiramis, which means Dove in the Syrian language. Her further career, up to her autocratic rulership, thanks to her masculine energy, is a matter of history.

Other exposure myths are told of Atalante, Kybele, and Aërope (v. Roscher).

11 Freud: Three Contributions to the Sexual Theory, Nervous and Mental Disease Monograph, No. 7. Also: Psychopathologie des Altagslebens, II ed., Berlin, 1909. Also: Hysterische Phantasien und ihre Beziehung zur Bisexualität.

12 This is especially evident in the myths of the Greek gods, where the son (Kronos, Zeus) must first remove the father, before he can enter upon his rulership. The form of the removal, namely through castration, obviously the strongest expression of the revolt against the father, is at the same time the proof of its sexual provenance. Concerning the revenge character of this castration, as well as the infantile significance of the entire complex, compare Freud, Infantile Sexual Theories and Analysis of the Phobia of a five year old Boy (Jahrbuch f. Psychoanalyse).

13 Compare the contrast between Tell and Parricida, in Schiller's Wilhelm Tell, which is discussed in detail in the author's Incest Book.

14 Compare in this connection the unsuccessful homicidal attempt of Tatjana Leontiew, and its subtle psychological illumination in Wittels: Die sexuelle Not (Vienna and Leipzig, 1909).

References

Abraham, K. (1913). *Dreams and Myths*: *A Study in Race Psychology*. New York: Jonson Repr. Corp.

Berger, A. (1904). *Feuilleton der Neue Freie Presse*, November 6, No. 14, p. 441.

Freud, S. (1910). *Zur Psychopathologie des Alltagslebens*: (*Über Vergessen, Versprechen, Vergreifen, Aberglaube und Irrtum*). Berlin: S. Karger.

Freud, S. (1910). *Three Contributions to the Sexual Theory*. New York: The Journal of nervous and mental disease publishing company.

Lessmann, H. (1906). *Die Kyrossage in Europa*. Charlottenburg: A. Gertz.

Meyer, E. (1905). Die Mosessage und die Leviten. *Berichte der königlichen preussischen Akademie der Wissenschaften* 31.

Müller, F. M. (1869). *Essays*. Leipzig: W. Engelmann.

Riklin, F. (1908). *Wunscherfüllung und Symbolik im Märchen*. Zurich: Fraz Deutiche.

The historical development of mythology

Joseph Campbell

Joseph Campbell (1904–1987) was an American scholar of comparative mythology. He attended Columbia University, where he received his BA in 1925 and an MA in 1927. After this, he travelled to Europe, living in France and Germany, where he also met the Theosophist Krishnamurti. This encounter sparked an interest in both Oriental religions and the value of viewing myth metaphorically. Campbell never completed his PhD but was nevertheless able to eventually become a Professor of Literature at Sarah Lawrence College, the United States, where he taught an introductory class on mythology. Teaching can be a basis for research, rather than simply the communication of it, and Campbell was inspired by his classroom exploration of myth to develop the concept of the monomyth, which is the idea that all hero myths are variants of a single hero's journey. This idea was to prove popular and helped fire many subsequent creative works, including the film *Star Wars*.

The hero's journey is widely available and neatly summarized in a number of freely accessible online locations. One of the advantages of the journey is that it can be simply expressed and apprehended: a hero must undergo a journey through several stages, typically including movement from the known to the unknown, triggered by answering (often reluctantly) a call to adventure. Several fantastic things happen on the adventure: there are dragons to slay, friends to make and mistakes to atone for. This not only transforms the wider world but also the hero, who ends by returning home with their new status. The journey's simplicity of form has helped its popularity and it does seem to be a structure that resonates with people, perhaps because of its similarity to a classic rite-of-passage. However, Campbell's myth theory is far broader than this; he developed highly influential ideas about the relation of myths across space and time, their importance for the individual and the challenges that we face when engaging with myth today. The reading that we have chosen to cover here showcases Campbell's approaches to these issues as well as his understanding of myth, truth and metaphor.

The comparative study of the mythologies of the world compels us to view the cultural history of mankind as a unit; for we find that such themes as the Fire-theft, Deluge, Land of the Dead, Virgin Birth, and Resurrected Hero have a world-wide distribution, appearing everywhere in new combinations, while remaining, like the elements of a kaleidoscope, only a few and always the same. Furthermore, whereas in tales told for entertainment such mythical themes are taken lightly – obviously in a spirit of play – they appear also in religious contexts, where they are accepted not only as factually true but even as revelations of the verities to which the whole culture is a living witness and from which it derives both its spiritual authority and its temporal power. No human society has yet been found in which such mythological motifs have not been rehearsed in liturgies; interpreted by seers, poets, theologians, or philosophers; presented in art; magnified in song; and ecstatically experienced in life-empowering visions.

Indeed the chronicle of our species, from its earliest page, has been not simply an account of the progress of man the toolmaker but – more tragically – a history of the pouring of blazing visions into the minds of seers and the efforts of earthly communities to incarnate unearthly covenants. Every people has received its own seal and sign of supernatural designation, communicated to its heroes and daily proved in the lives and experiences of its folk. And though many who bow with closed eyes in the sanctuaries of their own tradition rationally scrutinize and disqualify the sacraments of others, an honest comparison immediately reveals that all have been built from the one fund of mythological motifs – variously selected, organized, interpreted, and ritualized according to local need, but revered by every people on earth.

A fascinating psychological as well as historical problem is thus presented to us by our science. Man, apparently, cannot maintain himself in the universe without belief in some arrangement of the general inheritance of myth. In fact, the fullness of his life would even seem to stand in a direct ratio to the depth and range, not of his rational thought, but of his local mythology. Whence the force of these unsubstantial themes, by which they are empowered to galvanize populations, creating of them civilizations, each with a beauty and self-compelling destiny of its own? And why should it be that whenever men have looked for something solid on which to found their lives, they have chosen, not the facts in which the world abounds, but the myths of an immemorial imagination – preferring even to make life a hell for themselves and their neighbors, in the name of some violent god, rather than to accept gracefully the bounty the world affords?

Are the modern civilizations to remain spiritually locked from each other in their local notions of the sense of the general tradition? Or can we not now break through to some more profoundly based point and counterpoint of human understanding? For it is a fact that the myths of our several cultures work upon us, whether consciously or unconsciously, as energy-releasing, life-motivating, and directing agents; so that even though our rational minds may be in agreement, the myths by which we are living – or by which our fathers lived – can be driving us, at that very moment, diametrically apart.

[…]

It is obvious, surely, that we have here a potent mythical formula for the reorientation of the human spirit – pitching it forward along the way of time, summoning man to an assumption of responsibility for the reform of the universe in God's name, and thus fostering a new, potentially political philosophy of holy war. The first sociological expression of this new force was in the prodigious Persian empire of Cyrus the Great (*d*. 529 B.C.) and Darius the Great (*c*. 521–486? B.C.), which in a few decades reached from the bounds of India to those of Greece, and under the protection of which the postexilic Hebrews not only rebuilt their temple (Ezra 1:1–11) but also both reconstructed and reinterpreted their ancient Mosaic inheritance. The second formidable socio-political expression of the new progressive myth is therefore to be found in the Hebrew application of its message to themselves. The next application appeared in the world mission of Christendom, and the fourth in that of Islam.

'For the children of the desolate one will be more than the children of her that is married, says the Lord. Enlarge the place of your tent, and let the curtains of your habitations be stretched out; hold not back, lengthen your cords and strengthen your stakes. For you will spread abroad to the right and to the left, and your descendants will possess the nations and will people the desolate cities.' (Isaiah 54:1–3)

'And this gospel of the kingdom will be preached throughout the whole world as a testimony to all nations; and then the end will come.' (Matthew 24:14)

'And slay them wherever you catch them, and turn them out from where they have turned you out; for tumult and oppression are worse than slaughter. … And fight them on until there is no more tumult or oppression, and there prevail justice and faith in God; but if they cease, let there be no hostility except to those who practice oppression.' (Koran 2: 191; 193)

The Greeks, in a measure, participated in this mythos of the war of the Sons of Light with the Sons of Darkness. We find it reflected in some of the later developments of the mythology of Dionysos. Many conflicting earlier and later legends were told of the birth and deeds, death and resurrection of this great deity of the plant world, whose cult of divine ecstasy became the rage in Greece in the seventh century B.C. The ultimate origins of the wild rites are lost in the depths of an unrecorded past: indeed, as we shall see, they are certainly very much older than the history, or even the prehistory, of Greece itself. But we know a good deal concerning the later mutations through which the worship passed before the figure of the great lord of the grain and the vine – of bread and wine, of divine rapture, and of resurrection – became merged with that of Jesus in the sacramental system of the early Church.

According to one important version of his miraculous birth, death, and resurrection,[1] when the great goddess of the operations of agriculture and of the fruitful soil, Demeter, came to Sicily from Crete with her daughter Persephone, whom she had conceived of Zeus, she discovered a cave near the spring of Kyane. There she hid the maiden, setting to guard her the two serpents that were normally harnessed to the maiden's chariot. And Persephone there commenced weaving a web of wool, a great robe on which there was to be a beautiful picture of the universe; while her mother, Demeter, contrived that the girl's father, Zeus, should learn of her presence. The god approached his daughter in the form of a serpent, and she conceived of him a son, Dionysos, who was born and nurtured in the cave. The infant's toys were a ball, a top, dice, some golden apples, a bit of wool, and a bull-roarer.[2]

That is the first part of the story of the god Dionysos. The second tells of his death and resurrection. The infant in the cave was given a mirror, and while he was gazing into it, delighted, there approached him stealthily from behind two Titans, who had been sent by the goddess Hera, the jealous wife and queen of Zeus, to slay him. Now the Titans were divine beings of an earlier generation than the gods. They were the children of the Sky and the Earth, and from two of their number, Kronos and Rhea, the gods themselves, the Olympians, were born. The Titans and their mythology derived from an earlier stratum of thought and religion than the classical pantheon of the Olympians, and the episodes in which they appeared frequently had traits of an extremely primitive tone.

For example, in the present case, the two Titans stealing into the cave were painted with white clay or chalk – like the cannibals, whom we shall presently be meeting, at their feasts of ritual sacrifice. The Titans pounced upon the playing child, tearing him into seven parts, which they boiled in a cauldron supported by a tripod and then roasted on seven spits.[3] But when they had consumed their sacrifice – all except the heart, which had been rescued by the goddess Athene – Zeus, attracted by the odor of the roasting meat, entered the cavé, and when he beheld the scene, slew the white-painted cannibal Titans with a bolt of lightning. The goddess Athene thereupon presented the rescued heart in a covered basket to the father, who accomplished the resurrection, according to one version of the miracle, by swallowing the precious relic and himself then giving birth to his son.

The primitive aspects of this myth can be rediscovered, ritually enacted in a gruesome series of rites still practiced among the cannibals of the primitive equatorial regions. But for the present, let us turn our attention to the manner in which the crude inheritance was spiritually transformed and reinterpreted in the image of the concept of man's nature as a battleground of good and evil.

The chief channels through which this mythology was preserved and developed from the sixth century B.C. until about the fourth A.D. were the numerous, widely scattered Orphic conventicles, which, as we know, exercised a considerable influence on both the philosophical and the religious speculations of that crucial time. A direct and powerful line leads from the Orphic schools through Pythagoras (c. 582–c. 507 B.C.) and the Eleatic philosophers to Plato (427–347 B.C.), the Alexandrian mystery cults, and the great Neoplatonic thinkers, not only of the first millennium A.D. but also of the high Middle Ages and the Renaissance.

According to an important Orphic version of the myth of the killed and eaten infant Dionysos, it was from the ashes of the annihilated Titans that mankind arose. Man, therefore, is of mixed origin, containing a divine principle (Dionysos) and a wicked (that of the Titans). The image is analogous to that of the origin of the universe described by Zoroaster, and is actually an expression of the same idea of man's obligation to engage in a struggle of ethical significance, to release the godly substance from the grip of the dark and evil. However, in the Greek version of the problem we do not find any progressive, potentially political mythos of the ultimate salvation of the world. As in the Orient, we hear, rather, of the 'cycle of birth or becoming' *(kyklos tēs geneseōs)*; and the call to the individual is to save, not the world, but himself: to purge away the wicked portion of his nature and to cultivate the godly, by vegetarianism, asceticism, and assiduous practice of the Orphic rituals through many lives.

[...]

In the primitive world, where the clues to the origin of mythology must be sought, gods and demons are not conceived in the way of hard and fast, positive realities. The phenomenon of the primitive mask, for example, is a case in point. The mask is revered as an apparition of the mythical being that it represents, yet everyone knows that a man made the mask and that a man is wearing it. The one wearing it, furthermore, is identified with the god during the time of the ritual of which the mask is a part. He does not merely represent the god: he *is* the god. The literal fact that the apparition is composed of (a) a mask, (b) its reference to a mythical being, and (c) a man, is dismissed from the mind, and the presentation is allowed to work without correction upon the sentiments of both the beholder and the actor. In other words, there has been a shift of view from the logic of the normal secular sphere, where things are understood to be distinct from each other, to a theatrical or play sphere, where they are accepted for what they are *experienced* as being, and the logic is that of 'make-believe' – 'as if'. We all know the convention, surely! It is a primary, spontaneous device of childhood: a magical device, by which the world can be transformed from banality to magic in a trice. And its inevitability in childhood is one of those universal characteristics of man that unite us in one family. It is a primary datum, consequently, of the science of myth, which is concerned precisely with the phenomenon of self-induced belief.

Leo Frobenius wrote in a celebrated paper on the force of the daemonic world of childhood:[4]

A professor is writing at his desk and his four-year-old little daughter is running about the room. She has nothing to do and is disturbing him. So he gives her three burnt matches, saying, 'Here! Play!' and, sitting on the rug, she begins to play with the matches: Hansel, Gretel, and the witch. A considerable time elapses, during which the professor concentrates upon his task, undisturbed. But then, suddenly, the child shrieks in terror. The father jumps. 'What is it? What has happened?' The little girl comes running to him, showing every sign of great fright. 'Daddy, Daddy,' she cries, 'take the witch away! I can't touch the witch any more!'

Frobenius further observes:

> An eruption of emotion is characteristic of the spontaneous shift of an idea from the level of the sentiments *(Gemüt)* to that of sensual consciousness *(sinnliches Bewusstsein)*. Furthermore, the appearance of such an eruption obviously means that a certain spiritual process has reached a conclusion. The match is not a witch; nor was it a witch for the child at the beginning of the game. The process, therefore, rests on the fact that the match *has become* a witch on the level of the sentiments and the conclusion of the process coincides with the transfer of this idea to the plane of consciousness. The observation of the process escapes the test of conscious thought, since it enters consciousness only after or at the moment of completion. However, in as much as the idea *is*, it must have *become*. The process is creative, in the highest sense of the word; for, as we have seen, in a little girl a match can become a witch. Briefly stated, then: the phase of *becoming* takes place on the level of the sentiments, while that of *being* is on the conscious plane.

We may take this observation as a clue, not only to the origins of myth and of the fabulous rituals by which men and women have allowed themselves to be tortured as by demons, but also to the radical distinction between mythology as read by the Greek poets, artists, and philosophers and mythology as functioning in the primitive sphere.

Three categories are to be distinguished for mythology proper: daemonic, metaphysical, and humanistic. The first is characteristic of the earliest high civilizations, as well as of all primitive societies and folk cultures; the second achieved its apogee in medieval India, China, and Japan; while the last distinguishes the classical inheritance of the West.

According to the first, the gods and daemons represent something with a life and consciousness of its own, a 'something not ourselves' (to quote Cornford's felicitous paraphrase of the Greek term *theos*, 'god'),[5] which, though it is rather a force than a shape and works invisibly, yet appears in shapes. It appears in visions, where it works upon the spirit of the individual; and it appears in the paraphernalia of the ritual, to work upon the spirit of the group. Furthermore, many, if not all, rites have taken their rise from individual vision.

The Judeo-Christian-Islamic prophetic inheritance must be regarded (if we are to retain an objective distance) as a powerful variant of this first category of myth, wherein the daemons of Abraham, Jesus, Paul, Mohamet, and the rest, have been overinterpreted, not as personal patrons (like the daemon of Socrates) nor even as tribal patrons (like the deities of the Navaho), but as the father-creator of the universe, with a single program for the entire human race, to be administered by the representatives of this special visionary tradition. In fact, we may say that, just as the second of our categories of myth, the metaphysical, reached its apogee in the Far East and South Asia, so did the first, the daemonic, in the variously developed monotheistic theologies of the Synagogue, the Church, and the Mosque.

The second view, the metaphysical, seems to have taken its rise in the hermit groves and philosophically cultivated courts of India, in the eighth and seventh centuries B.C. It developed then, with increasing subtlety and sophistication as well as range of schools and peoples involved, until by the ninth century A.D. the whole of the Orient was a great symphony of metaphysical references.

We read already in the *Brihadāranyaka Upanishad* (eighth to seventh centuries B.C.):[6]

This or that people say, 'Worship this god! Worship that god!' – one god after another! This is his creation, indeed, and he himself is all the gods. ... He has entered into everything, even to the fingernail tips, as a razor would be hidden in a razor case, or fire in a fire holder. Him they see not; for, as seen, he is incomplete. When breathing, he is named the breath; when speaking, the voice; when seeing, the eye; when hearing, the ear; when thinking, the mind: these are merely the names of his acts. Whoever worships one or another of these – he knows not; for he is incomplete in one or another of these. One should worship with the thought that he is one's very Self; for therein all these others become one. But that thing, namely, this Self, is itself but the footprint of this All: by it one knows this All, just as, verily, one finds [one's quarry] by a footprint. ... So, whoever worships another divinity than his Self, thinking 'He is one and I another,' he knows not. He is like a sacrificial animal for the gods. Verily, indeed, just as many animals can be of service to a man, even so each single person is of service to the gods. And if even one animal is taken away, it is not pleasant. What, then, if many? Therefore, it is not pleasing to the gods that men should know this.

Much the same insight can be sensed in the sayings of the Greek Xenophanes of Colophon (fl. 536 B.C.), the reputed founder of the Eleatic school from which Plato derived certain mythologically colored strains of his philosophy. He said:[7]

There is one God, greatest among gods and men, neither in shape nor in thought like unto mortals. ... He is all sight, all mind, all ear. ... He abides ever in the same place motionless, and it befits him not to wander hither and thither. ... Yet men imagine gods to be born, and to have raiment, voice, and body, like themselves. ... Even so the gods of the Ethiopians are swarthy and flat-nosed, the gods of the Thracians, fair-haired and blue-eyed. ... Even so Homer and Hesiod attributed to the gods all that is a shame and a reproach among men – theft, adultery, deceit, and other lawless acts. ... Even so oxen, lions, and horses, if they had hands wherewith to carve images, would fashion gods after their own shapes and make them bodies like to their own.

Or again, we have the words of Antisthenes (born *c.* 444 B.C.): 'God is not like anything; hence one cannot understand him by means of an image.'[8]

In the Orient the tendency of the philosophical development was to retain the atmosphere of myth, employing its symbols and rites as adequate means by which to ready the mind for intuitive insights into the ineffable mystery of the universe:

There the eye goes not;
Speech goes not, nor the mind.
We know not, we understand not
How one should teach It.
For It is other, indeed, than the known,
And, moreover, above the unknown:[9]

In the Occident, however, the tendency has been progressively toward such a definitively humanistic point of view as that epitomized in Nietzsche's volume of disillusionment, *Human, All Too Human*, where he writes that all – morality and religion, art and prophecy – in spite of their pretensions to supernatural authority, transcendental insight, and ineffable inspiration, are finally 'human, all too human,' and are to be read, consequently, in terms rather of psychology than of theology or metaphysics. One may, if one likes, regard these two views – the metaphysical and the humanistic, these two poles of philosophy in the modern world – as representing a play in the human mind of Niels Bohr's principle of complementarity; as a pair of opposites, or a pair of aspects, beyond which (as beyond the clashing rocks of the Symplegades) an ultimate truth of some sort must abide (awaiting perhaps our heroic arrival). But for the present systematization of the materials available to a natural history of the gods and heroes, the view of Nietzsche will suffice. And we shall have to commence, furthermore, far back of the great period of the differentiation of our cultures into Orient and Occident, with the primitive dancing ground of the gods and the mystery of the primitive mask.

[…]

Belief, or at least a game of belief, is the first step toward such a divine seizure. The chronicles of the saints abound in accounts of their long ordeals of difficult practice, which preceded their moments of being carried away; and we have also the more spontaneous religious games and exercises of the folk (the amateurs) to illustrate for us the principle involved. The spirit of the festival, the holiday, the holy day of the religious ceremonial, requires that the normal attitude toward the cares of the world should have been temporarily set aside in favor of a particular mood of dressing up. The world is hung with banners. Or in the permanent religious sanctuaries – the temples and cathedrals – where an atmosphere of holiness hangs in the air, the logic of cold, hard fact must not be allowed to intrude and spoil the spell. The gentile, the 'spoilsport,' the positivist who cannot or will not play, must be kept aloof. Hence the guardian figures that stand at either side of the entrances to holy places: lions, bulls, or fearsome warriors with uplifted weapons. They are there to keep out the 'spoilsports,' the advocates of Aristotelian logic, for whom *A* can never be *B*; for whom the actor is never to be lost in the part; for whom the mask, the image, the consecrated host or tree or animal, cannot become God, but only a reference. Such heavy thinkers are to remain without. For the whole purpose of entering a sanctuary or participating in a festival is that one should be overtaken by the state known in India as 'the other mind' (Sanskrit, *anya-manas*: absent-mindedness, possession by a spirit), where one is 'beside oneself,' spellbound: set apart from one's logic of self-possession and overpowered by the force of a logic of indissociation, wherein *A* is *B*, and *C* also is *B*.

'One day,' said Ramakrishna, 'while worshiping Shiva, I was about to offer a bel-leaf on the head of the image, when it was revealed to me that this universe itself is Shiva. Another day, I had been plucking flowers when it was revealed to me that each plant was a bouquet adorning the universal form of God. That was the end of my plucking flowers. I look on man in just the same way. When I see a man, I see that it is God Himself, who walks on earth, rocking to and fro, as it were, like a pillow floating on the waves.'[10]

From such a point of view the universe is the seat (*piṭha*) of a divinity from whose vision our usual state of consciousness excludes us. But in the playing of the game of the gods we take a step toward that reality, which is ultimately the reality of ourselves. Hence the rapture, the feelings of delight, and the sense of refreshment, harmony, and re-creation! In the case of a saint, the game leads to seizure, as in the case of the little girl to whom the match revealed itself to be a witch. Contact with the orientation of the world may then be lost, the mind remaining rapt in that other state. For such it is impossible to return to this other game, the game of life in the world. They are possessed of God: that is all they know on earth and all they need to know. And they can even infect whole societies so that these, inspired by their seizures, may themselves break contact with the world and spurn it as delusory or as evil. Secular life then may be read as a Fall, a Fall from Grace – Grace being the rapture of the festival of God.

[...]

From the position of secular man (*Homo sapiens*), then, we are to enter the play sphere of the festival, acquiescing in a game of belief, where fun, joy, and rapture rule in ascending series. The laws of life in time and space – economics, politics, and even morality – will dissolve. Whereafter, re-created by that return to Paradise before the Fall, before the knowledge of good and evil, right and wrong, true and false, belief and disbelief, we are to carry the point of view and spirit of man the player (Homo *ludens*) back into life: as in the play of children, where, undaunted by the banal actualities of life's meager possibilities, the spontaneous impulse of the spirit to identify itself with something other than itself, for the sheer delight of play, transubstantiates the world – in which, after all, things are not quite as real or permanent, terrible, important, or logical as they seem.

Notes

1   *Nonni Dionysiaca* 6.121; *Orphei Hymni* 39.7; ibid., 253.

2   O. Kern, *Orphicorum fragmenta* (Berlin, 1922), 34.

3   Ibid., 34, 35.

4   Leo Frobenius, *Paideuma, Umrisse einer Kultur- und Seelenlehre* (3 Aufl., Frankfurt, 1928), pp. 143–145.

5   Cornford, *Greek Religious Thought from Homer to the Age of Alexander*, pp. x–xii.

6   *Brihadāranyaka Upanishad* 1.4.6–10.

7   H. Diels, *Die Fragmente der Vorsokratiker* (Berlin, 4th ed. 1922), Vol. I.

8   Cited by Clement of Alexandria, *Exhortation to the Greeks*, p. 61.

9   *Kena Upanishad* 1.3.

10   Ibid., 396.

References

Cornford, F. M. (1923). *Greek Religious Thought from Homer to the Age of Alexander*. London: J. M. Dent and Sons, Ltd.

Diels, H. (1922). *Die Fragmente der Vorsokratiker*. Berlin: Weidmann.

Frobenius, L. (1928). *Paideuma, Umrisse einer Kultur- und Seelenlehre*. Frankfurt am Main: Frankfurter Societäts-Druckerei.

Huizinga, J. (1949). *Homo Ludens*. London: Routledge and Kegan Paul, Ltd.

Kant (1838–1842). *Prolegomena zu einer jeden künftigen Metaphysik, die als Wissenschaft wird auftreten können*. Leipzig: Werke.

Kern, O. (1922). *Orphicorum fragmenta*. Berlin: Weidmann.

Rapson, E. J. (1922). *The Cambridge History of India*. New York: The Macmillan Company.

Swami Nikhilananda (1942). *The Gospel of Sri Ramakrishna*. New York: Ramakrishna-Vivekananda Center.

Zimmer, H. (1951). *Philosophies of India*. New York: Pantheon Press.

Section B: Myth and dreams

(Dis)embodied mythology

Where does myth exist: on the page, or in the vision of the person reading, in the voice of the narrator or the ears of the person who hears? Is myth something that helps us escape from our physical existence, or is it something that shapes our physicality, affecting the way we walk, talk, think and dream? From the perspective of a society steeped in the Cartesian dualism of mind and body, it is easy to imagine mythology as something purely intellectual and separated from our embodied existence; however, theorists of myth have long made the connection between physical experience and the world of myth. Frazer's *Golden Bough* suggests a strong connection between myth and the embodied reality of daily life, seasonal change and ritual engagement (see Part Two, Section A, Chapter 1). Whereas both Campbell's and Rank's hero's journeys draw profundity and appeal from their connection to common, visceral, life-events.

A good proportion of our life is spent sleeping and for much of the time that our body is engaged in sleep we experience dreams. These dreams are at once connected to our daily-life experiences and yet separate from them. They allow us to feel present in the situation at the same time as giving the impression of taking us beyond the limitations of the waking world. Dreams are then at once embodied and able to gift a sense of transcendence, which allows the dreamer to enter into other states of being. Mythographers have argued that dreams reflect our waking life (Freud 1932), yet others have suggested that they shape it (Campbell 2011), while others still have collapsed the boundaries between the wisdom of myth, dreams and experience (Hallowell 2002).

Two of the theorists whom we have chosen to include in this section, Jung and Dundes, imagine that dreams and myth are connected through the way they engage with waking life while remaining distinct to it. For Dundes, myths (and dreams) are symptoms of a subconscious engagement with the experiences and desires of waking life. Dundes utilizes Freud's classical psychoanalytical technique, with its libidinous focus, to interpret a wide range of mythological and folk material. Jung, in contrast, moves the concept of the libido away from sexual energy and towards a form of psychic energy, at the same time suggesting that both this and other core elements of myths and dreams could be as much the result of evolutionary experiences as personal ones. It is important to note, however, that for Jung, both dream and myth are related to these common, formative, evolutionary experiences, known as archetypes, but they are both also distinct elements of the human condition (Segal 1999: 81). Dreams for Jung are often personal, only sometimes connected to common archetypes, whereas myth more reliably engages with this level of operation. Yet, myth's increased regulation means that its connection to archetypes is less pure and therefore requires more interpretative work (Segal 1999: 81).

In many cultures, however, the interpretation of myth leads neither inward towards personal neurosis nor backwards, to some remnant of evolutionary history, but rather outwards to a dwelt in world (Ingold 2000: 89–110). This is excellently illustrated by Sepie's contribution to this section, which challenges us to take seriously the claims that various myth-tellers make about the value of information gained in myth and/or dreams for interpreting and engaging with the world. From this perspective, myths are neither merely stories, told around a fire for relaxation, nor narratives, read to escape the woes of the world. Rather, they are narratives that draw our attention to ways of being in the world and, in so doing, increase the range of our skilful engagement with the environment.

References

Campbell, J., and Moyers, B. (2011). *The Power of Myth*. New York: Anchor.

Freud, S. (1932). The Acquisition of Power over Fire. *International Journal of Psycho-Analysis* 13: 405–410.

Hallowell, A. I. (2002). Ojibwa Ontology, Behavior, and World View. *Readings in Indigenous Religions* 22: 17–49.

Ingold, T. (2000). *The Perception of the Environment: Essays on Livelihood, Dwelling and Skill*. London: Routledge.

Segal, R. A. (1999). *Theorizing about Myth*. Amherst, MA: University of Massachusetts Press.

Flying saucers: A modern myth

Carl G. Jung

1

Carl Gustav Jung (1875–1961) was a Swiss psychiatrist and psychoanalyst, who founded the technique known as 'analytical psychology'. He studied medicine at the University of Basel, before working at Burgholzli psychiatric hospital, where he began correspondence with Sigmund Freud. He worked closely with Freud for a number of years, collaborating on the development of a new vision for human psychology. However, with the publication of his first book, in 1912, it became clear that Jung's thought had important differences to Freud's, and around the same time, their personal relationship also deteriorated.

Jung's independent thought deemphasizes the libido and emphasizes the importance of shared evolutionary responses, known as the collective unconscious for the interpretation of mythology. Jung's explorations of mythology led him to posit theories for the origin and function of mythology as well as its relationship to both dreams and modern life. In the reading that we have chosen to include here, Jung's expertise in paranormal experiences combines with his interest in mythology to illuminate the phenomenon of contemporary UFO sightings, which he sees as a new form of living mythology.

S ince the things reported of UFOs not only sound incredible but seem to fly in the face of all our basic assumptions about the physical world, it is very natural that one's first reaction should be the negative one of outright rejection. Surely, we say, it's nothing but illusions, fantasies, and lies. People who report such stuff – chiefly airline pilots and ground staff – cannot be quite right in the head! What is worse, most of these stories come from America, the land of superlatives and of science fiction.

In order to meet this natural reaction, we shall begin by considering the Ufo reports simply as rumours, i.e., as psychic products, and shall draw from this all the conclusions that are warranted by an analytical method of procedure.

Regarded in this light, the Ufo reports may seem to the sceptical mind to be rather like a story that is told all over the world, but differs from an ordinary rumour in that it is expressed in the form of visions,[1] or perhaps owed its existence to them in the first place and is now kept alive by them. I would call this comparatively rare variation a *visionary rumour*. It is closely akin to the collective visions of, say, the crusaders during the siege of Jerusalem, the troops at Mons in the first World War, the faithful followers of the pope at Fatima, Portugal, etc. Apart from collective visions, there are on record cases where one or more persons see something that physically is not there. For instance, I was once at a spiritualistic séance where four of the five people present saw an object like a moon floating above the abdomen of the medium. They showed me, the fifth person present, exactly where it was, and it was absolutely incomprehensible to them that I could see nothing of the sort. I know of three more cases where certain objects were seen in the clearest detail (in two of them by two persons, and in the third by one person) and could afterwards be proved to be non-existent. Two of these cases happened under my direct observation. Even people who are entirely *compos mentis* and in full possession of their senses can sometimes see things that do not exist. I do not know what the explanation is of such happenings. It is very possible that they are less rare than I am inclined to suppose. For as a rule we do not verify things we have 'seen with our own eyes,' and so we never get to know that actually they did not exist. I mention these somewhat remote possibilities because, in such an unusual matter as the Ufos, one has to take every aspect into account.

The first requisite for a visionary rumour, as distinct from an ordinary rumour, for whose dissemination nothing more is needed than popular curiosity and sensation-mongering, is always an *unusual emotion*. Its intensification into a vision and delusion of the senses, however, springs from a stronger excitation and therefore from a deeper source.

The signal for the Ufo stories was given by the mysterious projectiles seen over Sweden during the last two years of the war – attributed of course to the Russians – and by the reports about 'Foo fighters,' i.e., lights that accompanied the Allied bombers over Germany (Foo = *feu*). These were followed by the strange sightings of 'Flying Saucers' in America. The impossibility of finding an earthly base for the Ufos and of explaining their physical peculiarities soon led to the conjecture of an extra-terrestrial origin. With this development the rumour got linked up with the psychology of the great panic that broke out in the United States just before the second World War, when a radio play,[2] based on a novel by H. G. Wells, about Martians invading New York, caused a regular stampede and numerous car accidents. The play evidently hit the latent emotion connected with the imminence of war.

The motif of an extra-terrestrial invasion was seized upon by the rumour and the Ufos were interpreted as machines controlled by intelligent beings from outer space. The apparently weightless behaviour of space-ships and their intelligent, purposive movements were attributed to the superior technical knowledge and ability of the cosmic intruders. As they did no harm and refrained from all hostile acts it was assumed that their appearance over the earth was due to curiosity or to the need for aerial reconnaissance. It also seemed that airfields and atomic installations in particular held a special attraction for them, from which it was concluded that the dangerous development of atomic physics and nuclear fission had caused a certain disquiet on our neighbouring planets and necessitated a more accurate survey from the air. As a result, people felt they were being observed and spied upon from space.

The rumour actually gained so much official recognition that the armed forces in America set up a special bureau for collecting, analysing, and evaluating all relevant observations. This seems to have been done also in France, Italy, Sweden, the United Kingdom, and other countries. After the publication of Ruppelt's report the Saucer stories seem to have more or less vanished from the press for about a year. They were evidently no longer 'news'. That the interest in Ufos and, probably, the sightings of them have not ceased is shown by the recent press report that an American admiral has suggested that clubs be founded all over the country for collecting Ufo reports and investigating them in detail.

The rumour states that the Ufos are as a rule lens-shaped, but can also be oblong or shaped like cigars; that they shine in various colours or have a metallic glitter;[3] that from a stationary position they can reach a speed of about 10,000 miles per hour, and that at times their acceleration is such that if anything resembling a human being were steering them he would be instantly killed. In flight they turn off at angles that would be possible only to a weightless object.

Their flight, accordingly, resembles that of a flying insect. Like this, the Ufo can suddenly hover over an interesting object for quite a time, or circle round it inquisitively, just as suddenly to dart off again and discover new objects in its zigzag flight. Ufos are therefore not to be confused with meteorites or with reflections from so-called 'temperature inversion layers'. Their alleged interest in airfields and in industrial installations connected with nuclear fission is not always confirmed, since they are also seen in the Antarctic, in the Sahara, and in the Himalayas. For preference, however, they seem to swarm over the United States, though recent reports show that they do a good deal of flying over the Old World and in the Far East. Nobody really knows what they are looking for or want to observe. Our aeroplanes seem to arouse their curiosity, for they often fly towards them or pursue them. But they also fly away from them. Their flights do not appear to be based on any recognizable system. They behave more like groups of tourists unsystematically viewing the countryside, pausing now here for a while and now there, erratically following first one interest and then another, sometimes shooting to enormous altitudes for inexplicable reasons or performing acrobatic evolutions before the noses of exasperated pilots. Sometimes they appear to be up to five hundred yards in diameter, sometimes small as electric street-lamps. There are large mother-ships from which little Ufos slip out or in which they take shelter. They are said to be both manned and unmanned, and in the latter case are remote-controlled. According to the rumour, the occupants are about three feet high and look like human beings or, conversely, are utterly unlike us. Other reports speak of giants fifteen feet high. They are beings who are carrying out a cautious survey of the earth and considerately avoid all encounters with men or, more menacingly, are spying out landing places with a view to settling the population of a planet that has got into difficulties and colonizing the earth by force. Uncertainty in regard to the physical conditions on earth and their fear of unknown sources of infection have held them back temporarily from drastic encounters and even from attempted landings, although they possess frightful weapons which would enable them to exterminate the human race. In addition to their obviously superior technology they are credited with superior wisdom and moral goodness which would, on the other hand, enable them to save humanity. Naturally there are stories of landings, too, when the saucer-men were not only seen at close quarters but attempted to carry off a human being. Even a reliable man like Keyhoe gives us to understand that a squadron of five military aircraft plus a large seaplane were swallowed up by Ufo mother-ships in the vicinity of the Bahamas, and carried off.

One's hair stands on end when one reads such reports together with the documentary evidence. And when one considers the known possibility of tracking Ufos with radar, then we have all the essentials for an unsurpassable 'science-fiction story'. Every man who prides himself on his sound common sense will feel distinctly affronted. I shall therefore not enter here into the various attempts at explanation to which the rumour has given rise.

[...]

As one can see from all this, the observation and interpretation of Ufos have already led to the formation of a regular legend. Quite apart from the thousands of newspaper reports and articles there is now a whole literature on the subject, some of it humbug, some of it serious. The Ufos themselves, however, do not appear to have been impressed; as the latest observations show, they continue their way undeterred. Be that as it may, one thing is certain: they have become a *living myth*. We have here a golden opportunity of seeing how a legend is formed, and how in a difficult and dark time for humanity a miraculous tale grows up of an attempted intervention by extra-terrestrial 'heavenly' powers – and this at the very time when human fantasy is seriously considering the possibility of space travel and of visiting or even invading other planets. We on our side want to fly to the moon or to Mars, and on their side the inhabitants of other planets in our system, or even of the fixed stars, want to fly to us. We at least are conscious of our space-conquering aspirations, but that a corresponding extra-terrestrial tendency exists is a purely mythological conjecture, i.e., a projection.

Sensationalism, love of adventure, technological audacity, intellectual curiosity may appear to be sufficient motives for our futuristic fantasies, but the impulse to spin such fantasies, especially when they take such a serious form – witness the sputniks – springs from an underlying cause, namely a situation of distress and the vital need that goes with it. It could easily be conjectured that the earth is growing too small for us, that humanity would like to escape from its prison, where we are threatened not only by the hydrogen bomb but, at a still deeper level, by the prodigious increase in the population figures, which give cause for serious concern. This is a problem which people do not like to talk about, or then only with optimistic references to the incalculable possibilities of intensive food production, as if this were anything more than a postponement of the final solution. As a precautionary measure the Indian government has granted half a million pounds for birth-control propaganda, while the Russians exploit the labour-camp system as one way of skimming off the dreaded excess of births. Since the highly civilized countries of the West know how to help themselves in other ways, the immediate danger does not come from them but from the underdeveloped peoples of Asia and Africa. This is not the place to discuss the question of how far the two World Wars were an outlet for this pressing problem of keeping down the population at all costs. Nature has many ways of disposing of her surplus. Man's living space is, in fact, continually shrinking and for many races the optimum has long been exceeded. The danger of catastrophe grows in proportion as the expanding populations impinge on one another. Congestion creates fear, which looks for help from extra-terrestrial sources since it cannot be found on earth.

Hence there appear 'signs in the heavens,' superior beings in the kind of space ships devised by our technological fantasy. From a fear whose cause is far from being fully understood and is therefore not conscious, there arise explanatory projections which purport to find the cause in all manner of secondary phenomena, however unsuitable. Some of these projections are so obvious that it seems almost superfluous to dig any deeper.[4] But if we want to understand a mass rumour which, it appears, is even accompanied by collective visions, we must not remain satisfied with all too rational and superficially obvious motives. The cause must strike at the roots of our existence if it is to explain such an extraordinary phenomenon as the Ufos. Although they were observed as rare curiosities in earlier centuries, they merely gave rise to the usual local rumours.

The universal mass rumour was reserved for our enlightened, rationalistic age. The widespread fantasy about the destruction of the world at the end of the first millennium was metaphysical in origin and needed no Ufos in order to appear rational. Heaven's intervention was quite consistent with the *Weltanschauung* of the age. But nowadays public opinion would hardly be inclined to resort to the hypothesis of a metaphysical act, otherwise innumerable parsons would already have been preaching about the warning signs in heaven. Our *Weltanschauung* does not expect anything of this sort. We would be much more inclined to think of the possibility of *psychic* disturbances and interventions, especially as our psychic equilibrium has become something of a problem since the last World War. In this respect there is increasing uncertainty. Even our historians can no longer make do with the traditional procedures in evaluating and explaining the developments that have overtaken Europe in the last few decades, but must admit that psychological and psychopathological factors are beginning to widen the horizons of historiography in an alarming way. The growing interest which the thinking public consequently evinces in psychology has already aroused the displeasure of the academies and of incompetent specialists. In spite of the palpable resistance to psychology emanating from these circles, psychologists who are conscious of their responsibilities should not be dissuaded from critically examining a mass phenomenon like the Ufos, since the apparent impossibility of the Ufo reports suggests to common sense that the most likely explanation lies in a psychic disturbance.

We shall therefore turn our attention to the psychic aspect of the phenomenon. For this purpose we shall briefly review the central statements of the rumour. Certain objects are seen in the earth's atmosphere, both by day and by night, which are unlike any known meteorological phenomena. They are not meteors, not misidentified fixed stars, not 'temperature inversions,' not cloud formations, not migrating birds, not aerial balloons, not balls of fire, and certainly not the delirious products of intoxication or fever, nor the plain lies of eyewitnesses. What as a rule is seen is a body of *round* shape, disk-like or spherical, glowing or shining fierily in different colours, or, more seldom, a cigar-shaped or cylindrical figure of various sizes.[5] It is reported that occasionally they are invisible to the naked eye but leave a 'blip' on the radar screen. The round bodies in particular are figures such as the unconscious produces in dreams, visions, etc. In this case they are to be regarded as *symbols* representing, in visual form, some thought that was not thought consciously, but is merely potentially present in the unconscious in invisible form and attains visibility only through the process of becoming conscious. The visible form, however, expresses the meaning of the unconscious content only approximately. In practice the meaning has to be completed by amplificatory interpretation. The unavoidable errors that result can be eliminated only through the principle of 'waiting on events'; that is to say we obtain a consistent and readable text by comparing sequences of dreams dreamt by different individuals. The figures in a rumour can be subjected to the same principles of dream interpretation.

If we apply them to the round object – whether it be a disk or a sphere – we at once get an analogy with the symbol of totality well known to all students of depth psychology, namely the *mandala* (Sanskrit for circle). This is not by any means a new invention, for it can be found in all epochs and in all places, always with the same meaning, and it reappears time and again, independently of tradition, in modern individuals as the 'protective' or apotropaic circle, whether in the form of the prehistoric 'sun wheel,' or the magic circle, or the alchemical microcosm, or a modern *symbol of order*, which organizes and embraces the psychic totality. As I have shown elsewhere,[6] in the course of the centuries the mandala has developed into a definitely psychological totality symbol, as the history of alchemy proves. I would like to show how the mandala appears in a modern person by citing the dream of a six-year-old girl. She dreamt *she stood at the entrance of a large, unknown building. There a fairy was waiting for her, who led her inside, into a long colonnade, and conducted her to a sort of central chamber, with similar colonnades converging from all sides. The fairy stepped into the centre and changed herself into a tall flame. Three snakes crawled round the fire, as if circumambulating it.*

Here we have a classic, archetypal childhood dream such as is not only dreamt fairly often but is sometimes drawn or painted, without any suggestion from outside, for the evident purpose of warding off disagreeable or disturbing family influences and preserving the inner balance.

In so far as the mandala encompasses, protects, and defends the psychic totality against outside influences and seeks to unite the inner opposites, it is at the same time a distinct *individuation symbol* and was known as such even to medieval alchemy. The soul was supposed to have the form of a sphere, on the analogy of Plato's world-soul, and we meet the same symbol in modern dreams. This symbol, by reason of its antiquity, leads us to the heavenly spheres, to Plato's 'supra-celestial place' where the 'Ideas' of all things are stored up. Hence there would be nothing against the naïve interpretation of Ufos as 'souls'. Naturally they do not represent our modern conception of the psyche, but give an involuntary archetypal or mythological picture of an unconscious content, a *rotundum*, as the alchemists called it, that expresses the totality of the individual. I have defined this spontaneous image as a symbolical representation of the *self*, by which I mean not the ego but the totality composed of the conscious *and* the unconscious.[7] I am not alone in this, as the Hermetic philosophy of the Middle Ages had already arrived at very similar conclusions. The archetypal character of this idea is borne out by its spontaneous recurrence in modern individuals who know nothing of any such tradition, any more than those around them. Even people who might know of it never imagine that their children could dream of anything so remote as Hermetic philosophy. In this matter the deepest and darkest ignorance prevails, which is of course the most unsuitable vehicle for a mythological tradition.

If the round shining objects that appear in the sky be regarded as visions, we can hardly avoid interpreting them as archetypal images. They would then be involuntary, automatic projections based on instinct, and as little as any other psychic manifestations or symptoms can they be dismissed as meaningless and merely fortuitous. Anyone with the requisite historical and psychological knowledge knows that circular symbols have played an important role in every age; in our own sphere of culture, for instance, they were not only soul symbols but 'God-images'. There is an old saying that 'God is a circle whose centre is everywhere and the circumference nowhere.' God in his omniscience, omnipotence, and omnipresence is a totality symbol *par excellence*, something round, complete, and perfect. Epiphanies of this sort are, in the tradition, often associated with fire and light. On the antique level, therefore, the Ufos could easily be conceived as 'gods'. They are impressive manifestations of totality whose simple, round form portrays the archetype of the self, which as we know from experience plays the chief role in uniting apparently irreconcilable opposites and is therefore best suited to compensate the split-mindedness of our age. It has a particularly important role to play among the other archetypes in that it is primarily the regulator and orderer of chaotic states, giving the personality the greatest possible unity and wholeness. It creates the image of the divine-human personality, the Primordial Man or Anthropos, a *chên-yên* (true or whole man), an Elijah who calls down fire from heaven, rises up to heaven in a fiery chariot,[8] and is a forerunner of the Messiah, the dogmatized figure of Christ, as well as of Khidr, the Verdant One,[9] who is another parallel to Elijah: like him, he wanders over the earth as a human personification of Allah.

The present world situation is calculated as never before to arouse expectations of a redeeming, supernatural event. If these expectations have not dared to show themselves in the open, this is simply because no one is deeply rooted enough in the tradition of earlier centuries to consider an intervention from heaven as a matter of course. We have indeed strayed far from the metaphysical certainties of the Middle Ages, but not so far that our historical and psychological background is empty of all metaphysical hope.[10] Consciously, however, rationalistic enlightenment predominates, and this abhors all leanings towards the 'occult'. Desperate efforts are made for a 'repristination' of our Christian faith, but we cannot get back to that limited world view which in former times left room for metaphysical intervention. Nor can we resuscitate a genuine Christian belief in an after-life or the equally Christian hope for an imminent end of the world that would put a definite stop to the regrettable error of Creation. Belief in this world and in the power of man has, despite assurances to the contrary, become a practical and, for the time being, irrefragable truth.

This attitude on the part of the overwhelming majority provides the most favourable basis for a projection, that is, for a manifestation of the unconscious background. Undeterred by rationalistic criticism, it thrusts itself to the forefront in the form of a symbolic rumour, accompanied and reinforced by the appropriate visions, and thus activates an archetype that has always expressed order, deliverance, salvation, and wholeness. It is characteristic of our time that the archetype, in contrast to its previous manifestations, should now take the form of an object, a technological construction, in order to avoid the odiousness of mythological personification. Anything that looks technological goes down without difficulty with modern man. The possibility of space travel has made the unpopular idea of a metaphysical intervention much more acceptable. The apparent weightlessness of the Ufos is, of course, rather hard to digest, but then our own physicists have discovered so many things that border on the miraculous: why should not more advanced star-dwellers have discovered a way to counteract gravitation and reach the speed of light, if not more?

Notes

1   I prefer the term 'vision' to 'hallucination,' because the latter bears the stamp of a pathological concept, whereas a vision is a phenomenon that is by no means peculiar to pathological states.

2   *The War of the Worlds*, radio adaptation by Orson Welles (1938). – Editors.

3   Special emphasis should be laid on the *green* fire-balls frequently observed in the southwestern United States.

4   Cf. Eugen Böhler's enlightening remarks in *Ethik und Wirtschaft* (Industrielle Organisation, Zurich, 1957).

5   The more rarely reported cigar-form may have the Zeppelin for a model. The obvious phallic comparison, i.e., a translation into sexual language, springs naturally to the lips of the people. Berliners, for instance, refer to the cigar-shaped Ufo as a 'holy ghost,' and the Swiss military have an even more outspoken name for observation balloons.

6   'Concerning Mandala Symbolism' in *The Archetypes and the Collective Unconscious*.

7   Cf. 'The Self,' in *Aion*.

8   Significantly enough, Elijah also appears as an eagle, who spies out unrighteousness on earth from above.

9   Cf. 'Concerning Rebirth,' in *The Archetypes and the Collective Unconscious*, pars. 240ff.

10 It is a common and totally unjustified misunderstanding on the part of scientifically trained people to say that I regard the psychic background as something 'metaphysical,' while on the other hand the theologians accuse me of 'psychologizing' metaphysics. Both are wide of the mark: I am an empiricist, who keeps within the boundaries set for him by the theory of knowledge.

References

Böhler, E. (1957). *Ethik und Wirtschaft*. Zurich: Industrielle Organisation.
Jung, C. G. (1959). *The Archetypes and the Collective Unconscious*. New York: Pantheon Books.

The vampire as bloodthirsty revenant: A psychoanalytic post mortem

Alan Dundes

2

Alan Dundes (1934–2005) was a folklorist, who played an important role in the establishment of folklore as academic discipline. Dundes first attended Yale, where he studied English. After working in the military for a time, maintaining artillery, Dundes attended Indiana University to pursue a PhD in folklore at a time when the university was known as the premier centre for the study of folklore in the United States, and here he made many important contacts. He was a prolific writer, and a year after the completion of his PhD, he had already published twenty-nine articles. He went on to publish twelve books across the course of his career, and he edited almost as many again. For the vast majority of his career, he held a position in the anthropology department at the University of California, Berkeley, the United States.

Dundes was heavily influenced by psychoanalytic approaches to the study of mythology, especially that of Freud. As such, he saw in myth and folklore traces of unconscious desires or psychosis. This approach naturally led him into controversy when he applied it to material that large amounts of the American public viewed as sacred: in particular, his work on the New Testament and the homoerotic basis of much of American Football. The following selection by Dundes is drawn from one of his many casebooks of Folklore. It demonstrates how the psychoanalytic technique can be applied to (largely Western) Vampire legends and how these relate to the category of myth.

The first characteristic is the vampire's invariable return to attack 'those who on earth have been his nearest and dearest' (Nixon 1979: 18; see also Schierup 1986: 179). There is even a Greek idiom, 'The vampire hunts its own kindred' (du Boulay 1982: 232) or, in an earlier rendering, the vampire 'feeds on his own' (Bent 1886: 397), which supports the notion that the vampire is connected somehow with family dynamics. Twitchell, in his essay 'The Vampire Myth' (the reader is reminded that narratives about vampires are *legends*, stories told as true and set in postcreation time, *not myths*, which are sacred narratives explaining how the world and humankind came into being), even goes so far as to comment, 'The most startling part of the folkloric vampire is that he must first attack members of his own family' (1980: 86).

The second curious characteristic requiring an explanation is the belief that the vampire sometimes drinks milk rather than blood. Ernest Jones in his pioneering essay on the vampire notes this feature when he comments: 'The German Alp sucks the nipples of men and children, and withdraws milk from women and cows more often than blood. The Drud also sucks the breasts of children, while the Southern Slav Mora sucks blood or milk indifferently' (1971: 119). In Romania, we are told that vampires on St. George's Eve 'take milk away from nursing mothers' (Murgoci 1926: 332).

These two features of vampires – the attempt to attack close family members and the reported efforts of the vampire to drink milk rather than blood – are at first glance somewhat puzzling. But surely the most perplexing question to be explained is, Why do vampires need to suck the blood (or milk) of the living to facilitate a kind of life after death? Why, in sum, is the vampire a 'bloodthirsty revenant'?

To answer this fundamental question, we need to place the vampire phenomenon in a wider theoretical framework. That structural framework, apparently common to Indo-European and Semitic worldview in antiquity, involves a set of bisecting humoral binary oppositions: hot and cold, and wet and dry. To this very day, folk disease theory depends upon combinations of these distinctions; for example, diseases (and cures) are classified as being 'hot' or 'cold.' The word *sick* in English – about which, by the way, the OED claims, 'Relationship to other Teutonic roots is uncertain, and no outside cognates have been traced' – is very likely a derivative of the Latin *siccus*, meaning 'dry' (cf. *see* in French). In classical Greek thought, we are told that 'the Greeks conceived the living as "wet" and the dead as "dry"' (Lloyd 1964: 101). Perhaps the best articulation of the principle that liquid is life and drying is dying was made by Richard Broxton Onians in his brilliant tour de force entitled *The Origins of European Thought about the Body, the Mind, the Soul, the World, Time, and Fate*, first published in 1951. According to Onians, life is perceived as a process whereby liquid gradually diminishes until the final desiccation, which is death (1973: 214–215). I myself have earlier observed that it is possible to argue by analogy. Indo-European peoples could easily see the evolution, or more aptly the devolution, of grapes into raisins, plums into prunes, and so on, with this secular transition marked by the appearance of wrinkles. So as older men and women became wrinkled with the onset of advancing age, these wrinkles could perfectly logically be interpreted as the consequences of a drying-out process (Dundes 1980: 102–103). In this context we can understand why the replenishment of liquid lost, as a means of rejuvenation, is such a common theme, with manifestations as varied as the search for the fountain of youth and the application of ointments and oils to aging skin.

Closer to the vampire issue, we can also appreciate the specifics of various death and burial practices. In modern Greece, we find the custom of 'breaking vessels filled with water on the tombs of departed friends' (Onians 1973: 272; see also Sarton 1908). Politis, the founder of Greek folkloristics, in an essay on this custom, comments that 'the water held by these broken vessels was an offering to the dead' and that 'it refreshes the departed' (1894: 35, 41). He reports further, 'In Crete a jar full of water is deposited at the grave, where it is left for forty days, the belief being that during all that time the departed soul wanders over the haunts where it lived, and returns every evening to drink of the water provided' (1894: 37). Some have argued that the broken vessel is a symbol of the deceased and that 'the pouring out of the water symbolizes the vanishing soul and the dead body will fall to pieces like the broken crock. Others say that they pour out the water "in order to allay the burning thirst of the dead man"' (Onians 1973: 275). The antiquity of this ritual is confirmed by the Babylonian custom whereby the nearest kinsman of the deceased was obliged to serve as 'pourer of water' at the grave or tomb. Hence a Babylonian curse: 'May God deprive him of an heir and a pourer of water' (Onians 1973: 285).

All this helps explain why the dead are perceived as being thirsty. Ever since Bellucci's 1909 essay, 'Sul bisogno di dissetarsi attribuito all'anima dei morti,' and Deonna's equally excellent 1939 discussion, 'La soif des morts,' this folkloristic conception of the thirsty dead has been amply documented. (There is also Sartori's 1908 cross-cultural survey, 'Das Wasser in Toten-gebrauche.') So the vampire as a thirsty dead corpse fits very well into the standard Indo-European and Semitic worldwide paradigm.

From this, we can now understand why the dead are so anxious to obtain liquid refreshment to become re-fleshed. But why the sucking act (which in the literary forms of the vampire was metamorphosed into biting)? To answer this question (as well as the associated question of why the very conception of life should be tied to liquid), we must have recourse to psychology.

The majority of psychological analyses of the vampire have concentrated almost exclusively on literary versions of this creature, with special emphasis on Bram Stoker's 1897 novel *Dracula*. (For useful reviews of this massive literature, see Margaret L. Shanahan's extensive entry, 'Psychological Perspectives on Vampire Mythology,' in *The Vampire Book* [in Melton 1994: 492–501], and the section 'Psychoanalytical Approaches' in Leatherdale's *Dracula: The Novel & the legend* [1985: 160–175] and Gelder 1994.) There are also several clinical studies of patients exhibiting what is adjudged to be vampirelike behavior (see Yvonneau 1990; and Gottlieb 1991, 1993). Psychological or psychoanalytic studies of the folkloristic vampire proper are many fewer in number. Let us begin with Freud.

One of the sources cited by Freud in his much maligned *Totem and Taboo* was an 1898 treatise by Rudolf Kleinpaul entitled *Die Lebendigen und die Toten in Volksglanben, Religion und Sage*. In that treatise which Freud praised, there is an entire section devoted to the vampire (1898: 119–129). In summarizing Kleinpaul's discussion, Freud stated, 'Kleinpaul believes that originally … the dead were all vampires, who bore ill-will towards the living, and strove to harm them and deprive them of life' (Freud 1938: 853). This prompted Freud to inquire: Why do the 'beloved dead' become 'demons'? Is it just that the soul of the dead 'envies the living' and wants to be reunited with them? His answer depended upon two premises. First, Freud contended that there is inevitably ambivalence towards the deceased loved one, that is, feelings of *both* love and hate. The latter may have involved an actual wish, albeit perhaps an unconscious one, for the death of the beloved person (1938: 854). When the person dies, the survivor not surprisingly feels some guilt (for having at some point wished for the death). In some cases, the survivor may feel anger that he or she has been abandoned by the deceased. The second premise, according to Freud, is that feelings of guilt and anger on the part of the survivor are *projected* onto the deceased. In other words, 'I feel anger towards the deceased' is transformed through projection into 'the deceased feels anger towards me, the survivor.' 'Even though,' said Freud, 'the survivor will deny that he has ever entertained hostile impulses towards the beloved dead,' the result is nonetheless the survivor's fear of being injured by a vengeful 'hostile demon' (1938: 855).

Freud's explanation of vampires is more fully articulated by his loyal disciple and biographer Ernest Jones, whose essay on the vampire was originally published in German in 1912, just one year before *Totem and Taboo* was published. Jones also interprets the vampire in terms of projection. The living survivors' ambivalent feelings of both love and hate (e.g., towards parents) are supposedly projected onto the deceased so that it is the corpse who feels both love and hate towards the living (1971: 99–100). That is why, according to Jones, vampires frequently return to visit their nearest relatives, for example, wives, husbands, or children. Jones also suggests that the vampire belief complex involves a form of regression to an infantile 'sadistic-masochistic phase of development' (1971: 110). As the infant may express anger towards a parent through biting, so, through projection combined with *lex talionis*, the adult fears that the dead parent will retaliate by returning to bite him or her (1971: 112). Jones, like Freud, believed that the 'hostile "death-wishes" nourished by the child against the disturbing parent or other rival' are, after the actual death of this parent, translated through projection to a guilty conscience and a fear that the dead parental figure will return to exact vengeance (1971: 112). The mixture of love and hate towards the parental figures is symbolized by sucking (love) and biting (hate), actions taken by vampires towards the living (1971: 121).

The sadistic component of vampirism was noted by many writers, for example, Krafft-Ebing in his *Psychopathia Sexualis* (1953: 129) and Havelock Ellis in his *Studies in the Psychology of Sex* (1928: 126). But the specific hypothesis relating oral sadism to infantile conditioning came from psychoanalysis. Karl Abraham in his important 1924 paper, 'The Influence of Oral Erotism on Character-Formation,' described a shift from sucking to biting in the so-called oral phase of infantile development. In Abraham's words, ' … the irruption of teeth … causes a considerable part of the pleasure in sucking to be replaced by pleasure in biting' (1953: 396), and in that same paper, Abraham actually speaks of 'regression from the oral-sadistic to the sucking stage,' which has an element of cruelty in it as well, 'which makes them [such individuals] something like *vampires* to other people' (1953: 401, my emphasis). Abraham's astute observation of oral phases was echoed by psychoanalyst Melanie Klein, who confirmed that 'normally the infant's pleasure in sucking is succeeded by pleasure in biting' (1960: 179). It is this line of reasoning which led ineluctably to such statements as 'The vampire becomes a projection of oral sadism left over from the early infant-mother relationship' (Henderson 1976: 610; see also Kayton 1972: 310).

Melanie Klein, however, went further than her mentor Karl Abraham. It was she who postulated the critical importance of the maternal breast. She contended that an infant may, because of either overindulgence or deprivation of the maternal breast, direct aggressive impulses at that breast, its initial contact point with the mother (1960: 185–186). Henderson's rendering of this situation is: 'When mothering is not available at the right moment or is intruded when the infant is not reaching out for it, the breast becomes hateful and persecutory' (1976: 610). Klein readily admits that this idea of an infant 'trying to destroy its mother' presents a 'horrifying not to say an unbelievable picture to our minds' (1960: 187). The possible linkage between the 'drying up of the breast' and vampirism is proposed by Copjec, who claims, ' Most visual images of vampirism center on the female breast' (1991: 34 n. 16).

From a folkloristic perspective, we can see that, with the principle of *lex taliouis*, the infant-child may fear retaliation for such aggressive impulses and that such retaliation by the parents might take the form of sucking or biting. Folklore fantasy is full of swallowing monsters who threaten to eat up children, while the 'vagina dentata' (MotifF 547.1.1; see Otero 1996) could represent for males the maternal teeth threatening to bite (off) their male projection, just as male infants sought to bite (off) the projecting breast of the mother. In any event, the nursing mother confronted with oral sadistic sucking or biting on the part of a frustrated or angry infant may withdraw her breast from the infant's mouth, a perfectly reasonable course of action under the circumstances. This withdrawal of the breast would, from the infant's point of view, constitute a form of 'object loss.' In other words, sucking (and/or biting) the breast leads to object loss, meaning the withdrawal of the maternal breast (which in infantile logic appears to be inexhaustible: every time the infant wishes nourishment, the breast seems to be magically full again). Object loss, in general, is related to so-called separation anxiety on the part of infants, an anxiety-provoking situation which is articulated in such games as peek-a-boo and later hide-and-seek, where the 'lost' object is in every case 'found' and the separation anxiety alleviated (Frankiel 1993).

Now if we understand that the death of a loved one is also a form of object loss, in the psychological sense, and if there is guilt on the part of the living as having caused that death (e.g., through wishful thinking at some point), then it is possible that through projective inversion that the lost object (the deceased loved one) will return to take revenge by means of sucking or biting. This, I maintain, is precisely what we have in the folkloristic figure of the bloodsucking revenant known as the vampire.

There is another aspect of the vampire phenomenon that needs elucidation and concerns the conception of death itself. It is once again Ernest Jones who provides the critical clue. In his brilliant 1924 essay, 'Psycho-Analysis and Anthropology,' delivered as an address to the British Royal Anthropological Institute in February of that year, Jones suggested that death is 'a reversal of the birth act leading to a return to the pre-natal existence within the maternal womb' (1951: 137–138). The tomb-womb symbolic equation is now pretty much taken for granted. Freud in a footnote in his *Interpretation of Dreams* went so far as to propose that 'the profoundest unconscious reason for a belief in a life after death' is 'a projection into the future of this mysterious life before birth.' Freud also claimed that the dread of being buried alive stems from the same prenatal experience (1938: 395 n. 1). As one analyst phrases the issue, 'The symbolism is obvious: Earth equals mother; coffin equals womb. The vampire is, thus, born anew each night and begins anew its search for sustaining lifeblood from another' (Henderson 1976: 618).

[…]

Now we can better understand why the dead are thirsty. The life-giving liquid can be water, blood, or milk, among other choices. This is why the vampire is said to 'suck' fluids from its victims. Sucking is the initial infantile response to the maternal breast, which according to Melanie Klein is the infant's 'first object relation' (1957: 3). Biting comes later (as it does in literary versions of the vampire plot) with a marked increase in oral sadism. As we've noted, the infant's teeth are its first weapon against the maternal breast. Just as the infant may want to suck the living (breast) dry, so the deceased is imagined as wanting to return to suck the living dry. Just as an infant appears to have an insatiable appetite or thirst for milk, so the vampire constantly has to seek more liquid refreshment or sustenance. However, whereas the maternal breast to the infant seems to be a magical, inexhaustible source of nutriment, the living victims of vampires are not. When they lose their vital fluids, they themselves become vampires in need of liquid replacement. Whether this is simply a folk recognition of the communicable nature of infectious diseases, or whether it is merely an affirmation of the principle of 'limited good' (Foster 1965), the end result is the same. In the latter case, if there is a finite amount of liquid 'good,' the vampire's gain is automatically the victim's loss. More important, by sucking on the victim, the vampire may be said to *merge* with the victim (Kayton 1972: 310), which would constitute a veritable replication of the prototypic infantile breast-feeding scenario. The victim then becomes a vampire, that is, also regresses to an oral sadistic infantile level.

I believe the theory of vampires here proposed has the advantage of explaining a good many puzzling details about the vampire belief complex. We can now understand why vampires are thirsty: they are thirsty because all the dead in the Indo-European and Semitic world are considered to be thirsty, not just vampires. They are thirsty because death is debirth; the transit to the other world is the reverse of the birth process, that is, the movement through the birth canal. To be reborn, the deceased must undo death, that is, be born again. If death is truly debirth, then reversing the death process would be equivalent to rebirth. It is almost mathematical. Death is the negation of life, but the negation of death is once again life. Minus a minus equals a plus! Being born again leads to a symbolic reinstatement of the initial nurturing process, that is, the reestablishment of the first object relationship: sucking the maternal breast. But as the dead are angry (at being dead – or so the living suppose), the sucking is quite vicious; the dead suck their victims to death. We can now also understand why the vampire attacks members of its own immediate family, and also why the vampire is said to sometimes attack cows and goats, obvious milk-giving substitutes for the original maternal breast. We can now better appreciate the various apotropaic measures employed to prevent vampires from carrying out their nefarious actions. Burning a corpse, like cremation, completes the desiccating process (see Čajkanović 1974). Once *all* the liquid is removed, the corpse is permanently dead. Decapitation is also effective because, if the deceased has no mouth, it cannot possibly mount an oral attack on the breast. Driving a stake through the purported vampire's heart is not an attempt to pinion the corpse by impalement, but rather an efficacious means of draining the last remaining liquid (blood) from it, which like burning or cremation completes the desiccating death of the only partly deceased.

The oral erotic basis of vampirism would also help explain why this belief complex can so easily serve as a convenient metaphor for adult sexuality ranging from 'normal' oedipal heterosexuality (in many literary texts, the vampire typically attacks a member of the opposite sex) to homosexuality (Dyer 1988) and lesbianism (Case 1991; see also Melton 1994: 301–302, 362–366; and Gordon and Hollinger 1997). The latter forms of sexuality, after all, often do involve oral-genital sucking activity. For that matter, even kissing is essentially an act of sucking, not to mention the 'love-bite' (Morse 1993: 193).

Finally, it is my contention that it is the underlying oral erotic basis of the vampire belief complex which partly explains the endless fascination of this enigmatic creature. In prudish Victorian times, the Bram Stoker novel provided a much-needed outlet for repressed sexuality (see Bentley 1972; Stevenson 1988), but even in the twentieth century, the vampire of popular culture and literature serves a similar function. The fear of being attacked by a vampire – at night, in one's own bedroom – can be constructed as a form of wishful thinking. The vampire in the grave is analogous to a sleeping parent. It is an incarnate expression of a child's ambivalence towards his or her parent of the opposite sex. While the initial sucking of the breast can be an expression of love, too much sucking (or certainly biting) can be an act of aggression. The vampire, though overtly carrying out an aggressive act, also approximates the original life-giving and partly erotic breast-feeding relationship. That is why the vampire is both feared and regarded as fascinating, even to young children watching vampire movies on television or vampires in animated cartoons.

In conclusion, we can now argue that the theory of the origin of the word *vampire*, which suggested that the term comes from a root *pī*, meaning 'to drink,' makes perfectly good sense. Drinking, or rather sucking, is an essential sine qua non of vampirism. And this is so even if one cannot accept the proposed infantile origin of this remarkable living legend, which will never die as long as it can continue to renew itself with future generations yet unborn.

References

Abraham, K. (1953). 'The Influence of Oral Erotism on Character-Formation'. In *Selected Papers on Psychoanalysis*. Edited by Karl Abraham, 393–406. New York: Basic Books.

Bent, J. T. (1886). 'On Insular Greek Customs'. *Journal of the Anthropological Institute* 15: 391–403.

Bentley, C. F. (1972). 'The Monster in the Bedroom: Sexual Symbolism in Bram Stoker's *Dracula*'. *Literature and Psychology* 22: 27–34.

Caikanović, V. (1974). 'The Killing of a Vampire'. *Folklore Forum* 7: 260–271. (See also herein, pp. 72–84.)

Case, S. –E. (1991). 'Tracking the Vampire'. *Differences: A Journal of Feminist Cultural Studies* 3 (2): 1–20.

Copjee, J. (1991). 'Vampires, Breast-Feeding, and Anxiety'. *October* 58: 25–43.

Dondes, A. (1980). *Interpreting Folklore*. Bloomington: Indiana University Press.

Du Boulay, J. (1982). 'The Greek Vampire: A Study of Cyclic Symbolism in Marriage and Death'. *Mon* 17: 219–238. (See also herein, pp. 85–108.)

Dyer, R. (1988). 'Children of the Night: Vampirism as Homosexuality, Homosexuality as Vampirism'. In *Sweet Dreams: Sexuality, Gender, and Popular Fiction*. Edited by Susannah Radstone, 47–72. London: Lawrence & Wishart.

Ellis, H. (1928). *Studies in the Psychology of Sex*. Vol. 3. Philadelphia, PA: F. A. Davis.

Foster, G. (1965). 'Peasant Society and the Image of Limited Good'. *American Anthropologist* 67: 293–315.

Frankiel, R. V. (1993). 'Hide-and-Seek in the Playroom: On Object Loss and Transference in Child Treatment'. *Psychoanalytic Review* 80: 341–359.

Freud, S. (1938). *The Basic Writings of Sigmund Freud*. New York: Modern Library.

Gelder, K. (1994). *Reading the Vampire*. London: Routledge.

Gordon, J., and V. Hollinger, eds. (1997). *Blood Read: The Vampire as Metaphor in Contemporary Culture*. Philadelphia, PA: University of Pennsylvania Press.

Gottlieb, R. M. (1991). The European Vampire: Applied Psychoanalysis and Applied Legend. *Folklore Forum* 24: 39–61.

Gottlieb, R. M. (1993). The Legend of the European Vampire: Object loss and Corporeal Preservation. *Psychoanalytic Study of the Child* 49: 465–480.

Henderson, D. J. (1976). 'Exorcism, Possession, and the Dracula Cult: A Synopsis of Object-Relations Psychology'. *Bulletin of the Menninger Clinic* 40: 603–628.

Jones, E. 1951. "Psycho-Analysis and Anthropology." In Ernest Jones, Essays in Applied plied Psychoanalysis, 114–144. of Essays in Folklore, Anthropology and Religion. London: Hogarth Press.

Jones, E. (1971). *On the Nightmare*. New York: Liveright.

Kayton, L. (1972). 'The Relationship of the Vampire Legend to Schizophrenia'. *Journal of Youth and Adolescence* 1: 303–314.

Klein, M. (1957). *Envy and Gratitude: A Study of Unconscious Sources*. New York: Basic Books.

Klein, M. (1960). *The Psychoanalysis of Children*. New York: Grove Press.

Kleinpaul, R. (1898). *Die Lebendigen und die Toten in Volksglauben, Religion und Sage*. Leipzig: G. J. Göschen.

Krafft-Ebing, R. v. (1953). *Psychopathia Sexualis*. New York: Pioneer Publications.

Leatherdale, C. (1985). *Dracula: The Novel & the Legend*. Wellingborough: Aquarian Press.

Lloyd, G. E. R. (1964). 'The Hot and the Cold, the Dry and the Wet in Greek Philosophy'. *Journal of Hellenic Studies* 84: 92–106.

Melton, J. G. (1994). *The Vampire Book: The Encyclopedia of the Undead.* Detroit: Visible Ink Press.

Morse, D. R. (1993). 'The Stressful Kiss: A Biopsychosocial Evaluation of the Origins, Evolution, and Societal Significance of Vampirism'. *Stress Medicine* 9: 181–199.

Murgoci, A. (1926). 'The Vampire in Roumania'. *Folklore* 86: 320–349. (See also herein, pp. 12–34.)

Nixon, D. (1979). 'Vampire Lore and Alleged Cases'. *Miorita* 6: 14–28.

Onians, R. B. (1973). *The Origins of European Thought.* New York: Arno Press.

Otero, S. (1996). '"Fearing Our Mothers": An Overview of the Psychoanalytic Theories Concerning the Vagina Dentata Motif F 547.1.1.' *American Journal of Psychoanalysis* 56: 269–288.

Politis, N. G. (1894). 'On the Breaking of Vessels as Funeral Rite in Modern Greece'. *Journal of the Royal Anthropological Institute* 23: 28–41.

Sartori, P. (1908). 'Das Wasser im Totengebranche'. *Zeitsebrift des Vereins fur Volkskunde* 18: 353–378.

Schierup, C.-U. (1986). 'Why Are Vampires Still Alive? Wallachain Immigrants in Scandinavia'. *Ethnos* 51: 173–198.

Stevenson, J. A. (1988). 'A Vampire in the Mirror: The sexuality of Dracula'. *PMLA* 103: 139–149.

Twitchell, J. (1980). 'The Vampire Myth'. *American Imago* 37: 83–92.

Yvonneau, M. (1990). 'Matricide et vampirisme'. *L'Evolution Psycbiatrique* 55: 575–585.

More than stories, more than myths: Animal/human/nature(s) in traditional ecological worldviews

Amba J. Sepie

3

Amba J. Sepie is an anthropologist and geographer, whose work makes an important contribution to the understanding that fieldwork data drawn from marginalized communities is of value for understanding a world that is dwelt in by the dominant community. It follows that this information is a significantly richer resource than is often imagined, providing insight into the world, rather than just other people's (vanishing?) worlds. This presents a significant challenge to mythographers, most of whom have sought to use mythological material to understand either a particular community or a symbolic, often internal, psychological truth.

In 2018 Sepie was awarded a doctorate in geography from the University of Canterbury, in New Zealand, for a thesis entitled *Tracing the Motherline*. She also holds an MA in religious studies and a BA in anthropology and religious studies, both from the University of Canterbury. At the time of writing, she has published five articles, which explore the entanglements of myth, ecology and worldview. The material that we have chosen to include here draws on her understanding of both mythology and ecology to develop a sophisticated argument about human relations with non-human people. Sepie here explains the relevance of myth for ecological engagement through a thoroughgoing exploration of the need to take seriously nondominant conceptions of dwelling. In so doing, Sepie significantly complicates the symbolists' cosy answer to the challenge of truth and opens the possibility for a mythography that seeks to neither debunk nor explain away non-Western mythology.

The idea of cultural evolution has rendered the folk story, or myth, as a quaintly accepted pre-modern error made by early or 'primitive' humans. As such, the art of listening to (or hearing) the speech of the animals has been kept alive (if barely) in folklore. In the mythologies of the world, comprehension of the language of the birds was revered as a divine boon: the Norse god, Odin, presided over the world with the help of two wise ravens; in tales from Wales, Greece, India, and greater Russia, an unlikely hero is granted the gift of hearing the prophesy of birds by magic; in Sweden, by the taste of dragons blood. King Solomon's wisdom, like that of Odin, was attributed to the birds, as were the stories of Aesop. For modern urban humans, these are generally thought of as folk tales and stories for children. Conversely, as cultural ecologist David Abram (2010) writes:

> [The] sacred language regularly attributed by tribal peoples to their most powerful shamans is often referred to as 'the language of the birds'. A keen attunement to the vocal discourse of the feathered folk has been a necessary survival skill for almost every indigenous community – especially for the active hunters within the group, and for the intermediaries (the magicians or medicine persons) who tend the porous boundary between the human and more-than-human worlds. (p. 196)

The value complex that underpins this division into truth and fiction has a long and convoluted history, and is based upon a combination of religious, philosophical, and scientific thought that has been incubated over at least two thousand years. Such questions, and the legitimacy of narrative as 'fact' or as 'useful knowledge', can be rendered very differently within indigenous, as compared with secular westernized contexts. As noted by the late Vine Deloria Jr. et al. (1999):

> In most tribal traditions, no data are discarded as unimportant or irrelevant. Indians consider their own individual experiences, the accumulated wisdom of the community that has been gathered by previous generations, their dreams, visions, and prophecies, and any information received from birds, animals and plants as data that must be arranged, evaluated, and understood as a unified body of knowledge. This mixture of data from sources that the Western scientific world regards as highly unreliable and suspect produces a consistent perspective on the natural world. (pp. 66–67)

Conversely, westernized frameworks categorize much of this content as religion or culture, myth, folktale or epic, and fable, or as genres that are studied within the areas of literature, folklore, religious studies, and anthropology. The study of narratology within the field of folklore, for instance, was initially focused upon forms, functions, and stylistic analysis (see Levi-Strauss 1963, 1966, 1968; Propp 1968; Propp and Liberman 1984). Early narratologists (such as Vladimir Propp) attempted to isolate aspects of narrative and develop typologies which were, in turn, used to extrapolate meanings or, in the case of Levi-Strauss, symbolic structures. In more contemporary times, narrative has come to be reimagined more broadly, as an active cultural force that 'enables us to make meaning out of a chaotic world' (Bal 2002: 10).

Traditional and indigenous ways of making 'story' can, however, be thought to challenge certain received wisdoms regarding the structure or form of narrative, especially regarding authorship, character, coherence, sequence and spatiality. In the specific area of *animal* narratology, indigenous narratives involve shifting concepts of personhood and identity as applicable to the 'characters' (who are often non-human), and a markedly different distinction between the fictional and non-fictional. This is not to suggest indigenous stories or literatures do not employ or recognize fiction, but that it is not set aside in quite the same manner as within 'westernized' categories of writing and thought. In traditional Native American contexts, for example, a distinction between ceremonial and popular genres makes more sense, or the sacred as juxtaposed with the pedagogical or humorous, soothing or entertaining (see Allen 1986).

Myth, in particular, has attracted a range of different uses across the disciplines. In folklore and religious studies, myth is used only to refer to a certain kind of narrative, or to quote Wendy Doniger (2011): 'a story that [is] good to believe in but unverifiable in the real world [… or] a story that a group of people believe for a long time despite massive evidence that it is not actually true' (p. ix). This meaning derives directly from the shift, in ancient Greece, from *mythos* (truth) to *logos* (lies and dissimulation), and eventually morphed into *fabula* in the Latin, or 'a persistent lie' (Kane 1998: 34). Bruce Lincoln (1996), a religious historian, speculates that the original shift in meaning (as concretized by the Romans) arose in ancient Greece with the rise of Platonic reason and the resultant unstable power relations between various 'regimes of truth'. This moment, preserved in etymological history, reveals a kind of colonization of thought and word in action; specifically, the overturning of traditional beliefs within an urban and 'progressive' political and economic context, in which a belief complex was eradicated and ultimately overthrown by a newer philosophy. The origin point for what now counts as 'true' and 'false' knowledge has to be set somewhere around the time of this transfer. One consequence of this was the creation of a distinct fictitious genre (myth and fable) into which non-Christian, pre-Christian, and other beliefs could be relocated.

Semiotician Roland Barthes (1984) defined myth as a type of speech, or a system of communication in which 'everything can be a myth provided it is conveyed by a discourse' (p. 109). These ways of thinking about myth – suggesting a radical divorce from historicity and how myths might be viewed within diverse cultural contexts – have significantly impacted upon the use of the term within the social sciences. Myth and discourse are often conflated whenever there is an emphasis on the 'truth' value of a claim, or a lack thereof. Myth can be broadly used to refer to anything that has persisted as 'true' and yet, can be shown to be only 'popularly true', for example, the 'myth of biological race' or the 'myth of the Communist threat'. In short, it is a term that often stands in for 'error' or 'fallacy', and it is *this* designation, when transposed onto the understanding of narratives of indigenous origin, that indigenous scholars have taken issue with.

Native American Laguna scholar, Paula Gunn Allen (1986: 102–103), writes that myth has been polluted by popular misuse to the point of being synonymous with 'lie'. Allen aligns the scholarly employment of 'myth' with other derogatory terms that imply backwardness, foolishness, and the general derision of native life-ways, arguing that the manner in which it has been used always points towards 'questionable accuracy'. As such, myth stands opposed to truth whenever it is considered as a part of a fiction-fact binary, and this is a problem which many social scientists (anthropologists, in particular) tend to recoil from resolving in concrete terms. Learning from animals, for example, or affording personhood and wisdom to non-human in general, can present enormous cosmological instability for those trained in westernized traditions. Modern humans are encouraged to speak *about* animals as part of a category called 'nature', or in the words of Abram (2010): 'Language is a human property, suitable for communication with other persons. We talk to people; we do not talk to the ground underfoot' (p. 174). Reading Abram, it's clear he is referring (somewhat tongue-in-cheek) to the conservative social norm which upholds the division between sentience and non-sentience, however the norm has a powerful hold on ethnographic scholarship. This is precisely how ethnographies of indigenous and traditional peoples become 'stories' and 'accounts' that are not assessed as 'true' or 'false', but truth claims that are 'true for them' or 'true enough'. As I have argued elsewhere, many ethnographers have gone to great lengths to suggest that it does not matter whether these stories are 'true' or not, but only that they are accurate representations of 'what people believe' (Sepie 2014, 2016a, 2016b). Anthropologist Paul Nadasdy (2007) describes the contradiction as follows:

> What to the Athapaskan or Cree hunter is a perfectly explainable – if not quite everyday – event becomes for the biologist (or anthropologist) an anomaly. Faced with stories of this sort, those of us wedded to a Euro-American view of human-animal relations have one of two choices: we can choose to disbelieve the account, or we can shrug it off as a bizarre coincidence. Either way, we avoid any attempt at explanation. (p. 36)

This avoidance presents serious problems for recognition of indigenous and traditional life-ways. Truth must matter if the dominant worldview is to be properly queried in areas where it is hegemonic: in areas where ascriptions of cultural relativism simply cannot compete with the abiding authority of the dominant worldview. Paul Rabinow [1983] (2011) writes that inscribed relations between truth and power are concealed by devices which 'bracket truth', thus taking no culture at its word: 'The anthropologist thus succeeds in studying what is serious and truthful to Others without it being serious and truthful to him' (p. 31). Claims as to the subjectivity of truth have served academics well, as these can be extended from religion and culture into the designated supernatural realm, to reduce and marginalize, as 'false', any realities which directly oppose the dominant norms.

Truth *matters* in westernized contexts, especially academic realms, and to suggest it does not matter, or that truth is 'relative' within an indigenous context appears structurally racist. Sami scholar Rauna Kuokkanen (2007) argues that these (and other) 'silences' which do not take metaphysical differences in worldview into account simply reproduce imperialism.

[...]

Learning to be human (again)

What are permitted as legitimate topics of inquiry in an academic context can be heavily restricted, with the exception of those modes of scholarship which engage a degree of political correctness with regards to 'cultural otherness'. Gillian Bennett (1987), a folklorist who studies afterlife beliefs, writes that: 'No-one will tackle the subject because it is disreputable, and it remains disreputable because no one will tackle it' (p. 13). I have elsewhere called this racist, as the 'magical gloss of cultural difference' allows for just about any phenomenon in non-westernized contexts, whilst simultaneously banning the serious investigation of intuitive faculties 'closer to home', aligning these with religion, or even madness (Sepie 2016a).

Intuition, like the religious 'miracle', is generally considered an oddity or anomaly. We do have some words for it, such as second sight (or, 'the sight'), the sixth sense, clairvoyance, clairaudience, and others, however, these are considered as 'spiritual beliefs' and studied by scholars of religion. They are not necessarily considered to be *real*, but 'true for those who believe'. Interestingly, (as I have quietly tested for over twenty years), when there is little to no chance of such experiences being documented or publicly exposed, many westernized individuals will readily recall at least a few anecdotal accounts of foresight, sixth sense, direct insight, or verified intuition.

There are also countless ethnographic examples the world over that document in great detail case studies such as the one Rose explores, and plenty of Old Jimmy Manngaiyarri's who will explain clearly and directly how the 'tell' works. Jeremy Narby, in his work alongside Ashaninca communities in the Peruvian Amazon, was regularly confronted with the statement that local ecological knowledge came from the *ayahuasqueros*, or shamans, who said that their knowledge of plants came from the plants themselves. In his discussion of ayahuasca (the primary visionary botanical brew used by the *ayahuasqueros* in their role as healers and mediators with the spirit world), he notes that the very combination of the elements required for the brew is beyond 'rationality', as the westernized mind may conceive of it:

> So here are people without electron microscopes who choose, among
> some 80,000 Amazonian plant species, the leaves of a bush containing a
> hallucinogenic brain hormone, which they combine with a vine containing

substances that inactivate an enzyme of the digestive tract, which would
otherwise block the hallucinogenic effect [...] and when one asks them how
they know these things, they say their knowledge comes directly from the
hallucinogenic plants. (Narby 1999: 11)

Although the botanical knowledge of indigenous Amazonians astonishes
scientists, there is no acceptable explanation beyond the assertion that their extensive
knowledge must be acquired through 'trial and error'. The related claim, that
ayahuasqueros acquire communications directly from the ayahuasca brew, detailing
the rest of their extensive medicinal repertoire (equally as impressive), is just beyond
the explanatory faculties of scientists. The discussion as to how their knowledge is
acquired, and how their medicine works, has been put aside in favor of the greater
objective of appropriating 'shaman pharmaceuticals' for western doctors. Much of
what is happening in these accounts comes down to understanding relationship, but
not in the manner assumed by Narby's scientists.

Consider the explanation of Arola, who conveys a Native American, yet
philosophical, position on 'knowing'. He writes that the only way to know what
a bird *is* (for example), comes via understanding the web of relations in which
it participates. It is in a *particular* place, at a *particular* time, and it plays a part
in a structure of relations that is larger than the bird itself. 'Knowing' the bird is
therefore dependent upon knowing its relation to the whole and yet, realizing that the
relationship is fluid and thus, ever changing. In Arola's work:

An indigenous comportment ... must perpetually attend to the fact that the
manner in which what is shows itself will be multifarious and unpredictable. Any
attempt to fully conceptualize how things will appear to us prior to our experience
of them will place undue limits on the presencing of things. (Arola 2011: 557)

In other words, any *predetermined* concept that an animal, a stone, or a storm
cannot speak (or exhibit other features that do not 'match' their designation), can
silence their 'tell'....

A. Irving Hallowell [1960] (2002), an anthropologist who made the very first
attempt to explain this in scholarship, was noted for using an Ojibwe example
regarding an old man's account of the 'aliveness' of a stone, and his openness to
regarding the stone as a potential teacher (for a contextual discussion of this, see Bird-
David 1999). Arola writes that there is simply no distinction in a Native American
worldview between natural and supernatural, animate and not. Hallowell's account
did not necessarily mean the old man *had* spoken to a stone, just that he would not
close off the possibility that such an interaction might teach him something. 'If we
approach the stone as an inanimate object in advance, assuming that it is nothing but
a mute object that sits in front of us [...] we will never encounter a stone as anything
more than such a mute object' (Arola 2011: 557). In this way of being, the same is
true of mountains, rivers, and weather.

In the documentary film, *The Grammar of Happiness*, there is an extremely brief
moment when the Pirahã men (in the Amazonia region) are hunting and listening to

the monkeys, and one man asks another if he heard what they said (Everett 2008; O'Neill and Wood 2012). This was by no means a 'mystical' moment, but one scene in a documentary that had nothing to do with hearing and understanding the monkeys. For the Pirahã, this was an ordinary event, and it remains ordinary, provided we do not (as Arola warns) close down ontological possibility, which is the prerequisite for what can, and cannot, 'be' or exist.

Indigenous cosmologies (also called origin stories, or charter myths) generally leave room for considerably more ontological possibility than the dominant cosmological frameworks which continue to inform the processes of westernization. Cosmology sets the 'order' of things, quite literally, in predetermining the set of objects, events, and so forth, that are the terms of reference in the ontological, epistemological (knowledge), and axiological (value) schema of any cultural complex.

This may sound rather complex, but it is actually quite simple – if the creation story sets up certain conditions of possibility (consider God, Adam and Eve in the Garden of Eden, or the Big Bang onset of a material universe), then values and beliefs about what is possible and what can exist (atoms, genes, talking birds) flow on from this. In the Big Bang version of events, and the cascading narratives of earth's beginning that fill in the time between then, and now, at no point does an animal, nor a stone, talk. In a fundamentalist view of the Christian Bible, however, this happened, but only in a 'special place' (the Garden) and the animal was evil. Nor can you find an ancestral spirit speaking to you in a dream in either of these origin stories. So ontology, or what is possible/what can exist, is fixed by these stories.

In the complex we refer to as 'western', these stories are a mixture of scientific beliefs and Abrahamic religious ideas (with a very healthy substratum of pagan-Christian dogma regarding the necessity of controlling errant spirits). These cosmological narratives ultimately inform what is 'allowed', and what is 'good' or 'useful' to believe or do. This worldview excludes everything being discussed herein, as it denies other species (and the more-than-human world) all potential for conscious interactions, personhood, and agency. The contrasts that can be drawn are stark.

All of these 'tells' are based, fundamentally, upon a core understanding of origin-in-the-sentient-land (earth as mother), on active attention to the kin relations for which we are responsible, and the other life forms with which we share a connection. Although they might be place-specific, origin in the land and kinship with a particular 'place' are not quite the same thing, in that land is the mother of connection to the specific places in which humans make home.

Rose (2013: 102–103) notes a number of 'tells' that all depend upon paying attention – those that are visually or habitually cued (such as the march flies 'telling' that the crocodiles are laying their eggs), and those that rely on an internal sort of communication. Intuitive knowing, good listening, and familiarity with the landscape are all integral to 'figuring out the tell' that comes from a combination of connection, observation, and communications with other species. Usually this is called 'seeing', and 'hearing', rather than 'knowing', as such. Holmes and Jampijinpa (2013: n.p.) note the *land can talk to Warlpiri people*. This includes the nonverbal body language of Country.

Anthropologist Nurit Bird-David (1999), who has studied with the Nayaka peoples (of South India), describes their concept of kin, or relatives, as 'anyone whom we share with'. 'Sharing with' makes kin into persons. She also describes the Nayaka explanation of 'talking with' other persons (in her example, trees) as something akin to 'attentiveness' to the variances (and invariances) in the behavior, and responses, of those with whom the Nayaka are in relation. Seeing, hearing, talking, knowing, and other divisions, are collapsed in Nayaka ways of being, or perhaps not delineated in these discrete ways. Nayaka, indigenous Australian, First Nations and Native American descriptions all concur that intimate and useful knowledge comes from these sorts of relations.

There are also, importantly, reminders from indigenous scholars not to reify (or concretize) such experiences to appear as magical or purposeless mysticism. Cordova, for example, who was trained in the western philosophical tradition and 'studied white people' (as she put it), warned against divorcing pragmatism from the popular trope of the Native American who speaks to trees and birds and receives all knowledge from a spirit guide. She writes 'If the American aboriginal peoples were truly of such a nature, they would never have survived. Embedded in the mythology, legends, and traditions, is a pragmatic core ... based on acute observation' (Cordova 2007: 213). In this defense against stereotyping Native Americans as 'mystics', Cordova might be misconstrued as suggesting a purely utilitarian connection with the more-than-human world, when in fact she eschews any such binary between myth and utility. Her perspective is inherently relational. Relationality, equally, collapses and disrupts privileged western categories of nature/culture and human/animal however this embedded ecological awareness is accompanied by responsibility, and what Cordova calls, reverence. Westernized people (beautifully phrased by Cordova as 'ghostly beings residing in decadent bodies on inanimate and alien ground) can, however, learn to be 'human' again (2007).[1]

Robert Wolff (2001), a psychologist and educator who has worked and lived in Indonesia and the Pacific Islands, writes of his experiences as follows:

> For many years my work took me to many parts of Southeast Asia and the Pacific. I recorded and collected what I could of methods of healing and herbal medicines ... It seemed that all such knowledge was being erased by our intolerance of other-ness. I was deeply saddened by what I believed was an irreparable loss. In our rush to create man-made chemicals, we rejected age-old knowledge of the riches of the earth that are freely available all around us. We invented machines, but ignored talents and abilities we must have in our very genes. (p. 5)

Wolff recounts a story from time spent in Sumatra (in an aptly titled chapter called *Learning to Be Human Again*) about a walk he takes with a man called Ahmeed, when they came upon a snake in some bamboo (Wolff 2001: 144–170). Ahmeed stops and motions, be silent – *no talking, stay still, quiet*. A large snake crawling along the ground crosses their path, maybe fourteen or more feet in length, uncommon in size and on the ground instead of a tree. Wolff, curious as to how Ahmeed knew the snake was there, questions him at length. All he would respond with, given the absolute lack of any signal from the snake prior to the encounter, was that he knew. He had neither seen, nor heard it, but he knew. The remainder of the chapter details how Wolff himself comes to learn how to pay attention, to find water, to hear the tell of a tiger (in Malay *'rimau*) and to recognize himself as a human in-relation to the knowledge and voices of the larger ecological unit in which he comes to recognize his connection to the whole. Once Ahmeed realizes the transformation that has taken place, he asks Wolff:

> 'Do you turn off the seeing?' Yes, I told him, I had to […] 'Good,' he said […] 'You are alone […] It will be difficult for you to see because you do not have the village around you.' He used the word *kampong*, suggesting not only a settlement, but especially the extended social relationships of a village, or a Sng'oi settlement. (Wolff 2001: 166–167)

This example highlights one of the biggest obstacles to actualizing some of the wisdom and praxis described here. To embody Macy's concept of the ecological self would be a necessary first step towards feeling less isolated, and heal the 'breach' that Graham mentioned in her description of an indigenous Australian worldview.[2] A necessary second step would be for westernized peoples to adopt a systems view of what is referred to as 'consciousness', in conceiving of the spaces-between-people as being *full* of communications and relationships, and our human selves as potential receivers to those communications.[3]

I, like many others, was not taught how to be in-relation-with the 'pattern that connects' – as Gregory Bateson (1991) famously phrased it – with the world around me, with other humans, and with other species. I was born *already colonized*. I descend from a variety of variously hued migrants without a clear blood memory or place to which I might *whakapapa* – to use a genealogical word borrowed from the indigenous nations of my country.[4] I have no such word that can mean anything close to the same thing and the English language is all I know. The processes of colonization have converted and distorted all histories that might have aided me in knowing to whom, and to where, I belong. I know only that I lack any ancestral memory of a relationship with place, and have no knowledge of how to find, nor kill, nor be respectful toward, my own food.

I can attest, however, to the idea that it is possible for us to become aware of what we are being 'told', and that we can learn, despite familial, social, or geographical disadvantages, to do this in modest ways. There is a *difference* between the chattering of my mind (in Abram's opinion, enhanced by literary culture), and the arrival of intuitive knowings or intuitive experiences with more-than-human nature as a component of waking consciousness. This confirms (to me) that we can begin from where we are, learn to pay attention to the conscious web of relations, and trust those intuitive moments that happen when we recognize what it really means to be a human, born on the earth, who is *also*, animal. We are not (as dictated by the fantasy of human exceptionalism) somehow *more* human according to the degree we move away from nature, but *less* human by way of this presumption.

Notes

1   None of these scholars are advocating for a 'seeker' culture in which westernized peoples descend upon indigenous communities for guidance (or appropriate ceremony etc.), and nor are they proposing that there is something 'more intuitive' about indigenous peoples in general. Many of the traditional ways of being discussed in this paper are endangered and have been for some time, in other instances they have been almost entirely eradicated from a people or region, as have the languages that help sustain them. It is not the responsibility of indigenous elders, scholars, or communities to 'save' the westernized peoples of the world; rather, pedagogical responsibility for un-learning has been occurring through networks of transmission which venerate these life ways without reduction, or through appropriations which have not been gifted. It is the responsibility of each individual within one's own community to help one another 'get right' with the world, and to understand/teach how to have 'right relations'. Gifting is nonetheless a part of what the Haudenosaunee, and others, see as part of the remedy for decolonizing the westernized. For instance, David Mowaljarlai, senior Lawman of the Ngarinyin peoples of the west Kimberley, has said: 'We are really sorry for you people. We cry for you because you haven't got meaning of culture in this country. We have a gift we want to give you. We keep getting blocked from giving you that gift […] And it's the gift of pattern thinking. It's the culture which is the blood of this country, of Aboriginal groups, of the ecology, of the land itself […] What we see is, all the white people that were born in this country and they are missing the things that came from us mob, and we want to try and share it. And the people were born in this country, in the law country, from all these sacred places in the earth. And they were born on top of that. And that, we call *wungud* – very precious. That is where their spirit come from. That's why we can't divide one another, we want to share our gift, that everybody is belonging, we want to share together in the future for other generations to live on. You know? That's why it's very important' (ABC Radio 1995).

2   There are a number of initiatives in this area (called nature-connection modeling) which have emerged in the last fifteen years. In addition to the long-term work of Joanna Macy (Macy 2007, 2013; Macy and Brown 1998; Macy and Johnstone 2012) it is instructive to look at the work of Jon Young (Young 2016; Young and Gardoqui 2012) as supported through his work with Native American and San communities in Botswana, and by Richard Louv (2005, 2011) and Darcia Narváez (2014, 2016a, 2016b).

3   This perspective is sustained by philosophy of consciousness researchers who pursue non-local ideas of consciousness, as supported by quantum physicists such as Amit Goswami (Goswami 2000, 2008, 2011; Goswami et al. 1993), David Bohm (Bohm 1994, 2002; Bohm and Edwards 1991; Bohm and Hiley 1993; Bohm and Peat 2000), F. David Peat (Briggs and Peat 1984, 1999; Buckley and Peat 1996; Peat 1994, 2000), and others. Unlike the old scientific view of consciousness as localized to individual minds, this view is consistent with the inherent principle of non-locality within indigenous and traditional cosmologies in numerous communities, throughout the world.

4   *Whakapapa* is a Māori term that is used to refer to kinship ties, as both a noun (my whakapapa, or family tree) and a verb or process (as in, I whakapapa to that river). In Aotearoa New Zealand (unlike many other countries) indigenous words and concepts are used cross-culturally, with respect, as recognition of indigenous sovereign status despite

on-going Crown ownership, and as recognition of *tangata whenua*, which refers to Māori ancestral and contemporary traditional guardianship of the land. Furthermore, the use of Te Reo Māori is a national language, and is encouraged and taught in schools. The adoption of appropriate words, such as the use of Māori greetings, is not considered to be cultural appropriation.

References

ABC Radio (1995). *The Law Report: Aboriginal Law (David Mowaljarlai)*. Radio Broadcast. New York: ABC Radio.

Abram, David. (2010). *Becoming Animal: an Early Cosmology*, 1st ed. New York: Pantheon Books.

Allen, Paula Gunn. (1986). *The Sacred Hoop: Recovering the Feminine in American Indian Traditions*. Boston: Beacon Press.

Arola, Adam. (2011). 'Native American Philosophy'. In *Oxford Handbook of World Philosophy*. Edited by William Edelglass and Jay L. Garfield, 554–565. Oxford: Oxford University Press.

Bal, Mieke. (2002). *Travelling Concepts in the Humanities: A Rough Guide*. London and Toronto: Toronto University Press.

Barthes, Roland. (1984). *Mythologies*. Translated by Annette Lavers. New York: Hill and Wang.

Bateson, Gregory. (1991). *A Sacred Unity: Further Steps to an Ecology of Mind*. Edited by Rodney E. Donaldson. New York: Cornelia & Michael Bessie Books.

Bennett, Gillian. (1987). *Traditions of Belief: Women and the Supernatural*. Harmondsworth: Penguin.

Bird-David, Nurit. (1999). 'Animism' Revisited: Personhood, Environment, and Relational Epistemology. *Current Anthropology* 40: S67–S91. [CrossRef].

Bohm, David. (1994). *Thought as a System*. London and New York: Routledge.

Bohm, David. (2002). *Wholeness and the Implicate Order*. London and New York: Routledge.

Bohm, David, and Mark Edwards. (1991). *Changing Consciousness: Exploring the Hidden Source of the Social, Political, and Environmental Crises Facing Our World*, 1st ed. San Francisco: HarperSanFrancisco.

Bohm, David, and Basil J. Hiley (1993). *The Undivided Universe: An Ontological Interpretation of Quantum Theory*. London and New York: Routledge.

Bohm, David, and F. David Peat. (2000). *Science, Order, and Creativity*, 2nd ed. London and New York: Routledge.

Briggs, John, and F. David Peat. (1984). *Looking Glass Universe: The Emerging Science of Wholeness*. New York: Cornerstone Library.

Briggs, John, and F. David Peat. (1999). *Seven Life Lessons of Chaos: Timeless Wisdom from the Science of Change*, 1st ed. New York: HarperCollins Publishers.

Buckley, Paul, and F. David Peat. (1996). *Glimpsing Reality: Ideas in Physics and the Link to Biology*, rev. ed. Toronto: University of Toronto Press.

Cordova, Viola F. (2007). *How It Is: The Native American Philosophy of V.F. Cordova*. Edited by Kathleen Dean Moore. Tucson: University of Arizona Press.

Deloria Jr., Vine, Barbara Deloria, Kristen Foehner, and Samuel Scinta, eds. 1999. *Spirits & Reason: the Vine Deloria, Jr., Reader*. Golden: Fulcrum.

Doniger, Wendy. (2011). *The Implied Spider: Politics and Theology in Myth*, updated ed. New York: Columbia University Press.

Everett, Daniel Leonard. (2008). *Don't Sleep, There Are Snakes: Life and Language in the Amazonian Jungle*. London: Profile.

Goswami, Amit. (2000). *The Physicists' View of Nature*. 2 vols; New York: Kluwer Academic/Plenum Publishers.

Goswami, Amit. (2008). *God Is Not Dead: What Quantum Physics Tells Us about Our Origins and How We Would Live*. Charlottesville: Hampton Roads.

Goswami, Amit. (2011). *How Quantum Activism Can Save Civilization: A Few People Can Change Human Evolution*. Charlottesville: Hampton Roads.

Goswami, Amit, Richard E. Reed, and Maggie Goswami. (1993). *The Self-Aware Universe: How Consciousness Creates the Material World*. New York: Putnam.

Hallowell, A. Irving. (2002). Ojibwa Ontology, Behavior, and World View. In *Readings in Indigenous Religions*. Edited by Graham Harvey. New York: Continuum, pp. 17–49. First published 1960.

Holmes, Miles C. C., and Wanta Jampijinpa. (2013). Law for Country: The Structure of Warlpiri Ecological Knowledge and Its Application to Natural Resource Management and Ecosystem Stewardship. *Ecology and Society* 18: 19. [CrossRef].

Kane, Sean. (1998). *Wisdom of the Mythtellers*, 2nd ed. Ontario and New York: Broadview Press.

Kuokkanen, Rauna Johanna. 2007. Reshaping the University : Responsibility, Indigenous Epistemes, and the Logic of the Gift. Vancouver: UBC Press

Levi-Strauss, Claude. (1963). *Totemism*. Boston: Beacon Press.

Levi-Strauss, Claude. (1966). *The Savage Mind*. London: Weidenfeld & Nicolson.

Levi-Strauss, Claude. (1968). *Structural Anthropology*. 2 vols. London: Allen Lane.

Lincoln, Bruce. (1996). Gendered Discourses: the Early History of Mythos and Logos. *History of Religions* 36: 1–12.

Louv, Richard. (2005). *Last Child in the Wood: Saving Our Children from Nature-Deficit Disorder*, 1st ed. Chapel Hill: Algonquin Books of Chapel Hill.

Louv, Richard. (2011). *The Nature Principle: Human Restoration and the End of Nature-Deficit Disorder*. Chapel Hill: Algonquin Books of Chapel Hill.

Macy, Joanna. (2007). *World as Lover, World as Self: Courage for Global Justice and Ecological Renewal*. Berkeley: Parallax Press.

Macy, Joanna. (2013). The Greening of the Self. In *Spiritual Ecology: The Cry of the Earth, a Collection of Essays*. Edited by Llewellyn Vaughan-Lee. Point Reyes Station: The Golden Sufi Center, pp. 145–156.

Macy, Joanna, and Molly Young Brown. (1998). *Coming Back to Life: Practices to Reconnect Our Lives, Our World*. Gabriola Island: New Society Publishers.

Macy, Joanna, and Chris Johnstone. (2012). *Active Hope: How to Face the Mess We're in without Going Crazy*. Novato: New World Library.

Narby, Jeremy. (1999). *The Cosmic Serpent: DNA and the Origins of Knowledge*. New York: Jeremy P. Tarcher/Putnam.

Nadasdy, Paul. 2007. The Gift in the Animal: The Ontology of Hunting and Human-Animal Sociality. American Ethnologist 34: 25–43

Narváez, Darcia. (2014). *Neurobiology and the Development of Human Morality: Evolution, Culture, and Wisdom*, 1st ed. London and New York: W.W. Norton and Company.

Narváez, Darcia. (2016a). Returning to Humanity's Moral Heritages. *Journal of Moral Education* 45: 256–260. [CrossRef].

Narváez, Darcia. (2016b). Revitalizing Human Virtue by Restoring Organic Morality. *Journal of Moral Education* 45: 223–238. [CrossRef].

O'Neill, Michael, and Randall Wood. (2012). *The Grammar of Happiness*. Annandale: Essential Media & Entertainment.

Peat, F. David. (1994). *Lighting the Seventh Fire: The Spiritual Ways, Healing, and Science of the Native American*. Secaucus: Carol Pub. Group.

Peat, F. David. (2000). *The Blackwinged Night: Creativity in Nature and Mind.* Cambridge, MA: Perseus Pub.

Propp, Vladimir. (1968). *Morphology of the Folktale,* 2nd ed. Publications of the American Folklore Society; Austin: University of Texas Press.

Propp, Vladimir I. A., and Anatoly Liberman. (1984). *Theory and History of Folklore.* Translated by Ariadna Y. Martin, and Richard P. Martin. Minneapolis: University of Minnesota Press.

Rabinow, Paul. 2011. Humanism as Nihilism: The Bracketing of Truth and Seriousness in American Cultural Anthropology. In The Accompaniment: Assembling the Contemporary. Edited by Paul Rabinow and Michel Foucault. Chicago: University of Chicago Press, pp. 13–39. First published 1983

Rose, Deborah Bird. (2013). Val Plumwood's Philosophical Animism: Attentive Inter-Actions in the Sentient World. *Environmental Humanities* 3: 93–109. [CrossRef].

Sepie, Amba J. 2014. Conversing with Some Chickadees: Cautious Acts of Ontological Translation. Literature and Medicine 32: 277–98

Sepie, Amba J. (2016a). 'No Limestone in the Sky: The Politics of Damned Facts'. In *Damned Facts: Fortean Approaches to the Study of Religion, Folklore and the Paranormal.* Edited by Jack Hunter. Paphos: Aporetic Press.

Sepie, Amba J. (2016b). Symbolic Malfunctions in the Failure of Nerve: Heretical Anthropology. *Symbolism: An International Journal of Critical Aesthetics* 16: 295–314.

Wolff, Robert. (2001). *Original Wisdom: Stories of an Ancient Way of Knowing.* Rochester: Inner Traditions.

Young, Jon. (2016). Effective Connection Modeling and Regenerating Human Beings. Paper presented at Sustainable Wisdom: Integrating Indigenous Knowledge for Global Flourishing Conference, University of Notre Dame, Notre Dame, IN, USA, September 11–15.

Young, Jon, and Dan Gardoqui. (2012). *What the Robin Knows: How Birds Reveal the Secrets of the Natural World.* Boston: Houghton Mifflin Harcourt.

Section C: Myth and history

The search for truth

In October 2015 *Secrets of the Dead*, an Emmy-nominated TV Series, ran a special exploration of Trojan Mythology (called *The Real Trojan Horse*). During the broadcast, Edith Hall (Professor of Classics at King's College, London) emphatically stated, 'I want to find out whether there was any real history behind … [the] myth' (Fowlie and Sanders 2015). In this statement Hall captures the way that myth is commonly positioned as simultaneously opposed to the category of the real, which contains history, and a potential source of insight into the historical and the real. In this view, neither the contemporary use of myth nor its cosmological insights are of central importance. The focus instead is on the analyst's skilful detection of elements of lost, or partially forgotten, truths. For it is only thanks to the analyst's reconstructive skill that a narrative worthy of interest in the modern age can be told.

This sense, that there must a be a hidden truth behind a seemingly trivial mythic narrative, is of course part of what Lévi-Strauss (see Part Three, Section A, Chapter 1) has described as the mythic systems of a steam engine, which views the past in a linear fashion (Lévi-Strauss and Charbonnier 1969: 33–39). On the one hand, the quest for lost truth requires the present to be the result of a process of cultural evolution. On the other hand, there is a sense that (in the rush for progress) something might have been lost. This soft primitivism combines with the remnant of the Protestant desire to cut out the reactor's hand, to create a sense that myth (at least as we have it today) is a corrupted form of an older, perhaps more valuable, narrative, which belonged to an ancient (forgotten) and yet advanced civilization (cf Hancock 2012).

The idea of a partially forgotten, advanced yet ancient, civilization may be viewed as harmless (if unhelpful) myth making were it not for the fact that it is notoriously connected to both the academic and popular construction of the Aryans. A seemingly innocent academic suggestion that moved quickly from a linguistic hypothesis to a cultural concept and then a racial truth, with devastating consequences. The origin of this movement can be located in the noticing of linguistic connections that stretch across Europe and into Asia. This so-called Indo-European hypothesis, reasoned that linguistic connections that can be found in literature as diverse as medieval Ireland and India could only be the residue of an ancient (and now-forgotten) language, which had once spread throughout the region, probably through invasion. It was therefore suggested that if language spread this way, then so too must have mythology and that the exploration of mythological connections between these distant regions could reveal something of a now-forgotten ancient mythology (see Part Two, Section C, Chapter 3).

Of course, none of the above, inductive, steps are without challenge, but the argument was to prove for a time dangerously persuasive to a politically receptive Europe. Two of the chapters in this section (Part Two, Section C, Chapter 2 and Part Two, Section C, Chapter 3) can be seen as broadly speaking to this Indo-European tradition, one from its beginning and the other from a contemporary perspective. We would encourage readers to engage critically with these chapters while bearing in mind three core facts: (1) the Indo-European hypothesis can only, at best, provide a hypothetical reconstruction; (2) there is nothing in the essence of this hypothesis that necessitates the invocation of the problematic concept of race; (3) the hypothesis could rest on assumptions of historical patterns of trade as much as those of invasion, or even mass folk movement.

The third offering in this section (a reading by Mercia Eliade) takes a different approach to the relation of history and myth, despite its author being closely aligned to the Indo-European movement. Politically, Eliade was known to have far-right leanings (Allen 2008), and this, combined with an interest in Indian religion, should have made him highly susceptible to Aryan ideology. Indeed, it is impossible to imagine that his politics did not negatively impact his work. However, Eliade is perhaps best known for contrasting myth with what he termed the terror of history, which he had witnessed first-hand during the turbulent times of the first half of the last century (Allen 1988). Through this (and other allusions to the value of non-Aryan mythology), it is possible to see the seeds of an argument against the damaging ideologies of race, nation, progress and purity.

Collectively, these challenging and problematic readings open the question of the relation of politics to mythography. They demonstrate both that speculation on myth is far from an innocent pursuit and that myth analysis can be myth creation. Although the Indo-European hypothesis has fallen out of favour among contemporary mythographers, we feel that it is important, in an age that has seen the theory revived by popularist, nationalist movements in both Europe and India (cf Beck 2002; Ozra 2013), for the next generation of mythographers to be confident in their ability to properly assess these theories, as well as have the capacity to detect within Aryan theories the cultural biases and flaws that can lead to the creation of dangerous ideologies. There is nothing wrong in being interested in the mythology of India and Europe, or indeed in a comparative exercise between the two. The danger comes when we switch from wanting to understanding a culture's mythology to projecting onto the material a politically fashioned and supposedly pure, or true, mythology.

References

Allen, D. (1988). Eliade and history. *The Journal of Religion* 68 (4): 545–565.
Allen, D. (2008). Prologue: Encounters with Mircea Eliade and His Legacy for the 21st Century. *Religion* 38 (4): 319–327.

Back, L. (2002). Aryans Reading Adorno: Cyber-culture and Twenty-First-Century Racism. *Ethnic and Racial Studies* 25 (4): 628–651.

Fowlie, T., Sanders, J. O. (2015). *The Real Trojan Horse*. Blink Films, Thirteen Productions, & PBS Distribution (Film).

Hancock, G. (2012). *Fingerprints of the Gods: The Evidence of Earth's Lost Civilization*. New York: Three Rivers Press.

Lévi-Strauss, C., and Charbonnier, G. (1969). *Conversations with Claude Lévi-Strauss* (Vol. 34). London: Jonathan Cape.

Oza, R. (2013). 'The Geography of Hindu Right-Wing Violence in India'. In *Violent Geographies*, 159–180. London: Routledge.

Myth and reality

Mircea Eliade

Mircea Eliade (1907–1986) was a historian of religion and a key figure in the phenomenological branch of religious studies, which should not be confused with philosophical phenomenology. By employing the term 'phenomenology', Eliade means to suggest that he is more interested in the experience that people have of the sacred than any beliefs that might lie behind that experience. Eliade is well known for his mapping of world religions, his work on myth and his forays into shamanism. Born in Romania, Eliade studied in Bucharest, before undertaking further studies in both India and Italy. His PhD work explored Indian religions, and his time spent in India was the subject (in 1988) of a hit film, *The Bengali Night*.

In 1933, Eliade returned to Romania, where he became involved in the Romanian nationalist movement – accusations of fascist sympathies were to eventually stain his legacy. Theoretically, Eliade drew inspiration from Jung, and this is reflected in his understanding of the importance of symbols in a spiritual life. Eliade's focus on mythology is a natural consequence of his insistence that to study myth as a living thing is to explore the foundation of religious life. That is to say that myth functions as a key revelation, which has the ability to collapse time and obviate the terrors of history. The selection that we have chosen to include here is from his book *Myth and Reality*. It provides his most developed definition of myth, as well as a discussion of the function of mythology and its relation to truth.

It would be hard to find a definition of myth that would be acceptable to all scholars and at the same time intelligible to nonspecialists. Then, too, is it even possible to find *one* definition that will cover all the types and functions of myths in all traditional and archaic societies? Myth is an extremely complex cultural reality, which can be approached and interpreted from various and complementary viewpoints.

Speaking for myself, the definition that seems least inadequate because most embracing is this: Myth narrates a sacred history; it relates an event that took place in primordial Time, the fabled time of the 'beginnings'. In other words, myth tells how, through the deeds of Supernatural Beings, a reality came into existence, be it the whole of reality, the Cosmos, or only a fragment of reality – an island, a species of plant, a particular kind of human behavior, an institution. Myth, then, is always an account of a 'creation'; it relates how something was produced, began to *be*. Myth tells only of that which *really* happened, which manifested itself completely. The actors in myths are Supernatural Beings. They are known primarily by what they did in the transcendent times of the 'beginnings'. Hence myths disclose their creative activity and reveal the sacredness (or simply the 'supernaturalness') of their works. In short, myths describe the various and sometimes dramatic breakthroughs of the sacred (or the 'supernatural') into the World. It is this sudden breakthrough of the sacred that really *establishes* the World and makes it what it is today. Furthermore, it is as a result of the intervention of Supernatural Beings that man himself is what he is today, a mortal, sexed, and cultural being.

We shall later have occasion to enlarge upon and refine these few preliminary indications, but at this point it is necessary to emphasize a fact that we consider essential: the myth is regarded as a sacred story, and hence a 'true history', because it always deals with *realities*. The cosmogonic myth is 'true' because the existence of the World is there to prove it; the myth of the origin of death is equally true because man's mortality proves it, and so on.

Because myth relates the *gesta* of Supernatural Beings and the manifestation of their sacred powers, it becomes the exemplary model for all significant human activities. When the missionary and ethnologist C. Strehlow asked the Australian Arunta why they performed certain ceremonies, the answer was always: 'Because the ancestors so commanded it.'[1] The Kai of New Guinea refused to change their way of living and working, and they explained: 'It was thus that the Nemu (the Mythical Ancestors) did, and we do likewise.'[2] Asked the reason for a particular detail in a ceremony, a Navaho chanter answered: 'Because the Holy People did it that way in the first place.'[3] We find exactly the same justification in the prayer that accompanies a primitive Tibetan ritual: 'As it has been handed down from the beginning of earth's creation, so must we sacrifice .... As our ancestors in ancient times did – so do we now.'[4] The same Justification is alleged by the Hindu theologians and ritualists. 'We must do what the gods did in the beginning' (*Satapatha Brāhmana*, VII, 2, 1, 4). 'Thus the gods did; thus men do' (*Taittiriya Brāhmana*, I, 5, 9, 4).[5]

As we have shown elsewhere,[6] even the profane behavior and activities of man have their models in the deeds of the Supernatural Beings. Among the Navahos 'women are required to sit with their legs under them and to one side, men with their legs crossed in front of them, because it is said that in the beginning Changing Woman and the Monster Slayer sat in these positions.'[7] According to the mythical traditions of an Australian tribe, the Karadjeri, all their customs, and indeed all their behavior, were established in the 'Dream Time' by two Supernatural Beings, the Bagadjimbiri (for example, the way to cook a certain cereal or to hunt an animal with a stick, the particular position to be taken when urinating, and so on).[8]

There is no need to add further examples. As we showed in *The Myth of the Eternal Return*, and as will become still clearer later, the foremost function of myth is to reveal the exemplary models for all human rights and all significant human activities – diet or marriage, work or education, art or wisdom. This idea is of no little importance for understanding the man of archaic and traditional societies, and we shall return to it later.

'True stories' and 'false stories'

We may add that in societies where myth is still alive the natives carefully distinguish myths – 'true stories' – from fables or tales, which they call 'false stories'. The Pawnee 'differentiate "true stories" from "false stories," and include among the "true" stories in the first place all those which deal with the beginnings of the world; in these the actors are divine beings, supernatural, heavenly, or astral. Next come those tales which relate the marvellous adventures of the national hero, a youth of humble birth who became the saviour of his people, freeing them from monsters, delivering them from famine and other disasters, and performing other noble and beneficent deeds. Last come the stories which have to do with the world of the medicine-men and explain how such-and-such a sorcerer got his superhuman powers, how such-and-such an association of shamans originated, and so on. The "false" stories are those which tell of the far from edifying adventures and exploits of Coyote, the prairie-wolf. Thus in the "true" stories we have to deal with the holy and the supernatural, while the "false" ones on the other hand are of profane content, for Coyote is extremely popular in this and other North American mythologies in the character of a trickster, deceiver, sleight-of-hand expert and accomplished rogue.'[9]

Similarly, the Cherokee distinguish between sacred myths (cosmogony, creation of the stars, origin of death) and profane stories, which explain, for example, certain anatomical or physiological peculiarities of animals. The same distinction is found in Africa. The Herero consider the stories that relate the beginnings of the different groups of the tribe 'true' because they report facts that *really* took place, while the more or less humorous tales have no foundation. As for the natives of Togo, they look on their origin myths as 'absolutely real'.[10]

This is why myths cannot be related without regard to circumstances. Among many tribes they are not recited before women or children, that is, before the uninitiated. Usually the old teachers communicate the myths to the neophytes during their period of isolation in the bush, and this forms part of their initiation. R. Piddington says of the Karadjeri: 'the sacred myths that women may not know are concerned principally with the cosmogony and especially with the institution of the initiation ceremonies.'[11]

Whereas 'false stories' can be told anywhere and at any time, myths must not be recited except *during a period of sacred time* (usually in autumn or winter, and only at night).[12] This custom has survived even among peoples who have passed beyond the archaic stage of culture. Among the Turco-Mongols and the Tibetans the epic songs of the Gesar cycle can be recited only at night and in winter. 'The recitation is assimilated to a powerful charm. It helps to obtain all sorts of advantages, particularly success in hunting and war …. Before the recitation begins, a space is prepared by being powdered with roasted barley flour. The audience sit around it. The bard recites the epic for several days. They say that in former times the hoofprints of Gesar's horse appeared in the prepared space. Hence the recitation brought the real presence of the hero.'[13]

What myths reveal

This distinction made by natives between 'true stories' and 'false stories' is significant. Both categories of narratives present 'histories', that is, relate a series of events that took place in a distant and fabulous past. Although the actors in myths are usually Gods and Supernatural Beings, while those in tales are heroes or miraculous animals, all the actors share the common trait that they do not belong to the everyday world. Nevertheless, the natives have felt that the two kinds of 'stories' are basically different. For everything that the myths relate *concerns them directly*, while the tales and fables refer to events that, even when they have caused changes in the World (cf. the anatomical or physiological peculiarities of certain animals), have not altered the human condition as such.[14]

Myths, that is, narrate not only the origin of the World, of animals, of plants, and of man, but also all the primordial events in consequence of which man became what he is today – mortal, sexed, organized in a society, obliged to work in order to live, and working in accordance with certain rules. If the World *exists*, if man *exists*, it is because Supernatural Beings exercised creative powers in the 'beginning'. But after the cosmogony and the creation of man other events occurred, and man *as he is today* is the direct result of those mythical events, *he is constituted by those events*. He is mortal because something happened *in illo tempore*. If that thing had not happened, man would not be mortal – he would have gone on existing indefinitely, like rocks; or he might have changed his skin periodically like snakes, and hence would have been able to renew his life, that is, begin it over again indefinitely. But the myth of the origin of death narrates what happened *in illo tempore*, and, in telling the incident, explains *why* man is mortal.

Similarly, a certain tribe live by fishing – because in mythical times a Supernatural Being taught their ancestors to catch and cook fish. The myth tells the story of the first fishery, and, in so doing, at once reveals a superhuman act, teaches men how to perform it, and, finally, explains why this particular tribe must procure their food in this way.

It would be easy to multiply examples. But those already given show why, for archaic man, myth is a matter of primary importance, while tales and fables are not. Myth teaches him the primordial 'stories' that have constituted him existentially; and everything connected with his existence and his legitimate mode of existence in the Cosmos concerns him directly.

[...]

Australian totemic myths usually consist in a rather monotonous narrative of peregrinations by mythical ancestors or totemic animals. They tell how, in the 'Dream Time' (*alcheringa*) – that is, in mythical time – these Supernatural Beings made their appearance on earth and set out on long journeys, stopping now and again to change the landscape or to produce certain animals and plants, and finally vanished underground. But knowledge of these myths is essential for the life of the Australians. The myths teach them how to repeat the creative acts of the Supernatural Beings, and hence how to ensure the multiplication of such-and-such an animal or plant.

These myths are told to the neophytes during their initiation. Or rather, they are 'performed,' that is, re-enacted, 'When the youths go through the various initiation ceremonies, [their instructors] perform a series of ceremonies before them; these, though carried out exactly like those of the cult proper – except for certain characteristic particulars – do not aim at the multiplication and growth of the totem in question but are simply intended to show those who are to be raised, or have just been raised, to the rank of men the way to perform these cult rituals.'[15]

We see, then, that the 'story' narrated by the myth constitutes a 'knowledge' which is esoteric, not only because it is secret and is handed on during the course of an initiation but also because the 'knowledge' is accompanied by a magico-religious power. For knowing the origin of an object, an animal, a plant, and so on is equivalent to acquiring a magical power over them by which they can be controlled, multiplied, or reproduced at will. Erland Nordenskiöld has reported some particularly suggestive examples from the Cuna Indians. According to their beliefs, the lucky hunter is the one who knows the origin of the game. And if certain animals can be tamed, it is because the magicians know the secret of their creation. Similarly, you can hold red-hot iron or grasp a poisonous snake if you know the origin of fire and snakes. Nordenskiöld writes that 'in one Cuna village, Tientiki, there is a fourteen-year-old boy who can step into fire unharmed simply because he knows the charm of the creation of fire. Perez often saw people grasp red-hot iron and others tame snakes.'[16]

This is a quite widespread belief, not connected with any particular type of culture. In Timor, for example, when a rice field sprouts, someone who knows the mythical traditions concerning rice goes to the spot. 'He spends the night there in the plantation hut, reciting the legends that explain how man came to possess rice [origin myth] .... Those who do this are not priests.'[17] Reciting its origin myth compels the rice to come up as fine and vigorous and thick as it was when *it appeared for the first time*. The officiant does not remind it of how it was created in order to 'instruct' it, to teach it how it should behave. He *magically compels it to go back to the beginning*, that is, to repeat its exemplary creation.

The *Kalevala*, relates that the old Väinämöinen cut himself badly while building a boat. Then 'he began to weave charms in the manner of all magic healers. He chanted the birth of the cause of his wound, but he could not remember the words that told of the beginning of iron, those very words which might heal the gap ripped open by the blue steel blade.' Finally, after seeking the help of other magicians, Väinämöinen cried: 'I now remember the origin of iron! and he began the tale as follows: Air is the first of mothers. Water is the eldest of brothers, fire the second and iron the youngest of the three. Ukko, the great Creator, separated earth from water and drew soil into marine lands, but iron was yet unborn. Then he rubbed his palms together upon his left knee. Thus were born three nature maidens to be the mothers of iron.'[18]

It should be noted that, in this example, the myth of the origin of iron forms part of the cosmogonic myth and, in a sense, continues it. This is an extremely important and specific characteristic of origin myths ....

The idea that a remedy does not act unless its origin is known is extremely widespread. To quote Erland Nordenskiöld again: 'Every magical chant must be preceded by an incantation telling the origin of the remedy used, otherwise it does not act .... For the remedy or the healing chant to have its effect, it is necessary to know the origin of the plant, the manner in which the first woman gave birth to it.'[19]

In the Na-khi ritual chants published by J. F. Rock it is expressly stated: 'If one does not relate ... the origin of the medicine, to slander it is not proper.'[20] Or: 'Unless its origin is related one should not speak about it.'[21]

... as in the Väinämöinen myth given above, the origin of remedies is closely connected with the history of the origin of the World. It should be noted, however, that this is only part of a general conception, which may be formulated as follows: *A rite cannot be performed unless its 'origin' is known, that is, the myth that tells how it was performed for the first time*. During the funeral service the Na-khi shaman chants:

'Now we will escort the deceased and again experience bitterness;
We will again dance and suppress the demons.
If it is not told whence the dance originated
One must not speak about it.
Unless one know the origin of the dance
One cannot dance.'[22]

This is curiously reminiscent of what the Uitoto told Preuss: 'Those are the words (myths) of our father, his very words. Thanks to those words we dance, and there would be no dance if he had not given them to us.'[23]

In most cases it is not enough to *know* the origin myth, one must *recite* it; this, in a sense, is a proclamation of one's knowledge, *displays* it. But this is not all. He who recites or performs the origin myth is thereby steeped in the sacred atmosphere in which these miraculous events took place. The mythical time of origins is a 'strong' time because it was transfigured by the active, creative presence of the Supernatural Beings. By reciting the myths one reconstitutes that fabulous time and hence in some sort becomes 'contemporary' with the events described, one is in the presence of the Gods or Heroes. As a summary formula we might say that by 'living' the myths one emerges from profane, chronological time and enters a time that is of a different quality, a 'sacred' Time at once primordial and indefinitely recoverable. ...

Structure and function of myths

These few preliminary remarks are enough to indicate certain characteristic qualities of myth. In general it can be said that myth, as experienced by archaic societies, (1) constitutes the History of the acts of the Supernaturals; (2) that this History is considered to be absolutely *true* (because it is concerned with realities) and *sacred* (because it is the work of the Supernaturals); (3) that myth is always related to a 'creation', it tells how something came into existence, or how a pattern of behavior, an institution, a manner of working were established; this is why myths constitute the paradigms for all significant human acts; (4) that by knowing the myth one knows the 'origin' of things and hence can control and manipulate them at will this is not an 'external,' 'abstract' knowledge but a knowledge that one 'experiences' ritually, either by ceremonially recounting the myth or by performing the ritual for which it is the justification; (5) that in one way or another one 'lives' the myth, in the sense that one is seized by the sacred, exalting power of the events recollected or re-enacted.

'Living' a myth, then, implies a genuinely 'religious' experience, since it differs from the ordinary experience of everyday life. The 'religiousness' of this experience is due to the fact that one re-enacts fabulous, exalting, significant events, one again witnesses the creative deeds of the Supernaturals; one ceases to exist in the everyday world and enters a transfigured, auroral world impregnated with the Supernaturals' presence. What is involved is not a commemoration of mythical events but a reiteration of them. The protagonists of the myth are made present, one becomes their contemporary. This also implies that one is no longer living in chronological time, but in the primordial Time, the Time when the event *first took place*. This is why we can use the term the 'strong time' of myth; it is the prodigious, 'sacred' time when something *new, strong,* and *significant* was manifested. To re-experience that time, to re-enact it as often as possible, to witness again the spectacle of the divine works, to meet with the Supernaturals and relearn their creative lesson is the desire that runs like a pattern through all the ritual reiterations of myths. In short, myths reveal that the World, man, and life have a supernatural origin and history, and that this history is significant, precious, and exemplary.

I cannot conclude this chapter better than by quoting the classic passages in which Bronislav Malinowski undertook to show the nature and function of myth in primitive societies. 'Studied alive, myth ... is not an explanation in satisfaction of a scientific interest, but a narrative resurrection of a primeval reality, told in satisfaction of deep religious wants, moral cravings, social submissions, assertions, even practical requirements. Myth fulfills in primitive culture an indispensable function: it expresses, enhances, and codifies belief; it safeguards and enforces morality; it vouches for the efficiency of ritual and contains practical rules for the guidance of man. Myth is thus a vital ingredient of human civilisation; it is not an idle tale, but a hard-worked active force; it is not an intellectual explanation or an artistic imagery, but a pragmatic charter of primitive faith and moral wisdom .... These stories ... are to the natives a statement of a primeval, greater, and more relevant reality, by which the present life, fates and activities of mankind are determined, the knowledge of which supplies man with the motive for ritual and moral actions, as well as with indications as to how to perform them.'[24]

Notes

1   C. Strehlow, *Die Aranda-und-Loritja-Stämme in Zentral-Australien*, vol. III (J. Baer and Company, 1907), p. i; cf. Lucien Lévy-Bruhl, *La mythologie primitive* (Paris, 1935), p. 123. See also T. G. H. Strehlow, *Aranda Traditions* (Melbourne University Press, 1947), p. 6.

2   C. Keysser, quoted by Richard Thurnwald, *Die Eingeborenen Australiens und der Südseeinseln* (=Religionsgeschichtliches Lesebuch, 8, Tübingen, 1927), p. 28.

3   Clyde Kluckhohn, 'Myths and Rituals: A General Theory,' *Harvard Theological Review* 35 (1942): 66. Cf. ibid. for other examples.

4   Matthias Hermanns, *The Indo-Tibetans* (Bombay, 1954), pp. 66 ff.

5   See M. Eliade, *The Myth of the Eternal Return* (New York, 1954), pp. 21 ff.

6   Ibid., pp. 27 f.

7   Kluckhohn, 'Myths and Rituals', quoting W. W. Hill, *The Agricultural and Hunting Methods of the Navaho Indians* (New Haven, 1938), p. 179.

8   Cf. M. Eliade, *Myths, Dreams and Mysteries* (New York, 1960), pp. 191 ff.

9   R. Pettazzoni, *Essays on the History of Religions* (Leiden, 1954), pp. 11–12. Cf. also Werner Müller, *Die Religionen der Waldlandindianer Nordamerikas* (Berlin, 1956), p. 42.

10 Pettazzoni, *Essays on the History of Religions*, p. 13.

11 R. Piddington, quoted by L. Lévy-Bruhl, p. 115. On initiation ceremonies, cf. M. Eliade, *Birth and Rebirth* (New York, 1958).

12 See examples in Pettazzoni, *Essays on the History of Religions*, p. 14, n. 15.

13 R. A. Stein, *Recherches sur l'épopée et le barde au Tibet* (Paris, 1959), pp. 318–319.

14 Of course, what is considered a 'true story' in one tribe can became a 'false story' in a neighboring tribe. 'Demythicization' is a process that is already documented in the archaic stages of culture. What is important is the fact that 'primitives' are always aware of the difference between myths ('true stories') and tales or legends ('false stories'). Cf. Appendix 1 ('Myths and Fairy Tales').

15 Strehlow, *Die Aranda-und-Loritja-Stämme in Zentral-Australien*, vol. III, pp. 1–2; Lévy-Bruhl, *La mythologie primitive*, p. 123. On puberty initiations in Australia, cf. *Birth and Rebirth*, pp. 4 ff.

16 E. Nordenskiöld, 'Faiseurs de miracles et voyants chez les Indiens Cuna,' in *Revista del Instituto de Etnologia*, vol. II (Tucumán, 1932), p. 464; Lévy-Bruhl, *La mythologie primitive*, p. 118.

17 A. C. Kruyt, quoted by Lévy-Bruhl, *La mythologie primitive*, p. 119.

18 Alil Kolehmainen Johnson, *Kalevala. A Prose Translation from the Finnish* (Hancock, MI, 1950), pp. 53 ff.

19 E. Nordenskiöld, 'La conception de l'âme chez les Indiens Cuna de l'Isthme de Panama,' *Journal des Américanistes*, N.S. 24 (1932): 5–30, 14.

20 J. F. Rock, *The Na-Khi Nâga Cult and related ceremonies*, vol. II (Rome, 1952), p. 474.

21 Ibid., p. 487.

22 J. F. Rock, *Zhi-mā funeral ceremony of the Na-Khi* (Vienna Mödling, 1955), p. 87.

23 K. T. Preuss, *Religion und Mythologie der Uitolo*, vols. I–II (Göttingen, 1921–1923), p. 625.

24 B. Malinowski, *Myth in Primitive Psychology* (1926; reprinted in *Magic, Science and Religion* [New York, 1955], pp. 101, 108).

References

Eliade, M. (1954). *The Myth of the Eternal Return*. New York: Pantheon Books.

Eliade, M. (1958). *Rites and Symbols of Initiation; the Mysteries of Birth and Rebirth*. New York: Harper.

Eliade, M. (1960). *Myths, Dreams, and Mysteries: The Encounter between Contemporary Faiths and Archaic Realities*. New York: Harper.

Hermanns, M. (1954). *The Indo-Tibetans: The Indo-Tibetan and Mongoloid Problem in the Southern Himalaya and North-Northeast India*. Bombay: I.L. Fernandes.

Johnson, A. K. (1951). *Kalevala: A Prose Translation from the Finnish*. Hancock, MI: Printed by the Book Concern.

Kluckhohn, C. (1960). *Myths and Rituals: A General Theory*. Indianapolis, IN: Bobbs-Merrill, College Division.

Lévy-Bruhl, L. (1963). *La mythologie primitive*. Paris: Presses Universitaires de France.

Malinowski, B. (1926). *Myth in Primitive Psychology*. New York: W.W. Norton.

Nordenskiöld, E. (1932). *Faiseurs de miracles et voyants chez les indiens cuna*. Tucumán: Universidad nacional de Tucumán.

Nordenskiöld, E. (1932). La conception de l'âme chez les Indiens Cuna de l'isthme de Panamá (la signification de trois mots cuna : purba, niga et kurgin). *Journal De La Société Des Américanistes* 24 (1): 5–30.

Pettazzoni, R. (1954). *Essays on the History of Religions*. Leiden: E.J. Brill.

Preuss, K. T. (1921). *Religion und Mythologie der Uitoto: 1*. Göttingen: Vandenhoeck & Ruprecht.

Preuss, K. T. (1923). *Religion und Mythologie der Uitoto: 2*. Göttingen: Vandenhoeck & Ruprecht.

Rock, J. F. (1952). *The Na-khi Naga Cult and Related Ceremonies*. Roma: Istituto Italiano per il Medio ed Estremo Oriente.

Rock, J. F. (1955). *The Zhi mä funeral ceremony of the Na-khi of Southwest China: Described and transl. from Na-khi manuscripts*. Vienna: Mödling.

Stein, R. A. (1959). *Recherches sur l'epopee et la barde au Tibet*. Paris: Presses universitaires de France.

Strehlow, C. (1911). *Die Aranda- und Loritja-Stämme in Zentral-Australien: 3, 2*. Frankfurt am Main: Baer.

Strehlow, T. G. H. (1947). *Aranda Traditions*. Melbourne: Melbourne University Press.

Thurnwald, R. (1927). *Die eingeborenen Australiens und der Südseeinseln*. Tubingen: Mohr.

The original elements of mythology

Max Müller

2

Max Müller (1823–1900) was a German philologist and Orientalist, who initially made his name by producing the first scholarly edition of the Rig Veda and was later better known for his contributions to both comparative religion and mythology. He attended Leipzig University, where he studied philology and philosophy and mastered an impressive range of ancient languages including Latin, Persian and Sanskrit. In 1868, he was appointed to the inaugural chair of Comparative Philology at the University of Oxford, where he worked for most of his career. In 1888, two years before his death, he was commissioned to deliver the prestigious Gifford Lecturers at the University of Glasgow, and these lecturers have proved to be some of his most influential material.

Müller was heavily influenced by the transcendentalist role of spirituality and criticized Darwinian ideas of human development. He, in turn, was led to develop a comparative approach to the exploration of mythology, which was (in) famous for its positing of a primal solar mythology. Müller is also widely considered to be a forerunner of the Indo-European school of mythography, which explored myths from India and Europe in search of a common ancestor. The following selection is taken from his longer work *Comparative Mythology* and is a masterly demonstration of the way that (largely ancient) myths from around the world can be compared to discover, either through attentiveness or inventiveness, core similarities, which can then be used to (re)create the lost worldview of prehistoric society.

We can best enter into the original meaning of a Greek myth, when some of the persons who act in it have preserved names intelligible in Greek. When we find the names of Eos, Selene, Helios, or Herse, we have words which tell their own story,... Let us take the beautiful myth of Selene and Endymion. Endymion is the son of Zeus and Kalyke, but he is also the son of Aethlios, a king of Elis, who is himself called a son of Zeus, and whom Endymion is said to have succeeded as King of Elis. This localises our myth, and shows, at least, that Elis is its birthplace, and that, according to Greek custom, the reigning race of Elis derived its origin from Zeus. The same custom prevailed in India, and gave rise to the two great royal families of ancient India – the so-called Solar and the Lunar races: and Purûravas, of whom more by and by, says of himself –

> The great king of day
> And monarch of the night are my progenitors;
> Their grandson I.

There may, then, have been a King of Elis, Aethlios, and he may have had a son, Endymion; but what the myth tells of Endymion could not have happened to the King of Elis. The myth transfers Endymion into Karia, to Mount Latmos, because it was in the Latmian cave that Selene saw the beautiful sleeper, loved him and lost him. Now about the meaning of Selene, there can be no doubt; but even if tradition had only preserved her other name, Asterodia, we should have had to translate this synonym, as Moon, as 'Wanderer among the stars.' But who is Endymion? It is one of the many names of the sun, but with special reference to the setting or dying sun. It is derived from ἐν-δύω, a verb which, in classical Greek, is never used for setting, because the simple verb δύω had become the technical term for sunset. Δυσμαὶ ἡλίου, the setting of the sun, is opposed to ἀνατόλαι, the rising. Now, δύω meant, originally, to dive into; and expressions like ἠέλιος δ' ἄρ ἔδυ, the sun dived, presupposes an earlier conception of ἔδυ πόντον, he dived into the sea. Thus Thetis addresses her companions, Il. xviii. 140 –

Ὑμεῖς μέν νύν δύτε θαλάσσης εὐρέα κόλπον.
(You may now dive into the broad bosom of the sea.)

Other dialects, particularly of maritime nations, have the same expression. In Latin we find,[1] 'Cur *mergat* seras aequore flammas.' In Old Norse, 'Sôl gengr i aegi' [The sun goes into the sea – Vigfusson, *Icel. Diet.*, p. 758]. Slavonic nations represent the sun as a woman stepping into her bath in the evening, and rising refreshed and purified in the morning; or they speak of the Sea as the mother of the Sun, and of the Sun as sinking into her mother's arms at night. We may suppose, therefore, that in some Greek dialect ἐνδύω was used in the same sense; and that from ἐνδύω, ἐνδύμα was formed to express sunset. From this was formed, ἐνδυμίων,[2] like οὐρανίων from οὐρανός, and like most of the names of the Greek months. If ἐνδύμα had become a common name for sunset, the myth of Endymion could never have arisen. But the original meaning of Endymion being once forgotten, what was told originally of the setting sun was now told of a name, which, in order to have any meaning, had to be changed into a god or a hero. The setting sun *once* slept in the Latmian cave, the cave of night – Latmos being derived from the same root as Leto, Latona, the night; – but *now* he sleeps on Mount Latmos, in Karia. Endymion, sinking into eternal sleep after a life of but one day, was *once* the setting sun, the son of Zeus – the brilliant Sky, and Kalyke – the covering night (from καλύπτω); or, according to another saying, of Zeus and Protogeneia, the firstborn goddess, or the Dawn, who is always represented either as the mother, the sister, or the forsaken wife of the Sun. *Now* he is the son of a King of Elis, probably for no other reason except that it was usual for kings to take names of good omen, connected with the sun, or the moon, or the stars – in which case a myth, connected with a solar name, would naturally be transferred to its human namesake. In the ancient poetical and proverbial language of Elis, people said 'Selene loves and watches Endymion,' instead of 'it is getting late'; 'Selene embraces Endymion,' instead of 'the sun is setting and the moon is rising'; 'Selene kisses Endymion into sleep,' instead of 'it is night.' These expressions remained long after their meaning had ceased to be understood; and as the human mind is generally as anxious for a reason as ready to invent one, a story arose by common consent, and without any personal effort, that Endymion must have been a young lad loved by a young lady, Selene; and, if children were anxious to know still more, there would always be a grandmother happy to tell them that this young Endymion was the son of the Protogeneia – she half meaning and half not meaning by that name the Dawn, who gave birth to the sun; or of Kalyke, the dark and covering Night. This name, once touched, would set many chords vibrating; three or four different reasons might be given (as they really were given by ancient poets) why Endymion fell into this everlasting sleep, and if any one of these was alluded to by a popular poet, it became a mythological fact, repeated by later poets; so that Endymion grew at last almost into a type, no longer of the setting sun, but of a handsome boy beloved of a chaste maiden, and therefore a most likely name for a young prince. Many myths have thus been transferred to real persons, by a mere similarity of name, though it must be admitted that there is no historical evidence whatsoever that there ever was a Prince of Elis, called by the name of Endymion.

Such is the growth of a legend, originally a mere word, a μύθos, probably one of those many words which have but a local currency, and lose their value if they are taken to distant places – words useless for the daily interchange of thought – spurious coins in the hands of the many – yet not thrown away, but preserved as curiosities and ornaments, and deciphered at last, after many centuries, by the antiquarian. Unfortunately, we do not possess these legends as they passed originally from mouth to mouth in villages or mountain castles – legends such as Grimm has collected in his *Mythology*, from the language of the poor people in Germany – not as they were told by the older members of a family, who spoke a language half intelligible to themselves and strange to their children – not as the poet of a rising city embodied the traditions of his neighbourhood in a continuous poem, and gave to them a certain form and permanence. Unless where Homer has preserved a local myth, all is arranged as a system, with the *Theogony* as its beginning, the *Siege of Troy* as its centre, and the *Return of the Heroes* as its end. But how many parts of Greek mythology are never mentioned by Homer! We then come to Hesiod – a moralist and theologian, and again we find but a small segment of the mythological language of Greece. Thus, our chief sources are the ancient chroniclers, who took mythology for history, and used of it only so much as answered their purpose. And not even these are preserved to us, but we only believe that they formed the sources from which later writers, such as Apollodorus and the scholiasts, borrowed their information. The first duty of the mythologist is, therefore, to disentangle this cluster, to remove all that is systematic, and to reduce each myth to its primitive unsystematic form. Much that is unessential has to be cut away altogether, and after the rust is removed, we have to determine first of all, as with ancient coins, the locality, and, if possible, the age, of each myth, by the character of its workmanship; and as we arrange ancient medals into gold, silver, and copper coins, we have to distinguish most carefully between the legends of gods, heroes, and men. If, then, we succeed in deciphering the ancient names and legends of Greek or any other mythology, we learn that the past that stands before our eyes, in Greek mythology, has had its present – that there are traces of organic thought in these petrified relics – and that they once formed the surface of the Greek language. The legend of Endymion was present at the time when the people of Elis understood the old saying of the Moon (or Selene) rising under the cover of Night (or in the Latmian cave), to see and admire, in silent love, the beauty of the setting Sun, the sleeper Endymion, the son of Zeus, who granted to him the double boon of eternal sleep and everlasting youth.

Endymion is not the Sun in the divine character of Phoibos Apollon, but a conception of the Sun in his daily course, as rising early from the womb of Dawn,[3] and after a short and brilliant career, setting in the evening, never to return again to this mortal life. Similar conceptions are frequent in Aryan mythology, and the Sun viewed in this light is sometimes represented as divine, yet not immortal – sometimes as living, but sleeping – sometimes as a mortal beloved by a goddess, yet tainted by the fate of humanity. Thus, *Tithonos*[,] being derived from the same root as Titan,[4] expressed originally the idea of the Sun in his daily or yearly character. He also, like Endymion, does not enjoy the full immortality of Zeus and Apollon. Endymion retains his youth, but is doomed to sleep. Tithonos is made immortal, but as Eos forgot to ask for his eternal youth, he pines away as a decrepit old man, in the arms of his ever youthful wife, who loved him when he was young, and is kind to him in his old age. Other traditions, careless about contradictions, or ready to solve them sometimes by the most atrocious expedients, call Tithonos the son of Eos and Kephalos, as Endymion was the son of Protogeneia, the Dawn; and this freedom in handling a myth shows, that at first, a Greek knew what it meant if Eos was said to leave every morning the bed of Tithonos. As long as this expression was understood, I should say that the myth was present; it was past when Tithonos had been changed into a son of Laomedon, a brother of Priamos, a prince of Troy. Then the saying, that Eos left his bed in the morning, became mythical, and had none but a conventional or traditional meaning. Then, as Tithonos was a prince of Troy, his son, the Ethiopian Memnon, had to take part in the Trojan war. And yet how strange! – even then the old myth seems to float through the dim memory of the poet! – for when Eos weeps for her son, the beautiful Memnon, her tears are called 'morning-dew' – so that the past may be said to have been still half-present.[5]

As we have mentioned Kephalos as the beloved of Eos, and the father of Tithonos, we may add that Kephalos also, like Tithonos and Endymion, was one of the many names of the Sun. Kephalos, however, was the rising sun – the head of light – an expression frequently used of the sun in different mythologies.[6] In the *Veda*, where the sun is addressed as a horse, the head of the horse is an expression meaning the rising sun. Thus, the poet says – *Rv.* i. 163, 6, 'I have known through my mind thy self when it was still far – thee, the bird flying up from below the sky; I saw a head with wings, proceeding on smooth and dustless paths.' The Teutonic nations speak of the sun as the eye of Wuotan, as Hesiod speaks of –

$$\pi \acute{a} \nu \tau a \ \emph{i} \delta \grave{\omega} \nu \ \Delta \emph{i} \grave{o} \varsigma \ \emph{o} \phi \theta a \lambda \mu \grave{o} \varsigma \ \kappa a \grave{i} \ \pi \acute{a} \nu \tau a \ \nu o \acute{\eta} \sigma a \varsigma;$$

and they also call the sun the face of their god.[7] In the *Veda*, again, the sun is called (i. 115, 1) 'the face of the gods,' or the face of Aditi [the Infinite] (i. 113, 9); and it is said that the winds obscure the eye of the sun by showers of rain (v. 59, 5).

A similar idea led the Greeks to form the name of Kephalos; and if Kephalos is called the son of Herse – the Dew – this meant the same in mythological language, that we should express by the sun rising over dewy fields. What is told of Kephalos is, that he was the husband of Prokris, that he loved her, and that they vowed to be faithful to one another. But Eos also loves Kephalos; she tells her love, and Kephalos, true to Prokris, does not accept it. Eos, who knows her rival, replies, that he might remain faithful to Prokris, till Prokris had broken her vow. Kephalos accepts the challenge, approaches his wife disguised as a stranger, and gains her love. Prokris, discovering her shame, flies to Kreta. Here Diana gives her a dog and a spear, that never miss their aim, and Prokris returns to Kephalos disguised as a huntsman. While hunting with Kephalos, she is asked by him to give him the dog and the spear. She promises to do so only in return for his love, and when he has assented, she discloses herself, and is again accepted by Kephalos. Yet Prokris fears the charms of Eos – and while jealously watching her husband, she is killed by him unintentionally, by the spear that never misses its aim.

Before we can explain this myth, which, however, is told with many variations by Greek and Latin poets, we must dissect it, and reduce it to its constituent elements.

The first is 'Kephalos loves Prokris.' Prokris we must explain by a reference to Sanskrit, where prush and prish mean 'to sprinkle,' and are used chiefly with reference to raindrops. For instance, *Rv.* i. 168, 8. 'The lightnings laugh down upon the earth,[8] when the Winds shower forth the rain.'

The same root in the Teutonic languages has taken the sense of 'frost' – and Bopp identifies prush with O. H. G. frus, frigere.

In Greek we must refer to the same root $\pi \rho \acute{\omega} \xi$, $\pi \rho \omega \kappa \acute{o} \varsigma$, a dewdrop, and also Prŏkris, the dew. Thus, the wife of Kephalos is only a repetition of Herse, her mother – Herse, dew, being derived from Sk. vrish, to sprinkle. The first part of our myth, therefore, means simply, 'the Sun kisses the Morning Dew.'

The second saying is, 'Eos loves Kephalos.' This requires no explanation: it is the old story, repeated a hundred times in Aryan mythology, 'the Dawn loves the Sun.'

The third saying was, 'Prokris is faithless; yet her new lover, though in a different guise, is still the same Kephalos.' This we may interpret as a poetical expression for the rays of the sun being reflected in various colours from the dewdrops – so that Prokris may be said to be kissed by many lovers; yet they are all the same Kephalos, disguised, but at last recognised.

The last saying was, 'Prokris is killed by Kephalos,' *i.e.* the dew is absorbed by the sun. Prokris dies for her love to Kephalos, and he must kill her because he loves her. It is the gradual and inevitable absorption of the dew by the glowing rays of the sun which is expressed, with so much truth, by the unerring shaft of Kephalos thrown unintentionally at Prokris hidden in the thicket of the forest.[9]

We have only to put these four sayings together, and every poet will at once tell us the story of the love and jealousy of Kephalos, Prokris, and Eos. If anything was wanted to confirm the solar nature of Kephalos, we might point out how the first meeting of Kephalos and Prokris takes place on Mount Hymettos, and how Kephalos throws himself afterwards, in despair, into the sea, from the Leukadian mountains. Now, the whole myth belongs to Attika, and here the sun would rise, during the greater part of the year, over Mount Hymettos like a brilliant head. A straight line from this, the most eastern point, to the most western headland of Greece, carries us to the Leukadian promontory – and here Kephalos might well be said to have drowned his sorrows in the waves of the ocean.[10]

Another magnificent sunset looms in the myth of the death of Herakles. His twofold character as a god, and as a hero, is acknowledged even by Herodotos – and some of his epithets are sufficient to indicate his solar character, though perhaps no name has been made the vehicle of so many mythological and historical, physical and moral stories, as that of Herakles. Names which he shares with Apollo and Zeus are Δαφνηφόρος, Αλεξίκακος, Μάντις, Ἰδαῖος, Ὀλύμπιος, Παγγενέτωρ.

Now, in his last journey, Herakles also, like Kephalos, proceeds from east to west. He is performing his sacrifice to Zeus, on the Kenaeon promontory of Euboea, when Deianeira sends him the fatal garment. He then throws Lichas into the sea – who is transformed into the Lichadian islands. From thence Herakles crosses over to Trachys, and then to Mount Oeta, where his pile is raised, and the hero is burnt, rising through the clouds to the seat of the immortal gods – himself henceforth immortal and wedded to Hebe, the goddess of youth. The coat which Deianeira sends to the solar hero is an expression frequently used in other mythologies; it is the coat which in the *Veda*, 'the mothers weave for their bright son' – the clouds which rise from the waters and surround the sun like a dark raiment. Herakles tries to tear it off; his fierce splendour breaks through the thickening gloom – but fiery mists embrace him, and are mingled with the parting rays of the sun, and the dying hero is seen through the scattered clouds of the sky, tearing his own body to pieces, till at last his bright body is consumed in a general conflagration, his last-beloved being Iole – perhaps the violet-coloured evening clouds – a word which, as it reminds us also of ἰός, poison (though the *i* is long), may perhaps have originated the myth of a poisoned garment.

Notes

1   Grimm's *Teutonic Mythology*, trans. James Steven Stallybrass, 4 vols (London: George bell and Sons, 1880–88), p. 704 [p. 742, ed. Stallybrass].

2   Lauer, in his *System of Greek Mythology*, explains Endymion as the Diver. Gerhard in his *Greek Mythology* gives ᾽Ενδυμίων as ὁ ἐν δύμῃ ὤν.

3   So in Psalm cx. 3, the Messiah has His birth 'from the womb of the morning.'

4   Ἀφελῶς δ' ἔλαμψε Τίταν. – *Anakreontea*, 47.

5   As an instance of the solidarity of classical myths with those of primitive peoples, this from New Zealand may be compared: 'Up to this time the vast Heaven has still ever remained separated from his spouse the Earth. Yet this mutual love still continues – the soft warm sighs of her loving bosom still ever rise up to him, ascending from the woody mountains and valleys, and men call them mists; and the vast Heaven, as he mourns through the long nights his separation from his beloved, drops frequent tears upon her bosom, and men seeing these term them dew-drops.' – Sir G. Grey, *Polynesian Mythology*, 1855, p. 15.

6   *E.g.*, '(Sol) caput obscura nitidum ferrugine texit.' – Vergil, *Georgic*, i. 467.

The mounting sun,

Through thick exhaled fogs his golden head hath run.

– M. Drayton, *Polyolbion*, Song 13, *sub init*.

7   Grimm, *Mythologie*, p. 666. [Eng. trans., p. 703. We may perhaps compare the Semitic use of *pani*, face, for the manifestation of a deity, *e.g.* Peni-el, 'face of God' (Gen. xxxii. 30, 31), equivalent to the Babylonian *páni-ili*, and 'the face (*pen*) of Baal,' a name given to the Carthaginian goddess Tanith. This explains a difficult passage in Hosea xi. 2.]

8   *Cf.* the Persian *khandah i barq*, 'the laughter of the lightning'; and Shelley makes the cloud say, 'I laugh as I pass in thunder.' So Lucretius, 'Æther lumine *ridet*' (iii. 22); 'the light of the righteous laugheth.' – Prov. xiii. 9.

9   'La rugiada Pugna col sole.' – Dante, *Purgatorio*, 1, 121.

10 The Leukadian rock faces the entrance to the under-world, 'the portals of the sun,' when he sinks into the darkness of the west (Homer, *Odyssey*, xxiv. 11, 12). It was the leaping-off place for despairing lovers and death-doomed criminals (Ovid, *Fasti*, v. 630; Hesiod, xv. 179). They were conceived as following the sun in his descent as –

A god gigantic, habited in gold,
Stepping from off a mount into the sea.

(C. Wells)

Similarly the New Zealanders regard Reinga, at the north end of the islands, as the leaping-off place which gives entrance to their Hades, 'the great Mother-Night' (R. Taylor, *Te Ika a Maui: Or, New Zealand and Its Inhabitants: Illustrating the Origin, Manners, Customs, Mythology, Religion, Rites, Songs, Proverbs, Fables, and Language of the Natives: Together with the Geology, Natural History, Productions, and Climate of the Country: Its State as*

Regards Christianity: Sketches of the Principal Chiefs, and Their Present Position [AH & AW Read, 1855], pp. 148, 231). In Mangaia the point of departure when they leap into the sea for spirit-land, Avaiki, faces the setting sun (W.W. Gill, *Myths and Songs from the South Pacific* [London: HS King, 1876], p. 159). At the west point of Upolu is the leaping-stone, giving a direct route to Fäfä (Hades). – J. B. Stair, *Old Samoa: Or, Flotsam and Jetsam from the Pacific Ocean* (Religious Tract Society, 1897), 219. The old Norsemen cast themselves from the Valhalla cliff into Odin's Pend (the sea) to gain immortality. – C. Elton, *Origins of English History* (London: B. Quaritch, 1882), pp. 91–92. See also R. Brown, *Semitic Influence in Hellenic Mythology: With Special Reference to the Recent Mythological Works of the Rt. Hon. Prof. F. Max Müller and Mr. A. Lang* (London: Williams & Norgate, 1898), pp. 257–260. So Cajae Raz, the extreme western point of Armorica, is held by the Bretons to be the place of departure of souls for the under-world (Procoplus, Claudian, Villemarqué).

References

Brown, R. (1898). *Semitic Influence in Hellenic Mythology: With Special Reference to the Recent Mythological Works of the Rt. Hon. Prof. F. Max Müller and Mr. A. Lang*. London: Williams & Norgat.

Drayton, M. (1612). *Polyolbion*. London: Lownes.

Elton, C. I. (1882). *Origins of English History*. London: B. Quaritch.

Gill, W. W. (1876). *Myths and Songs from the South Pacific*. London: HS King.

Grey, G. (1885). *Polynesian Mythology and Ancient Traditional History of the New Zealand Race, as Furnished by Their Priests and Chiefs. By Sir George Grey*. Auckland: Printed by H. Brett.

Grimm, J. (1882). *Teutonic Mythology*. Translated by James Steven Stallybrass, 4 vols. London: George bell and Sons, 1880–88.

Lauer, J. F. (1853). *System der griechischen Mythologie*. Berlin: Druck und Verlag von Georg Reimer.

Stair, J. B. (1897). *Old Samoa: Or, Flotsam and Jetsam from the Pacific Ocean*. London: Religious Tract Society.

Taylor, R. (1855). *Te Ika a Maui: Or, New Zealand and Its Inhabitants: Illustrating the Origin, Manners, Customs, Mythology, Religion, Rites, Songs, Proverbs, Fables, and Language of the Natives: Together with the Geology, Natural History, Productions, and Climate of the Country: Its State as Regards Christianity: Sketches of the Principal Chiefs, and Their Present Position*. AH & AW Read.

CúChulainn's women and some Indo-European comparisons

Nicholas J. Allen

3

Nicholas J. Allen is Emeritus Fellow at Wolfson College, Oxford. Prior to his retirement, in 2001, he was a Reader in the Social Anthropology of South Asia in the Department of Anthropology, at the University of Oxford and Governing Body Fellow at Wolfson College, Oxford. He studied medicine at Oxford and St. Mary's Hospital, before converting to graduate studies in social anthropology. Allen carried out fieldwork in Nepal and Northwest India and uses his knowledge of these regions to add an extra dimension to his comparative exploration of mythology. Theoretically, Allen draws from Durkheim, Mauss, Dumont and (especially) Georges Dumézil, an influential figure in the comparative exploration of the mythology of India and Europe. This Indo-European approach to mythology is tied to the Indo-European language hypothesis, which posits a hypothetical linguistic (and by extension societal) ancestor of a wide range of languages, which are distributed throughout the region.

The Indo-European hypothesis (and its allied studies) became problematically entangled with conceptions of an Aryan race, with devastating consequences, but it need not necessarily lead in that direction, and there is nothing necessary about the move from language, through society, to race. It is, nevertheless, important to be aware of these theories, their hypothetical nature and the possibilities of a dangerous slide to reactionary politics that can come from a seemingly innocent reading of myths. Allen's work is clearly distinct to these more problematic, historical theories and stands as one of the best examples of how the Indo-European approach continues (albeit at the margins) to operate today. In this chapter, Allen demonstrates both how this technique unfurls and explains why he remains committed to this method of engaging with mythology.

Of the five provinces of early Irish sacred, geography, Connacht, Ulster and Leinster represent respectively the first, second and third of the three Dumézilian functions (Rees and Rees 1961). However, that leaves unaccounted for the two remaining provinces which, by one account, were Munster and Meath, and were connected by the Reeses respectively with despised social outsiders and with the transcendent king. Over the last decade I have been trying to develop their ideas, and have proposed that Indo-European comparativists need to recognise a basic pentadic scheme, of which the Dumézilian triad is a subset or contraction. Rather than proposing five functions, I prefer the hypothesis of a single fourth function (pertaining to Otherness), which is split into positively and negatively valued half-functions or aspects. Support for this idea has come from a number of Indo-European areas, including Rome and Nuristan, but above all from ancient Greece and India. Comparative work on Homer and the *Mahābhārata* explains the origin of my interest in CúChulainn and the orientation of this paper, so a brief summary is needed.

Arjuna, the central hero of the Sanskrit epic, leaves his wife to go on a journey around India, and at each cardinal point he encounters one or more females; then he returns home to his main wife. Odysseus leaves Penelope for Troy and other adventures, but just before returning to her he has a string of encounters with other females. These take place at four locations – provided one treats as a single location the zone shared by the Sirens, Scylla and Charybdis, whom I refer to collectively as 'the Straits Monsters'. It turns out that the encounters of Arjuna and Odysseus can be matched, though the second encounter for one hero corresponds to the third for the other, and vice versa (see Figure 1).

The best explanation for these correspondences is that both epics derive via oral transmission from a protonarrative. Moreover, there is a reason why the proto-hero has precisely five relationships with females at this point in his career. Elaborating on Dumézil (1979), I argued (1996) that the proto-culture had a five-fold classification of modes of sexual or marital union, that this list manifested the four functions, and that the proto-hero's encounters provided a mythic charter for matrimonial custom. Let us consider the third encounter in Arjuna's journey. The hero meets a set of five crocodiles who were formerly singing temptresses/nymphs, and it corresponds to Odysseus' second encounter, which is with the Straits Monsters (Allen 1999b). Moreover, although Arjuna does not have sex with Vargā and her friends, his close bodily contact with them represents, I think, a bowdlerisation of the lowest-ranking form of sexual encounter, which is to be classified under the fourth function, negative aspect.

The Arjuna-Odysseus similarities, which go well beyond this particular journey, might in theory be due to some sort of Greece-India contact. This seems unlikely

I should like to thank the Royal Irish Academy for the invitation to a colloquium in 1998, which led to this paper. An earlier draft (January 1992) was given in Oxford at the seminar of Professor Ellis Evans.

	Sanskrit	Greak	Irish
hero's father	INDRA, Pāndu	(Sisyphus?) Laerres	LUG, Sualdam
hero	Arjuna	Odysseus	CúChulainn
main wife	Draupadi +	Penelope +	Emer +
female 1	N Ulûpī +	1 Circe +	1 Dornoll -, Dordmair +
female 2	E Citrāngadā	3 Sirens, Seylla, Charybdis	4 Uathach +, d. 1 Scathach +
female 3	S Varga & 4 friends	2 Calypso +	2 Aífe +
female 4	W Subhadra +	4 & 5 Nausicaa d. Arete	3 Eis Enchenn
female 5	Urvasi	5 (Callidice +)	6 Derbforgaill -,+
female 6	Uttara	6 (Nausicaa)	5 Fand +
hero's son	Babhruvahana	(Telegonus)	Conlai

Figure 1 The first two columns mostly summarise previously published comparisons between Arjuna, with special reference to his Penance, and Odysseus, with special reference to the second half of his *nostos*. The Irish column summarises the additional comparison argued for in this paper. Gods are shown in capitals, 'monsters' in italics. A plus sign indicates that the relationship between female and hero is sexual, a minus in two Irish cases that it is not; none of the relationships with 'monsters' are sexual. In all cases females 1–4 are encountered by the hero in the course of a single journey. The last row refers to a son *who fights his father*. Bracketed entries in the Greek are non-Homeric. The numerals show the correspondences, while the vertical order within a column shows the real sequences of meetings (*ordo naturalis*). 'd.' means 'daughter of'.

Structure	Sk	Gk	W	Tr	Encounter 4	Sk	Gk	W	Tr
1 Framework	+	+	+	o	31 Complex	+	+	+	+
2 Monsters	+	+	+	+	32 Crowds	+	+	(+)	+
3 Transits	+	o	+	o	33 Skin	o	+	o	+
4 Revisits	+	+	+	+	34 Mother	o	+	+	+
					35 Cupid	+	+	+	+
The hero					36 Helper	+	+	+	+
5 Central	+	+	+	+	37 Reluctance	o	+	+	+
6 Fathers	+	(+)	+		38 Female cry	o	+	+	o
7 Chastity	+	o	+	o	39 Sport	o	+	(+)	+
8 Duel	+	+	+		40 Advice	o	+	+	+
					41 Dowry	+	+	+	+
Main wife									
9 Suitors	+	(+)	+	o	**Encounter 1 & 2nd Irish episode**				
10 Faithful	o	+	+	o	42 Foreseen	+	+	o	+
11 Jealousy	+	o	+		43 Drug	o	+	o	+
					44 Threat	o	+	+	+
Encounter 1 & transit					45 Prediction	+	+	+	o
12 Ordering	+	+	+	+	46 Seashore	(o)	+	+	o
13 Magician	+	+	+	+	47 Pairing	+	+	+	o
14 Randy	+	+	+	o					
15 Leftalone	+	+	+	+	**Encounter 5 (ignoring Nausicaa episode)**				
16 Prophet	(o)	+	o	+	48 Otherworld	+	(+)	+	
17 Domestic	+	+	+	o	49 Advances	+	(+)	+	
18 Guidance	o	+	+	o	50 Privation	+	o	+	
19 Objests	o	+	+	o	51 Chariot	+	o	+	
					52 Enemics	+	(+)	+	
Encounter 2									
20 Son	+	(+)	+	+	**Encounter 6**				
21 Struggle	o	+	o	o	53 Tribute	+	o	+	+
22 Sex	+	o	+	o	54 Reticence	+	o	+	+
23 Durations	+	+	+	+	55 Identify	+	o	o	+
24 Dissuasion	o	+	o	+	56 Reward	+	o	+	+
					57 Transfer	+	+	+	
Encounter 3									
25 Bird	(+)	+	o	+					
26 Passage	+	+	+	o					
27 Hanging	o	+	+	o					
28 Back	+	+	o	+					
29 Leap	+	+	o	+					
30 Merit	o	o	o	+					

Figure 2 Each point of comparison (1–57) is marked as either present (+) or absent (o), a few doubtful cases being bracketed. A blank represents an absence which is due to the absence of a whole corresponding stretch of narrative. The columns show Sanskrit, Greek, *Wooing* and *Training* from left to right except for Encounter 5, where the Irish source is *Serglige Con Culainn*.

for various reasons, and becomes even more so if, as I hope to show here, there is a cognate narrative in Irish. That is the main aim of this paper. In short, I shall argue that CúChulainn's journey to improve his military skills is cognate with Arjuna's journey (supposedly a penance) and with the second half of Odysseus' *nostos*.[1] CúChulainn, the central hero of the Ulster cycle, leaves Emer, his fiancée, and before he returns to marry her, he goes on a journey and encounters females at four main locations. Here again, one encounter is with a 'monstrous' female, and is asexual. The implication is that all three stories go back to a common ancestor, presumably proto-Indo-European.

[…]

Structure

1   *Framework*. All three traditions share the framework of main wife at home plus (essentially) four encounters on journey, though *Training* omits the main wife.

2   *Monsters*. In all cases, one of the encounters is with a female or females who are somehow monstrous or aberrant. Eis is a witch or hag, apparently with a bird's head.

3   *Transits*. Though transits between locations are generally uneventful, the Sanskrit and Irish traditions treat at some length the transit between locations 1 and 2.

4   *Revisits*. In each tradition the hero's onward journey is interrupted at least once by a doubling back. Arjuna revisits Citrāngadā, Odysseus revisits the Scylla-Charybdis Straits, and CúChulainn revisits Scáthach. The encounter that is repeated is always the second in the story (not necessarily the one labelled '2'!).

The hero

5   *Central*. Although formally subordinate to others, the hero is central to his particular epic. Thus, Arjuna is formally subordinate to his eldest brother, who becomes king, but he is central in birth order, and demonstrably central in role. In the Trojan War as a whole Odysseus is formally subordinate to Agamemnon, but arguably central. CúChulainn is formally subordinate to King Conchobar, but central to the Ulster Cycle.[2]

6   *Fathers*. Both Indian and Irish heroes have two fathers, one divine, one human. Supreme within their respective pantheons, how far Indra and Lug are comparable in other respects is outside my present scope. In post-Homeric sources Sisyphus is said to have made Anticleia pregnant before she settled down with Laertes. Although Sisyphus is not a god, he is the craftiest of mortals – cf. Lug's description as *samildánach*, 'master of all arts'?

7   *Chastity*. Though Arjuna marries during encounters 1, 2 and 4, during his pilgrimage he should in principle be living as a *brahmacärin, a* chaste student of religion. Odysseus may or may not be under a similar obligation, but CúChulainn certainly is: when he and Emer part, each promises chastity (*genas*) to the other.

8   *Duel*. Each tradition has a father-son duel, but the outcome varies. Father kills son (Conlaf) in Ireland; son (Telegonus) kills father in Greece; in India son (Babhruvähana) apparently kills father and himself falls dead of grief, but both revive.[3] Both in India and Ireland responsibility for the event falls squarely on the father. The father-son duel is often discussed by comparativists (who usually cite Sohrab and Rustum from Iran), but the duel is isolated from the rest of the story and the comparison of the mothers is missed.

Main wife

9   *Suitors*. Draupadï is won by Arjuna's archery at a concourse of princes, but the occasion ends in violence. In extra-Homeric sources, Penelope is won by Odysseus in a foot-race, but it is probably better to think of the archery contest before the slaughter of the Suitors as a renewed wooing. *Wooing* begins with CúChulainn outdoing the other Ulster warriors in martial exercises, and ends with his killing twenty-four men in Emer's *dún*. Although the notion of rival suitors is not made explicit at either point, it may be implicit.

10 *Faithful*. Both Penelope (in Homer) and Emer remain faithful to their absent males in spite of strong provocation. Penelope's suitors are prominent both in the *Telemachy* and when the hero returns to Ithaca. The Irish equivalent forms a brief sub-narrative within the Scáthach episode: Emer's father arranges for her to wed Lugaid Noes of Munster, but she rejects him.

11 *Jealousy*. Later in the story, the main wife shows jealousy of one of the hero's other women – Draupadï of Subhadrä (1,212.15-20), Emer of the otherworldly Fand.

Encounter 1 and transit

12 *Ordering*. The encounter labelled 1 is in all traditions the hero's first encounter, whatever discrepancies arise thereafter in the ordering (cf. also §3).

13 *Magician*. This first female is always in some sense a magician. Ulüpï uses a magic stone to resuscitate Arjuna after his duel, and can confer invulnerability in water. With her wand and potions Circe can transform men into swine and back again. Dornoll (in *Wooing*) has supernatural powers (*batar erdrach a cumachtae*), and can send visions telepathically. As for *Training*, Dordmair's martial feats may be no more magical than those of the other teachers, but she alone is a *bhandráoi*, a druidess.

14 *Randy*. In all cases the first female makes sexual advances, which are received by the hero reluctantly or not at all. Arjuna is worried by his religious duties, Odysseus by Hermes' warnings; as for Dornoll, she has big fists and knees, and her ugliness deters CúChulainn. But whatever his reasons, the hero lacks enthusiasm.

15 *Left alone*. The hero starts out in company, but before the end of the second encounter is alone. Arjunas companions turn back just before he meets Citrängadä in the East. Odysseus' crew, who ask him to set off home after the year with Circe, are all drowned between his first passage of the straits and his second. As for CúChulainn's two or three friends, Lóegaire Búadach and Conall Cernach or Conchobar, they return home either because of the visions sent by the angry Dornoll or because Dordmair judges them so inferior to CúChulainn.

16 *Prophet*. After his year with Circe, Odysseus is sent by her to Hades, primarily to consult the blind seer Tiresias about his future. The dialogue takes place where two rivers join, not far, apparently, from the stream of Ocean, in near darkness. After his year with Dordmair, CúChulainn meets beside the sea a large black man who tells him to continue his journey and study with Scáthach. After meeting the prophets, both heroes spend a restless night at location 1 before departing at dawn.

17 *Domestic*. *Wooing* ignores the dark-skinned prophet, but instead gives the hero, after he has left Dornoll, a curious pair of interviews. After parting from his lion, CúChulainn first meets a maiden in a glen who recognises him from the days when the two of them were learning sweet speech as foster children in the same household. But after meeting Tiresias, Odysseus talks with his mother Anticleia. Both conversations concern domestic memories, and are inconsequential.

18 *Guidance*. Secondly, CúChulainn meets a warrior who teaches him the way ahead across the two halves of the Plain of Ill-luck. This figure, with

his practical advice, is the equivalent in *Wooing* of the large black man in *Training*, and again parallels Tiresias.

19 *Objects*. CúChulainn receives from the warrior two enigmatic objects, a wheel and an apple, perhaps corresponding to the puzzling oar and winnowing fan in Tiresias' prophecy. The matter is complicated, however, for the sweet speech (*bindius*) of the maiden, and the warrior's wheel and apple, may also relate respectively to Sirens, the whirling Charybdis and the crunching Scylla. Or is this fanciful?

Encounter 2

20 *Son*. After the complex transit mentioned in §3, we must now, following the Sanskrit ordering, leap ahead in the Irish to Aífe (female 2), who corresponds to Citrängadä. Both of these are mother to the son who fights his father (§8). Post-Homeric Greece in general makes Telegonus son of Circe (female 1), and the variant statement that he was the son of Calypso (female 2) is often played down.

21 *Struggle*. Before the sexual liaison, both stories present an episode of violence. In *Wooing*, CúChulainn behalf of Scáthach fights Aífe on a 'rope' (narrow on path?) above a glen. Aífe snaps the shaft of CúChulainn's sword near the hilt, but the hero pretends that her beloved charioteer, horses and chariot behind her have fallen from the rope into the glen. Her attention is diverted: she looks round and is overpowered. This struggle probably parallels the storm which precedes Odysseus' arrival at Calypso's island. The snapped sword parallels the snapped mast, and the fictive precipitation of charioteer, horses and chariot parallel the drowning or sinking of Odysseus' pilot, crew and ship respectively.

22 *Sex*. This time (cf. §14) the sexual initiative lies with the hero. Arjuna bargains for Citrängadä with her father, [and] CúChulainn demands sex with Aífe at the point of a sword (*Wooing*). The other versions leave the issue open.

23 *Durations*. The hero's stay regularly lasts longer than with female 1. The figures are: Sanskrit, 3 years: 1 night; Greek 7 years: 1 year; *Training* 2 years: 1 year (*Wooing* does not give durations).

24 *Dissuasion*. The female does not want the hero to pursue his journey. Thus, in spite of Zeus's instructions transmitted via Hermes, Calypso tries to dissuade Odysseus from leaving. Similarly, after the first year Aífe successfully urges CúChulainn to stay, and after the second she tries again but fails.

Encounter 3

25 *Bird*. As regards the female monster(s), there is a gradient of complexity. The Greek has three separate types of being, viz. the Sirens on their grassy island, Scylla on one cliff, Charybdis on the other. The Sanskrit has two phases in the life of a single set of nymphs, a Siren-like phase and (as punishment) a crocodile phase. The Irish is simpler still: Eis is an old woman blind in her left eye (*Wooing*), or a strange and horrible hag carrying obscure objects including some smelted iron (*Training*). But I think she retains hints of the two phases. Her name Bird-head (En-chenn) parallels the extra-Homeric bird body of the Sirens (normal on vase paintings), and the encounter takes place on a sea cliff.

26 *Passage*. The difficulty of passing between Scylla and Charybdis is proverbial, and when Eis tells CúChulainn to get out of her way the narrowness and difficulty of the passage is stressed. 'The route is narrow as a hair … slippery as an eel's tail' (*Training*).

27 *Hanging*. In *Wooing* the hero lets himself down from the path so that only his toes cling to it. Odysseus hangs, *like a bat*, from the fig tree over Charybdis.

28 *Back*. In *Training* CúChulainn closes his arms and legs around the bridge, lying 'supine athwart' it, as Stokes translates, while the hag batters him. I suspect two images are relevant: Odysseus clinging to the fig tree with hands and feet, but also Odysseus tied to the mast, with his back against it.

29 *Leap*. In any case, after the hag has attacked, the hero performs his salmon-leap feat upwards, and beheads her. Odysseus too performs dramatic movements at this point in his story. He dives downwards from the fig tree into the sea, and probably he correspondingly had to leap to reach it.

30 *Merit*. When Arjuna wrestles Vargä out of the pool, she regains her form as a beautiful nymph. His act of redemption is clearly presented as meritorious, as religiously virtuous. The killing of Eis is also explicitly a good act (*fa maith an marbadh*).

Encounter 4

31 *Complex*. In all versions encounter 4 shows the greatest length and narrative elaboration – far the greatest if one ignores the *Nekuia* which complicates the Circe episode.

32 *Crowds*. Ignoring the *Nekuia* again, this is the only section of the journey which involves crowd scenes, and which lists the names of warriors. There

are fifteen names in the Sanskrit, twelve in the Greek, six in *Training* (on the second visit), though the text later implies that there should have been eight.

33 *Skin*. Early in the episode the hero may lose some skin. Odysseus, paddling close to the Scherian shore, buoyed up on Ino's headband, is cast by a great wave against a rock, which he grabs. As the wave retreats, he is sucked away from it and skin is stripped from his hands. On his second day with Scáthach, CúChulainn kills her son Guar in a duel, and as the giant falls, his tooth removes a strip of the hero's flesh from shoulder to fingers. Cuar's fall may parallel the ebbing wave.

34 *Mother*. Uniquely, this section brings together a powerful mother and a nubile daughter. The Sanskrit barely alludes to Subhadrä's father, not at all to her mother, but Nausicaa's mother Arete, in spite of the significant role of King Alcinous, enjoys in the kingdom a preeminence puzzling to Homerists. In the Irish, Scáthach's preeminence is unquestioned, and Uathach's father goes totally unmentioned. It is with Uathach that the hero initially sleeps, but he also enjoys 'the fellowship of thighs' with Scáthach.

It may seem odd that the hero sleeps with both daughter and mother… Scáthach fuses two proto-narrative figures: as mother she corresponds to Arete, as lover to Circe. In other words, in *Wooing* she has taken over from female 1 (now Dornoll) the sexual relationship that originally belonged in that episode. Seen from the other end, the original female 1 has split and part of her persona has, as it were, slipped over into the next episode and been given to the mother of female 4.[4]

35 *Cupid*. The encounter between hero and the nubile female 4 is characterised by love at first sight, or virtually first sight. In India it is the male who is smitten, in the other two traditions the female.

36 *Helper*. One of the girl's primary relatives encourages the affair, or potential affair. This role is taken by Krishna (Subhadrä's brother), by Alcinous (Nausicaa's father), or by Scáthach (Uathach's mother).

37 *Reluctance*. However, in Greece and Ireland, the hero is reluctant. The Nausicaa affair never takes off, and Uathach (in *Training*) has to use both persistence and bribery.

38 *Female cry*. When Uathach attempts to enter CúChulainn's bed, he wounds her finger and she cries out. In *Wooing* this cry precipitates the fight with Cochar (cf. the Cuar of *Training*). Nausicaa's handmaidens cry out when the princess loses the ball in the river.

39 *Sport*. This is the only location associated with sport. Although exhausted, Odysseus participates triumphantly in the Phaeacian games. On arrival in Scáthach's location the weary CúChulainn finds some youths playing hurley and games, and outshines them all. Both heroes find local

supporters. The Greek is encouraged by Athene when she marks the length of his discus throw; the Irish is congratulated and kissed by four compatriots.

40 *Advice*. In both cases the nubile daughter advises the hero on when and how to gain his ends by approaching the powerful mother: Uathach's advice parallels Nausicaa's.

41 *Dowry*. Arjuna eventually abducts Subhadrä, but a formal marriage is arranged and later a vast dowry is delivered to the hero. Odysseus, having arrived on Scheria destitute, leaves as a rich man. CúChulainn demands wealth from Scáthach, cither point blank after his first night (*Training*), or as dowry (*tinnscra*) along with his other demands a little later. No doubt he receives it.

[...]

The broader picture

Clearly the three traditions need eventually to be presented more fully so as to fill in the context for individual points; and each point needs to be examined in greater detail, so as to show conclusively that the similarities are too precise and too specific to be dismissed. The most important arguments are §§1–2,the structure of the main journey. If a few of the other 55 fall by the wayside, no matter.

In any case there are further issues to explore, of which I mention only three. Firstly, why are none of the non-Irish females military instructors, and why are the Irish teachers (curiously) female? What has happened, I think, is that Irish tradition has merged two things that are distinct in the Sanskrit – the females encountered by Arjuna on a journey connected with his primary marriage, and the male instructors with whom he and his princely contemporaries have recently studied the martial arts. In brief, as teacher of young warriors, Scáthach corresponds to Drona the archery specialist who (curiously, again) is a Brahman. Consider for instance the 'rope of darts' motif, and its placement. Drona uses a string of arrows, one shot into the end of the next, to extract an object from a well (1,122.12-19), while it is on his first night with Scáthach (*Training*) that CúChulainn uses a similar string as a ladder to descend from a roof-top. Moreover, it is during their period of training that the Indian Karna begins to nourish the jealousy that will make him the arch-enemy of his half-brother Arjuna; and the relationship between Ferdiad and his arch-enemy and foster-brother CúChulainn is consolidated during the equivalent period.

Secondly, we can glance at the end of the story. Back at Emain Macha CúChulainn is infuriated that, by a sort of *jus primae noctis*, Emer must spend the night with Conchobar, and he assuages his anger by gathering together all the swine and wild deer and birds that he can find on Sliab Fuait. But towards the end of the *Mahäbhärata*, during the great Horse Sacrifice, we find two motifs juxtaposed:

a curious sexual ritual in which Draupadï mimes copulation with a horse, and a gathering of all types of animal from land, air and water (14,87.6-9, tr. Ganguli 1993, vol. IV (bk. 14): 147).

Finally, we must ask whether the idea of the three functions plus the two half-functions is relevant here. The functional pattern that is so clearly recognisable in Arjuna's Penance by no means leaps to the eye either in the Greek or the Irish. But this is not surprising, for the general trend of world history has been towards the blurring and dissolution of forms of primitive classification (Allen 1994), of which the Indo-European ideology provides one example. What is more surprising is how much of the old pattern has survived across the millennia.

Notes

1   The comparison of CúChulainn with Achilles or others (Sergent 1999) is not in principle incompatible with the comparison made here. Different parts of the career of a single Indo-European proto-hero might have been kept together in the Irish but given to different heroes in the Greek; or a single part in the original might have been given to more than one hero in the Greek.

2   On the functional analysis of Arjuna, see Allen 1999a. Since I here focus on women, I do not draw on the persuasive paper by Hiltebeitel 1982, which is too often neglected (for instance in McCone 1990 and in Mallory and Stockman 1994).

3   CE 14, 78–82; translation of the older edition (14,79–81) b Ganguli 1993, vol. IV (bk 14): 135–141.

4   *Training* presents a more complex picture in that both Dordmair and Scáthach have sex with the hero.

References

Allen, N.J. (1994). '*Primitive Classification*: The Argument and Its Validity'. In *Debating Durkheim*. Edited by W.S.F. Pickering and H. Martins, 40–65. London: Routledge.

Allen, N.J. (1996). 'The Hero's Five Relationships: A Proto-Indo-European Story'. In *Myth and Myth-Making: Continuous Evolution in Indian Tradition*. Edited by J. Leslie, 1–20. London: Curzon.

Allen, N.J. (1999a). Arjuna and the Second Function: A Dumézilían Crux. *J. Royal Asiatic Society,* Series 3, 9, no. 3: 403–418.

Allen, N.J. (1999b). Les crocodiles qui se transforment en nymphes. *Ollodagus* 13: 151–167.

Dumézil, G. (1979). *Mariages Indo-Européens*. Paris: Payot.

Ganguli, K.M. (1993). *The Mahabharata* (trans). [1st p'back ed.] (Vols. I–IV). New Delhi: Munshiram Manoharlal.

Hiltebeitel, A. (1982). 'Brothers, Friends and Charioteers: Parallel Episodes in the Irish and Indian Epics'. In *Homage to Georges Dumézil*. Edited by E.C. Polomé [JIES Monograph 3], 85–111. Washington.

Mallory, J.P. and Stockman, G. (1994). *Ulidia*. Belfast: December.

McCone, K. (1990). *Pagan Past and Christian Present in Early Irish Literature*. Maynooth: An Sagart.

Rees, A. and Rees, B. (1961). *Celtic heritage*. London: Thames and Hudson.

Sergent, B. (1999). *Celtes et Grecs. I. Le livre des héros*. Paris: Payot.

part three

What do myths do?

Section A: Structuralist approaches

Myth and meaning

Structuralism was undoubtedly the most important and far-reaching development of the twentieth century for the analysis of mythology. Although structuralism is a broad label, with several forms, it was the structuralism of Claude Lévi-Strauss (and his followers) that was to have the largest impact on the world of mythography. This brought a clear and unified system to the exploration of comparative mythology, which was also subtle enough to account for localized conceptions of myth. In his landmark essay, 'The Structural Study of Myth', Lévi-Strauss outlines the need for his approach by arguing that myth at the time of writing was the play thing of all sorts 'of amateurs' who used it in ways that were both widely competing and wholly inadequate (1955: 428). In this muddle of approaches, there were some who claimed that myth was a form of defective science, others who claimed it was about personal psychology, while still others claimed it was about supernatural beings (1955: 428). Lévi-Strauss argued that this confusion resulted all too often in the myth not being valued in its own right, viewed instead as only a gateway to crude speculation about history, psychology, or science (1955: 428). It was time, he claimed, for a new approach, which would take myth as an object worthy of study in itself – this he called structuralism after the structural movement in linguistics (Lévi-Strauss 1955: 430).

The linguist Ferdinand De Saussure had earlier noted that just because words sound the same in different languages, it does not mean that they are meaningfully related (De Saussure 2011 [1916]). This is because there is nothing that essentially ties a word to the thing that it is describing; instead, the relationship is developed through a culturally contextualized process of naming, which is largely arbitrary (De Saussure 2011 [1916]). Inspired by Saussure's work in linguistics, Lévi-Strauss proposed that those mythographers (see Section 2C) who hypothesized that a certain similarity between myths meant that there must be a common origin from which the myths are drawn are as mistaken as a linguist who postulates that two languages are connected because they both have words, with quite different meanings, that sound the same (Lévi-Strauss 1955: 430). A structural analysis of myth, by contrast, would explore the symbolic elements of the myth (known as mythemes) by first grounding them in a contextualized discussion of the society that they are drawn from (Lévi-Strauss 1969: 1). Only then could the analysis proceed to compare them to surrounding mythemes within the same myth (Lévi-Strauss 1969: 1). The attention should not be, however, on typologizing the mythemes, so much as exploring how they relate, for it is in the exploration of these relations that we come to appreciate the structure of a myth (Lévi-Strauss 1955: 431). By comparing the structures of several myths from the same community, we can build up a sense of a more profound socio-cultural structuring system (Lévi-Strauss 1969). By comparing how the myth transforms as it moves through space and time, we can map the way that distinct cultural units relate and eventually move to an understanding of the fundamental structuring system of all human existence (Lévi-Strauss 1955).

Structuralism was not without its critics (see, for example, Part Three, Secton B, Chapter 3 in the Reader); however, its impact was undeniable and the analyses of myth that structuralism produced continue to reward those who engage with them today. It is debatable how flawed the techniques are, whether these issues are fundamental, or merely accidental. At their best, they reveal something about the relationship between myth, society and the world, which is verifiable through renewed engagement. At their worst, they are good to think with, as both a landmark moment in the study of myth and a highly engaging (often-insightful) example of how a social scientific analysis of myth might proceed.

References

De Saussure, F. (2011). *Course in General Linguistics*. New York: Columbia University Press.

Lévi-Strauss, C. (1955). The Structural Study of Myth. *The Journal of American Folklore* 68 (270): 428–444.

Lévi-Strauss, C. (1969). *The Raw and the Cooked: Introduction to a Science of Mythology* (Vol. 1). New York: Harper & Row.

Jewels and wounds

Claude Lévi-Strauss

1

Claude Lévi-Strauss (1908–2009) was perhaps the most significant mythographer of the last century. His approach to mythology, known as structuralism, spread into neighbouring disciplines and has left a significant legacy that still influences mythography today. After an initial period studying philosophy, Lévi-Strauss accepted a position in sociology at Sao Palo University, Brazil. This post also afforded him the opportunity to undertake several trips to the Amazon, where he engaged in a form of multi-sited fieldwork that allowed him to gain a sense of the way that neighbouring Amazonian cultures related and differed, and this influenced his later analyses of mythology.

During the Second World War, Lévi-Strauss returned to France, where he opposed the Nazi advance until he was forced to flee to the United States. In the postwar period he returned to Paris, and in 1948, he was awarded a doctorate from the Sorbonne. He went on to teach at the College de France, where he became the chair of social anthropology in 1959. At the College de France, Lévi-Strauss developed his myth laboratory, from which he both published the results of his many analyses of mythology and introduced the world to his ever-evolving structuralist analysis technique. Central to this technique was the combination of an in-depth understanding of a myth's cultural contexts and the ability to use a form of mathematical notation to render the essence of any given myth in simple and easily comparable forms. Much of this notation worked on the detection of a series of binary oppositions that moved towards a transformative twist (often noted by shorthand such as, ':' for is to, '::' for as is). At the most abstract level, Lévi-Strauss believed that this system told us something profound about the way that all of humanity understood the world. At more detailed and culturally specific levels, it revealed both specific worldviews and the relationality of neighbouring cultures. Over a protracted period, Lévi-Strauss mapped these relations and transformations in a series of books known as the *Mythologiques*. The text that we have chosen here is drawn from a second series of books, which Lévi-Strauss intended to be more accessible to the wider public. Despite this intent, the thought in this short extract is complex, yet it will reward the reader who takes time to reflect on it.

The extract opens with an exploration of the mythology of the Pacific Northwest Coast of America. Here, there are several linguistically and culturally related groups (Thompson, Shuswap, Chilcotin) that can be termed Salish. All the Salish people seem to have a form of a myth about Lynx, Coyote and their sons. The myth begins with two girls who marry Coyote and Lynx (the masters of wind and fog) after encountering them making dentalia (magical shells). After marriage, Lynx has a son who is captured by Owl, but the boy escapes and enters a lake, from which he is reborn as the master of the dentalia, but with a repulsive skin (like that of his father). The skin, however, is burnt, and this creates fog, and when the fog clears, he is handsome once more. In the extract that follows Lévi-Strauss maps the way that the idealized myth that we have sketched here transforms as it moves through the related Salish peoples (and beyond), noting not how the motifs transform so much as how the relationships between the motifs remain largely consistent, despite surface-level transformations.

Beyond the Thompson, the Shuswap, the northernmost members of the Salish ensemble, change the myth of the stolen child in two ways. On the one hand, they take a part away from it, which they incorporate in another context (the myth indexed M_{738} in *The Naked Man*, pp. 471–473); on the other hand, they impoverish the original by reducing it to the episodes of the hero's kidnapping and liberation. Transformed into a Bird, Owl is to fill the function usually given to nocturnal birds of prey: that of announcing an upcoming death. And instead of acting like a tyrant as in the Thompson myth, or like an ogre as in the Kutenai one, Owl in the Shuswap version is a wise and powerful magician; he does not enslave the hero but imparts his knowledge to him and even makes him superior to himself.

The Chilcotin, the Shuswap's neighbors, belong to the Athapaskan linguistic family. In their midst, the myth of the stolen child regains all of its richness while also undergoing important transformations. I have noted many times this double phenomenon, observable when crossing either together or singly a linguistic and a cultural boundary or again an ecological one.

Here is the Chilcotin version.

Under the pretext of offering him some treats, Owl led a naughty boy outside. He captured him, raised him, made him grow through magical means, and gave him lots of presents, among them a dentalia necklace. The parents set off looking for their son. When they found him, he was in no hurry to leave Owl's place, where he enjoyed himself. His parents succeeded in convincing him and, taking advantage of Owl's absence, they burned his cabin down. Owl chased after them, and they hid in ambush at the end of a small bridge. When Owl was on the bridge, the hero appeared on the other shore brandishing his fingers, each covered with a goat horn. The terrified Owl fell into the water, swam to the shore, and gave up the pursuit. Upon the hero's return to his village, a feast was given in his honor. He presented himself adorned with the shells he had brought along, and he distributed them to everyone. 'And that is where the Indians first got dentalia shells.'

One day, the hero's mother found him dirty and sent him to bathe. He first refused, but she insisted. He dived in and disappeared. The disconsolate mother remained at the edge of the lake, from which she refused to move.

Winter came soon after. The women of the village went to the lake to make holes in the ice to draw water. The hero, who lived at the bottom of the lake, had fun breaking their buckets. Two sisters succeeded in attracting him to the shore by getting him to grab onto a richly decorated bucket. The hero was covered with mud, his skin was all loose, and his aquatic stay had made him so weak that he could not walk anymore. The two women tried in vain to scratch off the mud; they carried him to their cabin to warm him up, and they nursed him.

It got colder; snow covered the ground. It was not even possible to find wood to make the snowshoes necessary for hunting.

The hero dragged himself outside, where he discovered just enough wood to make one pair of snowshoes. He told one of the women to bring in this wood and to shake it when she was halfway down the ladder through which one entered the cabin in winter (These cabins were half-buried; they were entered through the smoke hole and by going down a ladder made out of a notched tree trunk). When the wood was shaken, it multiplied and filled the cabin so it was possible to make snowshoes. And yet the hunters returned empty-handed day after day. There was nothing left to eat.

Even though still weak and covered with mud, the hero announced he would go hunt Caribou if each man gave him an arrow. The one he received from Raven was made out of leather and thus soft. The hero left, took off his mud skin 'like a shirt,' and hid it. With each good arrow he killed a Caribou, and with the bad one a Coyote. He put his mud skin back on and sent each man to get the animal he had coming.

The hero was now hunting successfully every day. Raven spied on him and discovered the mud shirt hanging between two adjacent tree trunks. Raven ripped it apart and spread the pieces about, but the hero succeeded in mending it. The next time, Raven succeeded in surprising the hero without his skin on; he saw him young, handsome, strong, adorned with shells. From then on, the hero kept his natural appearance and married the two sisters.[1]

I have discussed at length in *Structural Anthropology*, volume 2 (p. 262) and in *The View from Afar* (pp. 105–108) the specific reasons the Chilcotin had for surrounding the origin of dentalia shells with mystery. Now it is other aspects of the Chilcotin myth that need to be discussed. Because of the constraints I have just alluded to, though the theme of the dentalia thieves is echoed among the Chilcotin, it could only be so in a disguised form: instead of the women *taking out* of the water the shells produced by their *brother* as *he bathes*, here the women pull out of the water a nonkinsman, a future *spouse*, who *had not wanted* to bathe, and they pull him out by *immersing into* the water a richly decorated bucket. This bucket tempts him, and he gives in to covetousness, just like the dentalia thieves, who too were incapable of resisting the covetousness that shells, these other precious objects, aroused in them.

The Thompson myth explained the origin of fog … meteorological phenomenon that mixes up the sky and the earth. In the Chilcotin version, the 'fog skin' is replaced with a 'mud skin' – mud being a mixture of water and earth. The fog originates from the sick skin of an old man and is thus a symptom of an internal pathological state. The Chilcotin hero's mud skin has an external origin: the aquatic milieu in which the hero lived, as stressed by the fruitless efforts of the women to scrape it off – which, incidentally, shows well that, in a mythological narrative, the smallest detail can have a meaning and fill a function.

The most remarkable transformation is that affecting the relationship of the hero and his mother (or the woman who returns him to the human condition) with water. I have given five versions of the myth. Four come from peoples belonging to the Salish linguistic family – that is, Coeur d'Alene, Thompson, and Chehalis – while one comes from the Chilcotin, who are Athapaskan.

In a Coeur d'Alene version, the hero's mother is thirsty. She asks her son for water, which he is slow to bring her or, in an Okanagan version, even refuses to bring her.[2] A Thompson version replaces this motif with a bath that the overheated hero wants to take but his mother tries to talk him out of. The Chehalis version from the lower Fraser basin includes an extra constraint in that the child stolen by Owl is a girl. It is thus necessary to introduce a male character into the story and to give him a spouse who tries to talk her husband out of going to the lake to drink: she prefers to bring him herself what he needs to quench his thirst.

In all three cases, the protagonists are thus a man and a woman close to him, mother or spouse. One of the two protagonists – sometimes the man, sometimes the woman – puts up obstacles to the fulfillment of the desire for water expressed by the other. Finally, this desire can take two forms: either for a drink (thus, water contained in the body), or for a bath (that is, for water that contains the body).

In addition to the three permutations illustrated respectively by the Coeur d'Alene, Thompson, and Chehalis versions:

Drink desired by the woman; obstacle raised by the man

—   —   —   man,   —   —   —   woman

Bath   —   —   —   —   —   —   —

it is clear that we would expect a fourth one:

Bath desired by the woman; obstacle raised by the man.

There are no grounds to think that this formula did not exist in the versions remaining unknown to the researchers. We cannot forget that we know only a small part of the mythological corpus in this as in all other areas of America. At the time when the major part of the research was done – roughly in the second half of the nineteenth century and the first half of the twentieth – the native cultures were already dying. Older informants were becoming rare, and the memory of certain myths or versions had probably gone.

It is nonetheless striking that we do not encounter the expected permutation when crossing the linguistic boundary separating the Thompson and the Chehalis from the Chilcotin. Instead, we come across another one that the versions discussed above did not lead us to foresee. Instead of the woman desiring a bath for herself, she wants to impose one on her son … using the pretext that he is dirty, a reproach that nothing in the narrative explains, which he refuses to accept. From the role of subject, the woman passes to that of agent, and the refusal by the other is not anymore aimed at a need felt by oneself; it translates an absence of need felt by the other. Indeed, a bath desired by oneself for oneself, in spite of the other, is the contradictory of a bath wanted not by and for oneself, but for the other, who does not want it.

If, for the reasons I have explained, we can set aside as not pertinent the change in the identity of the woman in the Chehalis version, the double twist that one observes when passing from the Salish versions to the Athapaskan one can be written up as follows:

$$F_{man} \quad : \quad F_{woman} \quad :: \quad F_{man} \quad : \quad F_{wanted \, both}$$
$$\text{(wanted bath)} \qquad \text{(wanted drink)} \qquad \text{(wanted drink)} \qquad \textit{(woman)}$$

in which the four terms correspond (from left to right respectively to the Thompson, Coeur d'Alene, Chehalis, and Chilcotin versions).

This mythical set does not disappear beyond its major area of diffusion. Toward the northwest it is transformed into legendary tradition by the Tsimshian and gravitates toward the fictional genre among the Carrier, while to the east the Cree have incorporated it into their recent history. I have used this as an example in my study of 'How Myths Die' (*Structural Anthropology*, vol. 2, chap. 14) and need not come back to it here.

Anyone doubting that myths do come out of the same mold in North and South America should look to myths M_{254}, and M_{273} in *From Honey to Ashes*. Of course mythology is universally full of werewolves who steal children. But even if we limit ourselves to a single example – M_{273}, a Guyan myth – it exhibits, along with those I have just summarized, analogies that are too specific to be fortuitous. Thus there are the expeditions of the kidnapper to his prisoner's village to bring to her everything that she is missing: clothing, household utensils, vegetables (because he feeds her only with meat); and, in the North American myths, the journey of a helpful character to the village of a starving captive to get the food which he was fed since his childhood, or, in another version, to fetch roots so as to vary a diet made up exclusively of insects.

Two sequences of the North American myths are clearly seasonal in nature. After having run away from his kidnapper, and on the way to his village, the hero is too hot; he feels the pressing need to bathe in a lake or to drink of its water. There, he transforms himself into a Loon and thus becomes the master of dentalia shells, the natural adornment of this bird.[3] It is during the summer that these Loons live on inland lakes; they winter on the coast, as the lakes are then frozen. In contrast, when the hero arrives at his young wife's village, he complains of the cold and enters the cabin of an old man to warm himself. It is there that he puts on a skin covered with wounds and sores, forming a pair of opposition with the healthy skin adorned with precious shells that is really his. All the rest of the myth occurs in a winter climate: lack of wood for heating, snow making hunting difficult, and so on. The Loon that makes up the hero's first avatar announces the wind. His second avatar, the sick skin, gives birth to the fog. The myth thus implicitly or explicitly elaborates a series of oppositions: summer/winter; water/fire; wind/fog; jewels/wounds. And these oppositions, when laid out next to each other, reproduce an armature with which we are already familiar.

In *The Raw and the Cooked*, this armature resulted from the transformative relation of certain Bororo myths. As we have seen regarding the problem of twinness, North and South American myths often send back to each other. In the present case, the recourse to the Bororo should not be surprising since, as I wrote in 1964 (*The Raw and the Cooked*, pp. 141–142):

> the Bororo way of thinking was greatly influenced by Tupi mythology. In both groups the same myth – the one about the jaguar's human wife, who is the mother of the two civilizing heroes – occupies an essential position. And the

modern Bororo versions remain astonishingly close to the one that Thevet
recorded as existing among the Tupinamba in the sixteenth century.

Let us now look at two other Bororo myths, pertaining respectively to the origin
of water and adornments (M_2) and to the origin of illness (M_5). I have shown that
these myths partake of the same single transformation. Both have for protagonist a
character, male or female, whose name Birimoddo means 'pretty skin.' (This name
brings us already quite close to the North American hero, who hides his beautiful
skin, 'as smooth and soft as that of his wife,'[4] underneath that of an old man covered
with pus.) In the Bororo myth M_5, a woman named Pretty Skin exudes illnesses,
and later changes into a rainbow – rainbows being seen as the cause of illnesses
according to belief found in South America from Guyana all the way to the Chaco
(*The Raw and the Cooked*, pp. 246–250).

Amerindian thought, which often compares fever to a warm garment, sets in
correlation and in opposition, on the one hand, wounds and skin diseases, which are
natural coverings, and on the other, adornments, which likewise are visible from the
outside but are a cultural covering.[5] These latter have magical properties that heighten
the vitality of the wearer while, on the contrary, the natural coverings weaken him.
But even though these coverings act in opposite ways, both are intermediaries
between life and death. They thus occupy a median position, comparable from a
formal viewpoint to that of the rainbow and the fog existing between the sky and
the earth.

However, we need to note a difference between the myths of the two hemispheres.
In order to pass from adornments to illness (or the inverse), the South American
transformation needs two distinct myths, at least in appearance. In North America,
the homologous transformation requires only a single myth, which incorporates
wounds and jewels into a single framework. It is this ambiguity that enables us to
understand why the personality of the heroine – or of the two heroines – oscillates all
through the mythical ensemble that is the object of the present book. A young girl,
shy and rebellious against marriage, changes into a shameless sister, whose lack of
reserve borders on incest. The myths in which these two types of heroines appear
associate them respectively with wounds and adornments. Married against her will
to Lynx, the rebellious young girl nurses him and cures him of the wounds he has
received. As for the indiscreet sister, she takes away from the hero the adornments
he has produced.

The dialectic of the myths does not stop there: at a later stage of the
transformation, one sister, by using gestures that are too free, gives back to the
hero the human form he has lost, or alternatively she makes it possible for her
double to do so. In this sense she cures him. Likewise, by becoming her own
inverse, a young girl who first rejects all of her suitors chooses the most wretched
and repulsive one, thanks to whom she obtains rich adornments not for her own
use and against the will of her parents but for their benefit and without them being
aware of it:[6]

$$F_{wounds} : F_{adornments} :: F_{wounds} : F_{rebellious\ daughter-1}$$

F_{wounds}	$F_{adornments}$	F_{wounds}	$F_{rebellious\ daughter-1}$
(rebellious daughter)	(indiscreet sisters)	(indiscreet sisters)	(*adornments*)

Notes

1   Farrand 2: 36-27.

2   Cline: 228 (indexed M_{746a}, Levi-Strauss 8: 479).

3   'The loon was a great shaman, and used to kill and eat his friends. He made his body spotted with white by touching it with his finger-tips during his period of training. Some of the Uta'mqt say the spots on his body were originally dentalia' (Teit, *Mythology of the Thompson Indians*, p. 336).

4   Hill-Tout 2: 350.

5   Our popular language does likewise. Under the heading *rubis* ['ruby'] the dictionary Littré gives as its meaning 'red bumps or rash that appear on the nose and the face.' And under the heading *perle* ['pearl']: 'one of the common names for albugo or white spot in the cornea.' Medical vocabulary is full of metaphors borrowed from the jeweler's an: *vésicule perlée* ['pearled blister'], *douleur en bracelet* ['braceleted pain'], *lesion en médaillon* ['lesion in the form of a medallion'], *eruption en collier* ['necklace rash'], and so on. The surgeon 'sets a wound.'

   A version of die Thompson myth summarized earlier well brings out this equivalency: Tsa'au'z took off his sores or spotted covering, and became clothed in dentalia instead. On the following morning the dentalia fell off, and, by the time the people awoke he was clothed in sores again. This happened four nights, so Tsa'au'z' parents-in-law became rich in dentalia (Teit, *Mythology of the Thompson Indians*, pp. 241, 265–268).

6   When I proposed this formula for the first time in 1955 (*Structural Anthropology*, p. 224) it was shrugged off, but during these last few years, it has been met with interest and used in various applications ranging from rural architecture to the *Cogito*. See R. Bucaille et al., *Pigeons de Limagne* (Université Populaire de Clermont-Ferrand, 1987), p. 140; J. F. Bordron, *Descartes. Recherches sur les contraintes semiotiques de la pensée discursive* (Paris: P.U.F., 1987), pp. 80–82; J. Petitot, 'Approche morphodynamique de la formule canonique du mythe,' *l'Homme* 106–7 (1988): 24–50; Mark S. Mosko, *Quadripartite Structures* (Cambridge University Press, 1985), pp. 3–7; 'The Canonic Formula of Myth and Non-Myth,' *American Ethnologist* 18/1 (1991): 126–151; A. Coté, 'L'Instauration sociale. Du schème cononique à la formule canonique,' *Anthropologie et sociétés* 13, no. 3 (1989): 25–36.

References

Bordron, J. F., and Greimas, A. J. (1987). *Descartes: Recherches sur les contraintes sémiotiques de la pensée discursive*. Paris: Les Éditions G. Crès et Cie.

Bucaille, R. et al. (1987). *Pigeons de Limagne: Approche ethologique et interprétation ethnologique*. Clermont-Ferrand: Université populaire de Clermont-Ferrand.

Cline, W. et al. (1938). The Sinkaietk or Southern Okanagon of Washington. *General Series in Anthropology* 6, Menasha.

Côté, A. (1989). L'instauration sociale. Du schème canonique à la formule canonique. *Anthropologie et sociétés* 13 (3): 25–35.

Farrand, L., and Mayer, T. (1919). Quileute tales. *The Journal of American Folklore* 32 (124): 251–279.

Hill-Tout, Ch. (1905). Report on the Ethnology of the Stlatlumh of British Columbia. *JRAI* 35.

Lévi-Strauss, C. (1996). *The Raw and the Cooked*. Chicago: University of Chicago Press.

Lévi-Strauss, C. (1981). *The Naked Man*. New York: Harper & Row.

Lévi-Strauss, C. (1983). *From Honey to Ashes*. Chicago: University of Chicago Press.

Lévi-Strauss, C. (1984). *Structural Anthropology*. Chicago: University of Chicago Press.

Mosko, M. S. (1991). The Canonic Formula of Myth and Non-myth. *American Ethnologist* 18 (1): 126–151.

Mosko, M. S. (2009). *Quadripartite Structures: Categories, Relations, and Homologies in Bush Mekeo Culture*. Cambridge: Cambridge University Press.

Petitot, J. (1988). Approche morphodynamique de la formule canonique du mythe. *L'homme* 28 (106): 24–50.

Teit, J. (1981). Mythology of the Thompson Indians. Leiden: E J Brill Ltd.

Pulleyar and the Lord Buddha

Edmund Leach

2

Sir Edmund Leach (1910–1989) was Professor of Social Anthropology at the University of Cambridge and Provost of King's College Cambridge. He came to anthropology after an initial education in engineering and travels throughout Asia. These field experiences led him to Malinowski and the London School of Economics (LSE), from where he was awarded a PhD in anthropology in 1947, for a large and detailed thesis that explored the hill tribes of Burma and Assam. After graduation he worked as a lecturer at the LSE for a time before moving to Cambridge in 1953. He was elected President of the Royal Anthropological Institute in 1971 and made a fellow of the British Academy in 1972; in 1975 he was Knighted.

During his time at Cambridge, Leach was introduced to the structuralism of Claude Lévi-Strauss, which he found immediately highly stimulating. He quickly published a landmark structuralist analysis of Genesis, before becoming known as the key interpreter of Lévi-Strauss in Britain. Leach's structuralist approach, however had important differences to Lévi-Strauss's structuralism. It was more grounded and commonly combined with Malinowskian functionalism. Leach was also highly suspicious of the more universal elements of Lévi-Strauss thought and his claim to uncover a fundamental, universal structuring system, which Leach termed a meaningless abracadabra. Leach's structuralism serves to illuminate the structuring systems that lie behind particular myths and societies, while lacking the more philosophical dimension of Lévi-Strauss's thought. In the material that we have chosen to include here, Leach seamlessly combines structuralist, functionalist and psychoanalytical theory to explain how shared myth and symbol both unifies and distinguishes Hindus and Buddhists in Sri Lanka.

Let me start by explaining my title. Pulleyar is the Sinhalese version of the Tamil word *Pillaiyar* (Pillear). In Tamil, but not in Sinhalese, this word means 'the son' and is the name given to Ganesha, the elephant headed Hindu deity who is rated the son of Shiva and Parvati. In the Hindu system Shiva (God) has many aspects. Because he is a potent warrior his emblems include the *lingam* (phallus), trident and spear; because he is an ascetic monk they include a rosary and a begging bowl (Zimmer 1946).

The philosophic dialectic which makes such contradictions sensible is not easily understood; in village Hinduism the various aspects of Shiva are distributed among secondary deities who are thought of as members of his family. His consort Parvati, like Aphrodite, represents sexual love; his sons Skanda and Aiyanar are warriors, and his third son Ganesha is, after a fashion, an ascetic. But Ganesha's qualities are ambiguous and it is with this ambiguity that this essay is largely concerned.

If Parvati be equated with Aphrodite, then Ganesha is the equivalent of Hermes, 'breaker of the way and guide of the soul' (Zimmer 1951). He is the doorkeeper of heaven, a trickster whose friendly help can clear all obstructions but whose enmity can cause disaster. Now one of Ganesha's special characteristics is that he has a broken tusk which he carries around in his hand, and in the context of heavenly tricksters such symbolism is familiar. The American Indian Winnebago Trickster 'takes his phallus off and carries it around in a box,' 'the phallus is Trickster's double and alter ego'(Kerenyi 1956; Radin 1956). In Ancient Greece, Hermes' most characteristic representation was as an erect phallus, yet his sexuality was equivocal. Contrasted with his twin sister Aphrodite he stood as Shiva stands to Parvati, but Hermes' union with Aphrodite produced the sexually ambiguous Hermaphroditos (Kerenyi 1951). Moreover, although Hermes started his career as a bearded adult, he ended as a graceful, though athletic, adolescent. Even the ecstatic Dionysus is sexually ambiguous; 'he is never represented as a noticeably phallic deity; he is shown either clothed in a long robe, or in some other effeminate form. The carrying around of a phallus, its erection and unveiling, played some part in his cult; … even though separated from him, it was something peculiarly his own'(Radin 1956). Ganesha is one of this crew.

It is part of my thesis that Ganesha's broken tusk is a phallic emblem and that its detachability denotes a certain ambivalence about Ganesha's sexual nature. There are contexts in which the *lingam*-phallus, which is properly an emblem of Shiva, may serve as a manifestation of any one of Shiva's sons, Ganesha included (Dumont 1957). In such a context Ganesha may be virile and potent. But there are other contexts where Ganesha seems to be an effeminate eunuch.

This ambivalence is not haphazard. Ganesha does not exist by himself but in association with other members of Shiva's family. The sexual qualities which are

This paper was prepared while the author was the holder of a Fellowship at the Center for Advanced Study in the Behavioral Sciences, Stanford, California. Acknowledgments are made to various Fellows of the Center for their comments upon earlier versions of this paper and to sundry correspondents but particularly to Dr. Nur Yalman, Professor McKim Marriott and Mr. Michael Ames.

attributed to Ganesha depend upon context and, generally speaking, are the opposite of those attributed to his father (Shiva) or to one or other of his two brothers Skanda and Aiyanar.[1] As Shiva varies so also Ganesha varies, but in the inverse direction.

Now, although Ganesha is a Hindu deity he also receives worship from Sinhalese-speaking Buddhists and this is particularly the case in the district of Nuvarakalaviya in Northern Ceylon which lies just to the south of a zone inhabited by Tamil-speaking Hindus. In the cult of the Nuvarakalaviya Buddhists, Ganesha is known by the name Pulleyar, and is thought of as the elephant lord of the forest. Aiyanar his elder brother is revered as guardian of the village reservoir and of the village itself. There is no cult of Shiva and no mother goddess, but instead a reverence for the Lord Buddha.

For Hindus, Ganesha and his mother and brothers are simply appendages and aspects of Shiva, the Great God (Mahadeva), who is virile;[2] but among the Sinhalese of Nuvarakalaviya, Pulleyar and his brother Aiyanar are without specific parents. Instead they are the feudal dependants of the Lord Buddha, and the Lord Buddha is the supreme ascetic. So we can investigate a relatively simple question; what happens to Shiva's son Ganesha when he is transferred to a Buddhist context as a servant of the Lord Buddha?

(To avoid ambiguity, I shall hereafter use *Pulleyar* to refer to the special form of the elephant headed deity that is worshipped by the Sinhalese Buddhists of Nuvarakalaviya and I shall use *Ganesha* to refer to all other forms whether Ceylonese or Indian, Hindu or Buddhist.)

[...]

The mythological tales which surround Ganesha's personality are mostly concerned with how he got his elephant's head and how he broke his tusk. A thinly masked theme of castration, mother-love, and sexual frustration pervades all these stories. I give below a selection of these. I also include a few associated myths in which Ganesha himself does not appear.

A. 1 – Shiva left home to go hunting. He took all his servants with him. Parvati wished to take a bath, but there was no one to guard the door so she made a guardian out of the dirt from her own body. Shiva, returning, was furious that he was prevented from entering his own house and struck off the head of the guardian, Ganesha. Parvati in turn was furious and ordered her husband to restore Ganesha to life. Shiva could not find the head so replaced it with the head of an elephant which was the first animal that his servants happened to see when they went out into the forest. Thereafter Ganesha became the favorite son of Parvati and Shiva and is above all the guardian of entrances (Wilkins 1913).

In association with this kind of Shiva, Ganesha is corpulent and sedentary. In relatively rare representations Ganesha appears in Dionysiac guise, dancing and drinking wine (e.g. Zimmer 1955 Vol. 2 Pl. 319; Getty 1936 Pl. 7). I postulate that this 'ecstatic' Ganesha is always associated with an ascetic aspect of Shiva.

A. 2 – Ganesha was born from Shiva's head while Shiva was gazing upon the beauty of his *sakti* Uma. This Ganesha was a youth of outstanding beauty endowed with the qualities of Shiva himself. Uma in jealousy put a curse of ugliness upon him so that he acquired an elephant's head and a pot belly (Getty 1936; Yalman 1954–55).

A. 3 – Maha Ishvara (Shiva) is God. Uma his wife lives in his turban because from the turban it is very easy to have sexual intercourse. One day Uma saw a man of great beauty. She had sex relations with the man. When Maha Ishvara heard of this he was angry and gazed on the man with his third eye. The man was reduced to ashes. Uma craved Maha Ishvara's pardon and begged him to recreate the man. The man was recreated but he was without genitals (Yalman 1954–55).

A. 4 – One day Uma wanted to go visiting so she made a man to look after the house. When Maha Ishvara came the man would not let him in. (Then follows the last part of the story recorded in A. 1) (Yalman 1954–55).

A. 5 – Ganesha was the offspring of Shiva and Kali. When Kali first looked at her child its head was burnt to ashes. Shiva sent servants to bring in the head of the first animal they found asleep with its face to the North. This proved to be an elephant. Shiva fixed the elephant head to the child's decapitated body (Mayo 1935).

B. 1 – Vishnu, at Shiva's request, manifested himself as a female, (Mohini). Shiva, enraptured at the sight, had an ejaculation. He caught the divine sperm in his hand. This turned into a *lingam* which was the godling Aiyanar. Mohini changed back into Vishnu (Dumont 1957).

B. 2 – Parasurama (Rama with the Axe) was a manifestation of Vishnu and a devotee of Shiva to whom Shiva gave his magic axe. Parasurama was fifth son of Jamed Agni and his wife, Renuka. Renuka observed an act of copulation and the purity of her mind was sullied with sexual thoughts. Jamed Agni, indignant at his wife's fall from grace, ordered his sons to kill her. The elder sons refused but Parasurama obeyed. For this act of filial piety he was rewarded with invulnerability and a single wish. He wished that his mother be restored to life, forgetful of the past and with a pure mind (Dowson 1903).

B. 3 – Parasurama paid a visit to his lord and master Shiva. The gate was barred by Ganesha. Parasurama and Ganesha fought. Parasurama threw his axe. Ganesha recognized his own father's axe and bowed before it, catching it on his tusk which was immediately severed (Wilkins 1913).

B. 4 – The union of Shiva and Parvati was sterile. Vishnu in pity manifested himself as an infant and became their son. The gods assembled to admire this child of outstanding beauty. Sani (Saturn) had neglected the caresses of his wife and he had cursed him, saying that the first child he looked at would be burnt to ashes. Sani attended the gathering of the gods but warned Parvati of the consequences. Parvati resigned herself to fate. Sani looked at the child which was immediately destroyed. At Brahma's behest Parvati was allowed to recreate the child in the deformed Ganesha shape (Wilkins 1913).

C. 1 – There was a beautiful mango (*amba*) in the garden. Ganesha and his brother Kataragama (Skanda) both wanted the mango. They were told by their mother to race around a salt sea. Kataragama set off around the sea but Ganesha ran around a salt dish in the kitchen. Ganesha won the mango but Kataragama hit him and broke off his tusk (Yalman 1954–55). (The mango, in Ceylon, is an explicit vagina symbol and is one of the main emblems of the mother goddess Pattini. In India, Amba is one of the names of Shiva's *sakti*, more particularly of Durga. It is also the name of one of the semi-divine heroines in the Mahabharata).

C. 2 – Skanda was courting a Vedda Princess (Valli Amma). Ganesha offered to assist. Skanda turned Ganesha into an elephant headed monster who frightened Valli who ran for help to Skanda. Skanda lost the magic formula so Ganesha forever retains his monstrous form (Cartman 1957).

C. 3 – Ganesha and his brother Karttikeya (Skanda) were both courting the same two girls, Siddhi and Buddhi. It was agreed that the brother who could first circumnavigate the world should win the girls. Skanda made the journey, but Ganesha stayed at home and 'proved by his logical talents and his aptness for quotation' that he had already completed the journey. Ganesha won the girls who are described as his *sakti* (Yalman 1954–55). (This is a North Indian story).

C. 4 – In South India and Ceylon it is said that Ganesha has no wife but that he is sought after by many girls. He refuses them all because he is looking for someone as beautiful as his own mother, Parvati (Cartman 1957). (Reported by an Indian graduate student, Chicago, 1961).

D. – Shiva was too kind and granted remission of sins and final bliss to all who worshiped at his shrine at Somnath. The Gods complained. Parvati created Ganesha so that 'he should create obstacles to men and by deluding them will deprive them of all wish to visit Somnath so that they shall fall into Hell' (Wilkins 1913). (This story from Western India stresses the 'ascetic' aspect of Shiva. I include it here because it displays Ganesha very plainly as a 'trickster' who frustrates man's efforts to unite himself with God).

[...]

Devata rituals

Whereas, in this area, the principal annual Buddhist festivals, *Wesak* and *Katina Pinkama*, synchronize with the beginning of a Yala cultivation period and the end of a Yala harvest, the principal *devata* festivals, *Mutti Mangalaya* and *New Rice*, are timed for the period when the rice is green and in ear and for the beginning of harvest respectively. They relate to living crops rather than to dead seed. But apart from these occasions, Pulleyar, as distinct from the other *devata*, receives a great deal of special attention. It is Pulleyar who makes women and cattle pregnant, who assures bountiful crops, who gives success in hunting, who heals sick children. And it is especially Pulleyar who may be consulted through the vehicle of a medium priest (*kapurala*) concerning the outcome of village quarrels, lawsuits and so on. I observed that private ceremonials took place at the Pulleyar *kovil* every few days, whereas the rituals at the Buddha *vihare* and at the *devale* of the other *devata* were reserved for formal occasions.

The symbols of Pulleyar were *lingam*-shaped phallic objects which in India would be more appropriate to Shiva than to Ganesha. Except when mediumistic trance seances were involved, the actual rites of Pulleyar were broadly similar to those made at Buddhist shrines. Buddhist devotees offered flowers and to a lesser extent vegetable foods. Pulleyar devotees offered food rather than flowers. But here we may note a contrast. Contact with the Buddha shrine gives the offerings the pollution of death and feces so they are later thrown away. Contact with the Pulleyar shrine makes the food magically beneficial to humans and it is usually consumed by children.

In some situations contact with Pulleyar is achieved directly, for when the *kapurala* priest goes into a trance he is thought to speak with the voice of Pulleyar himself. Here the contrast between Buddha and Pulleyar is exact. The priests of the Buddha are yellow-robed monks who from an early age live a life cut off from the ordinary world. Their whole training is concentrated on the avoidance of emotion; they achieve enlightenment by detachment from the tribulations of the ordinary world. They are, as it were, men who, among the living, are already half dead. They are revered as the dead are revered; they are admired but not loved.

In contrast, the typical priest of Pulleyar (or Aiyanar) is a medium who has learned how to go into ecstatic trances. Where the Buddhist priest wears his head shaved and moves always at a sedate steady pace, the Pulleyar priest wears his hair in long pigtails and achieves a state of ecstasy by violent dancing. The Buddhist priest bridges the gap between this world and the next by moving himself half way into the next world. The medium priest of Pulleyar bridges the same gap by bringing the deity himself into this world. The Pulleyar priest, a human being, becomes incarnate of his deity and manifests his power visibly for the congregation to see.

To summarize, these details are consistent with a binary antithesis: Pulleyar is what Buddha is not.

On the one hand we have the Buddha cult – the concern of the elderly, asceticism, contemplation of death, absence of emotion, polluted food offerings.

On the other hand we have the Pulleyar cult – the concern of the young, ecstasy, preoccupation with fertility and sex, food offerings fit for children.

But we should notice also how the qualities of this Nuvarakalaviya Pulleyar differ from those of his historical prototype Ganesha. Ganesha is seemingly a eunuch in contrast to his virile father Shiva. Nuvarakalaviya Pulleyar is sexually potent in contrast to the ascetic Buddha.

At the same time, although the Pulleyar cult and the Buddha cult stand opposed as ecstasy and asceticism are opposed, they are also integrated as part of one system. The monks insist that Pulleyar is a servant of the Lord Buddha; the force of this was brought home to me when I learned that the local *Kapurala*, the medium priest of Pulleyar, worked as a personal servant for the local Buddhist monk (*Bhikku*). (Diagram 1, Section D).

Let us compare this structure with that of the Christian Holy Family and the Saivite Holy Family, remembering that, in the Nuvarakalaviya situation, there is no mother goddess – no equivalent of either Parvati or of the Virgin Mary; the role contrast is based simply upon the sexuality or asexuality of males. In Christianity, sexuality is kept in the background and described as Holy Spirit, the potency of God the Father; Mary, the Mother, remains a virgin; Jesus is a sexless, effeminate figure. In South Indian Saivite Hinduism, sexuality is a central theme and is the main attribute of God the Father, and also of Parvati, the Goddess Mother; Ganesha, the son, is again an effeminate figure – a castrated male.

In Nuvarakalaviya, Buddha is treated as God but retains his characteristic of the supreme ascetic, sexless and devoid of emotion; there is no mother goddess; Pulleyar, the son, becomes the essence of sexuality. Whereas Ganesha has only one tusk but carries the other in his hand, Pulleyar has both tusks intact; he is moreover the source of fertility in women, in crops and among animals.

As between Christianity and the Sinhalese situation the contrast seems complete: God the Father is sexual – Jesus is sexless; Buddha is sexless – Pulleyar is sexual.

Yet again in certain other respects the Christian and the Sinhalese patterns are similar. In both cases it is God the son who is the friend of the children and in both cases God the son is only a secondary divinity, a mediator between the other world and this. Furthermore Pulleyar, (Ganesha) is, like Jesus Christ, the slain 'Son of God' who has been restored to life.[3]

In these two patterns, the European Christian and the North Sinhalese Buddhist, the same set of ideas appear, though arranged in a different fashion. We have various contrasts, the contrast between the authority of virility and the authority of age. The contrast between the mystery of creative life and the horror of destructive death. The common need for some deity who is a divinity in something less than a complete sense so that he or she can bridge the gap between the other world and this world, and again the common element of filiation, of parenthood and sonship, as a symbol for the representation of this bridge.

But as between Christianity and Sinhalese Buddhism the different and contradictory aspects of deity are differently distributed between the symbolic figures of the trinity. Arbitrary power which, for the Christian, is an attribute of God the Father, appears in the Sinhalese story as an aspect of 'God the Son,' the unpredictable elephant lord of the forest. But the passive ascetism of the suffering Christ is here an aspect of Buddha, supreme lord, who replaces Shiva, the God and Father of the Hindu trinity.

I would draw particular attention to the fact that the most typical devotional act in Buddhism is to sit in quiet contemplation within the *Vihare* precincts and ponder on the close approach of death, while the most characteristic ritual activity in the Pulleyar-*devata* cult is to invoke the presence of Pulleyar himself in the person of a trance-bound medium.

These are complementary aspects of a single idea and I suggest that the passive and active elements in divine worship are always complementary in this way, for always the active ecstatic element involves the notion that God comes down to earth, while the passive ascetic behavior implies that man reaches up to heaven. I think too that these two complementary types of religious behavior are nearly always found in close association.

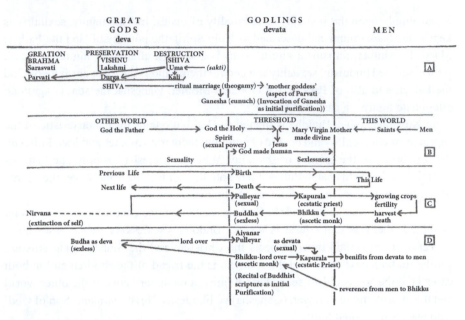

Diagram 1: Classification of gods, godlings and men.

On one hand, supernatural power seems to be located in the other world of the dead, so that we can reach that power only through the practice of asceticism and the appeal to ascetic, sexless, mediating divinities. On the other hand, supernatural power seems to be located here in this world and is manifested in the mystery of creative fertility. This latter kind of potency implies the existence of deities who are close at hand, sexually vigorous, ecstatic. The theologians may devise their elaborate theoretical systems and (in terms of theology) the Lord Buddha may be far removed from any Hindu god, but Buddhism alone is not a practical religion. Ordinary human beings cannot sustain at all times a totally ascetic view of the relation between man and God. In practice (as opposed to theory) every religious system is made up of complementary behaviors. Holidays are mixed with holy days, feasts are mixed with fasts. Indeed these pairs of words are one and the same.

I think I may be able to pull this together by going back to the beginning. The ordinary members of a religious congregation are not greatly concerned with the subtleties of theology. What matters is that their toal religious ideology should seem to them consistent. In the religions of the West consistency is provided by the Book which incorporates the whole body of sacred dogma. In the East consistency is provided by the totality of symbols. The theology is not consistent. One of the major functions of religion is to provide man with reassurance in the face of threatened danger. In active life he needs to be assured that life will go on, that sickness and threatened dangers will not succeed. But in old age Man needs to be reconciled with his inevitable fate; the fearfulness of death must be eliminated. It is perfectly logical that these two concerns of religious activity – the maintenance of life and the reconciliation with death – should be separated out and emphasized as separate sets of ritual.

So I come back to my title and my original question. Is this usefully considered a situation of syncretism at all? Are we concerned here with a merging of different religious ideas or is it just one particular manifestation of a complex of ideas which appears in a great variety of religious systems and even within the sacred precincts of the psychoanalyst's consulting room?

Notes

1 Skanda (Kumara-Subrahmanya-Karttikeya) and Aiyanar were both formed from Shiva's semen without Parvati's intervention; Ganesha was formed from the dirt of Parvati's body without Shiva's intervention. The classical Holy Family triad is Father (Shiva), Mother (Parvati) and Son (Ganesha) but Shiva may be replaced by either Skanda or Aiyanar, and Parvati by any one of a great variety of 'mother goddesses'. For a case where Aiyanar replaces Shiva see Dumont (1953, 1957: 325, 401–403) who is writing of a South Indian Tamil community. It is relevant that in Tamil, *aiyar* means father/chief, and carries an implication of overlordship, whereas in Sinhalese the word *aiya* means 'elder brother' and carries an implication of frustrated rivalry.

2 'In Shiva's company are worshipped Parvati, Ganesha, Subrahmanya, the Bull Nandi and minor attendants. Shiva is shown leaping in the ecstasy of the dance and on temple walls are often depicted his 64 sports or miracles (*ilia*). For the imagination of the Dravidians he is a great rhythmic force, throbbing and exulting in all the works of nature and exhibiting in kindly playfulness a thousand antics and a thousand shapes' (Eliot 1954).

3 This slightly stretches the ethnography. Pulleyar-Ganesha is the 'son of God' (Shiva). Shiva in his ascetic manifestation and Buddha in his enlightenment are, theologically, very close but I do not think that a Nuvarakalaviya villager would ever say that Pulleyar is the 'son of the Lord Buddha'; yet it seems to me that this is in fact his status.

References

Cartman, J. (1957). *Hinduism in Ceylon*. Colombo: M.D. Gunasena, p. 66, 68.

Dowson, J. (1903). *A Classical Dictionary of Hindu Mythology*. London: Kegan Paul, p. 230.

Dumont, L. (1953). Definition structurale d'un dieu populaire tamoul: Aiyanar, le Maitre. *Journal Asiatique* CCXLI: 255–270.

Dumont, L. (1957). *Une sous-caste de l'inde du Sud*. Paris: Mouton, p. 402, 401.

Eliot, Sir C. (1954). *Hinduism and Buddhism, an Historical Sketch*. 3 vols. New York: Barnes and Noble. Vol. 2, p. 222.

Getty, A. (1936). *Ganesha, a Monograph on the Elephant Faced God*. With introduction by Alfred Foucher. Oxford: Clarendon Press, pp. xv–xvii, 6.

Harper, E. B. (1959). A Hindu Village Pantheon. *Southwestern Journal of Anthropology* 15, no. 3: 227–234.

Kerenyi, K. (1951). *The Gods of the Greeks*. London: Thames and Hudson. Ch. 10, p. 176.

Kerenyi, K. (1956). 'The Trcikster in Relation to Greek Mythology', translated by R. F. C. Hull. In *The Trickster: A Study in American Indian Mythology*, by P. Radin. New York: Philosophical Library.

Mayo, K. (1935). *The Face of Mother India*. New York: Harper.

Radin, P. (1956). *The Trickster: A Study in American Indian Mythology*. With commentaries by Karl Kerenyi and C. G. Jung. New York: Philosophical Library, pp. 182; 183–184.

Wilkins, W. J. (1913). *Hindu Mythology: Vedic and Puranic*. Calcutta: Thacker Spink, pp. 333, 337, 338, 336, 334, 339, 351; ibid.

Yalman, N. O. Personal communication based on field work undertaken in Central Ceylon in 1954–55.

Zimmer, H. R. (1946). *Myths and Symbols in Indian Art and Literature*. New York: Pantheon Books.

Zimmer, H. R. (1951). *Philosophies of India*. Ed. Joseph Campbell. New York: Pantheon Books, p. 568n.

Zimmer, H. R. (1955). *The Art of Indian Asia: Its Mythology and Transformations*. 2 vols. Ed. Joseph Campbell. New York: Pantheon Books.

An outline of Propp's model for the study of wondertales

Manuel Aguirre

3

Manuel Aguirre is a senior lecturer in English literature at Universidad Autónoma de Madrid, Spain. He obtained a BA in English and Spanish studies from the University of Saragossa, followed by a BA in Germanic linguistics, from the University of Antwerp in Belgium. He then received an MA in philosophy from University College Cardiff and finally (in 1987) a PhD in English and comparative literature from the University of Antwerp. His research focuses on Gothic literature and narrative structures in epic, saga and fairy tale. He is the founder of the Northanger Library Project in 2006, which seeks to recover Gothic texts, which are often neglected.

The material that we have chosen to include by him here is a newly produced version of an article that previously featured in the Northanger Library. The article presents in clear terms the way that the structuralism of Vladimir Propp can be applied to the analysis of fairy tales and (by extension) wider mythology. Propp, like Lévi-Strauss, was influenced by linguistic structuralism, but he was to move in a different direction to Lévi-Strauss, focusing instead on mapping elements into a morphology, aided by an extensive system of notation. Propp's work failed to make the impact (at least in the West) that Lévi-Strauss's structuralism was to have, yet it stands as an important alternative structural approach that helps us to understand the limits of formalism.

The findings of structuralism, Russian formalism and the new critics since the early twentieth century led to numerous efforts towards developing a discipline nowadays known as narratology.[1] A great many of these are inspired by a classic text which is commonly viewed as one fountainhead of the entire discipline: Vladimir Propp's *Morphology of the Folktale*.[2] The aim of this outline is to place a tool at the disposal of researchers in the fields of folklore and popular culture.[3]

Published in 1928, Propp's *Morfológija skázki* received Western recognition only thirty years later, with the publication of an English (USA) translation in 1958. Based (like the later Italian version)[4] on a very faulty first Russian edition, and riddled with problems of its own, this translation was the subject of much criticism until a thoroughly revised version appeared in 1968.[5] Two years later, the French translation – based on a second, revised Russian edition – dispelled many of the obscurities still clinging to Western reception of Propp's work.[6] The best introduction to the theory to date is found in Liberman 1984.[7]

Propp pointed out that, whereas he had meant his book to be a morphology of the *wondertale* (*volsébnaja skázka*), his editor changed the title because he thought 'folktale' (*skázki*) would make it more attractive.[8] Wondetales are conventionally classed as a special subcategory within the more general set of folktales. Propp defines wondertales as 'those tales classified by Aarne under numbers 300 to 749'.[9] The reference is to the classic index *The Types of the Folktale*, first published by Antti Aarne over one hundred years ago and revised and expanded at various times since and generally known as the Aarne-Thompson Index (*AT*).[10] The index is arranged thematically and lists not tales but tale-types from all over the world. Each type receives a number, and this helps identify individual tales easily as belonging to this or that type. *AT* contemplates five categories of folktales:

I.   Animal tales (AT1-299)

II.   Ordinary folk-tales

    A.   Tales of magic (AT300-749)

    B.   Religious tales (AT750-849)

    C.   Novelle (Romantic tales) (AT850-999)

    D.   Tales of the Stupid Ogre (AT1000-1199)

III. Jokes and anecdotes (AT1200-1999)

IV.   Formula tales (AT2000-2399)

V.   Unclassified tales (AT2400-2499)[11]

Wondertales, also referred to as 'tales of magic' (*Zaubermärchen, contes merveilleux*), fall under II.A. This is the category to which Propp's research applies.[12]

Propp based his study on Aleksandr N. Afanás'ev's classic collection *Russian Folktales* (1855–1864).[13] This included over six hundred folktales, of which Propp used as his corpus numbers 50–151 from Afanás'ev's wondertales section – exactly 102 tales. Propp's structural model is based on the following criteria:

1   All wondertales are constructed on the basis of one single string of actions or events called 'functions'.

2   Function is significant action or event defined according to its place in the plot.

3   Function, and not theme, motif, character, plot or motivation, is the fundamental unit of analysis.[14]

4   Functions are independent of how and by whom they are fulfilled; from the standpoint of structural analysis, not doers, their method, their motivations or their psychology but the deed alone matters.

5   The number of functions available to wondertale-tellers is thirty-one.

6   With (codifiable) exceptions, functions always follow a strict order.

7   Tales are organized into *sequences* (see below); each sequence is composed of a selection of functions in the appropriate temporal order and constitutes a narrative episode.

8   Each function is susceptible of realization by different means ('forms of function'): Propp offers lists of the *function forms* that appear in his corpus (but warns that others are possible).

9   Only seven characters are available to wondertale-tellers: hero, false hero, villain, donor, helper, dispatcher, princess (sought-for person) and/or her father.[15]

10   All wondertales are composed of the same functions, though not every function need appear in every tale.

11   All wondertales share the same fundamental structure.

The standard presentation is a list of the thirty-one functions which provides number (in Roman numerals), summary of the function, definition (usually one single word) and the conventional sign given to it for identification purposes – a Greek letter for the first seven functions (the 'preparatory sequence'), Roman capitals for the rest (Departure and Return are assigned arrows instead of letters). Though structurally sound, in practice this method is cumbersome since it identifies functions by a number, whereas they will actually be referred to mostly by their letter. Furthermore, in the construction of a string, say I, V, VIII, XII, XVII (or 1, 5, 8, 12, 17), numbers would tend to be jumbled together and on the whole fail to give a clear picture. Because the visual quality of Propp's nomenclature is of great help, our first operation will be to invert the order of presentation, identifying the functions by their letter or sign (Propp himself resorted to this strategy in his synoptic presentation of tales). This is particularly necessary in that the English, French and (in a different way) Italian translations made an effort towards adjusting the definitions of functions to the letter chosen (alphabetically in many cases) for each. Thus, although the match could not be maintained in every instance, it helps that the appearance of the Donor should correspond to *D*, or that *G* should stand for Guidance.

THE THIRTY-ONE FUNCTIONS

α	Initial situation	(0)
β	Absentation	*One of the members of a family absents himself from home* (1)
γ	Interdiction	*An interdiction is addressed to the hero* (2)
δ	Violation	*The interdiction is violated* (3)
ε	Reconnaissance	*The villain makes an attempt at reconnaissance* (4)
ζ	Delivery	*The villain receives information about his victim* (5)
η	Trickery	*The villain attempts to deceive his victim in order to take possession of him or of his belongings* (6)
θ	Complicity	*Victim submits to deception and thereby unwittingly helps his enemy* (7)
λ	Preliminary misfortune	*Preliminary misfortune caused by a deceitful agreement* (7a)
A	Villainy	*The villain causes harm or injury to a member of a family* (8)
a	Lack	*A member of a family lacks something or desires to have something* (8a)
B	Mediation	*Misfortune or lack is made known; the hero is approached with a request or command; he is allowed to go or he is dispatched* (9)
C	Beginning counteraction	*The hero agrees to or decides upon counteraction* (10)
↗	Departure	*The hero leaves home* (11)
D	First function of the Donor	*The hero is tested, interrogated, attacked etc., which prepares the way for his receiving either a magical agent or a helper* (12)
E	The hero's reaction	*The hero reacts to the actions of the future Donor* (13)
F	Provision of a magical agent	*The hero acquires the use of a magical agent* (14)
G	Guidance	*The hero is led to the whereabouts of an object of search* (15)
H	Struggle	*The hero and the villain join in direct combat* (16)
ᐻ I	Branding	*The hero is branded* (17)
J	Victory	*The villain is defeated* (18)
K	Liquidation of Lack	*The initial misfortune or lack is liquidated* (19)
	Return	*The hero returns* (20)
Pr	Pursuit	*The hero is pursued* (21)
Rs	Rescue	*Rescue of the hero from pursuit* (22)
O	Unrecognized arrival	*Unrecognized, he arrives home or in another country* (23)
L	Unfounded claims	*A false hero presents unfounded claims* (24)

M	Difficult task	*A difficult task is proposed to the hero* (25)
N	Solution	*The task is resolved* (26)
Q	Recognition	*The hero is recognized* (27)
Ex	Exposure	*The false hero or villain is exposed* (28)
T	Transfiguration	*The hero is given a new appearance* (29)
U	Punishment	*The villain is punished* (30)
W	Wedding	*The hero is married and ascends the throne* (31)

The Initial Situation, though vital to the series, is no 'function' and accordingly receives no number (but it does receive a letter). 'Function' is an action or event 'defined from the point of view of its significance for the course of the action' (Propp 1928: 21). This is a fundamental tenet in Propp's system; in practice this means that FUNCTION = SIGNIFICANT ACTION (or EVENT) + POSITION IN THE SEQUENCE. The same action will have different morphological values depending on its place in the story. A wedding may be a reward (*W*) only if it occurs at the end of a sequence or of the tale; it may amount to a test if it occurs at *E*; while if it takes place in the preliminary sequence, it may signal the entrance of the Villain (e.g., as stepmother; function ε) and the onset of misfortune for a young heroine. Other values are possible.

Functions may fail of their purpose, in which case Propp identifies them by a *neg.* sign; or they may yield a result contrary to that expected, and are then identified by a *contr.* sign. Thus, F_{neg} means that the seeker failed to respond adequately to the Donor's test and in consequence received no help; while F_{contr}. means that instead of help the seeker's conduct towards the Donor earned him a punishment. Here follow additional remarks about specific functions.

1 'Function' α speaks of 'a family'; an extended family or just a community is often meant.

2 Function γ is defined as 'Interdiction' (Propp 1928: 26). Since the two function forms available here are 'interdiction' and 'command', we might opt for the general term 'Injunction'. Injunctions may be followed or disobeyed, and it is interesting here that the character's decision to do either will *not* change the course of the story: either way, the Villain will appear and act. We may extract from this an argument as to the *determinism* of wondertales and note that it entails assigning a 'semantic' value to narrative structure.

3 Function θ is defined as 'Complicity' in the English translation (Propp 1928: 30). But this word suggests a conscious participation in self-deception; this is no part of Propp's meaning – as his adverb 'unwittingly' makes clear (nor indeed does it reflect the reality of tales). We might therefore prefer to use 'Compliance'.

4   Function λ offers an interesting instance of variable function spread. Propp uses η for the villain's attempt at tricking the victim, θ for the victim's compliance with the villain. However, at Propp 1928: 30 we read:

A special form of deceitful proposal and its corresponding acceptance is represented by the deceitful agreement. ('Give away that which you do not know you have in your house.') [...] This element may be defined as preliminary misfortune. (Designation: λ, differentiating between this and other forms of deception.)

It is clear that, whereas Propp viewed η and θ as two different functions, here he proposes one single function to cover the (structurally identical) exchange: λ is the equivalent of $\eta + \theta$. This means something extremely important, of which he may not have been aware: if a given action may be represented by a single letter in a tale but may be 'decomposed' into two or more functions in another, then the converse holds, too: two or more functions may 'contract' into one, and therefore the entire string may be reducible to a much smaller number.[16]

5   Functions A and a are to be seen as variants of each other, and count therefore as one: the adventure is motivated by a misfortune or lack (a), or by an act of villainy (A) which creates misfortune or lack.

6   Function D is defined as 'The first function of the Donor' (p. 39). It is implied that the second function of the Donor is F. But whereas the definition of F (Provision of a magical agent) is self-explanatory, that of D does not clarify much, and it will be more useful to replace it with 'A Donor tests the hero' or 'The hero is tested'.

7   At p. 52 [Propp 1928], the letter J is used to designate the Branding of the Hero, I to designate Victory over the Villain; in actual fact, the circa-alphabetical order requires I for Branding, J for Victory. To complicate matters, at p. 152 [Propp 1928] the alphabetical order of the two letters IJ is preserved, but 'Branding' is now made to follow 'Victory'. Clearly there is confusion here. Let us agree with the French translator (who everywhere else adopts the letter choices made by the American edition) on the following:

H Struggle with the Villain

I Branding or Marking of the Hero

J Victory over the Villain

8   At pp. 60 and 154 [Propp 1928], lower case o is used to indicate 'Unrecognized arrival'. I have preferred a capital O to bring this function in line with the other letters.

9   Function W, 'Wedding'. As often, the abbreviated definition does not do justice to the concept (though seeing the letter W as the initial of

'Wedding' is helpful). Wedding is only one (albeit the most characteristic) of the possible function forms for *W*; other forms include monetary or other reward, or ascent to the throne.

The system does not contemplate tales as mere agglomerations of functions. Rather, as indicated earlier, functions appear in series, each series constituting a narrative episode. For such series Propp employs the Russian term *xod*. This word in fact means several things. The term adopted in the English translation is 'move', in the sense in which we speak of a move in a game such as chess. But every time a character acts or an event takes place we could, on the analogy of games, speak of a move; there would then be as many moves as there were functions in a given tale, which defeats the purpose – by *xod* Propp had in mind a *series* of these rather than single actions. Therefore the term 'move' is not quite accurate for such a series, and another rendering might be 'sequence', which tallies much better with the sense of the text. [17]

For the breakdown of tale elements Propp uses a three-tier arrangement (a variation on the system employed in the AT Index). A first level concerns major blocks of events ('sequences'). The second level consists of major, significant actions ('functions'). The third level offers alternative versions of these functions ('function forms'). In Lévi-Strauss's nomenclature the functions shape a *syntagma*; the forms a function can take in a given corpus shape an open *paradigm* of options.[18] The syntagma-paradigms arrangement can be illustrated with function ε:

ε *The villain makes an attempt at reconnaissance*

ε^1 *reconnaissance by the villain*

ε^2 *reconnaissance by the hero*

ε^3 *reconnaissance by other persons*

Notice that the main event here is not the hero's or the villain's action but the deed itself: reconnaissance takes place. In other words, structure has primacy over the identity of the agent.

The syntagma is one, and closed. The paradigms are open, and subject to expansion; this last point is important in any attempt at applying the model to other narratives than wondertales, since there is in principle no reason why further function forms could not be found in alternative texts. Paradigmatic variation is envisaged by the model itself, whereas syntagmatic variation is not; the latter, but not the former, will therefore, whenever it occurs, constitute the textual equivalent of a mutation or, for a more accurate metaphor, a graft.[19]

The construction of tales follows a double strategy. The storyteller chooses certain functions from the 31-string, and for each function chosen he or she chooses a certain form of it. Insightfully, if perhaps unknowingly, this system takes cognizance of a decisive feature of wondertales – their *oral* nature. From the work of Parry and Lord on South Slavic epic[20] we know that oral composition consists neither in repeating memorized texts nor in mere improvisation; singers (and the reasoning may be extended to oral storytellers) can create *extempore* because they have mastered a toolbox of possibilities which include repertories, patterns, formulas, systems of options. The 'discovery' that tales operate as aggregations of sequences is again of great value for the study of the orality of tales, for the use of sequences gives tales a recursive structure, and iteration is one of the basic principles of all oral narrative.

The complete string looks as follows (the simplified paradigms of function forms for A and K are offered by way of illustration):

$\alpha \beta \gamma \delta \varepsilon \zeta \eta \theta (\lambda) A a B C \uparrow D E F G HIJ K \downarrow Pr Rs O L M N Q Ex T U W$	
A^1	K^1
A^2	K^2
A^3	K^3

The following is an example of analysis of a two-sequence tale ('Pokatigoróšek,' Afanase'ev 133) offered by Propp (1928: 129–130). Between square brackets I have added a few succinct remarks to clarify the issue of iteration:

Sequence I.

A man, his wife, two sons, a daughter (α). The brothers, on leaving for work, request their sister to bring lunch to them ($\beta^1 \gamma^2$); they show the road to the field with shavings (thereby betraying their sister to the dragon ζ^1). The dragon rearranges the shavings (η^3), the girl goes out to the field with the lunch (δ^2), and follows the wrong road (θ^3). The dragon kidnaps her (A^1). The brothers' quests ($C \nearrow$). Herdsmen say: 'Eat up my biggest ox' (D^1). The brothers are unable to do so (E^1_{neg}). [New demand concerning a ram, then a hog. In all, three requests.] The dragon says: 'Eat up twelve oxen', etc. [then twelve rams, then twelve hogs.] (D^1), $E^1_{neg.}$ follows. The brothers are thrown beneath a stone (F_{contr}).

Sequence II.

Pokatigoróšek is born. The mother tells of the misfortune (B^4). Quests ($C \nearrow$). Herdsmen and dragon – as before ($D^1 E^1$, testing remains without consequences for the course of the action). Battle with the dragon and victory (H^1-J^1). Deliverance of the sister and the brothers (K^4). Return ($\swarrow$).

Propp's synoptic table for this tale (again, slightly adapted) is as follows:

I. $\alpha \beta^1 \gamma^2 \zeta^1 \eta^3 \delta^2 \theta^3 A^1 C \uparrow [D^1 E^1_{neg.}]^{\times 3} [D^1 E^1_{neg.}]^{\times 3} F_{contr.}$

II. $B^4 C \uparrow [D^1 E^1]^{\times 3} [D^1 E^1]^{\times 3} H^1 J^1 K^4 \downarrow$

I use the superscript $[]^{\times 3}$ to indicate threefold repetition of the bracketed segment. The model is able to convey this fundamental property of wondertales – iteration – but not (as it stands) its structural and narrative significance.[21] This remains a problem for subsequent work.

A second sequence is introduced, not necessarily because we have the birth of a hero but because it brings in a number of functions which make more sense as a new departure than as continuations from F_{contr} (this last function is a bit of a dead end; only a new departure will resolve the situation). The new sequence tells basically the same adventure with a different outcome. Other tales offer much greater complexity and several sequences (even interrupted sequences) may be necessary.

It is not quite exact that 'the testing remains without consequences for the course of the action' since only through his ability to gulp large animals does the hero earn a chance (denied to his brothers) actually to fight the dragon; while such impossible ability presages his impossible victory eventually. It is true that 'truncated' or 'blind' motifs are found in wondertales[22] but, as the example shows, we should not too readily assume that structural material occupies semantically empty slots. On the other hand, the hero's early prowess, though semantically significant, is not syntactically relevant since we *know* he will eventually fight and defeat the dragon (the way this knowledge arises in us has to do with narrative techniques I cannot discuss here). Once again, a deterministic principle rules the narrative.[23]

In the first sequence above, δ appears after $\zeta\ \eta$ whereas theoretically the order should be the reverse; but although it is standard for the villain to appear *right after* the victim has disobeyed the injunction (or unquestioningly followed it), nothing prevents the villain logically from intervening *so as to* make the victim disobey (or comply). Whence another important proposition ensues: not only is it immaterial for the course of events whether or not the victim fails to follow instructions but the very causal nexus between functions may be specious: whatever characters do, the sequel is defined not by their actions but by the structure of the tale. We may have here yet another structural basis for the determinism of wondertales; and the 'semantic' value of their 'form' becomes an inescapable issue.

Lastly, at pages xxv, 19 [Propp 1928] and elsewhere Propp writes of a 'morphology'. His is a botanical analogy, but in actual fact he is constructing a 'syntax' of the wondertale. Though his term is consecrated by use and it will be well to retain it, it opens the way for an examination of the 'grammar' of functions.

The efficacy of Propp's system is hard to dispute. All the same, numerous loose ends remain to be dealt with, and they may force a reconsideration of at least aspects of the model: both the 'grammar' and the semantics of functions must be studied in detail. If form has semantic content, we must approach issues like the significance of structural iteration or the deterministic nature of tales. The number of both functions and characters, too, may turn out to be an issue of much import. And the possibility of applying the model to at least certain literary genres must be seriously considered. These remain matters for subsequent study.

Notes

1   Tzvetan Todorov coined the word in his *Grammaire du Decameron* (Mouton: The Hague, 1969).

2   See Gerald Prince, 'Narratology and Narratological Analysis', in *Oral Versions of Personal Experience: Three Decades of Narrative Analysis*, special issue of *Journal of Narrative and Life History* 7: 1–4, ed. Michael G. W. Bamberg (1977), pp. 39–44.

3   This is a revised and shortened version of an article that first appeared in *The Northanger Library Project* (Madrid: The Gateway Press, 2011), http://www.northangerlibrary. com/documentos/AN%20OUTLINE%20OF%20PROPP'S%20MODEL%20FOR% 20THE%20STUDY%20OF%20FAIRYTALES.pdf

4   Gian Luigi Bravo, trans. *Vladimir Propp: Morfologia della fiaba* (Torino: Einaudi editore, 1966).

5   Vladimir Propp *Morphology of the Folktale*, trans. L. Scott, 2nd rev. edn. (Austin: University of Texas Press, [1928] 1968, 1994) (henceforward *Morphology*).

6   See Marguerite Derrida, trans., *Vladimir Propp: Morphologie du conte*. Suivi de *Les transformations des contes merveilleux*, trad. Tzvetan Todorov, et de E. Mélétinski *L'étude structurale et typologique du conte*, trad. Claude Kahn (Paris: Éditions du Seuil, 1970).

7   Anatoly Liberman, ed. *Vladimir Propp: Theory and History of Folklore*, trans. A. Y. and R. P. Martin (Minneapolis: University of Minnesota Press, [1984] 1993).

8   'The Structural and Historical Study of the Wondertale', in Liberman (ed.), 1984, pp. 67–81, 70.

9   *Morphology*, p. 19.

10   Antti Aarne, *Verzeichnis der Märchentypen* (Helsinki: Folklore Fellows Communications (FFC) 3, 1910); second edition, Antti Aarne and Stith Thompson, *The Types of the Folktale: A Classification and Bibliography* (FFC 74, 1928); third edition, AT 1961 (FFC 184); fourth edition, revised by Hans-Jörg Uther in 2004 as *The Types of International Folktales* (FFC 286, 3 vols.) (ATU 2004).

11   In ATU 2004 this fifth category has been eschewed.

12   There are sound reasons for reserving the term 'fairytale' (a translation of the seventeenth-century French *conte de fées*) for such folklore-inspired *literary* narratives as were written by Perrault, Grimm, Andersen and so on. See Neil Philips, 'Creativity and Tradition in the Fairy Tale', in *A Companion to the Fairy Tale*, eds. H. D. Davidson and A. Chaudhri (Cambridge: D. S. Brewer, 2003), pp. 39–55, 39.

13   Leonard A. Magnus's early translation, *Russian Folk-Tales* (London: Kegan Paul, Trench, Trubner & Co., 1915), contained only 73 of Afanas'ev's tales. The standard American reference, *Russian Fairy Tales*, trans. Norbert Guterman (New York: Pantheon Books, 1945), offered less than one third of the original collection.

14   That wondertales hinge on *action* has been conclusively argued by other researchers. See Axel Olrik, *Principles for Oral Narrative Research*, trans. K. Wolf and J. Jensen (Bloomington: Indiana University Press, [1921] 1992), p. 45; Max Lüthi, *The European*

Folktale: Form and Nature, trans. D. J. Niles (Bloomington: Indiana University Press, [1948] 1986), p. 13.

15 After assigning to each character a 'sphere of action', Propp situated the princess and her father jointly in one such sphere. His choice can be defended on empirical grounds, though its significance and ideology will merit further study.

16 Something like this was attempted by Algirdas Greimas, *Sémantique structurale: recherche de méthode* (Paris: Larousse, 1966), but his dry, quasi-algebraic treatment of functions does little to foster understanding.

17 *Séquence* is the term chosen in the French translation.

18 Claude Lévi-Strauss 1960 'La structure et la forme. Réflexions sur un ouvrage de Vladimir Propp', in *Cahiers de l'Institut de Science Economique Apliquée* 99 (s.M. 7), 1–36. Trans. as 'Structure and Form: Reflections on a Work by Vladimir Propp', in Libermann (ed.), 1984, pp. 167–188.

19 For the argument that Gothic fiction may be an instance of such a graft see my 'A Gothic-Folktale Interface', to appear in Gothic Studies.

20 See Albert B. Lord, *The Singer of Tales* (Cambridge: Harvard University Press, 1960).

21 See Propp's cursory remarks on trebling at pp. 74–75.

22 Lüthi, *The European Folktale*, pp. 60–64.

23 For discussion see my *The Thresholds of the Tale: Liminality and the Structure of Fairytales* (Madrid: The Gateway Press, 2007), pp. 72–83.

References

Aarne, A. A., Thompson, S. (1973). *The types of the folktale: A classification and bibliography; Antti Aarne's Verzeichnis der Märchentypen*. Helsinki: Suomalainen Tiedeakatemia.

Afanas'ev, A. N. (1915). *Russian folk-tales*. London: K. Paul, Trench, Trübner & Co.

Afanas'ev, A. N. (1945). *Russian fairy tales*. New York: Pantheon Books.

Aguirre, M. (2007). *The thresholds of the tale: Liminality and the structure of fairytales*. Madrid: Gateway Press.

Bamberg, M. G. W. (1997). *Journal of narrative and life history: Volume 7, numbers 1–4.*

Davidson, H. E., & Chaudhri, A. (2003). *A companion to the fairy tale*. Cambridge: Brewer.

Greimas, A. J. (1966). *Sémantique structurale: Recherche de méthode*. Paris: Librarie Larousse.

Lévi-Strauss, C. (1960). La structure et la forme: Réflexions sur un ouvrage de Vladimir Propp. *Cahiers De L'institut De Science Économique Appliquée*, 99, 3–36.

Lord, A. B (2000). *The singer of tales*. Cambridge, Mass: Harvard University Press.

Lüthi, M. (1986). *The European folktale: Form and nature*. Bloomington: Indiana University Press.

Olrik, A. (1992). Principles for oral narrative research. Bloomington: Indiana Univ. Press.

Propp, V. (1966). *Morfologia Della Fiaba*. Torino: G Einaudi.

Propp, V. (1968). *Morphology of the folktale*. Austin: University of Texas Press.

Propp, V. (1970). *Morphologie du conte: Suivi de Les transformations des contes merveilleux*. Paris: Seuil.

Propp, V. (1993). *Theory and history of folklore*. Minneapolis: University of Minnesota Press.

Todorov, T. (1969). *Grammaire du Decameron*. The Hague: Mouton.

Section B: Neostructuralist approaches

Beyond binaries

Lévi-Strauss's structuralist method for the analysis of mythology (covered in the previous section) was so popular at its height that it was almost inevitable that it would be met with an equally strong turn away, and this is, of course, what happened towards the end of the last century (Parker 2000: 15). Many surveys of the history of theory have consequently sorted myth analysis material into two academic epochs: the structuralist and the poststructuralist (cf Campbell 2002). Although certain prominent figures (see, for example, Derrida 2008) put forward alternative techniques for the analysis of literary texts, many of the (theoretically diverse) mythographers who are labelled poststructuralists work with Lévi-Strauss's thought, as much as they move beyond it. There is, however, a greater problem in the overextension of the category of poststructuralism, which can be explained by Lévi-Strauss's theory of Hot and Cold cultures (Lévi-Strauss and Charbonnier 1969). Western societies tend to value myths that highlight their progression through stages of increasing development (Lévi-Strauss and Charbonnier 1969). This neither does justice to the lasting influence of Lévi-Strauss's thought nor does it accurately map the way that knowledge is generated. It is for this reason that Frank posited the term 'neostructuralism', as a better way to describe the various techniques that were developed in the wake of Lévi-Strauss's analysis (Frank 1989).

In the Anglo-American world, Kunin has popularized the term 'neostructuralism' as a way of indicating that Lévi-Strauss has a lasting legacy, which nevertheless can be added to by those mythographers who follow in his wake. Kunin's understanding of structuralism resonates with the dominant approach to structuralism of the British school of structuralist analyses, which is exemplified by Edmund Leach (as detailed in the previous section). This approach has always viewed structuralism as a useful tool for understanding material rather than as a dogmatic, untouchable philosophy and, from this perspective, it is only natural to imagine that the tool can be further honed by successive experiments with it and should, by its nature, be open to a degree of transformation.

The neostructuralist contribution to theory that is offered by the readings we have collected in this section are together proposing a far more radical development of Lévi-Strauss's approach than Leach. In particular, there is a strong commitment to a detailed exploration (typically through protracted participant observation) of the surrounding society that the mythic material is drawn from. What is more, all the readings share a sense that the technique is useful only in so far as it tells us something interesting about a particular body of mythology, at the same time every society's mythology is understood as opening transformative possibilities within the analytical tool itself. Mary Douglas's article represents the most antagonistic of the three approaches that we have selected, yet in this early work, her willingness to think with structuralism is as at least as prevalent as her distrust of its promises. Hugh-Jones and Kunin are more clearly marked as favourable to the technique, yet each is also able to point to the issues that exist with the analysis technique. Taken together, the chapters represent an important development of structuralism that offers the analyst a neostructuralist approach that is indebted to Lévi-Strauss without being bound to his work.

References

Campbell, A. (2002). 'Tricky Tropes: Styles of the Popular and the Pompous'. In
     Popularizing Anthropology. Edited by MacClancy and MacDonaugh, 70–94. London:
     Routledge.
Derrida, J. (2008). *The Animal That Therefore I Am*. New York: Fordham University Press.
Frank, M. (1989). *What Is Neostructuralism?* Minneapolis: University of Minnesota Press.
Lévi-Strauss, C., and Charbonnier, G. (1969). *Conversations with Claude Lévi-Strauss*.
     London: Jonathan Cape.
Parker, J. (2000). *Structuration*. London: Open University Press.

We think what we eat

Seth Kunin

1

Seth Kunin is a Deputy Vice Chancellor at Curtin University in Australia. Before moving into university management, he was Professor of Religion and Head of the Department of Religious Studies at the University of Aberdeen (UK). He has also taught at the University of Nottingham (UK) and Durham University (UK) and held management positions at both Durham and Aberdeen. Kunin's earliest work, *The Logic of Incest*, appears (at first glance) like a straightforward application of structuralism to Israelite mythology; however, it represented innovation within the structuralist technique through its application of structuralism to a distinct kind of society to that which dominated Lévi-Strauss's analyses. In his later work, Kunin increasingly pushes out of traditional Structuralism and into what he terms neostructuralist arenas. Much of this later work blends ethnographic fieldwork with structuralist analysis and moves out of the realms of historical Hebrew mythology to explore contemporary groups: first the Crypto-Jewish communities of New Mexico and then the Crypto-Christian communities of Japan.

The material that we have included here is perhaps the clearest statement of Kunin's neostructuralsim. In the extract, it is clear that Kunin has found Lévi-Strauss's analyses highly rewarding, yet it is also equally clear that Kunin has found aspects of Lévi-Strauss's structuralism problematic. Kunin here, despite his awareness of the limitations of Lévi-Strauss work, remains nevertheless committed to the core of Lévi-Strauss's vision, and this leads Kunin to propose his own modified, or neostructuralist, version of the technique. This chapter, therefore, both opens the possibility of a certain way of working with structuralism and puts forward the foundations of a neostructuralist approach that is demonstrated to be of immense value for contemporary mythography.

References

Kunin, S. D. (1995). *The Logic of Incest: A Structuralist Analysis of Hebrew Mythology*. Vol. 185. A&C Black.

While the theoretical model developed, here is unashamedly structuralist (or due to the changes suggested, neo-structuralist), drawing inspiration from the work of Claude Lévi-Strauss, there are several aspects of our approach that either develop some of the implications inherent in that theoretical apparatus or which take structuralist theory in new directions. One of the key areas of enhancement is in respect of levels of structure. This aspect of our discussion should not be seen as a deviation from the work of Lévi-Strauss. In spite of the fact that he does not distinguish between the levels of structure presented here, they are all implied by his analysis, that is, he uses structure in different ways throughout his discussions. The different usages are analogous to those levels presented here.

The issue of diachrony, particularly in relation to structural transformation, is also a development of theoretical implication. Although his work rarely traced diachronic development of structure, it did substitute geographic movement for movement in time. While this analogy may be questionable, the theoretical issues he raises in that respect can usefully be applied to diachronic transformation. This issue, however, does lead us to one of the significant differences between the analysis presented here and classical structuralism, that is the distinction between cold and hot societies. The argument presented here suggests that this is not a useful distinction.

There are additionally two other key areas of difference, Lévi-Strauss' analysis often moves from culture specific analysis to hypothesizing about either universal underlying structure in an abstract sense, or occasionally in a specific sense (that is, that a particular structural relation, for example that implied by his discussion of raw and cooked, is universal). While we are not arguing against universal underlying structure in the former sense, we are arguing against the imposition of particular content or meaning on a biological or universal level. The argument presented here is also more interested in the culture specific aspects of structure rather than the biological. The second fundamental difference is in relation to agency. Many readings of structuralism viewed it as denying human agency both in the creation of cultural artefacts and in practice – they saw it as suggesting a highly deterministic model for human behaviour. While Lévi-Strauss' understanding that structure is unconscious and provides the foundation for culture both in respect of individuals and groups forms the foundation of our theoretical perspective, we do see room for agency and structural difference. It is argued here that agency comes into play in the process of emphasizing or de-emphasizing aspects of structure, particularly in cases of cultural overlap. This process leads to possible transformation in structure, and thus removes the static view of culture that is often associated with structuralism.

The concept of transformation underlies many of the analyses presented in this volume. Due to our interest in underlying structure, we are largely interested in transformations at that level; these transformations must be examined in either a diachronic, as applied here, or a geographic context, as found in Lévi-Strauss' analyses. While many analyses, either anthropological or literary, focus on transformation at the narrative or surface level, for example, the narrative movement of a hero from ignorance to knowledge, or changes in technology, these elements must be seen as separate from underlying structure. Nonetheless, underlying structure is not static,

[and] its processes of change are usually much slower and are often associated with significant cultural changes; these changes arise or are associated with significant changes in the way the world is constructed, that is, changes in how we categorize the world and how those categories are related to each other. Cultural change, due to the complex nature of cultural interactions, is a given, thus structural transformation will be found in all societies. Structure and its relationship with culture in this sense is relatively conservative but it is not petrified. The arguments relating to agency are closely associated with one of the mechanisms for transformations in culture. Agency provides one of the motors for structural transformation. Agency, which is largely conscious, does not directly change underlying structure, rather it privileges different aspects of the structural equation, and by so doing leads to a slow process by which models of categorization and thinking can change.

[...]

Lévi Strauss' distinction between hot and cold societies ... suggests that 'hot' societies perceive themselves as undergoing rapid change, and thus have a concept of linear diachronic development and therefore of history. He assumes that structural transformation in hot societies is equally rapid and thus they are less amenable to structuralist analysis than cold societies. Nonetheless, hot societies are still seen as structured and in more recent work (for example, 1981) Lévi-Strauss applies structuralist methodology to modern, western literary works. Cold societies are those that do not perceive themselves as changing. They usually do not have a concept of linear development or history. Lévi-Strauss sees these societies as undergoing relatively slow change and thus their structures tend to be more static and thus amenable to analysis.

This distinction, however, is problematic on several levels. Its concept of history privileges a particular western view as a means of distinguishing between cultures. If history is seen as a model of self and time, rather than something qualitatively distinct, then there seems little reason to see it as fundamentally different from other models of self and time. Thus history or perception of linear diachrony cannot be the basis for distinction. If change is the significant factor, then the distinction becomes slightly more supportable. While all cultures are constantly undergoing process of transformation, it is likely that some are changing more quickly than others. Nonetheless, provided the material under analysis is specifically contextualized there seems little reason to make a strong distinction.

It seems likely that all societies include aspects reflecting these two models of time/self. This is likely both in respect of different subgroups having different models and to the community as a whole being relatively hot or cold. This critique is supported by Hill; he suggests that all societies are conscious of both myth and history, that is cold and hot perceptions of self (Hill 1988: 5 see also Turner 1988: 235–246). Although we would not agree with Hill's usage of myth and history as distinct categories, his view of the relative and composite nature of societies fits closely with the approach taken here.

One of the issues that is raised by discussion of hot and cold societies is the conventional distinction between myth and history (this discussion is necessarily brief, as it could encompass an entire volume). In order to deconstruct this distinction it [is] necessary to introduce the definition of myth used here. The definition of myth works on two levels both of which arise from structuralist theory. The underlying structure of the definition is 'highly structured narrative (or related) material'. This definition arises from the understanding of the structuring process discussed above; it sees myth as that body of material in which the structures are most strongly articulated. The definition at this level is open-ended: it makes no determination either of content or function. The next level of the definition narrows this range to narrative or related material (for example genealogies) that is used by a particular community to structure its understanding of self and the world. This level builds upon the structuring principle inherent in the underlying structural level, and focuses on a particular range of structuring.

On the basis of this definition there seems little value in the issue of dichotomy within either myth or history. Both of these types of narrative are means of structuring reality and defining the place of self in that reality. There are two primary areas of apparent difference, the diachronic linear framework of history, as opposed to the non-linear models of some mythological systems, and the aspects of factuality, that is, history is perceived or understood as being built upon documentable objective facts.

The first area of difference, the very notion of diachrony, is as suggested above a model of past and present, thus it should be examined in the context of other models. On this basis there seems no logical reason for privileging it by defining it as categorically different, particularly if the category which it defines is taken as being in some sense qualitatively distinct – the term history implies a certain legitimacy that is not given to the term myth. This difference is also weakened by the observation that even in societies whose model of self is seen as myth there is evidence of a diachronic linear understanding of time. This is specifically the case with biblical material. The narratives are given an historical framework; nonetheless they seem to work in the same way as mythological material.

The second area of difference is equally problematic – it privileges a concept of objective fact as a qualitative or categorical marker. It is possible to deconstruct the concept of historical fact. All events in histories (as opposed to the objective events) are models of past, choosing or privileging events on the basis of an understanding of significance – some models are more conscious of this process of selection, for example the Marxist, while in others it is implicit. Nonetheless, all descriptions of events are artificial constructs, isolating particular moments in the ongoing flow of time. While we are not denying that the past occurred, we are denying the possibility of recovering the past in an unmediated/unstructured form.

On the basis of these brief observations we suggest that both myth and history are highly structured narratives that model self and the world and thus are functionally identical. The difference is one of content: myth uses events that may or may not be fictional (it can use historical events), history uses events understood to be factual. This difference in content suggests that the two forms are based on cultural choices: our society chooses to privilege fact, and therefore we construct our significant narratives out of factual/objective (self-defined) data. Thus, science as a model of causality uses 'objective' data to create its understanding of reality and history uses analogous information. In other societies that do not have the same emphasis on 'objective' reality other material may be privileged. On this basis myth, history and science can only be distinguished on the basis of an ethnocentric privileging of our model of understanding. From a structuralist perspective they are identical: we choose to apply the single term myth to all of these cultural objects.

One of the interesting aspects of the emphasis on a scientific, factual model is its cultural pervasiveness. Most realms of modern western society attempt to utilize this type of model to validate their views or principles. This is perhaps surprisingly found in various forms of fundamentalist Christianity. One of the most obvious uses is in relation to the concept of Creationism or its close relation Intelligent Design. Both of these arguments used to counter Darwinism utilize (pseudo) scientific arguments to support their particular views. The significant feature is the prevalence of a model of knowledge that is shared by both scientific and religious argumentation. If we look at the legitimizing use of religious experience, it can also be seen as requiring 'empirical' data as the basis for truth. Religion must be legitimized through experiences that are accepted as objective, not merely on the basis of faith.

This discussion can also be focused on the individual. Human beings as structuring entities not only create structural models of self at the societal level, the same process of model-making occurs at the level of the individual. This model-making is structured in the same way as the higher levels of model-making, with interplay of the different levels shaping the underlying structure; this interplay is both on the conscious and unconscious levels. The conscious aspect is discussed below in relation to agency. It is due to the unconscious aspect of this process that when individuals create cultural objects, for example, tell their own stories, these constructs are structured in the same way as traditional stories. The presence of structuring is also found in constructions of self – with memory an analogous form to myth. Memory is a selection of events, true or fictional, that are used to construct a model of self or an explanation of self. The events chosen are constructs and viewed through the mediation of current understandings of self. Memory like other aspects of myth is culture and context specific – in different contexts different content may be privileged as significant or insignificant. Perhaps the only distinctive quality of memory is that it appears to be much more fluid than other forms of myth. This fluidity is particularly evident in a postmodern cultural situation in which individuals on the conscious level are reflexively attempting to redefine themselves; such redefinition leads to a restructuring of memories in line with the perception of self.

Agency

One aspect of the process of transformation at all levels involves individual agency. Agency comes into play through the individual's conscious and unconscious emphasis or privileging of aspects of the underlying structural equation. Thus, for example, in a system that is characterized by a negative relation between categories but with some degree of positive mediation, individuals or groups can differentially emphasize either the negative aspect of the equation or the aspect of positive mediation. Their differing emphasis will shape their own conscious and unconscious use of the underlying structure, and can, through pushing at the edges of the system, shift it as it transforms through time. This process is facilitated in cultural situations in which different cultural equations come into contact, particularly where there are dominant and subordinate cultural systems. In such cases the individuals can unconsciously work, to some degree, within both systems, leading to structural transformation of both models creating new structural forms. It is assumed, however, that long-term compart-mentalization is not possible and that the differing structural equations will have to be synthesized or in part rejected.

The conscious articulation of this form of agency is found in *jonglerie*, or identity juggling. This concept encapsulates the process by which individuals privilege different elements of their cultural repertoire at different points in time depending on context and individual choice. *Jonglerie* is not a random process, it allows the individual to highlight or select different aspects of their identity and thereby to shape and reshape different levels of their use and experience of structure. The theoretical concept *of jonglerie* highlights the constant process of conscious and unconscious negotiation of identity and the fact that all identities are in some sense contested. It is through this process that underlying structural patterns, and to some degree culture on a broader level, are transformed through time. As individuals and groups push the envelope, expand the realms of possibility, different types of development can occur. These include the levels of change highlighted above and also possibly a reaction against change, characterized as non-transformation.

Although the type of agency suggested here is not found in traditional structuralist theory, which sees underlying structure as deterministic and autonomous, the arguments presented should not be understood as undermining the original model. As argued above, structure is unconscious and shapes cultural understanding, communication and action. Nonetheless, culture is not static nor is structure: both transform in response to new contexts. The concept of *jonglerie* provides one of the mechanisms for cultural transformation. It suggests that individuals through the processes of articulating and defining their identity emphasize or de-emphasize different aspects of the underlying structural equation. While the individual choice does not change the equation, it can, if it is shared by a large segment of the group in question, lead to a process by which the model of thinking is transformed. It seems likely that this process is facilitated in contexts in which cultural boundaries are weak or people have the ability to move between several cultural identities or subcultural identities.

Both the concepts of bricolage and *jonglerie* are directly relevant to the material under discussion in this volume. The process of bricolage is highlighted in the use in one scripture of mythemes developed in an earlier scripture. Thus, the Death/ Rebirth mytheme is first found in the Hebrew Bible (though by saying this we are not assuming that the Hebrew Bible originated this mytheme; like all other mythemes and themes, it almost certainly had a long history prior to it being 'taken up' by the bricoleur to be restructured and reused in Israelite myth); it worked with concepts of death, birth, genealogy and difference to exemplify its underlying structural equation. These mythemes are then used in the New Testament, perhaps seven hundred years later. They no longer arise from the same cultural environmental context, as the Christian model of self was different from that of the Israelites; nonetheless, they were available in the textual context/environment. The bricoleur takes the elements, which were available to him from Israelite culture, and unconsciously restructures them to fit the new underlying structural pattern. A similar process of reusing the identical mythemes, traced from the Hebrew Bible, the New Testament through the Book of Mormon, also reveals the same process of bricolage and transformation.

[…]

Practice

Practice, or lived experience (both in terms of historical experience and practices), is the forum that brings together the conscious and unconscious levels of structural articulation; bricolage and *jonglerie* are brought together through action. The fact of practice or acting upon enables individuals and groups to articulate or relate underlying structure to the materials of the contextual or lived environment. It equally and simultaneously allows the relevant actors to articulate the materials of practice to the underlying structure. Neither the structure nor the practices can be given priority; both are common features of the system. Although we have suggested that structure has its basis in the biological nature of humanity, specific structures have their locus in individuals and communities; they exist not solely in the cognitive models or the practices but in the interrelationship of the two.

Due to the theoretical move away from fixed biological structures, our position moves closer to that of Bourdieu, particularly in his definition of *habitus*. *Habitus* can be seen as the unconscious 'strategy-generating principle' through which the individual and groups respond to different situations leading to the creation of meaningful practices (Bourdieu 1977: 72). The creation of these practices and their interrelated *habitus* arise from previous practices and thus serve as the basis for future practice. This suggests that subtle changes in practice can lead to transformation of *habitus* and thus in our terms structural transformation. Although it is tempting to think of practice in relation to acts, or perhaps rituals, there is no reason why it cannot be extended to the practice of writing and thereby texis. Texts, particularly because of their potentially authoritative nature, are useful indicators of the underlying role of systems of legitimization and authority found in all forms of practice and reproduced by forms of practice.

The articulation of the structures in lived experiences, however, is not merely reproductive or the bases of conformity; practice also allows or provides the basis for pushing and shaping the boundaries. Lived experience or practice both validates and is validated by structure; it is also shaped by and equally shapes underlying structural relations. Both action and narration (particularly but not exclusively spoken narrative or story-telling) are loci in which structure and content are articulated through interaction with the world, other individuals, groups or texts. The significance of the role of practice is emphasized in a recent review in the New York Review of Books (Flam 2001: 10). The author of the review, paraphrasing the book by John Golding, states: 'he constantly keeps in mind the ways in which the physical activity of painting can generate its own ideas and may be regarded as a form of thinking' (Flam 2001: 10). This expresses the role of practice as a means by which structure is both expressed and transformed.

References

Bourdieu, P. (1977). *Outline of a Theory of Practice*. Cambridge: Cambridge University Press.

Flam, J. (2001). Space Men. *New York Review of Books* 48: 11–13.

Hill, J. (1988). *Rethinking History and Myth*. Chicago: University of Illinois Press.

Lévi-Strauss, C. (1981). *The Naked Man*. New York: Harper & Row.

Turner, T. (1988). 'Commentary Ethno-Ethnohistory: Myth and History in Native South America Representations in Contact with Western Society'. In *Rethinking History and Myth*. Edited by J.D. Hill. Chicago: University of Illinois Press.

The gun and the bow

Stephen Hugh-Jones

2

Stephen Hugh-Jones is an Emeritus Associate of Cambridge University's Anthropology Department and Life Fellow of King's College, Cambridge. A graduate of Cambridge, he joined the Anthropology Department in 1971 and worked there as Lecturer, Senior Lecturer and Head of the Department, before retiring in 2010; he was also heavily involved in college life and was both Director of Studies and Assistant Senior Tutor at Kings. Throughout his time at Cambridge, Hugh-Jones combined a highly nuanced understanding of the structuralist method with deep engagement with Amazonian society and mythology. He carried out several long-term periods of fieldwork with the Barasana and always looked to use this fieldwork as a way of both refining and expanding structuralism, at the same time as using structuralism to reveal aspects of Amazonian mythology and wider practice. This is evident from his earliest work, such as the magisterial *The Palm and the Pleiades* (1979), to his most recent work, such as 'Writing on Stone; Writing on Paper' (2016).

The text that we have chosen to include here brings together Hugh-Jones's understanding of both the realities of Barasana life and structuralist theory, to present an important reflection on (and amendment to) the way that myth and history are dealt with in Lévi-Strauss's analysis technique. Here, Hugh-Jones works with Lévi-Strauss's much-maligned concepts of 'hot' and 'cold' culture to generate valuable insight into the way that analysts of myth can sensitively explore issues of colonial contact through a rich engagement with mythology.

References

Hugh-Jones, S. (1979). *The Palm and the Pleiades. Initiation and Cosmology in Northwest Amazonia*. Cambridge: Cambridge University Press.

Hugh-Jones, S. (2016). Writing on Stone; Writing on Paper: Myth, History and Memory in NW Amazonia. *History and Anthropology* 27, no. 2: 154–182.

The discovery of the New World was part of the wider process of European mercantile expansion and it is the impact of this expansion on the tribal peoples of the world that forms the theme of Eric Wolf's book *Europe and the Peoples Without History*. In his book Wolf seeks to give back history to those who, up till now, have been denied it. But the history he provides is doubly our own for not only is it dominated by our European world but it is also seen through our Western eyes. This he makes clear when he writes 'the global processes set in motion by European expansion constitute *their* history as well. There are thus no "contemporary ancestors" no people without history, no peoples – to use Lévi-Strauss' phrase – whose histories have remained cold" (Wolf 1982: 385).

Alongside this kind of ethnohistory there is room for another: in addition to one global history of tribal peoples in the world there are also many tribal peoples' histories of their worlds. To recognize and return this other kind of ethnohistory is no mere patronizing act of charity. It is a step in the direction of demythologising our own view of tribal peoples and a recognition that construction of the world and action within it are inseparable. Tribal peoples did not only suffer history but also made it and continue to do so.

Wolf's reference to Lévi-Strauss is perhaps misplaced for, as Lévi-Strauss himself makes clear, it is not history that is supposed to remain 'cold'. Rather 'hot' and 'cold' have to do with the opposed orientations and practices of different societies with respect to history and thus refer to the realm of culture and not to the kind of history that Wolf has in mind. And yet Wolf's hint of criticism may still be justified for another reason because, although he recognizes that even 'cold' societies are subject to historical change, Lévi-Strauss himself pays little attention to the impact of such change on the cultural systems which he analyses and makes no allowance for an historical consciousness within them. Thus if White People do not figure in the pages of *Mythologiques* they certainly do figure in Amerindian myth and thought.

[...]

I shall examine the way in which White People, their activities, possessions, and beliefs have been incorporated into the mythology of the Barasana and other Tukanoan Indians of the Vaupés region of the Colombian northwest Amazon.[1] Although it is the essence of timeless tradition, myth is nonetheless subject to a constant process of change which allows it to keep pace with reality. I am interested in the mechanisms of this change, in how novelty is incorporated into myth, in why this incorporation takes the form it does and in what the content of such myths can tell us about more general ideas and attitudes that the Indians hold towards White People.

Although lack of space precludes a proper discussion of historical narrative, ritual speech and oratory, or daily conversation, I want to stress that an excessive focus on myth, in isolation from other narrative and verbal genres, is liable to lead to a very distorted impression of how small-scale tribal societies view and react to historical events and changes, whether these have to do with relations internal to the society, with relations with other tribal groups, or with contact with Western society. Whilst there is no doubt that myths do play an important role in their views of the past and present, to pretend that such societies have no consciousness of history and that they have only one mode of thought ('mythic thought'), displayed in a specific mode of discourse (myth) and which marks them as being a particular kind of society ('cold'), is unwarranted. Ideas such as these belong ultimately to the mythology of the Noble Savage which came into play after the discovery of the Americas.

[…]

My first point then is that for the Vaupés Indians… myth and history are not mutually incompatible but co-exist as two separate and complementary modes of representing the past, each with its own appropriate narrative style and each with its own context of relevance. This point, obvious enough in itself, would hardly be worth making if it were not for the fact that it is often minimized, ignored or denied. All too often it is assumed that in 'totemic' societies with a 'cyclical' view of time, history is dominated by and subsumed under a mythic mode of thought or only exists after the trauma of contact with Western society.[2] This argument, based on precisely those modes of symbolic discourse – myths and totemic classifications – which do indeed appear to negate history, is both circular and has probably diverted attention away from the recording and analysis of oral history in such 'cold' societies thus reinforcing the impression of the dominance of myth. Mythic thought or structure does not engulf history but distills from events and individuals, memories and experiences, an ordered set of categories but it does not obliterate its sources from consciousness.

[…]

An immediately striking feature of occurrence of White People in Barasana myth is that virtually all reference to them is confined to a single mythic cycle.[3] The cycle concerns a culture hero called Wãribi ('He who went away') or Sie ('Bitter') who is often identified with Christ and the Christian God. Here is a brief summary of his story.

Wãribi was the child of an incestuous union between the Moon and his sister Bẽderiyo. As a punishment, the girl's father Bẽdi Kũbu, sent her up into the sky. Later she returned to earth, by now very pregnant, and arrived at the house of the Jaguars, her fathers's affines. The Jaguars' mother tried to hide and protect her granddaughter but she insisted in joining in with their dancing and they killed her. Their mother took her body to the river where she allowed Wãribi to escape from his mother's womb into the water.

Wãribi swam to his grandfather Bẽdi Kũbu's house where he played with the children swimming in the river. He caught butterflies and painted patterns on their wings, the origin of the White People's writing. To catch him, the children buried a young girl in the sand, urinated on the spot above her crotch to attract the butterflies and then went and hid. As Wãribi played with the butterflies the girl caught him between her legs and, though previously a bodyless spirit, he was now born as a real baby.

Wãribi grew supernaturally fast and later accompanied his grandfather on a visit to his affines the Jaguars. The Jaguars were playing football with Bĕderiyo's head, the origin of the White People's game, and Wãribi joined in their game, kicking the head across a river. He made a bridge of snakes disguised as logs and vines and sent the Jaguars to fetch the ball. At Wãribi's command, the bridge came undone sending the Jaguars into the river where they were eaten by piranhas.

Although he lost a leg, one Jaguar managed to get to the other bank and became the ancestor of White People and foreign Indians. His name was Steel Tapir or One Leg and it is through him that White People acquired steel and he explains why there are so many amputees in their towns. Wãribi made One Leg's descendants strong and fierce and gave them the power to make all kinds of manufactured goods but he sent them far to the East where they would not cause trouble. As one informant put it 'Wãribi left us Indians with nothing. To him we were like animals living amongst the trees and eating wild fruit'.

Later, Wãribi obtained loads of manufactured goods from the spirits of White People in the sky. As his grandfather was angry with him for killing his affines, he did not visit him but instead took the goods in a large canoe downstream to the White People living in the East. After many further adventures in which he stole curare poison, invented the gun and blowpipe and killed a man-eating eagle, Wãribi finally created true human beings.

This is a summary of a small fragment of what is in fact a very long myth but even the full version reveals little that can be readily identified with the people and events of the history of the region discoverable either from documentary sources or from the historical narratives of the Indians themselves.[4] The fact that the Jaguars live at Yauareté ('Jaguar Rapid') on the Vaupés river suggests a link between them and the Tariana Indians who live there today and who are known to have sold individuals from more isolated groups to White People as slaves in the past. Wãribi's killing of the Jaguars might then be taken as the expression of an actual or desired revenge against the Tariana but although the Barasana emphasize that the Jaguars are White soldiers and policemen, the agents of foreign oppression, they do not accept this specific interpretation. However the more general identification of White People with Jaguars is consistent with the Indians experience of them as powerful, murderous and predatory and as being outside the bounds of civilized society, themes which are repeatedly expressed in more historical narratives.[5]

Wãribi is described as the ancestor of all White People but, as the prototype shaman, he is above all identified with God and Christ and, through them, with the religious component of White Society. Although the Jaguars are also described as the ancestors of White People, they are most closely identified with soldiers, policemen and other of their secular and more violent manifestations. Wãribi's hostility to the Jaguars might thus reflect the historical antagonism between the religious and secular elements of White society for the missionaries have traditionally defended the Indians against the worst abuses of the traders, soldiers and police. But apart from possible instances such as these, the myth has only a very general relation to the specific individuals and events of history.

The story of the creation of true human beings follows the section of the myth summarized above and it repeats and amplifies some of its themes. Variants of this part of the myth are known from a number of different Vaupés groups and what follows is a composite version designed to bring out specific points.

When he had finished preparing the world, Wãribi created the first people. They came from the East in the belly of an anaconda and when it reached the Vaupés region, they emerged from the water as true people, the ancestors of the different exogamous language groups of the area. Last to be born was the ancestor of the White People but when the culture hero ordered the people to bathe it was he who plunged into the water first and came out clean and white. He was followed by the ancestor of the Blacks who acquired his colour from the now dirty water. The Indian was frightened of the water and did not bathe at all and so became inferior to White People.

The culture hero then offered the people a gun, a bow and some ritual ornaments. Given first choice, the Indians chose the bow and ornaments leaving the White Man with the Gun. Because they came from the same ancestral body, the people all spoke one language but, when given salt to lick, each began to speak in his own tongue. (In a Barasana version of the story, they were offered beeswax mixed with coca, a key symbol of contemporary ritual.[6]) The Indians refused to eat but women, snakes, spiders, and White People all ate the wax which is why women menstruate, snakes shed their skins, and White People wear clothing. Their common ability to shed their skins explains why snakes never die, why women live longer than men, and why White People are so numerous, healthy and long-lived. The Barasana liken the burning of beeswax to the Catholic use of incense in the Mass and the Indians' refusal to eat the wax and their refusal to bathe are both seen as a refusal to accept Christianity.

The ancestor of the Whites then began to threaten the others with his gun. To keep the peace, the culture hero sent him far away to the East and declared that war would be the White Peoples' equivalent of Indian ritual and that through war they would obtain the wealth of other people.

This story of the differentiation from a common ancestor may be told to account either for the origin of all the groups in the Vaupés or for the origin of the different, ranked clans which make up each one. In the former case, although the ancestors of each group are brothers ranked according to the order of their emergence or birth from the ancestral anaconda, the acquisition of different languages converts them into affines of equal status in accord with the principles of linguistic exogamy which apply in the area. In the latter case, no differences of language are introduced and the clans remain ranked according to the birth order of their respective ancestors.

Mention of White People is often omitted altogether but when they are introduced into the story they are treated initially as if they should have had equal status to any other Vaupés group, each of which is traditionally associated with a different language and with the manufacture of a particular material object (stool, canoe, basketry, etc.). They are thus treated as if they were to have been equal partners in the system of marital and ritual exchanges which regulates Vaupés Indian society.

The myth first sets up an initial distinction between an animal-like anaconda ancestor and true people or *bãsa*, a category which applies equally to Whites and Indians and which is sub-divided by linguistic and cultural markers. This initial situation is then transformed into a straight opposition between Whites and Indians as generic and ethnic categories between whom exchange is no longer possible. White people are banished from the social space of the Vaupés Indians and turned from potential affines into real enemies. They are now excluded from the category *bãsa* in its more restricted sense of 'true people' or 'people like us' (i.e. Vaupés Indians) and put into the category *gawa* which also applies to people such as the acculturated Baré and Carijona who acted as the allies of White People in the past.

This transformation from affine to enemy and the denial of exchange is prefigured in the earlier part of the myth. Whereas Bẽdi Kũbu has the Jaguars as affines with whom he exchanges women and basketry, his son, the Moon, prefers incest with his sister over marriage to these affines, and his grandson Wãribi kills all but one of these affines and banishes the survivor to the East, a separation also marked by a piranha-filled river.

Wãribi is the prototype shaman who sent all White people far away to the East and it was from the East that the first White people, the Portuguese slavers and Brazilian traders and missionaries, began to enter the Vaupés region. If Westerners saw, and still often see, Indians in temporal terms as representing an earlier stage in the development of humanity, the Indians see these differences more in spatial terms and not as a matter of relative progress. In the Indians' myths White People share an equal creation but one which is followed by an original separation and moral decline. However, the progressive incursion of White People into Indian territory, an incursion described in historical narratives, is seen in temporal terms as a cumulative change which results from the failure of later shamans to keep the foreigners at bay.

The establishment of an opposition between Whites and Indians and the denial of the possibility of exchange and affinity between groups who are in principle equal but different also introduces the question of their relative status. As a brother who was last to emerge, the ancestor of White People is logically younger and inferior to his Indian counterpart but his acquisition of the gun allows him to usurp his elder brother's status and to become dominant over him. This theme of a fateful choice between two brothers who swap status through one's cunning or the other's stupidity is common to many South American myths about the origin of White People and it is usually represented as a choice between the gun and the bow. I want now to examine this theme in more detail as it applies to the Vaupés Indians.

The contrast between Whites and Indians is characterized by an ambiguity which is also evident in contexts other than that of myth. Although in reality it is the more powerful White People who have largely determined the Indians present situation and although it was they who imposed the category 'Indian' which the Indians themselves now use, the myth suggests otherwise. By failing to choose the gun and by refusing to accept baptism and incense, the symbols of Christianity, the Indians are presented as having determined their own status and as being responsible for their present situation. In the same way, because it was Bẽdi Kũbu, the Indian, who was angry with Wãribi for having killed his Jaguar affines, Wãribi went off and gave his merchandise to the White People instead. This same theme of responsibility for one's own fate also occurs in a number of other Barasana myths in which, through their own doing, different animals either miss the opportunity to become human or lose their original human status.

The goods chosen by the Whites and Indians stand for whole differences in economy, life style, and values which define each group socially and which determine the relations between them. The choice of the bow implies a forest-based economy and condemns the Indians to be powerless against White men armed with guns. Their refusal to bathe reinforces the Indians' weakness by giving them a lower status and a declining population. To quote the culture hero of a Tukano version of the myth, 'after the arrival of the Colombians and Brazilians in your land, you shall have only one wife and she shall have only one or two sons; your brother's wife will have no sons and that is how the Tukano will die out [...] They will humiliate you and have you as their slaves' (Fulop 1954: 132). The Indians' choice of ritual ornaments also represents a system in which goods are obtained through ritualized exchange rather than through warfare, theft and coerced labour backed by the gun.

The myths reveal a fatalism which is also manifest in the ordinary talk of many of the elder Barasana who are aware of themselves as the last and rapidly disappearing representatives of a culture that was once common to the whole Vaupés area and whose last shreds are now being abandoned by a mission-educated youth. Such myths concern the recognition, interpretation and acceptance of White domination and by placing it at the beginning of time they present it as something inevitable and beyond human influence. They cannot serve as the basis of political action and they stand in marked contrast to the more aggressive political rhetoric of the younger Indian leaders.

The myths show also that, in their thinking about the place of White People in their cosmology, the Indians have been influenced by the negative values and inferior position assigned to them in the cosmology of the Whites. This influence is clear in the following passage from a Tukano myth in which the culture hero declares 'the Indians of the Vaupés are like animals. One day I shall send you chickens, dogs and pigs so that you can compare yourselves with them. I am cursing you. Look at the Colombians and Brazilians. They are really fine people' (Fulop 1956: 367).

But if Indians seem to invert the values of the White People so also do White people invert the values of Indians. Alongside the self-blame and self-denigration of the myths there also runs a countercurrent which suggests the Indians' moral superiority. For the Vaupés Indians, the idea of language embraces notions of character, essence, behaviour and temperament. It was their greedy, uncontrolled and thoughtless character, received by White People along with their language, which made it inevitable that they should bathe without fear, grab the gun and not share their possessions.

Whilst recognizing their intelligence and inventive powers, Indians frequently stress the poor memories, unsharing habits and uncontrolled aggression of White People. The myths draw an explicit contrast between these negatively evaluted [*sic*] qualities and the tranquil, reflective, controlled, and ritualized character of Indians which is epitomized in the person of the shaman. It was this character which lay behind their refusal to bathe and grab the gun. If the Indians chose to be Indians it was because they chose as Indians who rejected the values of life-style of the Whites. The bow implies powerlessness but it also represents an adaptation to the forest in which White People are so inept. The ritual possessions stand for a ritual ordering and mastery of the human and natural worlds by the shaman-priest or *kūbu*. The Indians' shamanic powers are seen as the counterpart of the religious powers that lie behind the technology and life-style of the Whites. As the creator of the gun and the Bible, the sources of power of the Whites, and the creator of Indian material culture and shamanic power, Wãribi is both God and shaman and personifies ambiguity.

[…]

Whenever the Barasana tell the eternal myths of the past they do so with reference to some contemporary pretext which exerts an influence on what is said. The myth must be made relevant to the pretext and the teller must use his judgment as to what to elaborate upon or omit. The myth of Wãribi is often told with almost no reference at all to White People but when it is told to me, as one of them, my informants will usually make sure to lace the myth with as many such references as they can muster. Some of these references, such as the invention of writing and football, function almost as an obligato accompaniment to the myth; others are less well known and are rarely mentioned and yet others are clearly invented on the spur of the moment. Here is an example of one such invention.

I once told a shaman, who had never heard of them before, about submarines – big underwater canoes full of people and firing great arrows from their bows. Later, I heard him tell a friend the episode of the myth of Wãribi in which the hero is swallowed by an anaconda, takes two of its ribs, makes a pair of scissors, cuts a hole in the side, and fires out an arrow. 'And that', he added nonchalantly with me as his other audience, 'that is how White People have those things they call submarines. That's what my grandfather told me'.

Examples such as these are common for this same creative analogical matching between myth and life is constantly employed to make any myth relevant to new experience and daily issues.…

[…]

I have shown how White People are integrated into myth at levels which range from off-the-cuff parallels drawn between new phenomena and elements of myth through to higher-level contrasts and oppositions between whole myths which emphasize the differences between Whites and Indians and systematize the relations between them. The unknown is constantly matched with the known and brought into myth through analogies of much the same kind as those which lead the *conquistadores* to see tigers in jaguars and fir-cones in pine-apples. I have suggested that this same kind of thinking probably allowed the historical integration of White People into myth for even they had a precedent in the form of mythological jaguars and very real stranger Indians with whom the Whites were often allied.

However, I have also suggested that this process of classification and matching must be set against real differences in power, wealth and prestige of which the Indians are fully aware. White People are not simply the equivalent of another Indian group, the Bible is not just another myth, guns are not merely the alternatives to bows and writing is much more than the patterns on the wings of a butterfly. For this reason, each time the system of myth is applied to new experience it is transformed and the values of its elements are changed ....

Through looking at the way White People are treated in myth we can gain insight into both the workings of myth itself and into the way in which Indians view outsiders, a view which is a reflex of their image of themselves. In addition, because the different representations of the contact situation, held by both sides, are an integral part of the way in which that situation evolves, a proper history of contact between native and Western society must take such representations into account. But in this context, as in any other, it should not be assumed that native representations will only and always take the form of myth.

Notes

1 Fieldwork amongst the Barasana (1968–1970, 1979, 1981, 1984) was variously supported by the Social Science Research Council; King's College, Cambridge, the Museum of Mankind and Central Television. This support is gratefully acknowledged.

2 See for example Da Matta's (1971) analysis of a Timbira myth concerning the origin of White People where he asserts that the myth 4 introduces historical awareness into tribal consciousness fp. 288) and that such consciousness begins with the contact of a tribal society with the outside world (p. 272). On the evidence he provides there seem to be few grounds for claiming either that the myth has to do with historical consciousness or that such consciousness was absent prior to the invention of the myth or to the arrival of White People.

3 The tendency to restrict reference to White People to only one or two myths is common throughout the Vaupés region and, judging from the compilations published by Wilbert (1978) and by Wilbert and Simoneau (1982), appears to be true of lowland South America more generally.

4 For fuller version of this myth, see Hugh-Jones (1979b: 274–283).

5 The animal-like status of White People is expressed not only in the very fact that they are identified with Jaguars but also by the fact that although their second creation occurs simultaneously with that of the Indians, their first creation as Jaguars precedes the creation of true human beings. By the logic of Barasana myth, this would imply that White People are on a par with the spirits of the dead, an inference supported by Barasana accounts of

the exploits of the shaman-prophet leaders of last-century millennial cults. These men are said to have made regular visits to the world of the dead, a world described as being identical to the towns of White People.

6   See Hugh-Jones (1979b: 163–192) for a fuller discussion of this ritual.

References

Da Matta, R. (1971). 'Myth and Anti Myth among the Timbira'. In *The Structural Analysis of Oral Tradition*. Edited by E. Maranda and P. Maranda. Philadelphia: University of Pennsylvania Press.

Fulop, M. (1954). 'Aspectos de la cultura tukana: cosmogónia'. *Revista colombiana de Antropología* 3: 97–137.

Fulop, M. (1956). 'Aspectos de la cultura tukana: mitología'. *Revista colombiana de Antropología* 5: 335–373.

Hugh-Jones, C. (1979a). *From the Milk River*. Cambridge: Cambridge University Press.

Hugh-Jones, S. (1979b). *The Palm and the Pleiades*. Cambridge: Cambridge University Press.

Lévi-Strauss, C. (1966). *The Savage Mind*. London: Weidenfeld & Nicolson.

Lévi-Strauss, C. (1969). *The Raw and the Cooked*. London: Jonathan Cape.

Lévi-Strauss, C. (1973). *From Honey to Ashes*. London: Jonathan Cape.

Lévi-Strauss, C. (1978). *The Origin of Table Manners*. London: Jonathan Cape.

Lévi-Strauss, C. (1981). *The Naked Man*. London: Jonathan Cape.

Wilbert, J. (1978). *Folk Literature of the Gê Indians*. Los Angeles: University of California Press.

Wilbert, J. and Simoneau, K. (1982). *Folk Literature of the Tobe Indians*. Los Angeles: University of California Press.

Wolf, E. (1982). *Europe and the Peoples Without History*. Berkeley: University of California Press.

The meaning of myth

Mary Douglas

3

With special reference to 'La Geste d'Asdiwal'

Professor Dame Mary Douglas (1921–2007) was one of the most well-known figures of social anthropology in the latter half of the twentieth century. After graduating from the University of Oxford, she spent a short period as a lecturer there, before moving to the University of London, where (in 1978) she was appointed to the post of Professor of Social Anthropology in University College, London. She later moved to the United States of America, where she held posts, first, as director of research at the Russell Sage Foundation, New York, and then as the Avalon Foundation professor in the humanities at Northwestern University (USA). After her retirement, in 1985, she worked as a visiting professor at Princeton University (USA), before moving back to the UK, where she held an honorary fellowship at St Anne's College Oxford.

Throughout her career, Mary Douglas was a vocal critic of what she saw as the widespread uncritical reception of Lévi-Strauss's work. However, arguably her most influential book, *Purity and Danger*, shows strong affinities with structuralism and could itself be classed as a structuralist work. In the text that we have chosen here, Mary Douglas demonstrates both her reasons for having reservations about the elements of structuralism and the potential value of the technique. In particular, she highlights her concerns about the way that the evolving nature of Lévi-Strauss's thought can make it seem at times contradictory. What is more, Douglas highlights many of the teething issues that can be found in Lévi-Strauss's earliest attempt to apply the technique to Oedipus mythology. Her concluding statement asks questions of structuralism's supporters but also offers the opportunity for Lévi-Strauss (and others) to allay her fears and address her concerns.

References

Douglas, M. (2003). *Purity and Danger: An Analysis of Concepts of Pollution and Taboo*. London: Routledge

[**B**ritain] is the home of philosophical scepticism, an attitude of thought which has insulated us more effectively than the North Sea and the Channel from Continental movements of ideas. Our intellectual climate is plodding and anti-metaphysical. Yet, in spite of these traditions, we cannot read much of Lévi-Strauss without feeling some excitement. To social studies he holds out a promise of the sudden lift that new methods of science could give. He has developed his vision so elaborately and documented it so massively from so many fields of our subject that he commands our attention.

He has developed most explicitly in connection with myth his ideas of the place of sociology within a single grand discipline of Communication. This part of his teaching draws very broadly on the structural analysis of linguistics, and on cybernetics and communication theory in general, and to some extent on the related theory of games. Briefly, its starting-point is that it is the nature of the mind to work through form. Any experience is received in a structured form, and these forms or structures, which are a condition of knowing, are generally unconscious (as, for example, unconscious categories of language). Furthermore, they vary little in modern or in ancient times. They always consist in the creation of pairs of opposites, which are balanced against one another and built up in various (algebraically representable) ways. All the different kinds of patterned activity can be analysed according to the different structures they produce. For example, social life is a matter of interaction between persons. There are three different types of social communication. First, there is kinship, the structure underlying the rules for transferring women; second, there is the economy, that is the structure underlying transfer of goods and services; third, there is the underlying structure of language. The promise is that if we can get at these structures, display and compare them, the way is open for a true science of society, so far a will-o'-the-wisp for sociologists.

So far myth has not been mentioned. Lévi-Strauss recognizes that its structures belong to a different level of mental activity from those of language, and the technique of analysis must be correspondingly different. The technique is described in his 'Structural Study of Myth' (1955) and is also made very clear in Edmund Leach's two articles (1961, 1962) in which he applies the technique to the Book of Genesis. It assumes that the analysis of myth should proceed like the analysis of language. In both language and myth the separate units have no meaning by themselves, they acquire it only because of the way in which they are combined. The best comparison is with musical notation: there is no musical meaning in a single isolated note. Describing the new science of mythologies which is to parallel linguistics, Lévi-Strauss unguardedly says that the units of mythological structure are sentences. If he took this statement seriously it would be an absurd limitation on analysis. But in fact quite rightly, he abandons it at once, making great play with the structure underlying the meaning of a set of names. What are sentences, anyway? Linguists would be at a loss to identify these units of language structure which Lévi-Strauss claims to be able to put on punched cards and into a computing machine as surely and simply as if they were phonemes and morphemes. For me and for most of us, computer talk is a mysterious language very apt for prestidigitation. Does he really mean that he can chop a myth into semantic units, put them through a machine, and get out at the other end an underlying pattern which is not precisely the one he used for selecting his units? The quickness of the hand deceives the eye. Does he further believe that this underlying structure is the real meaning or sense of the myth? He says that it is the deepest kind of sense, more important than the uninitiated reader would suspect. However, I do not think it is fair to such an ebullient writer to take him literally. In other contexts it is plain that Lévi-Strauss realizes that any myth has multiple meanings and that no one of them can be labelled the deepest or the truest. More of this later.

From the point of view of anthropology, one of his novel departures is to treat all versions of a myth as equally authentic or relevant. This is right, of course. Linguistic analysis can be applied to any literary unit, and the longer the better, so long as there is real unity underlying the stretches of language that are analysed together. Why stop short at one of Shakespeare's historical plays? Why not include the whole of Shakespeare? Or the whole of Elizabethan drama? Here Lévi-Strauss gives one of his disturbing twists of thought that make the plodding reader uneasily suspect that he is being duped. For by 'version' we find that Lévi-Strauss means both version and interpretation. He insists that Freud's treatment of the Oedipus myth must be put through the machine together with other earlier versions. This challenging idea is not merely for the fun of shocking the bourgeois mythologist out of his search for original versions. Freud used the Oedipus myth to stand for his own discovery that humans are each individually concerned with precisely the problem of 'birth from one' or 'birth from two' parents. On Lévi-Strauss's analysis of its structure, this problem is revealed as underlying the Oedipus cycle. So there is no inconsistency between Freud and Sophocles....

[...]

A summary of 'La Geste d'Asdiwal' best demonstrates how [Lévi-Strauss method] is to be understood. It is a cycle of myths told by the Tsimshian tribes. These are a sparse population of migratory hunters and fishers who live on the Pacific coast, south of Alaska. They are culturally in the same group with Haida and Tlingit, northernmost representatives of Northwest Coast culture. Topographically their territory is dominated by the two parallel rivers, Nass and Skeena, which flow southwest to the sea. In the summer they live on vegetable products collected by women, and in winter on marine and land animals and fish killed by the men. The movements of fish and game dictate their seasonal movements between sea and mountains, and the northern and southern rivers. The Tsimshian were organized in dispersed matrilineal clans and lived in typical Northwest Coast composite dwellings which housed several families. They tended to live with their close maternal kin, generally practising avunculocal residence at marriage and the ideal was to marry a mother s brother's daughter.

The myth begins during the winter famine in the Skeena valley. A mother and daughter, separated hitherto by their marriages but now both widowed by the famine, set out from East and West, one from upstream and one from downstream of the frozen Skeena, to meet each other half-way. The daughter becomes the wife of a mysterious bird who feeds them both and when she gives birth to a miraculous child, Asdiwal, its bird father gives him a magic bow and arrow, lance snow-shoes, cloak, and hat which make him invisible at will, invincible, and able to produce an inexhaustible supply of food. The old mother dies and the bird father disappears. Asdiwal and his mother walk West to her natal village. From there he follows a white bear into the sky where it is revealed as Evening-Star, the daughter of the Sun. When Asdiwal has succeeded, thanks to his magic equipment, in a series of impossible tasks, the Sun allows him to marry Evening-Star, and, because he is homesick, to take his wife back to the earth generously supplied with magic food. On earth, because Asdiwal is unfaithful to her, his sky wife leaves him. He follows her half-way to the sky, where she kills him with a thunderbolt. His father-in-law, the Sun, brings him to life and they live together in the sky until Asdiwal feels homesick again. Once home, Asdiwal finds his mother is dead and, since nothing keeps him in her village, he continues walking to the West. This time he makes a Tsimshian marriage, which starts off well, Asdiwal using his magic hunting-weapons to good effect. In the spring he, his wife, and her four brothers move along the coast northwards, towards the River Nass, but Asdiwal challenges his brothers-in-law to prove that their sea-hunting is better than his land-hunting. Asdiwal wins the contest by bringing home four dead bears from his mountain hunt, one for each of the four brothers, who return empty handed from their sea expedition. Furious at their defeat, they carry off their sister and abandon Asdiwal, who then joins some strangers also going North towards the Nass for the candlefish season. Once again, there are four brothers, and a sister whom Asdiwal marries. After a good fishing season, Asdiwal returns with his in-laws and wife to their village, where his wife bears them a son. One day, however, he boasts that he is better than his brothers-in-law at walrus-hunting. Put to the test, he succeeds brilliantly, again infuriating his wife's brothers, who abandon him without food or fire to die on a rocky reef. His bird father preserves him through a raging storm. Finally, he is taken by a mouse to the underground home of the walruses whom he has wounded. Asdiwal cures them and asks in exchange a safe return. The King of the Walruses lends Asdiwal his stomach as a boat, on which he sails home. There he finds his faithful wife, who helps him to kill her own brothers. But again Asdiwal, assailed by homesickness, leaves his wife and returns to the Skeena valley, where his son joins him. When winter comes, Asdiwal goes hunting in the mountains, but forgetting his snow-shoes, can go neither up nor down and is changed into stone.

This is the end of the story. In the analysis which follows, Lévi-Strauss draws out the remarkably complex symmetry of different levels of structure. Asdiwal's journeys take him from East to West, then North to the Nass, then Southwest to the sea fishing of walrus, and finally Southeast back to the Skeena River. So the points of the compass and the salient points of order of Tsimshian migration are laid out. This is the geographical sequence. There is another sequence concerned with residence at marriage.

The two women who open the tale have been separated by the daughter's virilocal residence at marriage. Living together, they set up what Lévi-Strauss calls a 'matrilocal residence of the simplest kind, mother and daughter'. Lévi-Strauss counts the first marriage of the bird father of Asdiwal as matrilocal. Then the sky marriage of Asdiwal himself with Evening-Star is counted as matrilocal, and matrilocal again the two human marriages of Asdiwal, until after he has come back from the walrus kingdom, when his wife betrays her brothers. So, Lévi-Strauss remarks that all the marriages of Asdiwal are matrilocal until the end. Then the regular pattern is inverted and 'patrilocahsm triumphs' because Asdiwal abandons his wife and goes home, accompanied by his son....

The same symmetry is traced in the cosmological sequence. First, the hero sojourns in the sky where he is wounded and cured by the sky people; then he makes an underground sojourn where he finds underground people whom *he* has wounded, and whom *he* cures. There is a similar elaboration of recurring themes of famine and plenty. They correspond faithfully enough to the economic reality of Tsimshian life. Using his knowledge of another myth of the region, Lévi-Strauss explains their implication. The Northwest Coast Indians attribute the present condition of the world to the disturbances made by a great Crow, whose voracious appetite initiated all the processes of creation. So hunger is the condition of movement, glut is a static condition. The first phase of the Asdiwal tale opposes Sky and Earth, the Sun and the earthly human. These oppositions the hero overcomes, thanks to his bird father. But Asdiwal breaks the harmony established between these elements: first he feels homesick, then, once at home, he betrays his sky wife for a terrestrial girl, and then, in the sky, he feels homesick again. Thus the whole sky episode ends on a negative position. In the second phase, when Asdiwal makes his first human marriage, a new set of oppositions are released: mountain-hunting and sea-hunting; land and sea.

Asdiwal wins the contest as a land-hunter, and in consequence is abandoned by his wife's brothers. Next time Asdiwal's marriage allies him with island-dwellers, and the same conflict between land and sea takes place, this time on the sea in a boat, which Asdiwal has to leave in the final stage of the hunt in order to climb onto the reef of rock. Taken together, these two phases can be broken down into a series of unsuccessful mediations between opposites arranged on an ever-diminishing scale: above and below, water and earth, maritime hunting and mountain-hunting. In the sea hunt the gap is almost closed between sea- and mountain-hunting, since Asdiwal succeeds where his brothers-in-law fail because he clambers onto the rock. The technique by which the oppositions are reduced is by paradox and reversal: the great mountain-hunter nearly dies on a little half-submerged rock; the great killer of bears is rescued by a little mouse; the slayer of animals now cures them; and most paradoxical of all, the great provider of food himself has provender become – since he goes home in the stomach of a walrus. In the final dénouement, Asdiwal, once more a hunter in the mountains, is immobilized when he is neither up nor down, and is changed to stone, the most extreme possible expression of his earthly nature.

Some may have doubted that myths can have an elaborate symmetrical structure. If so, they should be convinced of their error.

Lévi-Strauss's analysis slowly and intricately reveals the internal structure of this myth. Although I have suggested that the symmetry has here and there been pushed too hard, the structure is indisputably there, in the material and not merely in the eye of the beholder. I am not sure who would have argued to the contrary, but myths must henceforth be conceded to have a structure as recognizable as that of a poem or a tune.

But Lévi-Strauss is not content with revealing structure for its own sake. Structural analysis has long been a respectable tool of literary criticism and Lévi-Strauss is not interested in a mere literary exercise.

He wants to use myth to demonstrate that structural analysis has sociological value. So instead of going on to analyse and compare formal myth structures, he asks what is the relation of myth to life. His answer in a word is 'dialectical'. Not only is the nature of reality dialectical, and the structure of myth dialectical, but the relation of the first to the second is dialectical too.

[...]

The meaning of a myth is partly the sense that the author intended it to convey, and the sense intended by each of its recounters. But every listener can find in it references to his own experience, so the myth can be enlightening, consoling, depressing, irrespective of the intentions of the tellers. Part of the anthropologist's task is to understand enough of the background of the myth to be able to construct its range of reference for its native hearers. To this Lévi-Strauss applies himself energetically, as for example when he finds that the myth of the creative Great Crow illuminates the themes of hunger and plenty in Tsimshian life.

From a study of any work of art we can infer to some extent the conditions under which it was made. The maidservant who said of St Peter, 'His speech betrays him as a Galilean' was inferring from his dialect; similarly the critic who used computer analysis to show that the same author did not write all the epistles attributed to St Paul. This kind of information is like that to be obtained from analysing the track of an animal or the finger-prints of a thief. The anthropologist studying tribal myths can do a job of criticism very like that of art critics who decide what 'attribution' to give to a painting or to figures in a painting. Lévi-Strauss, after minute analysis of the Asdiwal myth, could come forward and, like a good antiquarian, affirm that it is a real, genuine Tsimshian article. He can guarantee that it is an authentic piece of Northwest Coast mythology. His analysis of the structure of the myth can show that it draws fully on the premises of Tsimshian culture.

Inferences, of course, can also be made within the culture; the native listener can infer a moral, and indeed myths are one of the ways in which cultural values are transmitted. Structural analysis can reveal unsuspected depths of reference and inference meaning for any particular series of myths. In order to squeeze this significance out, the anthropologist must apply his prior knowledge of the culture to his analysis. He uses inference the other way round, from the known culture to the interpretation of the obscure myth. This is how he discerns the elements of structure. All would agree that this is a worthwhile task. But in order to analyse particular structures, he has to know his culture well first.

At this stage we should like to be able to judge how well Lévi-Strauss knows the social reality of the Tsimshian. Alas, very little is known about this tribe. He has to make do with very poor ethnographic materials. There are several minor doubts one can entertain about his interpretation of the facts, but the information here is altogether very thin. A critic of Lévi-Strauss (Ricoeur) has been struck by the fact that all his examples of mythic thought have been taken from the geographical areas of totemism and never from Semitic, pre-Hellenic, or Indo-European areas, whence our own culture arose. Lévi-Strauss would have it that his examples are typical of a certain kind of thought, a type in which the arrangement of items of culture is more important and more stable than the content. Ricoeur asks whether the totemic cultures are not so much typical as selected, extreme types? This is a very central question which every anthropologist has to face. Is *La Pensée sauvage* as revealed by myth and rite analysis typical, or peculiar, or is it an illusion produced by the method? Here we are bound to mention Lévi-Strauss's idea of mythic thinking as *bricolage*. The *bricoleur*, for whom we have no word, is a crafts-man who works with material that has not been produced for the task he has in hand. I am tempted to see him as an Emmett engineer whose products always look alike whether they are bridges, stoves, or trains, because they are always composed of odd pieces of drainpipe and string, with the bells and chains and bits of Gothic railing arranged in a similar crazy way. In practice this would be a wrong illustration of *bricolage*. Lévi-Strauss himself is the real Emmett engineer because he changes his rules as he goes along. For mythic thought a card-player could be a better analogy, because Emmett can use his bits how he likes, whereas the *bricolage* type of culture is limited by pattern-restricting rules. Its units are like a pack of cards continually shuffled for the same game. The rules of the game would correspond to the general structure underlying the myths. If all that the myths and rites do is to arrange and rearrange the elements of the culture, then structural analysis would be exhaustive, and for that reason very important.

At the outset of any scientific enterprise, a worker must know the limitations of his method. Linguistics and any analysis modelled on linguistics can only be synchronic sciences. They analyse systems. In so far as they can be diachronic it is in analysing the before-and-after evolution of systems. Their techniques can be applied to any behaviour that is systematic. But if the behaviour is not very systematic, they will extract whatever amount of regularity there is, and leave a residue. Edmund Leach has shown that the techniques of Lévi-Strauss can be applied to early Greek myths, to Buddhist, and to Israelite myths. But I suppose he would never claim that the analysis is exhaustive.

Lévi-Strauss in his publications so far seems blithely unconscious that his instrument can produce only one kind of tune. More aware of the limitations of his analysis, he would have to restrict what he says about the attitude of mythic thought to time, past and future. Structural analysis cannot but reveal myths as timeless, as synchronic structures outside time. From this bias built into the method there are two consequences. First, we cannot deduce anything whatever from it about the attitudes to time prevailing in the cultures in question. Our method reduces all to synchrony. Everything which Lévi-Strauss writes in *La Pensée sauvage* about time in certain cultures or at a certain level of thinking, should be rephrased to apply only to the method he uses. Second, if myths have got an irreversible order and if this is significant, this part of their meaning will escape the analysis. This, as Ricoeur points out, is why the culture of the Old Testament does not fit into the *bricolage* category.

We know a lot about the Israelites and about the Jews and Christians who tell and retell these stories.[1] We know little about the Australian aborigines and about the no longer surviving American Indian tribes. Would this be the anthropologist's frankest answer to Ricoeur? We cannot say whether the *bricolage* level of thought is an extreme type or what it is typical of, for lack of sufficient supporting data about the examples. But we must say that the *bricolage* effect is produced by the method of analysis. For a final judgement, then, we can only wait for a perfect experiment. For this, richly abundant mythical material should be analysed against a known background of equally rich ethnographic records. We can then see how exhaustive the structural analysis can be and also how relevant its formulas are to the understanding of the culture.

Notes

1   Lévi-Strauss's own justification for *not* applying his method to Biblical materials seems to rest on the proposition that we do not know enough about the ancient Israelites! (See *Esprit*, November 1963, p. 632) but cf. Leach (1966) *passim* [E.R.L.].

References

Leach, E. R. 1961. Lévi-Strauss in the Garden of Eden: An Examination of Some Recent Developments in the Analysis of Myth. *Transactions of the New York Academy of Sciences*. Series 2: 386–396.

Leach, E. 1962. Genesis as Myth. *Discovery*, May: 30–35.

Leach, E. 1966. The Legitimacy of Solomon: Some Structural Aspects of Old Testament History. *European Journal of Sociology* 7: 58–101.

Lévi-Strauss, C. 1955. The Structural Study of Myth. *Journal of American Folklore* 28: 428–444. Reprinted with modifications in C. Lévi-Strauss, 1963a.

Section C: Spatial theories

From page to place

It is common for the student of mythology to encounter, within mythological texts, long lists of place names that can seem (to the contemporary reader) like an unwanted break in the narrative flow. Although such myths are frequently encountered today on the page, they would have previously been understood (and in many cases encountered) in relation to place. These onomastic references are not simply fillers, residue from oral cultures that had to pass long winter nights, they are rather crucial parts of the myth's communicative story that anchor it in place (cf Basso 1996: 37–70); to ignore the spatial element of mythology is to gain a diminished understanding of the material.

In this section we examine three readings that each aim to redress this balance by demonstrating (in distinct ways) the importance of geography for the interpretation of mythology. These arguments may be seen to fit into the recent spatial turn (Warf and Arias 2008), which broadly suggests that scholars have historically focused overly on the temporal and intellectual aspects of mythology at the expense of the equally, if not more, important spatial elements (Arias 2010). While it is true that there has been a tendency to focus on the characters and epochs of myth, it is important not to overstate the situation. Creation myths are found in many cultures, and several classical interpretations see these as attempts to explain the world without the aid of science. Both psychological and sociological theories quite rightly reject a simplistic and ethnocentric understanding of the relation between myth and place, yet the best of them never entirely abandons an interest in the geography of the mythology. Indeed, many of the writings in the early sections of this Reader demonstrate attentiveness to space, even if it is not the analyst's primary concern.

Eliade's well-known arguments about myth and 'the time before time' have to be balanced with his conception of a mythic axis mundi and the important act of sacred space in dissolving time. Although Malinowski stresses myth's act in social organization, he also follows Yeats's understanding that mythology is married to rock and hill (cf Yeats [1916] 1999: 167, Malinowski 1922: 330). Finally, it should not be overlooked that Lévi-Strauss's *Mythologiques* series has a strong spatial argument which he finds particularly useful in the absence of recorded history. The three articles that we have selected here all demonstrate awareness of the fact that they are writing into a tradition of spatial analysis. They do not seek to so much revolutionize the study as to innovate, through careful engagement with the classical texts of mythography (including Lévi-Strauss, Malinowski and Eliade). Collectively, they both highlight the spatial element of classical theories of mythology and suggest new and important ways that the analyst can engage spatially with myth.

References

Arias, S. (2010). Rethinking Space: An Outsider's View of the Spatial Turn. *GeoJournal* 75, no. 1: 29–41.

Basso, K. H. (1996). *Wisdom Sits in Places*. Albuquerque: University of New Mexico.

Malinowski, B. (1922). *Argonauts of the Western Pacific: An Account of Native Enterprise and Adventure in the Archipelagoes of Melanesian New Guinea*. New York: Dutton.

Warf, B., and Arias, S. (eds.). (2008). *The Spatial Turn: Interdisciplinary Perspectives*. London: Routledge.

Yeats, W. B. (1999). *The Collected Works of W.B. Yeats: 3* (Collected Works of W.B. Yeats/ Richard J. Finneran and George Mills Harper general editors). New York: Scribner.

Myth, memory and the oral tradition: Cicero in the Trobriands

Frances Harwood

Frances Harwood (1943–2003) was a social anthropologist, an accomplished mythographer and an environmental visionary. Her initial doctoral research, at Chicago, focused on the anthropology of Christianity, in general, and Christian practice in Melanesia, in particular. This involved prolonged fieldwork in the Solomon Islands and resulted in a rich text that includes some reflections on mythology. After completing her PhD, she spent periods as both a visiting fellow at Harvard University and a faculty member at Wesleyan University, where she further developed her theories of mythology, especially in relation to indigenous spiritualties. She eventually settled in Colorado, where she spent nineteen years as a faculty member of Naropa University. Her early interest in mythology was tied to an appreciation for the environment, and at Naropa, she both taught mythology and founded the Environmental Studies Department. Towards the end of her life, she laid the foundation of the Ecoversity in Santa Fe (USA). This was intended to be a place that would both practically teach and live out sustainability, or cultural ecology.

In the following article we see how Harwood's environmental sensitivities, when combined with fieldwork experience, led her to present an important spatial reading of mythology, which long predates fashionable talk of a 'spatial turn'. In this discussion she offers not only a spatial analysis of the mythology but also an important spatial reading of Malinowski, which both highlights the spatial aspects of Malinowski's own thought and demonstrates the need to move beyond this, if we are to truly understand the relationship between mythology and place.

As a child I remember being impressed by a memory trick which my father often performed. A random list of 18 words would be read to him slowly which he would commit to memory as they were spoken, and which hours later he could recite forward and backward, or retrieve any word when given its number in the series. The secret, which he later revealed to me, was to mentally place images suggested by the nouns on an 18-hole golf course well known to him. For example, he might envision a brown (Bron-) slavic (-slaw) skier (-ski) lying sick (Mal-) near a sand trap on the third green. When asked to recall the third word in the series he would envision this familiar third green with its associated image and, with luck, come up with the name Bronislaw Malinowski.

As it turns out, and unbeknownst to either of us, this memory technique of recall by a sequence of locations has a hoary tradition in the Western world (Crovitz 1970; Yates 1966) which can be dated at least from the time of classical Greek rhetoric. Moreover, the Greek mnemonic of location may be a residual form of an *aide mémoire* which serves to structure the myths and legends of nonliterate societies in all parts of the globe. Furthermore, I contend that the mnemonic device not only serves as a remembrance of things past, but is also a source of living tradition which informs, modifies, and is modified by systems of ongoing social relations. That is to say, location as a structural marker has both cognitive and instrumental functions.

Two quotations to set the scene may be of use here:

> Persons desiring to train the faculty [of memory] must select localities and form mental images of the facts they wish to remember and store those images in localities, with the result that the arrangement of the localities will preserve the order of facts, and the images of the facts will designate the facts ... (Cicero 1942: lxxxvi, 353–354)

> The mythical world receives its substance in rock and hill, in the changes in the land and sea. The pierced sea passages, the cleft boulders, the petrified human beings, all these bring the mythological world close to the natives, make it tangible and permanent (Malinowski 1922: 330).

Thomas S. Kuhn ... defines 'normal science' as being contingent upon acceptance by the scientific community of a paradigm which he defines as 'universally recognized scientific achievements that for a time provide model problems and solutions for a community of practitioners' (1962: x). In anthropological parlance, these paradigms might be termed the dominant *world view* of a culture, a subculture (e.g., the scientific community), or an epoch. In the Western tradition such paradigms range from the Medieval notion of the 'great chain of being' to Einstein's 'theory of relativity.' Given the acceptance of a paradigm, the development of 'normal science' unfolds through the solution of puzzles generated by the dominant paradigm. That is to say, development consists of ordering perceptions or 'facts' about the world in accordance with a set of puzzles generated by the paradigm. Such puzzles, according to Kuhn, fall into three domains, the 'determination of significant fact, matching facts with theory, and articulation of theory' (1962: 33).

This paper is an attempt to solve two puzzles, one having to do with a map I once drew plotting the locations of a series of Trobriand myths. The pattern which emerged falls under the class of problems designated by Kuhn as the 'determination of significant facts,' the puzzle being, what is the significance, if any, of the precise geographical place names which occur with such frequency in Trobriand mythology? The second puzzle, stemming in part from the first, involves 'articulation of theory,' the problem being to attempt a synthesis of the social functional approach to myth as propounded by Malinowski and the cognitive approach to myth stemming from the French school of anthropology, most powerfully and persuasively presented by Claude Lévi-Strauss. In trying to solve two puzzles at once, I take heart from Freud's maxim in *The Interpretation of Dreams* in which he claims that just as it is easier to crack two nuts together than either one alone, two problems are easier to solve than either one alone.

Myths as charters for social action

Malinowski's signal contribution to the study of myth derives from his concept of the interrelation between myth and social organization. For him myths were to be viewed as charters for social institutions. This formulation turns on two concepts – that of myth as a charter and that of an institution as an ethnographic category. He notes, for example, that for the Trobrianders

> The sacred tradition, the myths, enters into their pursuits, and strongly controls their moral and social behaviour. In other words … an intimate connection exists between the world, the mythos, the sacred tales of a tribe, on the one hand, and their ritual acts, their moral deeds, their social organization, and even their practical activities on the other (1948: 96).

As one of the first practitioners of long term and systematic fieldwork among nonliterate societies, Malinowski was in a position to appreciate firsthand the way in which myth is embedded within a functioning social system. He soon came to perceive that myth was 'not merely a story told but a reality lived' (1948: 100). It was this novel point of view that took the study of myth out of the hands of armchair students of mythology such as Leo Frobenius, Max Müller, and Sir James Frazer and gave it a central position in modern ethnography.

[…]

One component of an institution is the mythical charter itself which stands as a sacred precedent giving the stamp of legitimacy to the organized activity for each institution. Malinowski concentrates on the linkage between a particular institution and the mythical charter which gives it validation. He does not, however, concern himself with the linkages between the various mythical charters themselves. The lack of interest in pursuing the linkages between sets of mythical charters, an interest which has been neglected not only by Malinowski but by an entire generation of British anthropologists, may be traced to Malinowski himself who steered inquiry away from this area by his famous dictum, 'study the ritual, not the belief.' The type of ethnology produced by this dictum emphasizes social organization at the expense of the cognitive or intellectual ordering of a society.

[...]

Malinowski's fieldwork procedure consisted of drawing up a list of institutions such as gardening, fishing, and the kula trade. He was then faced with the problem of articulating the relations between these institutions, and solved the puzzle by introducing the theoretical framework of functionalism in which every institution is seen as being linked with and supportive of every other institution in a reverberating ring, such that a change in any one institution sets off a wave of repercussions affecting all other institutions. Malinowski, however, neglected to indicate the mechanisms by which the institutions are perceived, distinguished, and linked together in the minds of the Trobrianders themselves. It is at this point that the cognitive aspects of mythological charters come into play.

Myth is of a different order from the other institutional components with which Malinoswski was concerned. Whereas institutional components such as kinship, family, rank, and technology interpenetrate and impinge on one another on more or less an equal basis, it would seem that myth overarches these social and technological components and is itself of a different order. Myths stand behind the social order as charters, and give to social institutions an aura of rightness. That is to say, myths codify and sanction a set of activities, a set which Malinowski terms an institution. I maintain that these institutions are linked together not only by pragmatic considerations but by a coherent conceptual system marked by certain structural components common to all Trobriand myths....

The weakness of Malinowski's formulation of the uses of myth is that he ... relates specific myths to specific institutions, and does not concern himself with the horizontal linkages between the various mythic charters taken as components in the corpus of Trobriand mythology, how they are distinguished and demarcated one from the other, and the principles by which the charters are structurally related.

[...]

The spatial coordinate

In reading the Trobriand myths one feature is particularly striking. Each mythical event is closely associated with a particular location, or a series of locations, in the

Trobriand area. By plotting these locations, it is possible to construct a mythical geography of the Trobriands.

Malinowski speaks of the

> enlivening influence of myth upon the landscape. Here it must be noted also that the mythically changed features of the landscape bear testimony in the natives' mind to the truth of the myth. The mythical world receives its substance in rock and hill, in the changes in land and sea. The pierced sea passages, the cleft boulders, the petrified human beings, all these bring the mythological world close to the natives, make it tangible and permanent. On the other hand, the story thus powerfully illustrated reacts on the landscape, fills it with dramatic happenings, which fixed there forever, give it definite meaning (1922: 330).

The association with a locality as a prerequisite for the validity of a myth is brought out clearly in Malinowski's description of the difficulties which missionaries encountered in introducing Christianity to the Trobriands. The reaction of one native was reported as follows:

> If you go to Laba'i you can see the cave in which Tudava was born; you can see the beach where he played as a boy; you can see his foot mark at a place in the Raybwag. But where are the traces of Jesu Kerisu? Whoever saw any signs of the tales told by the misinari? Indeed they are not lili'u [sacred myths] (1922: 302).

Linking myths to particular localities would appear to be one means of dividing a corpus of myth into cognitively distinct segments. This mnemonic of location ties each portion of the corpus to a separate node on a geographic grid. Thus modifications or elaborations of one mythical charter tend to be prevented from setting up repercussions in other mythical charters and their linked social institutions.

[...]

The puzzle in this instance, then, is to work out a theory which might possibly account for the attachment of various myths to separate geographic localities …. Two possible solutions to the puzzle spring to mind. By analogy with rosary beads, it might be said that the localities constitute beads on a geographic chain. By telling these beads, one can run through the mythological sequence. The second suggestion is based on the observation that the Kula trading voyages are made from northwest to southeast. These voyages might then be assumed to be a ritual reenactment of the mythological corpus; a pilgrimage replicating the sequence of sacred geography. An analogy could be drawn to the stations of the cross. This theory of ritual reenactment modifies the recent emphasis given to economic interpretations of the Kula trade (Uberoi 1962).

Recapitulation and extension of Malinowski's theory

Malinowski was perhaps the first anthropologist to emphasize the close relationship between myths and social institutions, a relationship which is analyzed in terms of its pragmatic effect on social organization. For instance, in the myth of the flying canoe:

> If for each word [in the myth] describing the stages of canoe-building we insert a full description of the processes for which these words stand – we would have in this myth an almost complete, ethnographic account of canoe-building. We would see the canoe pieced together, lashed, caulked, painted, rigged out, provided with a sail, till it lies ready to be launched. Besides the successive enumeration of technical stages, we have in this myth a clear picture of the role played by the headman, who is the nominal owner of the canoe … and at the same time directs its building (1948: 101).

The myth of the flying canoe contains, as it were, a recipe for the materials, technology, procedure, and social organization needed for the production of a canoe; it functions as a mnemonic for a process. Therein lies the force of Malinowski's statement that myth is 'not merely a story told but a reality lived' (1948: 100).

The premise advanced in the previous section states that a myth such as that of the magical flying canoe which occurred at Monikiniki on the island of Kitava is thus bracketed by its locale and kept cognitively distinct from the other mythical charters occurring at other locations. I maintain, however, that this spatial bracketing has cognitive as well as pragmatic functions. Myths are not stable over time (as has sometimes been assumed by natives and anthropologists alike) handed down through countless generations verbatim. However tenaciously the natives and some anthropologists insist on the literal transmission through time, myths are forever changing. According to Vansina, the narrator's art 'consists not so much on learning through repetition the time-worn formulas as on the ability to compose and recompose the phrases for the idea of the moment on the pattern established by the basic formula' (1965: 5).

An improvement in canoe technology will in all probability be re-presented in the mythical charter in a way similar to which improvements in a recipe for apple pie will be touted as 'just like mother used to make.' However, what if the technological improvements in canoe building, or more importantly, revolutions in the social groups involved in canoe construction occur, such as a change from obligations of kinship to wage labor? Repercussions from such a shift might rapidly feed back upon such other key institutions as the family, subsistence gardening, and the Kula trade. All kinship obligations might be rapidly transformed into ones involving a cash nexus. The Trobriand design for living as Malinowski knew it would probably collapse.

[…]

Myth, I maintain, has built-in stabilizing mechanisms which prevent dramatic upheavals at least in the majority of instances. One mechanism, that of bracketing a myth and its associated social practices by tying it to a specific location, serves to insulate a myth from the rest of the corpus. Changes rung on the structural possibilities of any one myth are constrained from having a domino effect upon other myths, but they allow for a more gentle osmosis in which the mythical corpus and its associated social correlates move toward coherence through a long term process of accommodation....

Summing up and supporting examples

So far I have attempted to demonstrate that what seems to the Western reader a mere gratuitous insistence on a precise location for Trobriand myths is in reality an indispensable structural marker which serves at least three functions identified so far. Location segments the corpus of myth into separate cognitive units and it also serves as a mnemonic for recall of portions of the corpus. Secondly, a precise set of locations may serve as a series producer which organizes the totality of a Trobriand mythology along a temporal axis of logical precedence which is coextensive with the spatial axis of the sequence of locations. Thus the Trobriand narrator and his audience listening to the myth of the origin of mortality may be induced to recall the myth of first emergence which precedes it and the journeys of Tudava, the culture hero, which follow it. This might be analogous to a recital of the episode of Odysseus' dalliance with Calypso which would evoke the episodes of Scylla and Charybdis and the sojourn with Nausicaa which lie on either side of the Calypso story. For the listener well versed in his tradition, his mind would be speeded through the whole gamut of his culture from first things to last things aided by the positioning of each section of the narrative in one of a series of locales of a sacred geography. Conversely, we in the Western world emphasize temporality as our predominant mode of series producing. An account of the Napoleonic era is colored and informed by its position between the French Revolution and the Restoration – an observation which is strengthened by the insistence that Western fairy tales fall between two references to temporality, 'Once upon a time … and they lived happily ever after.' A satisfying Melanesien tale by contrast would fall between statements such as, 'She set out from X … and finally arrived at Y.'

The first two functions of location in myths, as segmentors and series producers, remain on the level of the oral tradition itself, its ordering and recall. A third point to be made about myth involves the relation of myth to the social order in which myth is seen to be constantly in flux rather than static. Thus, myth may through manipulation contain recipes for social change. However, the change induced by the reformulation and recombination of elements in one myth is prevented from having a shattering effect on the corpus and the culture as a whole by encapsulating each specific myth within specific geographical boundaries.

Three functions for a mnemonic of location have been made with reference to Trobriand mythology; it remains to be determined if they have a more general application.

The first example is taken from Zuni mythology of the southwestern United States. Matilda Coxe Stevenson, one of the first anthropologists to record the Zuni origin myth which is recited annually during the Shalako ceremony, was prepared for an informative recital of mythological occurrences from her Zuni informants. Instead she was rewarded with lengthy lists of place names almost devoid of elaboration. A brief excerpt from the myth reads as follows:

> We come to Corn mountain, here we get up and move on.
> We come to the spring at the base of the mesa; here we get up and move on.
> We come to the ant-entering place; here we get up and move on.
> We come to vulva spring; here we get up and move on.
> We come to the Middle place.
>
> … In a short time my fathers, whom I have there, will meet you on the road. You will meet together. They will come, and will give to all your children more of the great breath of A'wonawil:oha: the breath of the light of day (Stevenson 1904: 87–88).

This somewhat disappointing myth is, according to Dennis Tedlock (personal communication), an elaborate sacred geography. The place names given in the myth are familiar locations in the Zuni area which lie along a southwesterly to northeasterly transit. Recent archaeological evidence points to an *east to west* direction for Zuni migration, thus the origin myth bears little resemblance to the archaeological sequence. From his researches among the Zuni, Tedlock is convinced that each location recited in the Stevenson myth has, in most if not all cases, a well-known subsidiary myth telling of the mythical characters and occurrences associated with each location. The origin myth can thus be seen as a template which functions as a series producer and serves as a mnemonic device for the recall of the more extended myths which stem out from the main branch preserved in the Stevenson version of the origin myth.

The second example of the intimate relations found between geography and the mythical tradition in nonliterate societies is taken from accounts of Australian aborigines, where, in the absence of a written tradition, place names arranged in series take the place of chronology as a means of locating man within an ordered cosmos. Over most of Australia, aboriginal populations were organized into complex social organizations composed of sections, subsections, and moieties. Many of the groups so formed were entrusted with the ritual maintenance of their particular totems. Such rituals were carried out at sacred totemic sites, and were accompanied by elaborate mythologies. Elkin, among others, has noted the importance of place names on these myths:

> The portion of mythology and ritual and the sacred sites entrusted to such a
> cult group are determined by mythological history. It is basically the mythology

which records the travels and actions of the tribal heroes in its subdivision of the tribal territory. The country of each local group is crossed by paths or tracks, usually unmarked, along which there are a number of special sites where a hero performed some action which is recorded in myth …. (Elkin 1964: 151)

The Zuni and Australian use of locations as templates or mnemonic devices for the storage and retrieval of information to be used in extended treatments of particular myths is a fascinating and complex study in itself. Only the barest outline of the systems is given above.

A third example can be found among the Luapula, a group of Interlacustrine Bantu in East Africa, in which an extensive repertoire of traditional tales is tied to specific features of the landscape, tales which apparently are told only when passing these locations. Another form of narrative consists of narrations of the wanderings of groups now settled along the Luapula River. These tales consist in large measure of recitals of named places encountered in the migrations (Cunnison 1951). Narratives of this type are common to oral traditions of African tribes and are designated as 'wandersagen' by Vansina (1965). It is a type well known in the West from Biblical descriptions of the wandering tribes of Israel.

Thus it can be seen that the use of locations as mnemonic devices for the ordering of an oral tradition can be shown to have a worldwide distribution. Examples have here been cited from Melanesia, the American southwest, Australia, and Africa. Can traces of these mnemonic systems be found in the Western world?

Cicero and the artificial memory

Cicero in his treatise *De oratore* describes for his friends the theories and practices of Greek rhetoric. This work, together with the anonymous work *Ad Herennium* (circa 86–82 B.C.) are the most extensive accounts of the technique of memory which forms the last of the five parts of Greek rhetoric. It is to these brief Latin fragments on the art of memory that scholars of the Middle Ages and Renaissance turned for guidance in developing artificial memory systems from Albertus Magnus and Thomas Aquinas in Medieval times to more mystical systems such as the memory theatre of Guilio Camillo, Ramon Lull's wheels, and the mysterious *De umbris idearum* of Giordano Bruno (Yates 1966). A more recent, and perhaps independent use of the principles of artificial memory is contained in Luria's account of the Russian mnemonist, Vygotsky, who used Gorky street in Moscow for his mnemonic of location.

Transforming material to be remembered into images, and attaching the images to locations on an accessible map, allowed the recall of a great deal of information, in any sequence required – for sequence had become transformed into location on the mental map of that street (Crovitz 1970: 37).

[…]

Cicero gives practical advice for the acquisition of a good memory which he himself found indispensable when pleading law cases and delivering orations, both of which he accomplished without the aid of written notes or reminders:

> ... persons desiring to train this faculty [of memory] must select places and form mental images of the things they wish to remember and store these images in the places, so that the order of the places will preserve the order of the things, and the images of the things will denote the things themselves, and we shall employ the places and images respectively as a wax writing-tablet and the letters written on it (Cicero 1942: lxxxvi, 351–354).

[...]

In *Ad Herenium* the author suggests that the place chosen for the storage of images should be easily grasped by the memory, and might consist of a well-known building of many rooms in which the objects to be remembered are to be mentally placed. It is also advised that the building stand in a remote locale as 'crowds of passing people tend to weaken the impressions' (Yates 1966: 7). This observation tallies with locations used in Trobriand mythology for they also are unfrequented places or if close to human habitation they are left to grow up to thick bush. However, the Trobriand case differs from the Greek system of mnemonics in that the *loci* used by Trobrianders form part of a shared heritage whereas in the Greek case the *loci* chosen are based on strictly personal preference.

[...]

Conclusion

An attempt has been made to describe and substantiate a number of techniques used by a variety of oral traditions to locate mythical events and to give them meaning. Two axes for the organization of cultural materials have been mentioned – the spatial and the temporal. It would appear that a spatial axis predominates in nonliterate cultures whereas a temporal, that is to say historical, axis takes precedence in literate cultures.

It is argued that the precise geographical locations given with such frequency in the myths of nonliterate societies are not mere embellishments, but play a significant role as mnemonic devices for the recall of the mythical corpus. These locations also function as structural markers dividing a corpus into separate cognitive units. Furthermore, the discontinuity produced in the corpus by tying individual myths to specific locations has the pragmatic effect of restricting change if only temporarily to specific myths and their linked social institutions.

References

Cicero (1942). *De oratore, II*. Trans. E. W. Sutton and H. Rackham London: William Heineman.

Crovitz, H. F. (1970). *Galton's Walk: Methods for the Analysis of Thinking, Intelligence, and Creativity*. New York: Harper & Row.

Cunnison, Ian (1951). History on the Luapula. Rhodes-Livingston Papers, No. 21. Lusaka.

Elkin, A. P. (1964). *The Australian Aborigines*. Garden City: Doubleday.

Kuhn, Thomas S. (1962). *The Structure of Scientific Revolutions*. Chicago: University of Chicago Press.

Malinowski, Bronislaw (1922). *Argonauts of the Western Pacific*. London: Routledge.

Malinowski, Bronislaw (1948). *Magic, Science and Religion*. Glencoe: Free Press.

Stevenson, Matilda Coxe (1904). The Zuni Indians. 23rd Annual Report of the Bureau of American Ethnography.

Uberoi, J. P. Singh (1962). *Politics of the Kula Ring*. Manchester: Manchester University Press.

Vansina, Jan (1965). *Oral Tradition*. Chicago: Aldine.

Yates, Frances A. (1966). *The Art of Memory*. London: Routledge and Kegan Paul.

Implicit mythology in the Shimla hills

Jonathan Miles-Watson

2

Jonathan Miles-Watson is Associate Professor of the Anthropology of Religion in the Department of Theology and Religion at Durham University, UK. He has previously worked at Luther College, the United States; Tallinn University, Estonia; Swansea University, UK; and the University of Manchester, UK. He is the author of *Welsh Mythology: A Neo-structuralist Analysis* and *Christianity and Belonging in Shimla: Sacred Entanglements of a Himalayan Landscape*. He has co-edited both *Theories of Religion* and *Ruptured Landscapes* as well as being the author of numerous articles on the analysis of mythology and sacred space. He has carried out extensive fieldwork in both the UK and the Indian Himalayas.

In the article that we have chosen to include here, he brings together his interest in the structuralist analysis of mythology with his interest in the Himalayas and sacred space to put forward a nuancing of Lévi-Strauss's often-overlooked theory of implicit mythology. Through an application of the technique to the contemporary mythology of the former summer capital of British India, Simla/Shimla, he demonstrates the utility of this approach for understanding postcolonial, complex, hypermodern landscapes.

Lévi-Strauss's important contribution to the analysis of explicit mythology is well recognised, yet his interpretation of implicit mythology is less commonly discussed. There is, however, a small, but significant, body of literature that points to the promise of the idea (Galinier 2004; Houseman 1998; Hugh-Jones 1988, et al.). Drawing inspirationally on this work, I revisited Lévi-Strauss's concept of implicit mythology and found within it the seed of a theory that when fully developed has proved extremely useful for interpreting my own field research. In what follows, I will demonstrate how the concept of implicit mythology can be usefully developed through both embracing its generality and honing its specificity ….

The concept of implicit mythology can be traced back to Lévi-Strauss's brief mentions of the existence of a more disjointed type of mythology that often accompanies ritual action (1981 [1971]: 668–669, 1996 [1991]: 83) … This is profitably developed by the Hugh-Jonses (1979, 1988) in their analyses of Barasana culture and is encapsulated in Stephen Hugh-Jones's account of how they 'paid particular attention to … the kind of "implicit mythology" that is revealed in such things as hunting, fishing, gardening and food preparation, eating arrangements and manufacturing processes, as well as in ritual and ceremony' (1988: 14). In this description the concept of implicit mythology spreads out of its explicit ritual context to give meaning to a wide range of activities and actions, some of them directive, others consequential. It is an encompassing concept that joins together seemingly distinct meaning making processes and permeates through seemingly mundane daily acts of living ….

Implicit mythology, for the purpose of this article, is defined as the narrativization that both accompanies and contextualises ritual action, as well as being the trace of that ritual action. I take implicit mythology to be operating wherever there is material and action that is tumescent with mythic meaning. Implicit mythology can be … art and architecture, as well as found in activities … This is because implicit mythology, like explicit mythology, can refer to at once something specific and something general. This ability of implicit mythology to blur the boundaries of being makes it a powerful tool for accurately reflecting the way that specific and general understandings interweave in people's daily life ….

By its very nature implicit mythology therefore represents a more cohesive, holistic and grounded answer to these issues than explicit mythology, despite Lévi-Strauss's contrary suggestion (1981: 669). This is because implicit mythology is contextually situated and deals directly with problems that arise from navigating the world …. I have found that when implicit mythology is freed from the confines of Lévi-Strauss's cognitive model the potency and value of the concept increases. For, if we do not so much construct meaning out of a chaotic world as move along with a world of meaning (Ingold 2000: 98), then implicit mythology, anchored (as it is) to that movement through (and action within) the world, can reveal localised ecologies of being. In this understanding, implicit mythology is not a subsidiary category of explicit mythology; rather it is the other way around: explicit mythology forms a subsidiary category of implicit mythology ….

Shimla and Simla

Shimla, the state capital of Himachal Pradesh, is a migrant city of around 175,000 people, over half of whom are classed as being a floating population (Chandramouli 2011: 47). It is the home of the state government and the state university, as well as a wide selection of service and retail industries. Shimla is, in many ways, a hypermodern city (Coleman and Crang 2002: 1) …. Shimla's sites of postmodern capitalism are clearly places that relationships weave and knot around as people flow through the city. Moreover, they are also places with an obvious history that stretches back beyond the living and captures something of the actions (and desires) of those who are now dead. One of the reasons that so many tourists flow into Shimla each summer is the perceptible presence of colonial history, of the old colonial capital Simla, among Shimla's hypermodern spaces ….

The modern city of Shimla is a place where the trace of the past is inescapably present and as such it demands integration into the lives of its contemporary residents. Residents therefore grapple with questions about nationhood, identity and belonging. How is old Simla, reconciled with new Shimla? How can the past (in a modern city) be integrated with the present? The answer to these questions lies at the heart of the city in the nexus of implicit myths that knot around the site of The Cathedral on the Ridge ….

The Cathedral on the Ridge: Out of place sacred space

When … I first came to Shimla … I was instantly struck by (and drawn to) a large, Mock Gothic, Cathedral that sits at the very top of the ridge in the centre of the city. The sense that this Cathedral was somehow central stuck with me and a year later I wrote in my field journal that it was as if the rest of the city both physically and conceptually spirals around this central, sacred, place … The concept of spiralling is central to Lévi-Strauss's mythography. In both the *Raw and the Cooked* (1994: 1, 3) and *From Honey to Ashes* (1983: 30–47) he suggests that a Structuralist analysis should begin by locating a 'key myth'. This 'key myth' then forms the start of the analysis, which subsequently spirals out to incorporate new material that both is best understood in relation to the key myth and helps to further unlock the key myth's mysteries (1983: 30–47). The Cathedral on the Ridge is … the key myth of this article, but it is not, as Lévi-Strauss suggests (1994: 1–2), simply an arbitrary starting point that reflects the analyst's logic. Rather, engagement with the city allows the Cathedral to reveal itself as the key sacred place around which the implicit mythology knots and weaves ….

Most of the visitors to Shimla that I spoke to reported that upon arrival they made for The Cathedral on the Ridge. Once there they would take a photograph of it, or have a photograph taken with them stood outside, for only then would they feel that they had truly arrived. Similarly, many local residents would regularly walk the Mall until they came to The Cathedral on the Ridge where they would stop to enjoy the air and view before walking home. Indeed, this Cathedral has become synonymous with Shimla and it is no surprise that when the Facebook group 'Simla', which at the time of writing has over 170,000 members, came to choose its online avatar it chose an image of this Cathedral.

The building that people today flow steadily around began life in 1844 and was designed to evoke the spirit of a typical English parish church (Buck 1904: 118). Although today part of the welcoming Church of North India, it was originally an exclusive Anglican church, aimed at the Viceroy and other notables (Buck 1904: 118). Those dignitaries and their descendants are now gone and it would be reasonable to presume that this place had lost its importance, or had to radically transform its function. In the postcolonial, capital of Shimla, it may seem logical that the central function of the Cathedral has evaporated as the city's population transformed. Yet, the Cathedral is still geographically and mythically central. It is the logical problem that this place presents that makes it the ideal key myth for unlocking the wider mysteries of Shimla's implicit mythology ….

Implicit mythology and ritual action

When I first … entered the Cathedral my eyes were drawn to elements that I could recognise: the crucifix shape, the pews, the altar and the chancel window (depicting scenes from familiar Biblical mythology). I therefore began to interpret both the space and how to properly engage with it through reference to similar sacred spaces that I had a history of engagement with elsewhere. However, I had little knowledge of the historical actions that constituted this sacred space, or its wider implicit mythology. Years of attentive engagement transformed this situation as implicit mythologies of the place were shared in a variety of formal and informal addresses that drew my attention to the intentional and unintentional shaping of this space by past actors. I increasingly became skilled in the practice of discerning the trace of certain past historical action in the present sacred space. Today, I read the implicit mythology of the place as simultaneously transnational, transhistorical and situated (historically and spatially). Therefore, when I look today at the chancel window I do not simply read it as a material representation of Biblical explicit mythology … rather I associate it with a particular set of events and actors ….

Both the ability to reckon with the church environment that I arrived with and that which I subsequently developed may be seen as two subcategories of the kind of implicit mythology that Lévi-Strauss suggests accompanies ritual action (1981: 668–669). The first kind, which I will term 'standardised implicit mythology', refers to a widely held international understanding of Christian rituals in general, whereas the second, which I shall term 'vernacular implicit mythology', refers specifically to historical ritual and devotional action that has occurred within the Cathedral itself. Vernacular implicit mythology is in keeping with Lévi-Strauss's examples from small scale societies, whereas standardised implicit mythology is a logical development of Lévi-Strauss's thought when applied to an international religious organisation. There is also a third kind of narrativization that surrounds this Cathedral, this is a form of implicit mythology that contextualises both the sacred space and the action that unfolds there. This 'reflexive implicit mythology' is even more personal and powerful than the two types of implicit mythology that I have discussed so far and pushes the concept of implicit mythology beyond Lévi-Strauss's conception ….

We are now in a position to understand why The Cathedral on the Ridge is the key to resolving the tensions of the colonial past and the postcolonial present …. Shimla's Christians anchor themselves in the past of the city through the church. Thus, the church neither becomes a separated history, nor a dead space; rather, the processes of modernity and migration heighten the importance of the church as an anchoring device and situate it as the cypher for decrypting the mythological processes of the wider city. The Cathedral on the Ridge anchors the population through historical rupture because emotionally charged, reflexive implicit mythology is interwoven with vernacular implicit mythology, thus blending the memories of the individual with the collective memories of the landscape in a satisfying way.

It has to be admitted that the contemporary Christian does not experience the separate categories of implicit mythology in the way that I have categorised them here. Rather, they engage with the Cathedral in a way that effortlessly weaves the standardised, vernacular and reflexive implicit mythologies. Similarly, they continue to weave the implicit mythology of the building by continuously engaging in devotional practices that further alter the mythic landscape. Here, the utility of the term implicit mythology becomes manifest. For, the overarching nature of the term accurately captures the way that emotion, place, memory and space are unified in lived experience. What is more, the term also bridges from the sphere of the individual to that of the collective, wherein the individual actors themselves become part of the myth. Implicit mythology therefore (just as Lévi-Strauss predicted) captures the participatory value of mythology without the need to turn to complicating ritual theories.

The discussion so far has highlighted that at the centre of our mythic spiral stands The Cathedral on the Ridge. It is a site of powerful implicit mythology, which operates at three levels in the lives of some of Shimla's Christians: the global, the local and the personal. Shimla's Christians are a minority group that are intimately bound up with the city's majority Hindu population and yet are also distinct from it. We therefore still have to solve the logical problem of how our key implicit myth can resolve the wider tensions of the city. In order to do this I intend to summon evidence from the ghosts of Shimla, who can be found throughout the city as well as within this Cathedral ….

Widening the spiral: Worshiping with ghosts

The following implicit myths are taken from a conversation with a Hindu, elderly, long-term resident who spontaneously offered the following chronological narrativization of the presence of ghosts in and around the sacred Christian cathedral. During my time in Shimla I came to understand that it was common for Hindu residents to have much to say about this ostensibly Christian landscape. Indeed, I could have presented here (were space to allow) other strikingly similar, detailed, affectionate and highly formative accounts. The abundance of Hindu reflexive implicit myths of the Cathedral on the ridge demonstrates not only how alive a sort of polytropy is in Shimla (Carrithers 2000), but more importantly points to the way that this Cathedral operates as a key for transforming the disquiet of Shimla's general landscape. Although, in what follows, the chronology of the narrativization is retrospective, the temporal element of the events is, I hold, valuable as a reflection of the informant's structuring of their own history. For, this structure highlights the transformative abilities of implicit mythology, as well as the way that entering imaginatively into the weave of these mythologies answers wider questions of nationhood, identity and belonging.

(A) First memories

I remember as a child being drawn to the Cathedral. I would look up at it from the lower bazaar and think how wonderful it looked. Yet, whenever I expressed my desire to visit my grandparents would rebuke me saying that I should not travel up there, because the ghosts of Britishers could be found there. These ghosts were said to be very violent and to dislike Indians: if they caught you they would cut off the top of your head and hang you upside down. Despite my grandparents' warnings I did not stay away from the cathedral and I would join a group of children who would venture up to the Cathedral to play a game around the outside the building … when it started getting dark we would nervously hurry down the hill … the ghost of an English woman, who had died inside the church, haunted the place and she would get angry if children were too noisy or rowdy near the church.

This narrativization of early interaction with the Cathedral by a young Hindu is clearly a kind of reflexive implicit myth, for it relates to actions undertaken around a sacred space and (while that action is not strictly speaking ritual action) it is surrounded by ritualistic features. Perhaps more importantly these stories act as a pre-myth for the main implicit mythology that follows by creating dramatic tension. When the child encounters the Cathedral it first appears as a strange place, yet one that has to be reckoned with. The young Shimla resident is inescapably, almost against their will, drawn towards it. Like countless, classical, mythological landscapes, the place is at once central to the landscape and forbidden. What is more, as the grandparents warn, this is not only an alien place but a place of unreasonable aggression and perilous danger. The problem that the landscape presents (and that the mythology will seek a resolution to) is set. It is a problem that still potentially exists today: how does this imposing colonial, Christian, landscape relate to the life of a postcolonial Hindu?

An attempt to resolve this problem is found in the second movement of the reflexive implicit mythology. Here we see an attempt to claim the sacred central space represented by the colonial Cathedral. This attempt involves interlacing personal memories of childhood games around the outside of the building, yet this resolution is only partial and the place is still one fraught with danger and hostility, albeit now of a slightly more reasonable kind. For, a second ghost now emerges, that of the easily irritated female Britisher. Although she is less antagonistic than the head cleavers she is hardly welcoming, especially as she seems to view the young Indian's engagement with the space as inappropriate (*id est* noisy/rowdy) ....

(B) School days

During school days I attended … services at the church … The first time that I entered into the church it was a revelation … it was so peaceful to be there and be part of the worship. When I spent more time in the church it became more familiar and I came to know of all the people who had worshiped there before … To be honest, I became a bit angry with myself, I felt a bit foolish for having thought of it as a place of danger …. When we sang I liked to imagine … [that] the former choir girls [were] singing along with us … [We] talked … about a stained glass window [the Chancel window], designed by Lockwood Kipling, the father of Rudyard Kipling … that felt good.

In this second narrativization we move within the church and clearly into the realm of both reflexive implicit mythology and vernacular implicit mythology. Indeed, although directly absent from the narrative the account indirectly also suggests a familiarity with relevant elements of standardised implicit mythology. This narrative also shows the resolution to the problem posed by the first narrativization. Through increasing familiarity with the implicit mythology of the space, it is transformed from a foreboding realm of alterity into a comfortable and familiar realm. The ghosts have moved from first being violent, to then being angry, before becoming reassuring presences – all this is achieved without conversion or the compromising of a Hindu, Indian, identity. The completeness of this movement (and its relevance for wider Shimla life) is brought out in a final narrative.

(C) Homecoming

I returned [to Shimla], [and] I immediately went towards … [the] Cathedral … I wanted to feel connected with the city once more. It seemed to have changed, there were new shops and stalls on the Lower Bazaar and Mall and the whole place seemed busier than I remembered. I wanted to see something that had not changed, that I could relate to now, as I had done as a child and I thought that … [the] Cathedral would be the place for that. At first I could not see it clearly, there were too many crowds of people in the way, but I found my way through to Ladies' Park and standing there I looked

up and saw it again, just like I looked at it as a child. And I remembered
everything: my childhood days playing there, the fear of the ghost … singing
… how Lockwood Kipling had designed the chancel window, even my
Grandmother's tales … I knew then that I had come home.

In this final narrativization, which in many ways reflects the informant's current
view of their own relationship to the Cathedral, the degree to which the implicit
mythology has become internalised (and part of their identity) is clear. Through this
process the implicit mythology of The Cathedral on the Ridge has become a key for
understanding the wider landscape of Shimla. When taken together, these narratives
show a movement in the chronology of the implicit mythology. In the early ghost
stories the Cathedral is clearly the realm of the other: *Cathedral : Unreasonable
Violence : Alterity :: Lower Bazaar : Safety : Home.*

If we simplify these relations to two primary categories (and map the content of
those categories) we can see that Cathedral, along with Unreasonable Violence and
Alterity, falls into one category (A) and the Lower Bazaar, Safety and Home, are
united in a second (B). The two categories have little content overlap and movement
from one to the other is problematic. This suggests an underlying structure of negative
qualitative valence, which can be transcribed as A−B, or, A/B. As the narrative
progresses the young girl tries to reckon with the environment and engage with the
outside and this has some success in rehabilitating the place, but the resolution is
clearly incomplete: *Cathedral : Reasonable Violence : Somewhat Familiar :: Lower
Bazaar : Safety : Home.*

These mythemes possess a more mediated structure (A = B), yet the underlying
equation is still a weak form of opposition (A−B). Movement between the two
categories is attempted, but is severely restricted and fraught with danger. Some of
the categories' mythemes have a degree of overlap (Somewhat Familiar and Home),
but others are more oppositional (Reasonable Violence and Safety). However, by the
final set of narrativizations, a transformation has occurred, which results in category
overlap between the world of the Lower Bazaar and that of the Ridge. This effectively
rehabilitates the Ridge by overcoming the perceived difference between the colonial
Christian and the postcolonial Hindu worlds: *Cathedral : Timeless Peace (Safety) :
Home :: Lower Bazaar : Safety : Home.*

In this final set of mythemes movement between the two categories (and
locations) is unproblematic and the content of the two categories has become almost
identical, suggesting that the two categories have now dissolved into one (A + B).
By exploring the nexus of relations that wind around The Cathedral through the
concept of implicit mythology, we are therefore able to see the way that transnational
(standardised), vernacular and reflexive accounts are woven together through the
lives of both contemporary Christian and Hindu residents. This suggests that binary
categories of Hindu and Christian, colonial and postcolonial are of limited use in
this context. For, we see people existing along a continuum that cuts across faith
and time and relates to the level of the individual's engagement with the implicit
mythology of the place ….

Working with implicit mythology

In this article, we have seen how Lévi-Strauss's implicit mythology concept holds within it the inspirational seeds of an increasingly relevant analytic tool. For, as globalization increases and population movement intensifies, sacred spaces will increasingly find themselves in the same position. Whether traditional sacred spaces become non-places (Auge 1995) or places of profound value in this modern age may well increasingly depend on the implicit mythology that surrounds them ....

Lévi-Strauss's basic supposition, regarding the connectedness of the structure of mythology and implicit mythology[,] is here further validated .... For sure, the article has used personal and social contextualisation in order to analyse the implicit mythology, yet this is only following Lévi-Strauss's suggestion that the analyst begins by placing themselves at the heart of the culture under consideration (1994: 1–3) ... However, during his discussion of implicit mythology (1981: 668), Lévi-Strauss seems to go too far in marginalising the relation between mythology, action and emotion. I have here solved this problem by adding the subcategory of reflexive implicit mythology to his theory, which has proved to be (at least in this instance) a key tool in solving the structural puzzle presented by any given set of implicit myths. This subdivision of implicit mythology also allows the analyst to avoid the danger of having so general a category that it is of little empirical use.

The encompassing nature of the concept of implicit mythology is a great strength but also a potential weakness. However, by exploring subtypes of implicit mythology, we have here been able to maintain a sense of an overarching framework at the same time as introducing an important element of precision. This ability of implicit mythology to operate simultaneously at the level of the individual and the collective, as well as the mundane and the transcendent, allows it to open understanding of the complex ways that identity is formed as part of an ongoing system of nested relations in this postcolonial city .... It is clear that when some of the seemingly most abstract and least popular elements of Lévi-Strauss's thought are engaged with the messy reality of ethnographic research, they prove to be inspirationally valuable tools, whose usefulness is only heightened by contemporary social developments.

References

Augé, M. (1995). *Non-places: Introduction to an Anthropology of Supermodernity*. London: Verso.

Buck, E. J. (1904). *Simla, Past and Present*. Calcutta: Thacker and Spink.

Carrithers, M. (2000). On Polytropy: Or the Natural Condition of Spiritual Cosmopolitanism in India: The Digambar Jain Case. *Modern Asian Studies* 34, no. 4: 831–861.

Chandramouli, C. (2011). *Census of India 2011: Provisional Population Totals*. New Delhi: Office of Registrar General & Census Commissioner, India.

Coleman, S., and Crang, M. (2002). 'Grounded Tourists and Travelling Theory'. In *Tourism: Between Place and Performance*, 1–21. Oxford: Berghahn Books.

Galinier, J. (2004). A Lévi-Straussian Controversy Revisited: The Implicit Mythology of Rituals in a Mesoamerican Context. *Journal of the Southwest* 46, no. 4: 661–677.

Houseman, M. (1998). *Naven or The Other Self: A Relational Approach to Ritual Action.* Leiden: Brill.

Hugh-Jones, C. (1979). *From the Milk River: Spatial and Temporal Processes in Northwest Amazonia.* Cambridge: Cambridge University Press.

Hugh-Jones, S. (1988). *The Palm and the Pleiades: Initiation and Cosmology in Northwest Amazonia.* Cambridge: Cambridge University Press.

Ingold, T. (2000). *The Perception of the Environment: Essays on Livelihood, Dwelling & Skill.* London: Routledge.

Lévi-Strauss, C. (1981). *The Naked Man: Introduction to Science of Mythology, Volume 4.* New York: Cape.

Lévi-Strauss, C. (1983). *From Honey to Ashes.* Chicago: University of Chicago Press.

Lévi-Strauss, C. (1994). *The Raw and the Cooked: Introduction to a Science of Mythology.* London: Pimlico.

Lévi-Strauss, C. (1996). *The Story of Lynx.* Chicago, IL: University of Chicago Press.

The spatial anchoring of myth in Wamira, Papua New Guinea

Miriam Khan

3

Miriam Khan is Professor Emerita of Anthropology at the University of Washington, the United States, having previously been a Professor of Anthropology there for almost thirty years. She has carried out extensive fieldwork in both Papua New Guinea and French Polynesia, where she was led by the realities of the field to make key contributions to the emerging field of the anthropology of place/space, and these find full form in her award-winning book *Tahiti beyond the Postcard: Power, Place, and Everyday Life*.

In the reading that we have chosen to include here, Khan profitably employs her deep understanding of both pacific ethnology and spatial theory to give a rich reading of Wamira mythology. This stands as a powerful demonstration of the importance of both attending to the geography of mythology and mythology's potential to deepen our understanding of human relations with non-human people. The article also speaks to the issues of colonial contact and contemporary heritage management that the previous chapter in this book raised, demonstrating how the particularities of these engagements with mythology shift the focus of the analysis without ever entirely obscuring the shared realities.

A village of about 450 inhabitants, Wamira lies on the northeast coast of Milne Bay Province in Papua New Guinea.[1] Immediately behind the hamlets, which are scattered under trees along a stony beach, a grassy plain extends to the base of the mountains that begin their ascent a few kilometers inland. About two kilometers to the west of Wamira, perched on top of a lofty plateau, is Dogura, the headquarters of the Anglican Mission in Papua New Guinea.

On my first walk through Wamira, in 1976, I noticed several arrangements of stones, all various shades of gray, some small and round, others large flat slabs, some composed in circles, and others standing individually. Some of the arrangements were prominently located on the pebbly surface of the neatly swept hamlets. Others were shrouded by trees and bushes in areas that used to be hamlets but were since overgrown with vegetation. None of them seemed to be natural occurrences, nor did they seem to be placed arbitrarily. Each time I walked past these stones, people would point them out to me and tell their stories. Some stones were said to be sitting circles where important elders sat in the olden days. Some were reminders of mythological events. Some were said to be specific ancestors or ancestresses. And some were even known to walk around!

In Melanesian societies, mythological events are often articulated with places in the landscape. Various aspects of a people's past are perceived, recorded, and experienced spatially in terms of geographical features. These tangible, visible forms may be hills, mountains, rivers, lakes, or other features in the landscape. Often they are stones like those just mentioned. Stones that have mythical significance are said to be the paraphernalia of ancestral heroes or heroines – or the ancestors or ancestresses themselves – that have turned to stone. In noting this 'enlivening influence of myth upon the landscape,' Malinowski (1922: 330) said:

> The mythical world receives its substance in rock and hill, in the changes in land and sea. The pierced sea-passages, the cleft boulders, the petrified human beings, all these bring the mythological world close to the natives, make it tangible and permanent. On the other hand, the story thus powerfully illustrated, re-acts on the landscape, fills it with dramatic happenings, which, fixed there forever, give it a definite meaning.

I examine this humanized, petrified, and immortalized landscape in Wamira in order to gain insights into larger epistemological concerns that are applicable to the whole of rural village societies in Melanesia....

[...]

Specifically, let us look at as seemingly gray and colorless an aspect of their past as stones, memorials to history that anthropologists have noticed but to which they have paid little analytical attention. I suggest that anthropologists' lack of concern with stones as significant data is, in part, because anthropologists come from literate societies and are trained in a discipline that acknowledges language as the communicative vehicle of culture par excellence. They have focused primarily on what they, in their Western tradition, would acknowledge as mythology – namely, oral accounts of events chronologically linked in time. Other than granting it the briefest mention, they seem to neglect the very ground over which they stumble while recording ancestral myths. For a richer, more dynamic understanding of a Melanesian sense of mythology, and for one more in keeping with the recent focus on historical consciousness as an aspect of a people's culture, anthropologists must look not only at oral accounts of origin myths, which are limited to particular literary genres, but also at the way in which these myths are recorded and recalled by other devices, such as physical forms in the landscape. Stones, while not the only type of physical marker, provide pertinent and interesting examples of the Melanesian attachment to place and the recording of myth and history in terms of space.[2]

Ancestral stones in Melanesia

All across Melanesia, are traces of peoples' mythology recorded in the landscape, especially in stone (Riesenfeld 1950). Evidence of historically important stones exists as far east as Vanuatu (Rodman 1985; Rubinstein 1981) and New Caledonia (Clifford 1982; Leenhardt 1930)....

[...]

Of the places I visited on the northeast coast, Boianai is the village with the most fascinating stone memorials to its past. One cannot walk more than a few paces without encountering an important stone or group of stones. Several of the village's stones are deeply incised with geometric designs, the meanings of which are not known by the inhabitants today.[3] Each stone has a connection with Boianai's unwritten past. Usually they represent the paraphernalia of a mythical hero or heroine who turned into stone. One such example is the myth of Wakeke, a totemic snake whose house foundation remains in stone in the village. In the middle of the foundation is a small stone bowl; the pot in which Wakeke is believed to have cooked his food.

Occasionally, the stones themselves played a prominent role (as stones) in the mythological narrative. For example, the following myth explains why the people of Boianai are related to the cassowary. In the myth, some stones are boiled into broth and others are hurled at the fleeing cassowary. The contemporary record of these facts lies strewn over the landscape. The oral account is as follows:

Long ago, a young woman lived with her husband and child. Every day her husband went to the garden, but returned without any food. Being hungry, the woman boiled stones. She and her child drank the broth from the cooked stones. One day, angered by her husband's behavior, she decided to turn herself into a cassowary and leave. She constructed wings for herself from coconut fronds, knee caps from coconut husks, and legs from black palm sticks. That day, when her husband returned, she spread her wings and fled. In an attempt to call his wife back, he tempestuously hurled stones after her. But she escaped and now lives as a cassowary in the mountains behind Boianai.

Today, one can still see the stones in the village. There is a massive pile of stones, a full meter high, that is said to have accumulated as the hungry woman, each day, boiled them and tossed them aside. The boulders that her husband threw after her lie scattered along the path that leads from the village towards the mountains.

In Wamira, some 30 kilometers further east along the coast, mythologically significant stones, while slightly less numerous than in Boianai, are viewed in an equally important light. As in Boianai, these stones anchor mythological narratives to the land. Some serve the additional purpose of being charters for proper social behavior. For example, in one myth two women, named Maradiudiva and Marakwadiveta, turned to stones; the stones' presence today reminds Wamirans about the proper etiquette for sharing food. As the myth relates, each time Maradiudiva went down to the sea to fetch salt water, her sister, Marakwadiveta, with whom she lived, gobbled up all the food and later fabricated lies about relatives who had come and eaten it. Hungry and hurt, Maradiudiva walked into the sea and turned into stone. Now, with her stony countenance, she stands all alone in the bay. As the tide rolls in and out, the Wamirans perceive Maradiudiva rising and descending; a steady reminder to all that social living hinges on the sharing of food. Her sister, Marakwadiveta, also turned to stone and today is perched on the hillside overlooking the sea from where her sister rises and descends.

By far the most remarkable and spirited stone in Wamira is Tauribariba. It is to his tale that I now turn in greater detail and upon which I base much of my later analysis of how myth is anchored in space and recalled, and altered, in the present.

Tauribariba, the stone that wandered from the Cathedral

Tauribariba, a Wamiran ancestor, turned into stone when Wamira was first founded. In 1936, missionaries removed his stone form from the village and cemented him into the pulpit wall of the cathedral at the nearby mission Station of Dogura.

[…]

Tauribariba is a small stone, about fifteen centimeters long. Before being placed in the cathedral wall, he formed part of a large circle of stones, about five meters in diameter, in the center of the Wamiran seaside hamlet of Irere. His sister, Tauanana, is a sizable boulder, about half a meter in diameter. She sits in the middle of the circle, surrounded by their 'children'; numerous small stones, most of which are no more than six or seven centimeters in diameter. All of them are believed to have the ability to walk around, and their favorite time for this activity is at night. Wamirans say that occasionally new children appear at the shore, having surfaced from the sea at night. When children appear in this manner they are added to the circle of stones, which is thus continually fluctuating in number.

In 1936, when the Cathedral of St. Peter and St. Paul was completed at Dogura, Father John Bodger decided to cement Tauribariba into the pulpit wall. This move was seen by the missionaries as symbolizing the transference of the Wamirans' 'worship of stone' to that of God....

[...]

The ideological tug-of-war over altering Tauribariba's location, however, was not yet resolved. The day he was permanently removed, waves of discontent rippled through Wamira. According to oral tradition, as a result of his disappearance his grief-stricken sister, Tauanana, 'walked back into the sea with many of their children.' Wamirans say that it was not until August 1974 that Tauanana surfaced from her maritime hideaway, at which time she silently appeared on the beach. When the people of Irere recognized her they immediately helped her ashore and placed her in the circle of stones 'where she belonged.' Over the next several months, the children also wandered up from the sea.[4]

In May 1975, two Melanesian students from the History Department of the University of Papua New Guinea visited Wamira to view the stones. One history student noted in Irere that the 'female stone could not be found but is regarded as still being at the site of the stones when not moving around' (Loeliger 1975).[5] It is interesting to note that the student, who had come to examine the sacred stones, ended his report with the following comment: 'From here we walked back along the beach towards Wedau, to the monument [a cement shrine] commemorating the landing of the first Anglican missionaries in 1891' (Loeliger 1975). Little did he realize, perhaps, that Tauribariba and Tauanana were also such physical monuments. Nor did he realize that the Melanesians' need to record significant events in durable ways (a fact that was thought interesting enough to warrant a picture in a textbook and an educational outing for university students) was not that different from the missionaries' need to erect monuments.

Now, let us explore what all this – an ancestral brother and sister who turned into stone, their determined and spirited mobility, and the struggle between villagers and missionaries over the placement of one of the stones – tells us about the Wamirans. Specifically, what does it tell us about how they objectify mythology, how they rewrite it as the need arises, and how they represent the passage of time?

Place as record of the past and validation of fact

[...]

Recording and recalling the past is important in providing a group with a sense of collective identity. In Melanesia, mythological plots are often shared over wide geographical areas. Terrain, however, is not. Each village uses local landscape to make the myth its own. Specific points in the landscape are not only visual reminders of the mythical characters and their actions, but become details of knowledge, the accuracy of which validates the narrator's and group's ownership of the story. For example, while recording myths, I was told on several occasions that a version narrated by someone else was totally inaccurate because, in the circuitous progression of place names, one of the names was wrong. Or, I was often told that individuals discovered they were related to one another because they knew the identical details of place names in mythological narratives.[6]

Physical anchoring of facts is used not only to give authority to one's knowledge, but also to prove truth. For example, when having to account for an action, a Melanesian might say, 'Yesterday when I stood next to the mango tree at such-and-such a creek, I saw so-and-so going to her garden.' By thus anchoring themselves in the environment, they verify their words for those who hear. This manner of lending credence to one's actions and statements is extremely important when such heated topics as sorcery accusations or insinuations of food theft are disputed. From a Melanesian perspective, once the words are voiced aloud and anchored geographically to a place they take on a literal and credible quality.

[...]

We may turn to the Tauribariba myth to examine the process by which events become anchored to physical objects. The critical moment in which Tauribariba was transformed from human being to stone occurred after the waves thrashed against the canoe and Tauanana fell into the sea. The metamorphosis took place when people rescued Tauribariba and lifted him to shore. 'Everyone rushed to get Tauribariba and carry (*pawei*) him ashore. They set (*tonei*) him in the center of the hamlet where he still is today.' The word *pawei* means to carry by strapping onto a pole. Pigs or heavy loads (and also people, in the days of cannibalism) are transported in this way. The word *tonei* means to stab, pierce, or spear. In recalling their past, Wamirans perceive Tauribariba as sitting in the canoe as a person, as being transported from the shore in an inhuman way, and as being put down and jabbed into the ground like a stone. Thus, in the process of being carried onto land and being set down, Tauribariba is transformed from human lineage leader to stony ancestor and permanent marker of the group's history and identity. The Maibouni people thus immortalized the events of their settlement in spatial context and physical form.[7] Interestingly, the arrival of the Maibouni people as a group is not yet immortalized when they come ashore as individuals. They record the event only when they collectively fetch their leader, the symbol of their group, and carry him onto land.

In Wamira, the sea is often endowed with the sacred character of creator, transformer, immortalizer, or recycler of life. In many instances where, in a myth, a person turns to stone, such as with Maradiudiva and Marakwadiveta or Tauribariba and Tauanana, the transformation takes place as the individual emerges from, or wanders into, the sea. The sea also plays an important role during transitional phases of growth and decay. For example, the umbilical cord of a newborn infant, the cutting of which indicates the beginning of an individual's independent growth, is ritually tossed out to sea. People who come in contact with a dead body must wash in the sea to cleanse what they view as contamination with decay and death. After a corpse is buried, relatives of the deceased throw stones into the sea, explaining that this action is meant to parallel the departure of the deceased's spirit across the sea. Moreover, the pungent salty odor of the sea is taboo for the growth of taro plants. This pungent sea odor is likened to that of menstrual blood, believed to be the ultimate creative substance of human life. Thus, the sea is endowed with sacred qualities during phases of transition from fetus to infant, from life to death, and from death to afterlife. The passage of time itself, in its most naturally occurring and visible form, is marked by such transitions of growth and decay in people, animals, and plants. Symbolic markers of growth and decay are all brought back to the sea in Wamiran thought and action. In this light, it is not surprising that the transformation of human beings or their paraphernalia into stone (i.e., the immortalization of that which is mortal, the transference of life from one form to another, or the embodiment of the passage of time) also takes place in the sea.

[...]

The malleable nature of mythic 'words'

'But,' every Westerner who hears the tales of Tauribariba and the wandering stones exclaims, 'the stones don't *really* move, do they?' The answer is, 'yes, they do.' In almost every region of Melanesia where stones are markers of past events, they are also described as being capable of movement. For example, Strathern (1979: 50) discusses the 'itinerant quality' of the stones in the Western Highlands of Papua New Guinea. Near Buka, in the Solomon Islands, stones are known not only to walk about at night, but to fish, swim, dance, and even grow (Blackwood 1935). In the North Solomon Islands' village of Arawa, one man, in order to demonstrate his disbelief in the power of stones, heaved several ancestral stones over a cliff. When they reappeared the next morning, his skepticism disappeared (Spriggs personal communication).

Perhaps an even more accurate response than 'yes, the stones move' would be to say that the stones are helped in their movements. When Wamira was first settled, the people probably found a stone on the beach and placed it on the ground to commemorate their successful landing, or even returned to Iveive to fetch the appropriate stone. Likewise, we can assume that Tauribariba was assisted during his nighttime jaunt back from the cathedral to the village. And Wamirans readily say that when they see the children stones on the beach, they put them where they belong.[8]

In examining the fact of the stones' movements, concern should be focused less on how the stones move and more on why it is necessary that they move, or be moved, at all. The answer, I suggest, has to do with mythology being negotiable and subject to revision. It also has to do with the difference between literate and nonliterate societies' ways of recording events. After recording the past, one must occasionally amend and alter it in order to live with it in the present. Literate societies, which record their past primarily in books, can rewrite their books. They can ban them or revise them. Even their concrete or metal monuments can be altered, defaced, torn down, rebuilt, blown up, or quietly ignored. Nonliterate people who record their past in stone, however, must grant their stones some freedom of movement. The Wamiran past, like everyone else's, is not static, but represents a dynamic, ongoing relationship between past events and the present. Events that are recorded in stone can most easily be changed by the movement of the stones. A past recorded and illustrated by stones that walk up from the sea, wander in the night, disappear from cathedral walls, jump from boats bound for Australia, and so on, is dynamically and dramatically receptive to alterations and additions. Because a stone can mark time, like time, it can move.

People the world over, no matter how they conceive of the passage of time, mark important events in relatively permanent forms, whether these be cement columns, bronze statues, engraved plaques, or ordinary-looking stones. A superb example of how various cultures combined efforts and symbols to record a significant event occurred in 1978 when the centennial of Maurice Leenhardt's birth was celebrated in New Caledonia.

> Leenhardt's monument is a white cement column about seven feet high … On the stele the missionary's profile … has been modeled in bronze by a noted Paris artist. An engraved plaque has been supplied by the powerful mining conglomerate … At the narrow summit of the monument the local committee [of Melanesians] has placed an ordinary-looking smooth stone. (Clifford 1982: 226)

In its accounts of the centennial, the press dwelled on the speeches, the dignitaries who attended, and the monument. However, 'the stone was ignored' (Clifford 1982: 226). This is unfortunate because, to quote Leenhardt's biographer,

> Rocks are forms of local history, mythic 'words.' Traditionally, the spirit of an ancestor could be seized and solidified in the form of a rock gathered from a riverbed. The stone atop Leenhardt's monument is taken from a stream in the home valley of one of the missionary's original pastoral students. It solidifies, gathers, symbolizes the presence of the ancestors, of Leenhardt, and of the Melanesians who made his work possible. It gathers the landscape's past. Rocks are crucial in New Caledonia … They stake out the habitat, providing permanent markers around and over which flow the ongoing currents of social, historical, and natural life. (Clifford 1982: 226–227)

In the same way that reporters neglected the stone at Leenhart's centennial, anthropologists, on the whole, have neglected an essential ingredient in their analyses of Melanesian mythology. By focusing analyses of local mythology primarily on oral narratives, or by assuming that notions of the past are expressed in terms of temporality, they have restricted their understanding of the people. A much richer, deeper, more versatile and vibrant past might emerge if anthropologists also attend, as Melanesians themselves do, to what is physically in front of them on the ground.

Notes

1   The fieldwork upon which this paper is based was conducted in Papua New Guinea from June 1976 to March 1978 and from August 1981 to March 1982.

2   It must be noted that this desire for concrete expression of events as a way of recalling the past, substantiating knowledge, and creating a sense of identity is not unique to Melanesians. To name only a few examples among many, Christians point to the blood-stained cloth in the Cathedral of Orvieto to recall the miracle demonstrating the transubstantiation of wine into Christ's blood during the Communion. Or they cite the Holy Shroud of Turin in the Cathedral of San Giovanni (albeit recently proclaimed a fake) to demonstrate the existence of Christ. American families, especially those with children to whom to pass on historical knowledge and cultural traditions, make frequent journeys to historical markers. Although most are man-made, many, such as Plymouth Rock, occur naturally.

3   Incised stones have also been found in other regions of Melanesia. In most cases the local inhabitants can no longer interpret the designs (Blackwood 1935).

4   I was given no explanation for her surfacing at that time, 38 years after her disappearance into the sea.

5   When I first arrived in Wamira in 1976, she was again present in the oval of stones. I saw her there in 1981 as well.

6   The idea that sharing mythological knowledge demonstrates proof of past relationship, of course, works best when narratives are unwritten and privately owned.

7   Here we are again reminded of the missionaries who came ashore and later erected a cement monument at the spot where they first arrived.

8   The movement may also take the form of an upright stone 'falling down.' For example, in one Wamiran hamlet there exists a group of stones called Aritabu. These stones commemorate a lineage's collective action in the past and still symbolize its feelings of cohesion in the present. Several years ago, one of the Aritabu stones 'fell down because the members of the lineage were not working together harmoniously' (i.e., sorcery among the members threatened the cohesion of the group). I was told that if the lineage members 'work together the stone will prop itself up once again.' Upon further inquiry, I realized that the erection of the stone would, in fact, be accomplished by lineage men pouring pork broth into the ground below the stone while raising it into its place. Thus, the broth would physically soften the ground for the stone's upraising while simultaneously and symbolically indicating group unity through communal feasting on pork.

References

Blackwood, B. (1935). *Both Sides of Buka Passage*. Oxford: The Clarendon Press.

Clifford, J. (1982). *Person and Myth: Maurice Leenhardt in the Melanesian World*. Berkeley: University of California Press.

Leenhardt, M. (1930). Notes d'Ethnologie Néo-Calédonienne. *Travaux et Mémoires de l'Institut d'Ethnologie* 8. Paris.

Loeliger, C. (1975). Visit to Wamira Village, Wednesday, 14 May 1975. Dogura: Anglican Mission Library.

Malinowski, B. (1922). *Argonauts of the Western Pacific*. New York: Routledge.

Riesenfeld, A. (1950). *The Megalithic Culture of Melanesia*. Leiden: Brill.

Rodman, M. (1985). Moving Houses: Residential Mobility and the Mobility of Residences in Longana, Vanuatu. *American Anthropologist* 87: 56–72.

Rubinstein, R. L. (1981). 'Knowledge and Political Process on Malo'. In *Vanuatu: Politics, Economics and Ritual in Island Melanesia*. Edited by M. R. Allen, 135–72. New York: Academic Press.

Strathern, A. (1979). Men's House, Women's House: The Efficacy of Opposition, Reversal, and Pairing in the Melpa Amb Kor Cult. *Journal of the Polynesian Society* 88: 37–51.

part four

Where are myths going?

Section A: Myths and popular culture

What good are old stories?

If myth's purpose is to provide a prescientific explanation of the world (cf Tylor 1871), then it follows that the vast majority, if not all, of this book's readers will have been drawn to the subject for no greater reason than curiosity. From such a perspective, we would expect to find that today myth's key function is obsolete, it only remaining an area of interest for those who have the luxury of engaging in trivial amusements, or the indulgent exploration of both past and distant worldviews. However, it is not hard to find people in post-scientific cultures who still proclaim the value of mythology, and several academics have seen either traces of myth or the continuation/development of myth in contemporary popular culture.

In this context, it is possible to detect three classifications of contemporary mythopoiesis. The first of these is captured well in JRR Tolkien's poem 'Mythopoeia', where Tolkien (as both myth-critic and mythmaker) argues that in the post-scientific world, he will not cast his own 'small golden sceptre down', but will instead 'make anew' and 'make no lie' for he makes 'by the law' by which he was made (Tolkien 2001). Tolkien's writing is here imagined by him as a deliberate attempt to make a new mythology that, through a sort of law of *Imago Dei*, has an inherent value and veracity. Yet this inherently Christian vision is not the only way that mythopoiesis operates in the modern world. Previously marginalized groups and minority religions are also embracing digital media as a way of keeping their mythology current. The question that heads this chapter (what good are old stories?) is taken from the video trailer of 'Never Alone', a video game developed in collaboration with mythmakers from the Iñupiat of Alaska as an exploratory development of a responsive form of contemporary communication for mythology (Winter and Boudreau 2018).

A second approach, which many academics and creators of contemporary or popular culture take, argues that modern media does not so much create new myths as build a new form of creative expression on the foundations of aspects of ancient myth. The analyst interested in exploring this approach detects elements of ancient myth in contemporary works and examines how these both shape and are transformed by the new medium that they find themselves within. Finally, there is a school of thought that sees myth as an inescapable process, which must therefore find natural expression in contemporary outpouring. From this perspective, the movement from myth to history (or even, at its most extreme, science) is merely an ethnocentric way of describing the move from one sort of mythology to another.

The articles that we have chosen to include here speak to this range of ways of understanding mythology today. The Suttons effectively suggest that myth is inescapable through exploration of mythologization of science. Dundes tracks elements of myth (and patriarchal thought) in contemporary children's fiction. Wilkes suggests a complex relation between mythology and contemporary fan fiction. This leaves open the possibility for a highly positive form of contemporary mythopoiesis, which (as in Tolkien's vision) has the power to recalibrate society. Collectively, these chapters both introduce a range of approaches to the analysis of mythology and suggest ways that techniques of mythological analyses can be applied to contemporary popular culture.

References

Tolkien, J. R. R. (2001). *Tree and Leaf: Including Mythopoeia*. London: HarperCollins Publishers Ltd.

Tylor, E. B. (1871). *Primitive Culture: Researches into the Development of Mythology, Philosophy, Religion, Art, and Custom* (Vol. 2). London: J. Murray.

Winter, J., and Boudreau, J. (2018). Supporting Self-Determined Indigenous Innovations: Rethinking the Digital Divide in Canada. *Technology Innovation Management Review* 8 (2): 38–48.

Amateur mythographies: Fan fiction and the myth of myth

Ika Willis

1

Ika Willis is Senior Lecturer in English Literature at the University of Woolongong (Australia). She holds a PhD in cultural studies, awarded by Leeds University (UK), and BA in classics, awarded by the University of Oxford (UK), she has previously taught at the University of Bristol (UK). She is currently engaged in research into the thought of Roland Barthes and reception theory. In this chapter, Willis combines her understanding of cultural studies with her knowledge of both classical mythology and reception theory to create a provoking and influential analysis of the way that online communities receive, rework and create mythology. Her analytical technique moves beyond basic arguments about the universality of myth, the preservation of mythology and the power of folk culture to present a highly nuanced reading of the intricate relationship between mythology and popular culture that opens the door for further explorations into this complex and pertinent area.

The term *myth* recurs across multiple scholarly and popular contexts.... It is manifold in its referents: the word *myth* might be used to refer to ancient Greek and Norse stories about gods, heroes, and monsters; to margarine advertisements, Romans in films, or Greta Garbo's face (Barthes [1957] 1972); or, of course, to fan fiction. In this paper, I will draw on approaches to myth from both scholarly and amateur contexts in order to investigate the usefulness of the term *myth*, and the limits of its usefulness, for our understanding of fan fiction as narrative form and as social practice.

The concept of myth has been important to the practice and analysis of fan work, including fan fiction, on three levels: content, form, and theory. On the level of content, various traditional tales – including classical and Norse mythologies – have provided characters, narratives, monsters, and story worlds for fans to use in the generation of new fictions, as attested by the 1,520 stories in the Greek and Roman Mythology fandom on Archive of Our Own (AO3) and the 3,200 stories labeled Greek Mythology on FanFiction.net (as at November 7, 2015). Classical myth thus forms part of the rich and diverse content of fan fiction and its multiple, crisscrossing story worlds. More importantly, however, the idea of myth has been used by both scholars and fans to generate, structure, and analyze fan fiction on a formal and a theoretical level. As a narrative form, fan fiction, like classical myth, is characterized by its multiple, self-contained but (at least potentially) overlapping or crisscrossing story worlds; as a social practice, it has been theorized as a counterhegemonic or resistant practice of mythopoesis.

However, although 'the theme of the fan community creating a popular myth has been a central facet of fan studies,' as Hellekson and Busse put it (2014: 21), echoing the subtitle of Camille Bacon-Smith's foundational *Enterprising Women: Television Fandom and the Creation of Popular Myth* (1992), the idea of contemporary popular culture as myth has found little traction among classical myth scholars. Some classical scholars using a content-based definition of myth study contemporary popular forms which transmit or deliver ancient myth (for example, Kovacs 2011: 11: 'the masses have always been consumers of myth, though the mode of delivery changes frequently'). This approach, however, tends to lead to readings of contemporary popular texts which are entirely centered on and circumscribed by questions about the accuracy with which such texts transmit their ancient mythic content. Thus, for example, Amanda Potter's essay on the Furies in *Xena* (1995–2001) and *Charmed* (1998–2006) worries that 'viewers who had only the episodes on which to base their readings of the Furies could come away confused about the myth' (2009: 233–234); Ghita and Andrikopoulos, writing on the videogame *Rome: Total War* (2004), wonder whether they should 'condemn the product for propagating inaccuracies and creating false beliefs about the ancient world, or praise it for reviving the interest of the public in antiquity, by whatever means' (2009: 119). Either way, the contemporary text is seen only as a transmission or mediation of past content, not – as fan studies would usually have it – as a present-day contribution to the still-living tradition of myth.

Classical scholars who define myth not simply in terms of content but in terms of context or function are also disinclined to make connections between ancient and contemporary myth. Instead, they are concerned to emphasize the particularity of classical myth, and – particularly since the 1980s/1990s – have understood myth as being necessarily and irreducibly embedded in its social, historical, and cultural context. In his 1994 book *Imaginary Greece: The Contexts of Greek Mythology*, Richard Buxton defines myths as stories that are 'socially embedded' in contrast to 'idiosyncratic narratives' constructed by particular authors for particular ends (1994: 17). Citing Claude Calame's highly influential 1988 book *Métamorphoses du mythe en Grèce antique*, Buxton argues that if the terms *myth* and *mythology* 'are so used as to elide cultural differences in the context and content of story-telling, then they are doing more harm than good' (1994: 13).

Yet fans and pop culture audiences more often than not use these terms precisely to 'elide cultural differences,' to make connections between stories from widely different historical and cultural contexts. At the very same moment that classical scholars were turning away from comparativist decontextualizing models of myth toward an understanding of myth as 'socially embedded,' a strongly universalizing reading of Joseph Campbell's *Hero with a Thousand Faces* (1949) was infusing through popular storytelling, viewing, and critical practices, via George Lucas and Christopher Vogler (a story consultant at Disney who circulated a memo on the Hero's Journey in 1985, expanded into *The Writer's Journey: Mythic Structure for Storytellers and Screenwriters* in 1992). This model of myth sees it as an underlying universal pattern for storytelling which can be found – in the words of Vogler's memo – in 'every story ever told' since 'in his study of world hero myths Campbell discovered that they are all basically the same story,' one that 'springs from a universal source in the collective unconscious' (n.d.). This model has been influential on fans and remains important to at least some scholarly work on fan fiction: for example, Natalie Montano cites Campbell as 'one of the foremost scholars on myth' (2013: 695) in a paper on fan fiction and intellectual property law to which I will return below.

Classicists who follow Calame and Buxton in rejecting Campbell's model and moving to a definition of myth as socially embedded story have tended simply to dismiss popular cultural forms and practices which draw on this model, seeing them as fundamentally theoretically flawed and thus unworthy of scholarly analysis. However, instead of seeing these uses of myth in contemporary popular culture as irrelevant and/or incompetent contributions to scholarly discourse on myth, it might be more productive to see the interaction between fan fiction and classical myth as a site of intersection, negotiation, and contestation between different ways of doing myth. Indeed, as Bruce Lincoln points out in his book *Theorizing Myth*, the domain of myth has always been a site of exchange between amateur and scholarly knowledges: in the 19th century in particular, discourse on myth 'moved freely across academic and popular settings' (1999: 74). Moreover, Lincoln argues that discourse on myth is itself a form of mythmaking in that it tells 'a story with an ideological dimension' (216) about the past in order to situate us in the present. Thus the methodologies of the myth scholar should also be used to uncover and analyze the mythmaking aspects of discourses on myth, both popular and scholarly.

[…]

The myth of myth as folk culture

The term *myth* is persistently used in fannish and scholarly contexts to argue for common or popular ownership of stories, often explicitly or implicitly invoking parallels with ancient myth. Will Brooker addresses this point explicitly in his book on Batman, *Hunting the Dark Knight*, in which he distinguishes three modes of continuity in the Batman universe, three 'senses of Batman': myth, brand, and canon. He writes: 'We could call the first sense of Batman the *myth*. "Metatext" would also serve – in Reynolds's words, "a summation of all the existing texts plus all the gaps that those texts have left unspecified" – but "myth" captures better the sense that this Batman belongs to everyone; to the public, to popular memory, to a modern folk culture' (2012: 152).

As Brooker's discussion makes clear, the use of the term *myth* here specifically invokes a folkloric model linked to a particular understanding of intellectual and cultural property: 'Batman belongs to everyone' because he is part of 'a modern folk culture.' The same argument about myth as a mode of folklore and therefore as a mode of ownership is made, repeatedly and with particular intensity, about George Lucas's *Star Wars* (1977). One fan, Mark Magee, whose arguments have been given quasi-canonical status in academic fan studies by being cited in Henry Jenkins's book *Convergence Culture*, writes:

> If you were a kid in the seventies, you probably fought in schoolyards over who would play Han, lost a Wookie action figure in your backyard and dreamed of firing that last shot on the Death Star. And probably your daydreams and conversations weren't about William Wallace, Robin Hood and Odysseus, but, instead, light saber battles, frozen men and forgotten fathers. In other words, we talked about our legend (quoted in Jenkins 2006: 150).

One of the key functions of the appeal to myth (or legend) here is to refuse or deny one of the most obvious differences between ancient myth and contemporary mass culture: the economic conditions of its production and circulation. Unlike Robin Hood and Odysseus, Han Solo is trademarked; his name and likeness are the intellectual property of Lucasfilm. Through childhood play, parody, conversational references, and transformative fan works, Han circulates in contexts far beyond the original three films in which he appears – even far beyond the officially licensed novels, films, comics, video games, and merchandise – but he is not available for any playwright or vase painter to use at will for commercial gain.

[…]

Describing the texts of popular culture as myths is, then, a way of claiming commercial culture as common culture and ultimately as the basis for a genuine popular or folk culture – fan culture – that exists outside capitalist networks of production, distribution, and consumption (or at least in a tense or resistant relationship to those networks). Another *Star Wars* fan, Elizabeth Durack, also cited by Jenkins, takes this argument to its logical conclusion and claims that *Star Wars* belongs – morally, at least – to its fans:

> Perhaps the fans have a moral right to use *Star Wars*-related names and creative concepts at will because *Star Wars* is such a deeply ingrained part of our culture. The very success and ubiquity of the franchise is what makes it hover (dangerously?) close to the border of being something no longer privately-owned, but public cultural property. It has been observed by many writers that *Star Wars* (based purposely on the recurring themes of mythology by creator George Lucas) and other popular media creations take the place in modern America that culture myths like those of the Greeks or Native Americans did for earlier peoples. Holding modern myths hostage by way of corporate legal wrangling seems somehow contrary to nature (Durack 2000).

[...]

Durack suggests that *Star Wars* belongs to its fans because its place in the settler society of the modern United States is analogous to the place and function of myth in Ancient Greek and Native American societies: *Star Wars* as myth therefore has an organic and authentic cultural significance that means that it cannot be owned by corporations. This claim rests on the idea that myth works in the same way in both traditional and modern societies. However, Durack's argument also rests on a strong distinction between the two types of society – between the modern Enlightenment practices of legal wrangling and copyright and the natural practices of myth. In fact, the culture myths of Indigenous peoples in both North America and Australia are themselves the subject of a great deal of legal wrangling, precisely because the rights of the stories' owners have not been respected, and sacred stories have been appropriated, circulated, and sold for profit by settlers. Myth is thus being used here to elide or obscure the particular contemporary social, cultural, and legal dynamics of fan fiction rather than to illuminate them.

[...]

Fannish claims to ownership of popular texts on the basis of a myth about myth as folklore thus seem to justify some of the criticisms made by classical scholars about the poverty of a decontextualized understanding of myth that elides cultural and historical differences in storytelling practices as well as flattening out power differentials. However, as I turn away from fannish theories of myth to fan fictional practices in my next two sections, I hope to show that the practice of fan fiction is richer and more interesting than its theory. In particular, fan fiction is far ahead in its capacity to articulate arguments about story, hegemony, and power.

The myth of myth as counterhegemonic discourse

[…]

Lincoln argues that we should attend in more detail to the way in which agency operates in the 'act of narration' of myths and use 'a more dialectic, eminently political theory of narration, one that recognizes the capacity of narrators to modify details of the stories that pass through them, introducing changes in the classificatory order as they do so, most often in ways that reflect their subject position and advance their interests' (1999: 149).

Lincoln's call for a theory of narration that 'recognizes the capacity of narrators to modify details of … stories … in ways that reflect their subject position and advance their interests' precisely echoes the way in which fan fiction studies has understood transformative fan work ever since the pioneering work of Constance Penley and Henry Jenkins. Jenkins's and (especially) Penley's analysis draws on a theory of myth as female-voiced and counterhegemonic discourse, linking fan practices to the mythopoetic practices and theory developed in second-wave feminism in two interrelated contexts.

Mythopoesis appeared in second-wave feminism firstly via the return to the theory of originary matriarchy. This theory was developed in the mid-19th century by the Swiss anthropologist Johann Jakob Bachofen, was fleshed out at the turn of the 20th century by the pioneering feminist classicist and myth scholar Jane Ellen Harrison, and served as a potent source of inspiration to second-wave matriarchalists like Mary Daly: according to this theory, the earliest human societies were matriarchal. Patriarchy arrived later and violently, seeking to erase all traces of originary matriarchy; this historical event is registered in Greek myth through stories about the rise to dominance of the Olympian pantheon – particularly Zeus, who became King and Father of Gods by destroying his mother.

Secondly, myth emerged in second-wave feminist discourse in the theory of women's writing as revisionist mythmaking associated with poets like Adrienne Rich, Anne Sexton, and alta, and developed theoretically by second-wave poet-critics including Adrienne Rich (again), Hélène Cixous, and Alicia Ostriker. This theory sought to resolve debates about the nature of women's writing by arguing that differences between men's and women's writing arise not from essential differences between men and women but from the ways in which men and women are positioned differently with respect to culture and language.

Tina Passman brings both strands of feminist mythmaking together in an essay in a very early collection of feminist classical scholarship, writing:

> In this particular cultural moment when many of us cry for a revolution in human thought and action, some feminisms have anchored their visionary work firmly to the past, linking the notions 'ancient' and 'future' … The unearthing of evidence for early matriculture in the West – Europe, Asia Minor, and Africa – furnishes

the seed for this feminist re-visioning and re-construction of a matristic past and carries with it a web of ethics, aesthetics, history, and spirituality (1993: 182).

Passman's careful positioning of this matristic past as something that can only be accessed through feminist re-visioning and reconstruction – not through the disciplinary norms of history – echoes the attitude of most second-wave feminists, including Adrienne Rich. They are simultaneously doubtful about the reliability of historical accounts of ancient matriarchies, on the one hand, and, on the other, suspicious of the intensity with which such societies are declared impossible by mainstream scholars. Both Passman and Rich, tellingly, turn to the term *myth* to resolve (or dissolve?) this contradiction between history and ideology: Passman writes of a 'feminist myth of a matricultural origin for the West' that 'proposes a view of cultural history that challenges the basic values and assumptions of Western patriarchy' (1993: 182).

This powerful feminist myth of myth – the idea of a feminine origin for culture and history, erased by a late-coming patriarchy – is given equally powerful form in Lisztful's 2009 fan fic *The First Place* (2009). In the fic, the goddess Hera travels through a contemporary world, gathering several of her children and stepchildren – Dionysus, Apollo, Ares, Hephaestus, Artemis, Heracles, and Aphrodite – for a birthday party. At the party, she announces to her children: 'I fear I'd been made to believe that your father came first. That he made all of us, all of this. In that, I was incorrect ... I am the first ... I am the beginning. Life springs from me, and always shall.' When Zeus arrives, she says to him:

> Hera is not my only name. I have been many names. Ma Gu, Gaia, Ninhursag, Hathor, Isis, Spider Grandmother. I am Tiamat, Inanna, Ninsun, Asherah, Ashtart, Cybele, Danu. I am Frekka, Holda, Frau Holle, Potria Theron, Erda, and Umai, Mahimata, Shakti. I am all of these and more. I am the beginning, the first, the place from which all the rest is born. I am the mother of it all, and I love all of it ... From this point forward ... I intend to be all of these names, and all of these ideas. All of it. It is I, and you shall no longer wear it as your own. I know you can't, for in the naming, I've found all of the power I didn't before know was mine.

This moment draws on a number of important second-wave feminist re-visionings of myth and history. Firstly, the myth of an originary matriarchy, lost and erased with the advent of Zeus but still at least in principle retrievable. Hera's account of the loss of her originary status – 'I was made to believe that your father came first ... In that, I was incorrect' – closely echoes Harrison's account of the patriarchal-Olympian revisionist account of the birth of Pandora, who, Harrison argues, was an important goddess prior to the advent of Olympian religion:

> Zeus the Father will have no great Earth-goddess, Mother and Maid in one, in his man-fashioned Olympus, but her figure is from the beginning, so he remakes it; woman ... who made all things, gods and mortals alike, is become their

plaything, their slave … To Zeus, the archpatriarchal bourgeois, the birth of the first woman is but a huge Olympian jest (quoted in Passman 1993: 193).

Secondly, Lisztful's title, *The First Place*, invokes a tradition of second-wave (and later) feminist appropriations of the concept of *chora*. Plato introduces *chora* in the dialogue *Timaeus*, where he associates it with the terms *womb* and *nurse* and says that it 'provides a position for everything that comes to be.' *Chora*, which is closely associated with motherhood, is the originary space in which spatiality, signification, and life become possible – it is, literally, the first place. As has been traced, for example, by Alex Wardrop (2013), *chora* was taken up by a series of feminist philosophers, beginning with Julia Kristeva in *Revolution in Poetic Language*. Kristeva theorizes an originary maternity, which Lisztful's story superimposes on Bachofen's/Harrison's myth of originary matriarchy: Hera speaks from and as *chora* when she says 'I am the beginning, the first, the place from which all the rest is born.'

Finally, Hera's words 'in the naming, I've found all of the power I didn't before know was mine' allude, appropriately enough, to Mary Daly's *Beyond God the Father*, the founding text of matriarchalist feminism, which sets out from the premise that 'Women have had the power of *naming* stolen from us' and attempts to take that power back (Daly 1978: 8).

Lisztful's story thus also thematizes the stealing or reclaiming of language that Alicia Ostriker identifies as the fundamental characteristic of feminist mythmaking in her essay 'The Thieves of Language,' writing:

> Whenever a poet employs a figure or story previously accepted or defined by a culture, the poet is using myth, and the potential is always present that the use will be revisionist: that is, the figure or tale will be appropriated for altered ends, the old vessel filled with new wine, initially satisfying the thirst of the individual poet but ultimately making cultural change possible. Historic and quasi-historic figures like Napoleon and Sappho are in this sense mythic, as are folktales, legends, and Scripture (1985: 317).

Lisztful's story, I would argue, is genuinely mythic according to almost any of the criteria or models referred to in this paper. However, this is not because it includes subject matter, characters, or narrative structures drawn from classical mythology, but because it is embedded in a web of culturally meaningful and ideologically contested stories. That is, its mythic characters are not so much Hera, Zeus, and Aphrodite as they are Jane Harrison, Mary Daly, Julia Kristeva, and Hélène Cixous: it is from these characters and their stories that *The First Place* gains its narrative and social power. It is mythic not because of its content but because of its narrative form and its effectiveness as a social practice – two factors that, are interrelated.

Lisztful's use of feminist myths of myth is an example of fan fiction's capacity to elaborate a more sophisticated version of syncretism than does Vogler's reading of Campbell …. *The First Place* practices a mode of fannish mythmaking which does not simply assert an equivalence between all storytelling, all people, and all cultures, or between Greek myth, Native American myth, and *Star Wars*. Instead, it draws on both equivalence and difference to bring two mythic systems together and use them to interrogate one another.

[...]

Conclusion

The distinction between scholarly and popular models of myth with which I started has, I hope, been dissolved in the course of this paper: some popular models of myth can be traced back to scholarly sources (Herder, Campbell), but, simultaneously, the mythmaking practice of amateurs – fans and other writers, including second-wave feminist writers – converges with critical scholarly work on hyperseriality, producing fictocritical discourse on the crisscrossing story worlds of myth that itself crosses the border between academic and fannish work.

... In the reinvigorated discourse on myth today, I see opportunities for fans, pop culture scholars, and classicists to work together in order to recalibrate categories and redistribute privilege, including the categories and privileges that are used to divide the makers and readers of myth into scholarly and amateur communities, with little or no genuine dialogue going on between us.

References

Barthes, Roland. ([1957] 1972). 'Myth Today'. In *Mythologies*. Translated by Annette Lavers, 107–164. London: Jonathan Cape.

Brooker, Will. (2012). *Hunting the Dark Knight: Twenty-First Century Batman*. London: I.B. Tauris.

Buxton, Richard. (1994). *Imaginary Greece: The Contexts of Mythology*. Cambridge: Cambridge University Press.

Daly, Mary. (1978). *Gyn/Ecology: The Metaethics of Radical Feminism*. Boston: Beacon Press.

Durack, Elizabeth. (2000). 'fans.starwars.con'. *Echo Station*, 3 March. http://www.echostation.com/editorials/confans.htm.

Hellekson, Karen, and Busse, Kristina, eds. (2014). *The Fan Fiction Studies Reader*. Iowa City: University of Iowa Press.

Jenkins, Henry. (2006). *Convergence Culture: Where Old and New Media Collide*. New York: New York University Press.

Kovacs, George. (2011). 'Comics and Classics: Establishing a Critical Frame'. In *Classics and Comics*. Edited by George Kovacs and C. W. Marshall, 3–24. Oxford: Oxford University Press. http://dx.doi.org/10.1353/are.2015.0008.

Lincoln, Bruce. (1999). *Theorizing Myth: Narrative, Ideology, and Scholarship*. Chicago: University of Chicago Press.

Montano, Natalie. (2013). Hero with a Thousand Copyright Violations: Modern Myth and an Argument for Universally Transformative Fan Fiction. *Northwestern Journal of Technology and Intellectual Property* 11, no. 7: 689–705.

Ostriker, Alicia. (1985). 'The Thieves of Language: Women Poets and Revisionist Mythmaking'. In *The New Feminist Criticism: Essays on Women, Literature and Theory*. Edited by Elaine Showalter, 314–338. New York: Pantheon-Books.

Passman, Tina. (1993). 'Out of the Closet and into the Field: Matriculture, The Lesbian Perspective, and Feminist Classics'. In *Feminist Theory and the Classics*. Edited by Nancy Sorkin Rabinowitz and Amy Richlin, 181–209. London: Routledge.

Potter, Amanda. (2009). 'Hell Hath No Fury Like a Dissatisfied Viewer: Audience Responses to the Presentation of the Furies in *Xena: Warrior Princess* and *Charmed*'. In *Classics for All: Reworking Antiquity in Mass Culture*. Edited by Dunstan Lowe and Kim Shahabudin, 217–236. Newcastle-upon-Tyne: Cambridge Scholars Press.

Vogler, Christopher. (1992). *The Writer's Journey: Mythic Structure for Storytellers and Screenwriters*. Studio City, CA: Michael Wiese Productions.

Wardrop, Alexandra. (2013). 'Feminist Criticism and Plato's Timaeus-Critias: Rethinking Chora'. PhD diss., University of Bristol.

Storm power, an icy tower and Elsa's bower: The winds of change in Disney's *Frozen*

Lauren Dundes, Madeline Streiff
and Zachary Streiff

Lauren Dundes is Professor of Sociology at McDaniel College, the United States. Over an eighteen-year period she has been one of the most consistently influential analysts of Disney's Princess mythology. Her early work on Disney was carried out in collaboration with the folklorist Alan Dundes, whose work can be found elsewhere in this volume (Part 2, section B, Chapter 2). Together, Lauren and Alan published separate analyses of the Little Mermaid (2000), Pocahontas (2001) and Simba (2006). In more recent years, Lauren has collaborated in her Disney analyses with the younger family generation, especially Madeline and Zachary Strieff.

Dr Madeline Strieff is a research assistant for the journal *Regulation and Governance*. She has published articles that analyse *Mulan* (2016), *Moana* (2017) and *Frozen* (2017).

Dr Zachary Strieff is a research attorney for the superior court of California.

   The three authors (Dundes, Strieff and Strieff) collaborate in the article that we have chosen to include here to present a mythopoetic analysis of the character of Elsa, in the Disney film *Frozen*. It is possible to detect Freudian sympathies in their technique, and this is used to disrupt the cosy acceptance of *Frozen* as a myth that promotes equality. The article acts as a useful example of both how the study of myth is crucial to the understanding of contemporary politics/society and how something that is not readily classified as mythology can benefit from the application of the analyses techniques presented elsewhere in this volume.

Among Disney's blockbusters, Frozen (2013) has achieved resounding success as its most popular animated feature yet. Earnings exceeded a billion United States (US) dollars (Hibberd 2017) and YouTube views of just one version of its musical chart-topping hit, 'Let it Go', approached the 1.5 billion mark within five years of the film's debut (YouTube 2018). In the years subsequent to its release, interest in the movie has prompted plans for a *Frozen* sequel (due out in 2019 (Gander 2018)), as brisk sales of *Frozen* merchandise continue to drive this 'cultural behemoth' (Perry 2017). with influence that has been compared to Shakespeare (Dockterman 2018).... According to Zipes (2011), 'The telos of all Disney's fairy-tale films is to shape the vision of spectators so that they are convinced and believe that they share in the values and accomplishments of the narrative, thus obviating any or all contradictions ... through the systematic dissemination of images in books, advertising, toys, clothing, houseware articles, posters, postcards, radio, and other artifacts that have mesmerized us' (pp. 25–26). Yet despite delivering an 'annexed' version of family entertainment based on pre-existing fairy tales (Schickel 1997), *Frozen* has struck a chord in audiences, resulting in cultural tintinnabulation at a deep – and likely unconscious – level....

[...]

In this paper, we present a mythopoetic analysis of *Frozen* given the film's recapitulation of themes of Greek mythology. Myths are known for their adaptability and ability to 'encapsulate cultural patterns ... [and] projections of basic human dilemmas or impulses' (Dundes 1984: 3). In fact, archetypes from Greek mythology arguably bridge millennia with lasting resonance. Since popular Disney films tap into an 'era's complex and evolving' mores, they capture cultural shifts, especially gender-related conflicts (Davis 2007: 17). Our methodology involves content analysis with an unconventional emphasis on the symbolic and lexicographic manifestations of masculinity and effeminacy. Our analysis includes an examination of the portrayal of Olaf and Marshmallow, the snowflake emblem of Elsa's ice palace, and storm symbolism. A major theme explored is Elsa's command of storms as representative of her subversion of male power, which is imitative of the symbolism of Zeus, the Olympian king. As the Snow Queen, Elsa emulates Zeus in his position at the top of the social hierarchy in a cloud palace above Mount Olympus; Elsa lives in her palace atop the North Mountain, complete with a soaring steeple mounted on a phallic spire. Elsa conjures storm power associated with Zeus that denotes his consummate manhood (as symbolized by his phallic thunderbolt insignia). In taking on the role of Zeus, Elsa bucks the seemingly entrenched social order that defines males as the ultimate creators, with females as secondary.

[...]

Wind as fertilizing and gender

Historically, the wind as a fecundating agent explains the role of the Holy Ghost (or spirit) in the pregnancy of the Virgin Mary (see Jones 1951; Zirkle 1936). *Geist* (ghost) is related to spirit, breath, or wind, given the belief in wind-eggs (Zirkle 1936). *Spiritus* meant either breath or ghost with the 'consistent element that men seek to live without recourse to women' (Dundes 1976: 234). In *Genesis*, a wind moved over the waters (v1:2), after which God animated Adam by breathing life into his nostrils (v2:7). The conflation of breath and soul lends meaning to a newborn's initial breath that allows the spirit into the body while a person's last breath (or rattle) signals the spirit's exit from the body (Ryrie 1997). Wind power is also evident in the notion of fanning the flames (of passion or anger), as well as the expression 'as the spirit moves me', denoting when a person feels a sort of supernatural motivation that is beyond logic or consciousness.

Critical to this analysis is the portrayal of Elsa's various special powers derived through wind and storms as a curse. According to *Frozen* co-director Jennifer Lee, 'One sister [has] a superpower – or an *affliction* – and one [is] ignored because her sister's taking up all the energy in the room' (Solomon 2013, emphasis added). Her power serves as an apparently frightening reversal of traditional gender hierarchy in which a woman controls procreation in the context of a *Frozen* atmosphere, given that the title serves as a constant reminder that Elsa's 'affliction' resulted in an 'eternal winter', as Anna says (56:52), which is notable since creating something everlasting is normally enviable.

Elsa's power is clearly an affliction, because she initially abuses it to the detriment of the whole society, selfishly inviting the storm to 'rage' on while she grapples with the consequences of her emotional lability (in defiance of the expectation of women's self-sacrifice and altruism [Dundes 2001]); at one point, when she and Anna talk in her ice palace, she confesses to her sister, 'I can't control the curse' (57:16–18). Shortly thereafter, in a soliloquy, she watches in frustration as sharp icicles emerge from the walls of her palace, as she chants in vain, 'Control it. Don't feel – don't feel – don't feel.' In the film's representation of the 2013 zeitgeist (the ghost or spirit of the time), anxieties about rising female power (reflected in Elsa's selfishness and lack of control) may have been conflated with growing concerns that storms presage anthropogenic climate anomalies,…

[…]

Let it go – Bucking the trend of songs as evoking romantic enchantment

Elsa's first act of parthenogenesis occurs during 'Let it Go'. As a song, it is a form of incantation or en-*chant*-ment (see *chanter, cantar,* or cantor, related to singing). Typically, songs in Disney princess movies promote the heterosexual coupling of a female with a dominant male that can cause relative strangers to fall in love, especially in a magically short period of time; this phenomenon is parodied in *Frozen's* song 'Love is an Open Door', which precipitates the engagement of Hans and Anna the same day they met. 'Love is an Open Door' mocks characters such as *Sleeping Beauty's* Aurora, who falls for Prince Philip during a song in which they dance in the woods, and most classically Cinderella, who loves Prince 'Charming' after their ballroom dance, which is accompanied by singing.... Thus, the magic of singing is related to its ability to magically 'charm' a person (or 'charm' a snake in the case of blowing a phallic wind instrument called a *pungi*). The result is a person who might say he is *enchanté* (enchanted) by a woman who makes him feel spellbound. This is a fundamental concept in Disney princess movies, given the ubiquity of enchantment, a phenomenon linked to wind in the sense that the word 'air' is a synonym for song. Moreover, it indicates how the magic associated with men is charming, whereas magic performed by women is chilling (discussed below).

However, Elsa and her propensity for inducing freezing are the antithesis of an enchantress that mesmerizes men. At her coronation ball, Elsa tells Anna, 'No one is getting married' (26:22–23) after Anna and Hans tell her of their nuptial plans. Note that she does not say, 'It's too soon to get married' or 'You must ensure you've found the right person'. Instead, she implies permanent restrictions on sexual behavior for both her sister and herself, suggesting her own lack of interest in bewitching a man. In fact, Anna criticizes Elsa's tendency 'to shut people out' (26:41–43).

[...]

Women as nubile

Elsa's lack of interest in males in any capacity stands in sharp contradistinction to her sister, Anna. Elsa is more termagant than nubile nymph; she is the storm, raging on (as she sings in 'Let it Go'). She has no interest in assuming the passive female role.... Instead, similar to Zeus, she is capable of parthenogenesis, while wielding power that intimidates, and indeed emasculates men such as the unemployed icemen that describe Elsa as an 'icy force' in the first line of the film (in *The Frozen Heart: Ice Worker's Song*) and who see her as sexually inaccessible (see Streiff and Dundes 2017a). She not only prevents them from working but also usurps their role, as we see when Anna knocks on the doors of Elsa's ice palace. The doors open for her, but Kristoff is told not to enter. Anna is nervous about how Elsa will react to him and thus instructs him not to come inside, prompting him to stammer with frustration, 'But, but ... come on! It's a palace made of ice. Ice is my life' (53:36–38). Thus, Anna goes in alone (initially), showing that Elsa has both eclipsed the male role of ice harvester and has no desire for males to enter her (ice palace).

This scene cues the audience to see Elsa as hostile to men, tempestuous rather than nubile.... Nubile women are highly prized, and even likely to incite envy. We see ritualized protection against invidious reactions to their desirability in wedding 'toasts' that connote metaphorical drying, perhaps related to the evil eye in which enviable situations risk inviting desiccation committed by those who (often inadvertently) covet another person's good fortune (e.g., presumed impending fertility for newlyweds). Note that nubile women are young (not older, presumably infertile women). As cloudlike, they augur marital bliss of ascendance to the mythical cloud nine.

[…]

Elsa's parthenogenesis in 'let it go'

In a reversal of male womb envy, Elsa circumvents any male control as she explains in 'Let it Go'. She describes a howling wind and 'a swirling storm inside' as she lets loose her creative potential in the birth of Olaf (32:09–10), which is marked by a swirly gust (including a whooshing sound simulating wind that is blowing snow). Shortly thereafter, she uses her ungloved hands to send out gusts and release sparks that create a swirling whirlwind that morphs into Marshmallow (accompanied by the sound effects of a breath/small gust of wind) (58:12–15). The power of wind is also manifested in the terms 'whirlwind romance' and 'windfall', which are phenomena that suggest a supernatural element. Parthenogenesis through wind is an ancient concept: 'Most classical and medieval philosophers believed that certain mammals and birds could be impregnated by wind'; the wind's breath allowed conception 'without copulation' attributable to anemophily or wind pollination (Zirkle 1936: 95). The wind that Elsa conjures is similar to the Holy Spirit (or breath) responsible for Christ's virgin birth, and many other examples of impregnation by the wind in myths (Zirkle 1936).

[…]

Elsa conceives but does not carry her progeny in utero; she skips pregnancy, calling into question her ability to be a good mother. This point is demonstrated in an exchange occurring when Elsa is finally reunited with Olaf in her ice castle, where significantly more of her effort has gone (i.e., in her castle, not her children) – perhaps since it is 'a man's' home that is his castle, rather than a woman who should preside over such a lofty structure. The following scene poignantly exposes Elsa's maternal deficits:

Olaf (shyly):
You built me. You remember that?
Elsa (surprised):
And you're alive?
Olaf (unsure):
Um … I think so? (55:03–10)

Elsa then looks down at her hands, presumably contemplating their power to give life to the non-animated pre-pubescent version of the snowman in spite of her being a cold ice princess who lacks maternal warmth. In her capacity as a Snow Queen or a queen in a surrogate parent role, she fails, as her subjects suffer under her rule.…

[…]

The significance of gender non-conforming sons

At the end, similar to a pampered son or mama's boy (Coyle et al. 2016), Olaf receives his own personal flurry from Elsa, a salient gift that will protect him against the very-real male fears of (metaphorical) melting, but that also emasculates him, since males are supposed to take care of themselves and take risks. The need for the flurry reiterates that without men, the powerful woman's child is being reared in a way in which he will never be a real man. Although Marshmallow is a menacing palace guard, when he dons Elsa's crown, as Patterson and Spencer (2017) note, Marshmallow's cross-dressing is supposed to bring a laugh. The fact that this is a hidden scene that many viewers miss (because most people do not watch all of the credits) is a parting reminder to the audience that males who self-feminize are funny, and a means to leave audiences with a feel-good moment of superiority. A key part of this post-script is its sense of voyeurism in which Marshmallow hides his sexuality, as he furtively looks around to make sure no one sees his 'deviance' before he dons the crown. This contrasts with Olaf, who is more open about his sexuality as expressed in the carrot as phallus, including scenes of his carrot sagging due to melting, signaling a loss of a metaphorical erection (a fear known as medomalacuphobia). In any case, both snowmen escape the threat of melting, allowing them to retain a modicum of masculinity, and model different types of gender non-conformity.

[…]

Elsa as Zeus' daughter?

Anna's character develops in part within the context of her relationships with men and relatively mundane interactions. Yet it is hard to imagine Elsa in similar scenarios, even though the two women are sisters. We speculate that Elsa represents a daughter of Zeus, metaphorically, as intimated in the first line of the film, in the song 'The Frozen Heart (Ice Worker's Song)'. When the macho ice harvesters sing about Elsa (as suggested by Streiff and Dundes 2017a), their lyrics describe her as: 'Born of cold and winter air and mountain rain combining'. As discussed in this essay, someone 'born' from winter 'air' coupled with hydrating fluid from a mountain (where Zeus lives) suggests a supernatural birth (and the promiscuous Zeus was indeed the father of another Disney character,

Hercules). Elsa's parents do not understand her power (and there is no family history of her 'condition'); they must consult with a non-human being, a troll, about this 'condition'. Elsa's father is determined to quash her power, forcing her into a pariah existence because he sees her power as stigmatized rather than as a divine gift (that defies mortal origins). Her parents die due to a storm that appears to combine the powers of Zeus (with lightning striking the parents' ship) with the powers of Zeus' brother Poseidon, the god of the sea, as the ship is disabled by the storm and then swallowed by the sea (10:01–15).

Yet Elsa is no Zeus replacement: in a defining moment in the film, Elsa inadvertently 'strikes' her sister with ice, prompting Anna's senescence. In other words, because Elsa, the castrating, termagant sister, cannot properly wield power, her nubile sister sees her hair begin to turn white, which is reminiscent of the hoary tresses of a crone…. Anna's distress is a harbinger of her near-death by freezing at her sister's hand. Elsa's salvation comes in the form of stereotypically feminine tears that reverse her magic malfunction. Her weeping and empathy restore her humanity – or more specifically, her femininity – that replaces her masculine, castrating persona, propelling the story to an anachronistic happy ending.

Conclusions

We hope that by bringing attention to the complexities of meaning embedded in *Frozen* and its breathtaking success that we can elucidate contemporary societal struggles at a time when long-standing male dominance and traditional concepts of masculinity are changing. For example, according to *Carrot*, LGBTQ employees have, in many cases, been shut out of family planning coverage due to different fertility needs (O'Connor 2017), which is a manifestation of the challenges at the crossroads of sexuality and reproduction. Contemporary controversies include IVF (in vitro fertilization) treatment, which in at least one case resulted in a biological father paying child support for a son born without his permission post-divorce (Pearson 2018). With Elsa's snowmen progeny, Disney has sidestepped a procreation dilemma that they faced in their rendition of the mythical story of Hercules. In the original Hercules story, Zeus procreated with Alcmene, whose mortal husband fathered Hercules' other twin in an act of heteropaternal superfecundation. Yet in Disney's version of *Hercules* (1997), Hera and Zeus were presented as Hercules' parents, eliminating not only Zeus's infidelity, but also issues surrounding alternative methods of procreation. This means of reproduction also resulted in the Gemini astrological twins, when Zeus fathered Pollux but not his mortal twin Castor, yet another example of heteropaternal superfecundation.

Despite these options showcased in mythology long ago and increasingly available today through technological advances, Elsa's procreation is limited to snowmen that are not heteronormative. This suggests societal struggles with accepting a non-conventional means of reproduction, which is associated with gay couples. The snowmen's gender fluidity could show concerns about the possible outcomes of women procreating without male input, as *Frozen*'s 2013 release coincided with debates and changing opinions on gay marriage and transgender rights that were indubitably among the most visible and contentious social issues at the time.

Shortly after *Frozen*'s production, a *Time* cover story aptly encapsulated the socio-historical context for *Frozen* in its discussion of greater openness in discussing people who are transgender, and new policies reflecting efforts to enact 'changes in schools, hospitals, workplaces, prisons and the military' (Steinmetz 2014, para. 2) (see Drum 2016 for how the movement to install gender-neutral bathrooms began in 2012–2013). This relates to Elsa because she usurped Zeus' role at a time when trans men (born female) were seen as encroaching on men's bathrooms simultaneous with resistance to more unisex bathrooms that would detract from men's exclusive spheres,… even though in the first public bathrooms (latrines) in Rome, men and women sat side by side (Michaels 2016).

Elsa's virgin birth is a reversal of inveterate male creation aspirations that are so culturally inculcated that they are overlooked as normal. Elsa's appropriation of storms associated with virgin birth concludes 'happily' in her wielding power in a more gender-stereotypical manner: making ice sculptures, a skating rink, and snow confetti as she mingles with the commoners. Our concern is that Elsa's storm wielding and procreative powers were presented as a societal challenge that needed redress. At the end, when Elsa becomes nurturing and less castrating, her snowflake as a symbol that could ward off suitors becomes less central to her identity. As such, once rehabilitated, she conjures a giant signature snowflake in the sky (1:28:38), and then proceeds to obliterate it (1:28:40). This suggests that she is now available and open to suitors' advances, which qualifies as a happy ending for those partial to reinforcing gender stereotypes. Her tendency to slam doors, with connotations regarding restricted sexual access (Streiff and Dundes 2017a), changes in the finale when she embraces open gates, telling Anna, 'We are never closing [the gates] again' (1:31:56–57). Notably, she uses the pronoun we, but probably is not referring to Anna, who lacks power and never shut the gates in the first place. Instead, Elsa implies that she is relinquishing her status as a one-woman phenomenon and is perhaps open to the influence of a partner.

In addition, Elsa's lack of interest in men (see Streiff and Dundes 2017a) coupled with her father-absent births might reflect latent concerns about women balancing career, marriage, and children.

There is still the notion that marriage and children go hand-in-hand. In fact, the term 'Disney Princesses' has a proprietary, creationist nuance, as Walt Disney is the father of the company. It is through this lens that we can view her atypical motherhood, which is a twist on Mother Nature. The spirited discussion in the media about Elsa's sexuality (for example, Gander 2018) shows that viewers see the movie as a vehicle to discuss and advance causes related to sexuality.

The film also reflects women's rising power and their growing ability to perform in formerly all-male professions. These changes were highly visible in female inroads in both major political parties, notably in 2008, when Hilary Clinton competed against Barack Obama in the Democratic primary and Sarah Palin was the

Republican Vice Presidential candidate, John McCain's running mate. While both women were disparaged, Clinton earned the chilling moniker 'wicked witch of the left' (Miller 2018).

Elsa, discards her stigma as a sorcerer at the end of *Frozen*, because she is no longer wreaking havoc, but rather promoting a sense of community. She first saves her sister with love expressed as a tearful hug, literally a 'heartwarming' moment that stands in contradistinction to her acts of freezing. Yet her powers are to remain subdued and apparently should not emphasize that she is more powerful than the common villagers. This is the desired outcome, since the storms that Elsa conjures are a powerful force that is the dominion of men, with symbolic implications for fertility. Thus, Elsa's usurpation and misuse of the weather as well as her parthenogenesis present a crisis that must end in either her reform or her destruction. Fortunately, for the sake of *Frozen 2*, it is the former.

References

Coyle, Emily F., Fulcher, Megan, and Trubutschek, Darinka (2016). Sissies, Mama's Boys, and Tomboys: Is Children's Gender Nonconformity More Acceptable When Nonconforming Traits Are Positive? *Archives of Sexual Behavior* 45: 1827–1838. [CrossRef] [PubMed]

Davis, Amy M. (2007). *Good Girls and Wicked Witches: Changing Representations of Women in Disney's Feature Animation, 1937–2001*. Bloomington: Indiana University Press.

Dockterman, Eliana. (2018). The Ice Queen's New Kingdom. *Time*, 19 March, pp. 58–61.

Drum, Kevin. (2016). A Very Brief Timeline of the Bathroom Wars. *Mother Jones*, 14 May. Available at: https://www.motherjones.com/kevin-drum/2016/05/timeline-bathroom-wars/ (accessed on 3 April 2018).

Dundes, Alan. (1976). A Psychoanalytic Study of the Bullroarer. *Man* 11: 220–238. [CrossRef].

Dundes, Alan. (1984). Earth-diver: Creation of the Mythopoeic Male. In *Sacred Narrative*. Edited by Alan Dundes, 270–294. Berkeley: University of California Press.

Dundes, Lauren. (2001). Disney's Modern Heroine Pocahontas: Revealing Age Old Gender Stereotypes and Role Discontinuity under a Façade of Liberation. *The Social Science Journal* 38: 353–365.

Frozen (2013). Directed by Chris Buck and Jennifer Lee. Produced by Peter Del Vecho. Screenplay by Jennifer Lee. Story by Chris Buck, Jennifer Lee and Shane Morris. Burbank: Walt Disney Pictures.

Gander, Kashmira. (2018). Frozen 2: Disney's Elsa Shouldn't be a Lesbian Say Thousands of Backers in Anti-Gay Petition. Newsweek.com. Available online: http://www.newsweek.com/frozen-2-disneys-elsa-shouldnt-be-lesbian-sequel-say-thousands-backers-anti-846112 (accessed on 30 March 2018).

Hibberd, James. (2017). Frozen Original Ending Revealed for the First Time. EW.com. Available online: http://ew.com/movies/2017/03/29/frozen-original-ending/ (accessed on 5 April 2018).

Jones, Ernest. (1951). *Essays in Applied Psychoanalysis, Volume 2: Essays in Folklore, Anthropology and Religion*. London: The Hogarth Press.

Michaels, Samantha. (2016). N.C.'s Transgender Skirmish Is Just the Latest in a Long History of Bathroom Freakouts. *Mother Jones*, 11 May. Available online: https://www.motherjones.com/politics/2016/05/north-carolina-transgender-history-bathrooms-freakouts-timeline/ (accessed on 4 April 2018).

Miller, Madeline. (2018). From Circe to Clinton: Why Powerful Women re Cast as Witches. *The Guardian*, 7 April. Available online: https://www.theguardian.com/books/2018/apr/07/cursed-from-circe-to-clinton-why-women-are-cast-as-witches?CMP=fb_gu (accessed on 6 April 2018).

O'Connor. (2017). Carrot Fertility Raises $3.6M to Helop take IVF, Egg Freezing Benefits Mainstream. *Forbes*.

Patterson, Paul G., and Spencer, Leland G. (2017). What's So Funny about a Snowman in a Tiara? Exploring Gender Identity and Gender Nonconformity in Children's Animated Films. *Queer Studies in Media & Popular Culture* 2: 73–93.

Pearson, Alexander. (2018). German Man Ordered to Pay Child Support after Ex-Wife Forges Signature for IVF Pregnancy. *USA Today*, 3 May. Available online: https://www.usatoday.com/story/news/world/2018/05/ 03/german-man-child-support-ivf/576077002/ (accessed on 5 May 2018).

Perry, Spencer. (2017). *Frozen 2*. Details: Everything We Know about the Sequel. ComingSoon.net. Available online: http://www.comingsoon.net/movies/features/905423-frozen-2-details#Sbc3HrqVuGQwSfZ6.99 (accessed on 20 March 2018).

Ryrie, Charles C. (1997). *The Holy Spirit, Revised & Expanded*. Chicago: Moody Publishers.

Schickel, Richard. (1997). *The Disney Version: The Life, Times, Art and Commerce of Walt Disney*, 3rd ed. Chicago: Ivan R. Dee.

Solomon, Charles. (2013). *The Art of Frozen*. San Francisco, CA: Chronicle Books.

Steinmetz, Katy. (2014). The Transgender Tipping Point. *Time*, 29 May, 38–46.

Streiff, Madeline, and Dundes, Lauren. (2017a). Frozen in Time: How Disney Gender-Stereotypes Its Most Powerful Princess. *Social Sciences* 6: 38. [CrossRef].

YouTube. (2018). *Frozen: Let It Go* Sing-along. Official Disney UK. Available online: https://www.youtube.com/watch?v=L0MK7qz13bU (accessed on 2 May 2018).

Zipes, Jack. (2011). *The Enchanted Screen: The Unknown History of Fairy-Tale Films*. New York: Routledge.

Zirkle, Conway. (1936). Animals Impregnated by the Wind. *Isis: A Journal of the History of Science Society* 25: 95–130. [CrossRef]

Science fiction as mythology

Marilyn Sutton and Thomas Sutton

3

Marilyn Sutton is Professor Emeritus of English at California State University, Dominguez Hills (CSUDH), the United States. She was a Faculty member of CSUDH from 1973 until her retirement in 2008. She studied literature at Toronto University before engaging in graduate studies at Claremont Graduate University, where she was first named a Danfroth Fellow and then Distinguished Alumna; she graduated with a PhD in English in 1973.

Thomas Sutton moved from an academic background in mathematics and physics into management. He served as a director for the Public Policy Institute of California (2002–2015) and is currently a member of the Leadership Council of the School of Physical Sciences at the University of California, Irvine.

In the text that we have chosen for this volume, Thomas Suttons's interest in science is used to creatively power Marilyn Suttons's understanding of myth and literature. Together, they create an important early reflection on the way that science is mythologized into science fiction. The article talks to the issues surrounding myth and science that run throughout this volume at the same time as presenting a very early example of how myth theory can be profitably applied to emerging Western literature.

S cience fiction, it has recently been prophesied, will presently be shown to have contrived a 'mythology for our times.'[1] In fact science fiction has become so fully accepted as a mode of modern myth-making that the 1968 convention of the Modern Language Association devoted an afternoon forum, H. Bruce Franklin presiding, to 'Science Fiction: The New Mythology.' Despite this recognition, however, there remain a number of questions concerning the relative roles of myth and science in contemporary culture.

We have surely come a long way from the persistent idea, first put forth by Fontenelle in *The Origin of the Fables* (1724), that myth is essentially a primitive science, the imperfect result of a conscious search for causes of observable events.[2] A century later, despite their progressive contributions in other areas of myth study, both E. B. Tylor and Andrew Lang subscribed to the conception of myth as savage science. In his *Origins of Culture* (1871), Tylor states that 'savages have been for untold ages, and still are, living in the myth-making stage of the human mind.' He continues to argue that 'it was through sheer ignorance and neglect of this direct knowledge how and by what manner of men myths are really made, that their simple philosophy has come to be buried under masses of commentators' rubbish.'[3] Thirty-five years later, Lang noted that the followers of Tylor seemed unaware that they were only 'repeating the notions of the nephew of Corneille.'[4] Yet, indicative of how firmly entrenched the notion of myth as primitive science is, Lang too discusses the role of myth in primitive societies as man's 'first faint impulses of the scientific spirit' attempting a solution to the riddle of the world.[5]

Today if we can no longer characterize myth as prescience, we must ask what precisely is its relationship to science? Can we accept the sophisticated theory of Lévi-Strauss that myth is a mode parallel to science, similar in manner but differing in object? Lévi-Strauss suggests that both myth and science be considered as modes of structuring the universe; in fact, he goes so far as to posit a mathematical logic in the structural formation of myth.[6] His insistence that myth and science be considered as autonomous and mutually exclusive is a limiting feature even in his contemporary thesis. Since we are treating science fiction as the myth of modern technology, we are thereby committed to rejecting Lévi-Strauss' limitation of parallel autonomy and to posit a definite intersection of the mythopoeic and scientific modes.

Not all science fiction, of course, demonstrates such an intersection. We must recognize that science fiction in its current state encompasses a vast spectrum of works from the cartoons of Captain Video, Buck Rogers, and Flash Gordon, to the apocalyptic visions glimpsed by Arthur C. Clarke in *2001: A Space Odyssey*, the full-length novel elaborated from the film of the same title which Clarke had previously written in collaboration with Stanley Kubrick, and by C. S. Lewis in his *Perelandra* trilogy, a classic of science fiction.

Since both myth and science reflect man's irrepressible curiosity about his origins and his destiny, they each can be seen as a particular human means of structuring the universe. Paul Tillich in an essay on 'The Religious Symbol' suggests that wherever the objective world is recognized in its relatedness to the unconditioned transcendent, the unity of religion with the desire to understand the world is restored in the mythical symbol.[7] In this way science becomes myth despite its rational autonomy. Scientists themselves recognize the fact that science has moved from the immediate perception of empirical reality to a stage where the object of research is no longer nature in itself but rather nature as it is exposed to man's questioning.[8] In other words, contemporary science is conscious of its own symbolization.

Myth and science emphasize different aspects of the universe-structures they erect. Early myth is typically concerned with the study of origins whereas science generally focuses on the study of destiny. It is precisely because of the fundamentalism of primitive myth that C. Kerényi isolates for study the archetype of the divine child, 'the first-born of primeval times, in whom the origin first was.'[9] In his study Kerényi notes that the essential difference between the mode of the philosopher and that of the myth-teller is that the philosopher tries to pierce through the world of appearances in order to say 'what really is' while the myth-teller steps back into primordiality in order to tell us 'what originally was.' Underlying this concern with origins in myth seems to be an assumption that if tribal man can trace his beginnings through a narrative, he will simultaneously discover his *raison d'être* and thus be able to formulate a suitable mode of existence. In terms of cultural experience, a body of myth incorporates the essential beliefs of a tribe while ritual expresses the myth-embodied abstractions in concrete form. Through the performance of a particular ritual, a tribal man feels himself in harmony with the spirit pervading his body of myth. Science on the other hand tends to deny or at least ignore the issue of a supranatural purpose for existence and to employ the study of origins as one of numerous means to determine the form of future existence.

Both myth and science attempt to provide an overview of existence by bridging inner reality and outer reality. Here again the direction of the process differs: myth attempts to project inner reality (conscious desires, archetypal patterns) in the metaphor of outer reality, while science aims to illuminate inner reality through the study of outer, empirical forms. A body of myth forms an autonomous universe which stands in metaphoric relation to the actual world. Scientific hypotheses also form a universe, a universe which is not identical to objective reality but representative of man's understanding of it. Thus the question of validation or disproof is irrelevant to myth since the relation of myth to reality is analogical, but it is paramount for science because the worth of a scientific hypothesis is entirely dependent on the accuracy of its relationship to objective reality.

Before the advent of the scientific mode, the only means by which man could relate to his universe was through the mythopoeic mode. His acceptance of the narratives of gods and heroes as the meaning of his world served as an affirmation of intimacy with the most basic and therefore sacral structures of space, of time, of natural occurrence, and of historical event.[10] Prescientific man viewed everything outside himself as 'other' and to a large degree unknowable. For him myth served as the vehicle for his relationship with the 'other.' As the scientific or technological mode developed, man's orientation moved away from universal concepts to a more specialized focus on the individual empirical data. Historically this shift resulted in the sharp distinction between the two modes of thought, with the scientific recognized as the means to knowledge and the mythopoeic disenfranchised and relegated to the role of plaything for poets.

Perhaps we are now in a position to move beyond this convenient dissection of thought, for now that we can view the mythopoeic and the scientific modes in their matured states we can see the sharp distinctions disintegrating. In the field of contemporary theology, we have the example of Rudolph Bultmann, who attempts to apply scientific logic to the myth of Christianity and ends by 're-mythologizing' Christianity in the language of contemporary science rather than de-mythologizing it.[11] An example of the reverse process is provided by science fiction in which the scientific mode of thought is intentionally mythologized.

In the words of Fred Saberhagen, a science fiction author and critic, 'science fiction gives a chance to impose different coordinate systems upon the human condition and to try to see what will change and what will remain the same.'[12] A British scientist and poet, Peter Redgrave, provides in his short story 'Mr. Waterman'[13] an example of conscious imposition of a set of hypothetical time and space coordinates in order to mythologize science. Redgrave's story mythologizes evolution to produce a delightfully ironic narrative. It takes the form of a patient's reporting to his analyst the strange manner in which the creatures in his garden pool emerge during dewy evenings. The starfish couple on the ornamental stone steps and the barnacles brazenly affix themselves to the stems of rose trees. Eventually one such aquatic creature becomes so fully adapted to terrestrial existence that he takes up residence in the man's home and attempts to seduce his host's wife. At this point the analyst sends the patient off with a bit of routine advice and turns to his next client, who reports troubles with a 'married, air-breathing woman.'

We can see a relationship analogous to the myth-science dichotomy in the tension between the terms 'natural' and 'artificial.' All that preexisted human activity is generally considered to be natural. As man progressed, he developed both in self-awareness and tool-making ability. At the early stages of human development the contrast between natural object and human artifact was marked, largely because of the difficulty of bringing an artifact into existence. Modern technology has facilitated the production of artifacts to such a degree that the distinctions between the two categories are now being erased. Now that man can, in one sense, make man through the 'artificial' creation of a unit of 'natural' life in a DNA molecule, the terms 'natural' and 'artificial' have ceased to be antonyms.[14]

The mythopoeic mode flourished prior to the advent of empirical science. When man's entire surroundings were unknowable to him empirically, they elicited a response of awe and wonder. The meaning of existence was expressed for primitive man through the fashioning of a totem pole, the recounting of a myth, or even the ritual preparation of food. With the advent of empirical science, however, man came to learn objective facts about his universe. The fact that he could know some aspect of his world removed his sense of reverential awe and replaced it with a confidence that the 'other' was in fact knowable. It is only to be expected then that in the contemporary empirical context, a myth to be relevant must reflect human achievements and capacities rather than wonder in the face of a fore-ordained cosmic structure. Once man has become conscious of his position in the historical process, his attention shifts from the contemplation of the eternal structure to the action of the present moment.

The psychological interpretation of these observations is fully discussed by Jung in his fascinating book *Flying Saucers: A Modern Myth of Things Seen in the Skies*. After considering many contradictory pieces of evidence concerning the material existence of UFOs, Jung suggests, 'with all due reserve,' that UFOs

> are real material phenomena of an unknown nature, presumably coming from outer space, which perhaps have long been visible to mankind, but otherwise have no recognizable connection with the earth or its inhabitants. In recent times, however, and just at the moment when the eyes of mankind are turned towards the heavens, partly on account of their fantasies about possible spaceships, and partly in a figurative sense because their earthly existence feels threatened, unconscious contents have projected themselves on these inexplicable heavenly phenomena and given them a significance they in no way deserve.[15]

The possible future discovery of unknown physical phenomena as the outward cause of flying saucers would detract nothing from the myth for, typical of all myth, it does not operate as a scientific hypothesis but as a particular instance of the intersection of myth and science that we have posited at the outset of this essay.

Modern myth cannot be simply a representation of contemporary reality; it must resonate on multiple levels. Jung considers the 'living myth' of flying saucers as a golden opportunity to see how in a

> dark and difficult time for humanity a miraculous tale grows up of an attempted intervention by extra-terrestrial 'heavenly' powers – and at this very time when human fantasy is seriously considering the possibility of space travel and of visiting or even invading other planets.[16]

The present situation must be viewed in relation to a transcendent order of some description. For early mythopoeic man, this transcendent order was the cosmos with its gods, heroes, planets, and other inexplicable phenomena. In the area of scientific myth, the transcendent referent can no longer be the cosmos, since scientific research has shown that it is empirically knowable and as a consequence it is no longer entirely transcendent. As a referent, modern myth, especially science fiction, replaces the cosmos with the concept of space. Jung claims that it is the belief in this world and the power of man that is thrusting itself forward in the form of symbolic rumor and activating an archetype that has always expressed 'order, deliverance, salvation, and wholeness.' The visions of unidentified round shining objects are impressive manifestations of totality, their simple round form portraying the archetype of self which has been shown to play the chief role in uniting apparently irreconcilable opposites and is therefore best suited to compensate the split-mindedness of our age.[17] This archetype, so vital to humanity, has been expressed throughout human history in various forms, but it is characteristic of our time that it should take the form of a technological construction in order to avoid the anachronistic odiousness of a mythological personification.[18]

Space represents for science fiction an infinite, unknown extension which lends a grandeur to whatever actions are undertaken in it. Unlike a scientific hypothesis, a science fiction story is not formulated primarily to advance technological knowledge; rather it operates on a visionary, mythopoeic level. We might say that space provides for science fiction the context of *in illo tempore*, the usual location of myth; spatial distancing replaces temporal distancing. It is characteristic of science fiction that it is never set in the present time unless more than one time dimension is operative. This temporal distortion helps to secure a thematic universality, but there is a difference between this strategy and that employed in early myth. For in early myth the teller placed his narration in the realm of 'once long ago' to set the action outside the realm of actual possibility, but with science fiction the writer believes that his unusual time dimensions may be scientifically possible.

Both science fiction and myth deal primarily with beings of greater than ordinary power. Early myth presents semidivine beings who exhibit the quality of *mana* in their actions. Their source of power is something beyond the human. Since science fiction is being considered as the myth of technology, it is not surprising to find that man assumes the role of protagonist. His power, rather than being a suprahuman *mana*, is generally associated with superior knowledge, for knowledge is recognized as the motive force behind technological progress. The robot, a common motif in science fiction, being a thinking machine represents the ultimate refinement of technology, and many science fiction myths deal with the variety of relationships possible between the human and machine thinkers. But even this concern with the robot can be seen as humanistic inasmuch as the robot is simply an extension of man's scientifically most sophisticated quality, his power to reason and remember. Isaac Asimov, the father of 'robotics' in science fiction, eagerly envisions the day when scientists will design a computer capable of formulating the design of a computer more complex than itself. This moment will mark the beginning of a diverging series in which 'not only man-made man is possible, but man-made superman.'[19] This notion is not at all repulsive to Asimov; on the contrary, it is the fulfillment of an evolutionary pattern long ago projected in Greek mythology with the overthrow of the god Ouranos by Cronos.

Science fiction is a self-conscious form of myth in which man intentionally mythologizes scientific narrative. It is not infrequent to find themes from earlier mythologies serving as subplots for science fiction stories. Examples are readily afforded by Frank Herbert, who weaves a knowledge of ecology with allusions to Old Testament myths in his novel *Dune* (1965), and James Blish, who blends creation theology with echoes of demonism in his work *A Case of Conscience* (1958) to produce a myth in which a priest-scientist confronts an alien world of complete perfection and, aware that it is a theological impossibility, is forced to acknowledge it as a demonic creation.

Another excellent example of this technique is Arthur C. Clarke's short story 'The Star'[20] in which mythic material from Christianity furnishes the subplot. Clarke gives the mythology surrounding the star of Bethlehem and the birth of Christ a scientific explanation, proposing that the star was the result of the destruction of a completely idyllic race in a star system whose sun flared as a supernova at its death. Scientifically it is plausible that the star of Bethlehem, if there was one, was a supernova, but Clarke remythologizes extravagantly on this scientific basis. He suggests that God intentionally destroyed an entire people on the exploded star for His greater honor and glory. The underlying irony is made explicit by setting the narrative in Jesuit surroundings and playing on the Jesuit motto *Ad maiorem Dei gloriam*. In this particular myth, Clarke explodes a fiction concerning the star with scientific fact, and then goes on to mingle religion, psychology, and science to develop a mythopoeic vision. As myth, such a story is certainly much more conscious and literary than early myth, but it is not meant to be the myth of a tribe, rather it is the mythology concocted for the delight of technological man.

Notes

1   Albert B. Friedman, 'The Best Turnips on the Creek,' *N. Y. Rev. of Books*, 28 March 1968, p. 37.

2   See Richard Chase, *The Quest for Myth* (Baton Rouge, 1949), pp. 8–9.

3   (Reprint; New York, 1958), p. 283.

4   *Myth, Ritual, and Religion* (London, 1906), II, 339.

5   II, 49.

6   'The Structural Study of Myth,' in *Myth: A Symposium*, ed. Thomas A. Sebeok (Bloomington, 1965), p. 106.

7   In *Symbolism in Religion and Literature*, ed. Rollo May (New York, 1960), pp. 87–88.

8   Werner Heisenberg, 'The Representations of Nature in Contemporary Physics,' in *Symbolism in Religion and Literature*, pp. 230–231.

9   *Essays on a Science of Mythology* (New York, 1963), pp. 8–9.

10   Langdon Gilkey, 'Modern Myth-Making and the Possibilities of Twentieth-Century Theology,' in *Theology of Renewal* (Montreal, 1968), I, 286.

11   *Kerygma and Myth*, ed. Hans W. Bartsch (New York, 1961), pp. 43–44.

12   Quoted in *The Year's Best S-F*, ed. Judith Merril (New York, 1964), p. 34.

13   *Paris Review*, XXIX (1963), pp. 162–165.

14   Jacques Ellul, *The Technological Society* (New York, 1965), p. xix. In his treatment of technology Ellul includes techniques under the category of the 'natural,' which he seems to define as 'any environment able to satisfy man's material needs, if it leaves him free to use it as a means to achieve his individual internally generated ends.'

15   (London, 1959), p. 151.

16 p. 14.

17 p. 21.

18 p. 22.

19 'And It Will Serve Us Right,' *Psychology Today* II (1969): 64.

20 Reprinted in *A Century of Science Fiction*, ed. Damon Knight (New York, 1962).

References

Asimov, I. (1969). And It Will Serve Us Right. *Psychology Today*, April edition.

Bartsch, H. W. R. (1961). *Kerygma and Myth*. New York: Harper.

Blish, J. (1958). *A Case of Conscience*. New York: Del Ray Impact.

Chase, R. V. (1949). *Quest for Myth*. Baton Rouge: Louisiana State University Press.

Cowley, M. (1963). *Writers at Work: The Paris Review Interviews*. New York: Viking Press.

Ellul, J. (1964). *The Technological Society*. New York: Vintage Books.

Friedman, A. B. (1968). The Best Turnips on the Creek. *New York Review of Books*, March 28.

Herbert, F. (1965). *Dune*. Los Angeles: New English Library.

Jung, C. G. (1959). *Flying Saucers: A Modern Myth of Things Seen in the Skies*. London: Routledge & Kegan Paul.

Jung, C. G., and Kerényi, K. (1963). *Essays on a Science of Mythology; the Myth of the Divine Child and the Mysteries of Eleusis*. Princeton, NJ: Princeton University Press.

Knight, D. F. (1962). A Century of Science Fiction. New York: Dell Publishing.

Lang, A. (1906). *Myth, Ritual and Religion*, vol. 2. Longmans, Green, and Company.

May, R., and Riches, P. (1966). *Symbolism in Religion and Literature*. New York: George Braziller.

Merril, J. (1964). *The Year's Best SF*. New York: Delacorte Press.

Sebeok, T. A. (1965). *Myth: A Symposium*. Bloomington: Indiana University Press.

Shook, L. K. (1968). *Theology of Renewal: Proceedings of the Congress on the Theology of the Renewal of the Church; Centenary of Canada, 1867–1967*. Montreal: Palm Publishers.

Tylor, E. B. (1871). *Primitive Culture; Part 1: The Origins of Culture*. London: Murray.

Section B: The future of mythology

Mythological Terminalia

Have we reached the end of mythology? Are we entering a global post-mythological age? And did mythology in the West truly die long ago, even if it is only now that its afterglow is fading finally to black? These (or variants of the above) are common questions at the beginning of undergraduate mythology seminars, but we have reserved them here to the end of the volume precisely because the texts that go before this provide the basis for a good range of well-reasoned responses to the questions. This is partly because how you understand or define myth greatly affects the prognosis for its future.

From the perspective of a crude form of cultural evolution, myth lost its purpose long ago in the West and the other outlying areas, where it survives, are simply waiting to catch up (Rankin 2002: 48). This hard primitivism is inverted in the soft primitivism of the surrealists who (despite their lament for the loss of mythology) are still operating within the same evolutionary framework, as evidenced by their longing for a return to a 'pre-logical' state (Weibe 1987). Here the trope is of loss, but there is also some hope of continuation and even, through the adoption of alternative lifestyles, revival. Kerényi captures this well with his rallying cry that 'Mythology, like the severed head of Orpheus, goes on singing even in death and from afar' (2002: 4). Eliade (1974) also connects with this sense of loss and resistance (through both his conception of the terror of history and his desire to return to the sacred embrace of myth), while offering little indication, or hope, that myth has a robust future.

Campbell's monomyth (1949) may seem to offer the greatest hope for the future of mythology. We have repeatedly seen in this book how Campbell's model was accepted by mass-media producers, who used it to power a string of movies, television shows, toys, games and self-development programmes. What is more, it has proved highly attractive, being eagerly devoured by the public and becoming both the shared and formative narratives for successive generations, whose acts of mimesis do indeed seem to move people from individuals, existing in linear time, towards a collective, with the power to collapse time and space (Laycock 2010). Campbell's model may, therefore, be taken to suggest that the future of myth is positive, and yet it is also a monomyth – a singular myth that arises from a particular cultural, racial and gendered context that could be seen to be closing down the rich variety of ways of being that a more diverse mythology would reveal.

As such, Campbell's model could be tied to other issues of globalization, deterritorialization and the displacement of the physical by the virtual. Has the process of globalization (and its traumatic movements) severed our connection with local ecologies of being and the physical anchoring that they so often enjoy? Basso's (2010) troubling account of the way that the forced movement of the Apache caused a dislocation of their myths from relevant places suggests that the result of this dislocation of mythology is a breakdown of social systems. However, as both Hugh-Jones and Miles-Watson demonstrate in this book, it must also be remembered that many mythological systems have coping mechanisms that allow for both the continuation of the myth and the preservation of social order.

Hugh-Jones's Amazonian material and Miles-Watson's Indian examples remind us that much of what we have said here so far is itself a heavily positioned account that fails to adequately account for the complex ways that myth operates outside of the comfortable ground of Western mythographers. From the position of a modern, developing and increasingly globally assertive country like India, most of the foregoing argument seems like a parochial squabble that misses the reality all around. For sure, there are movements in India that would reject, in a Tylorian fashion, the modern relevance of myth, and there are those who are as influenced by *Star Wars* as anyone in the West, but these are at best two aspects of a rich and complex landscape. For the masses, mythology has never gone away, and if anything, it has become of increasing importance. That is not to say, however, that the mythological landscape is either unchanging or uncontested. Recent years have seen a rise in an authorized nationalist mythology that is tied strongly to geography, the preservation of hegemony and aims to override the many rich alternative myths that people live by. This is, of course, not an uncontested process, and the same period has also seen notable resistance movements, with both sides making extensive use of new media and technology.

We have chosen to call this section Mythological Terminalia partly because it is the last section of the book but also because we do seem to be at a more general moment of terminus. Drawing on the understanding put forward by the Ethnographic Terminali project, we suggest that this mythological terminus 'is the end the boundary and the border; [but] it is also a beginning, its own place, a site of experience and encounter' (Ethnographic Terminalia Collective 2014: i). As we write this, it is clear that the world is at a moment of mythological, social and natural endings, but also at an important crossroad, or meeting place. A place at once at the margins and yet a central place of new beginnings. As we move forward, new technology may be harnessed to facilitate acts of mythopoesis that unseat established structures and help steer the world towards a more helpful way of being. Alternatively, that same technology can be used by corporations to cynically pursue economic gain at the expense of social and planetary well-being. Or perhaps more worryingly still, technology can be harnessed by nationalist and misogynist movements to propagate myths that reinforce problematic boundaries of all sorts (territorial, social and sexual). As editors, we do, therefore, believe that mythology has a future, but what that future is (and whether that mythology will be beneficial) is something that at this historic moment is far from certain.

References

Basśo, K. H. (2010). *Wisdom Sits in Places: Landscape and Language among the Western Apache*. Albuquerque: University of New Mexico Press.

Campbell, J. (1949). *The Hero with a Thousand Faces*. New York: Pantheon Books.

Eliade, M. (1974). *The Myth of the Eternal Return, or, Cosmos and History*. Princeton, NJ: Princeton University Press.

Ethnographic Terminalia Curatorial Collective (2014). *The Bureau of Memories: Archives and Ephemera*. Installation catalogue. Washington, DC.

Kerényi, K. (2002). *Science of Mythology: Essays on the Myth of the Divine Child and the Mysteries of Eleusis*. London: Routledge.

Laycock, J. (2010). 'Myth Sells: Mattel's Commission of the Masters of the Universe Bible'. *Journal of Religion and Popular Culture* 22: 2.

Rankin, D. (2002). *Celts and the Classical World*. London Routledge.

Wiebe, D. (1987). The Prelogical Mentality Revisited. *Religion* 17 (1): 29–61.

Does myth have a future?

Robert Segal

1

Professor Robert Segal is a sixth-century chair in religious studies at the University of Aberdeen (UK) and director of the *Centre for the Study of Myth*. He came to Aberdeen from Lancaster University, where he was the professor of theories of religion for nineteen years. Prior to moving to the UK, he taught at Louisiana State University (USA) and Reed College (USA). He has held visiting positions at a wide range of North American institutions (including Stanford, Toronto, Tulane and Pittsburgh) and at Cambridge University, UK. Professor Segal has written extensively, perhaps more than any other living scholar, on the topics of mythology and myth analysis. His many publications include a four-volume exploration of theories of myth, the Oxford *Very Short Introduction to Mythology,* and an introduction to the thought of Joseph Campbell.

Segal's research into (and publications about) mythography covers a wide range of theorists; however, it is possible to detect concentrations of interest in the writings of Jung, Campbell and the Gnostics. These influences are also detectable in the material that we have chosen to include here, which gauges the future for mythology by using these theories/theorists (along with Tylor) as a springboard into the discussion. The result is a thoughtful (if somewhat pessimistic) reflection on the way that these theorists envisioned a future for mythology, and this strikes a somewhat discordant note with the material covered in the previous section.

Whether myth has a future depends on its capacity to meet the challenge posed by modern science. As Marcel Detienne and many others have shown, the challenge to myth does not begin in the modern era.[1] It goes back to at least Plato, who rejected Homeric myth as trivial and immoral. The Stoics defended myth against these charges by reinterpreting it as metaphysical and moral allegory.

Modern challenges to myth have been made on intellectual, theological, and political grounds. The chief modern challenge, however, has come from natural science, which does so well what myth had long been assumed to do: explain the origin and operation of the physical world. Where myth attributes events in the world to the decisions of gods, science ascribes events to impersonal, mechanical processes.... Science does not challenge the *origin* of myth. How and why myth arises does not matter. Science challenges the assumed *function* of myth by usurping that function.

The most facile response to the gauntlet thrown down by science has been to ignore science. An only slightly less facile response has been to pronounce science itself mythic. A more credible response has accepted science as the reigning explanation of the world and has then either 'surrendered' or 'regrouped.' Surrendering means simply replacing myth with science. Myth is here conceded to be an outdated and incorrect explanation of the world. Regrouping means altering either the function or the subject matter of myth in order to make myth compatible with science. Myth here becomes other than a *literal explanation* of the world. Either the function of myth becomes other than that of explanation, or the subject matter of myth becomes other than the literal one.

The surrender of myth to science: Tylor

The exemplars of the surrendering response to science are the pioneering anthropologists Edward Tylor and James Frazer. Tylor represents a purer case than Frazer, whose views on the function of myth are muddled and contradictory.[2] According to Tylor, myth arises and functions solely to explain events in the physical world. Like science, myth serves neither to endorse nor to condemn the world but only to account for it. Myth does not moralize, sanction, or emote. It explains.

Tylor's surrender of myth to science presupposes not only that the exclusive function of myth is explanatory but also that mythic explanations are unscientific. Tylor assumes that myth is unscientific because it employs personal rather than impersonal causes.[3] Tylor also assumes that personal explanations are inferior to impersonal ones. He therefore takes for granted that the rise of science spells the fall of myth. 'Primitives' have myth; moderns have science. Yet the rise of science somehow does not also dictate the end of religion. Even though for Tylor religion and myth operate in tandem to explain the world – religion identifies which god causes an event; myth tells how and why that god causes the event – religion can survive the rise of science where myth cannot. True, religion can survive only by ceding explanation to science and by becoming instead a mere espousal of ethics – a view epitomized by Matthew Arnold. But at least religion can change and thereby survive. For some unstated reason myth cannot.

In fact, Tylor rails against those theorists of myth who dare to make myth other than an explanation, including those who turn myth into moral allegory.[4] According to this group of theorists, Perseus, for instance, 'symbolizes war, and when of the three Gorgons he attacks only the mortal one, this means that only practicable wars are to be attempted.' A present-day moral allegorizer might take the story of Perseus as 'an allegory of trade: Perseus himself is Labour, and he finds Andromeda, who is Profit, chained and ready to be devoured by the monster Capital; he rescues her and carries her off in triumph.'[5] For the moral allegorizers, myth is compatible with science both because it is really about human beings rather than about gods and because it says how human beings ought to behave rather than how they do behave. The function of myth becomes normative rather than explanatory, and the subject matter of myth becomes symbolic rather than literal.

Tylor denounces the moral allegorizers not because they alter the function or subject matter of myth for themselves but because they do so for primitives. For Tylor, to cede the explanatory function of myth is to trivialize myth, and the explanatory function requires a literal reading. He thus says that 'the basis on which such [mythic] ideas as these are built is not to be narrowed down to poetic fancy and transformed metaphor. They rest upon a broad philosophy of nature, early and crude indeed, but thoughtful, consistent, and quite really and seriously meant.'[6] Tylor assumes that the allegorizers anachronistically project their own incredulity onto primitives. Scarcely taking myth seriously themselves, these theorists cannot imagine that anyone else ever has.

It is, then, in the *name* of myth that Tylor denies myth a future. For him, to take myth seriously is to take it as an explanation of the world. That that explanation has been vanquished by the scientific one does not, for Tylor, demean it. On the contrary, myth remains a competitor, albeit a losing competitor, in the grandest intellectual enterprise.

The regrouping of myth in the wake of science: Eliade, Bultmann, Jonas, and Jung

As common as the strategy of surrendering myth to science has been, even more popular has been the strategy of regrouping. Conceding to science only the explanatory function and the literal subject matter of myth, this strategy seeks alternative functions and subjects beyond the ken of science. Regrouping has taken several forms. One form has been to credit myth with one or more nonexplanatory functions, in which case myth runs askew to science and can therefore coexist with it…. A second form of response has been to interpret myth symbolically, in which case myth does not even refer to the physical world and so can likewise coexist with science…. The boldest form of response has been to alter both the function and the subject matter of myth, so that on neither count does myth compete with science….

Mircea Eliade

Mircea Eliade does not reject the explanatory function of myth. For him, as for Tylor, myth serves to explain how gods created and control the world: 'Myth narrates a sacred history; it relates an event that took place in primordial Time, the fabled time of the "beginnings." In other words, myth tells how, through the deeds of Supernatural Beings, a reality came into existence, be it the whole of reality, the Cosmos, or only a fragment of reality – an island, a species of plant, a particular kind of human behavior, an institution.'[7] Indeed, Eliade goes beyond Tylor in crediting myth with explaining not only natural phenomena but also social ones: 'Myths, that is, narrate not only the origin of the World, of animals, of plants, and of man, but also all the primordial events in consequence of which man became what he is today – mortal, sexed, organized in a society, obliged to work in order to live, and working in accordance with certain rules.'[8]

How, then, does Eliade meet the challenge of science? By proposing functions served by myth in addition to the explanatory one. Myth for Eliade justifies as well as explains phenomena. Myth does not, to be sure, pronounce phenomena good. But it does pronounce them inevitable and in that sense seeks to reconcile humanity to them. For example, myth justifies death less by postulating an afterlife, though Eliade notes myths that do, than by rooting death in an event in primordial time, when the world was still malleable but when any action made permanent whatever it effected. In primordial, or mythic, time the cosmic clay is soft; by subsequent, historical, ordinary time it has hardened. According to myth, human beings die because 'a mythical Ancestor stupidly lost immortality, or because a Supernatural Being decided to deprive him of it, or because a certain mythical event left him endowed at once with sexuality and mortality, and so on.'[9] Myth makes the present less arbitrary and therefore more tolerable by locating its origin in the hoary past.

Myth for Eliade does more than explain and justify. It regenerates. To hear, to read, and especially to reenact a myth is magically to return to the time when the myth took place, the time of the origin of whatever phenomenon it explains and justifies: 'But since ritual recitation of the cosmogonic myth implies reactualization of that primordial event, it follows that he for whom it is recited is magically projected *in illo tempore*, into the "beginning of the World"; he becomes contemporary with the cosmogony.'[10] In returning one to primordial time, myth reunites one with the gods, for it is then when they are nearest, as the biblical case of 'the Lord God['s] walking in the garden in the cool of the day' typifies (Genesis 3:8). That 'reunion' reverses the postlapsarian separation from the gods, a separation that is equivalent to the fall, and renews one spiritually: 'What is involved is, in short, a return to the original time, the therapeutic purpose of which is to begin life once again, a symbolic rebirth.'[11] The ultimate payoff of myth is experiential: encountering divinity.

Clearly, science offers no regenerative or even justificatory function. Science simply explains. Myth, then, has a future: it can do things that science cannot.

But Eliade offers another argument in favor of the future – in fact, the eternality – of myth. Myth not only serves functions that transcend the function served by science; it also serves them for moderns as well as for primitives. Moderns for Eliade fancy themselves scrupulously rational, intellectual, unsentimental, and forward-looking – in short, scientific. Nothing could veer farther from their collective self-image than adherence to myth, which they dismiss as egregiously outdated. Yet even they, according to Eliade, cannot dispense with myth.

[...]

Plays, books, and movies are mythiclike because they reveal the existence of another world alongside the everyday one – a world of extraordinary figures and events akin to those found in earlier, superhuman myths. Furthermore, the actions of those figures account for the present state of the everyday world. Most of all, moderns get so absorbed in plays, books, and movies that they imagine themselves to be back in the world before their eyes. Identifying themselves with the characters of the stories, they experience the same hopes and fears. If, argues Eliade, even self-professed atheists ineluctably have their own myths, then surely myth is panhuman, in which case it has a boundless future.

However appealing, Eliade's dual counterargument to Tylor – that myth serves functions that science cannot duplicate and that even moderns cherish myth – is dubious. First, the nonexplanatory functions of myth depend on the explanatory one, as Eliade himself recognizes in always characterizing myth as at least an explanation. But then myth can serve its other functions only if it can fend off science in serving its explanatory function. How it can do so, Eliade never says. Perhaps he is assuming that the phenomena explained by modern myths are entirely social – for example, the origin of tools, marriage, government, and nationalities – and not at all natural – for example, the origin of the sun and the moon. But *social* science seeks to account for social phenomena, so what is left for myth alone to explain?

Second, modern myths do not return one to the time of the gods. They may not even go backward in time but may instead go forward, as in science fiction, or go sideways, such as to other cultures around the world. Even myths that do move backward rarely go as far back as the time of the gods. They take one back to only 'post-primordial' time. These myths may provide escape from the present, but how much renewal can they provide? A hagiographical biography of George Washington may attribute the establishment of twentieth-century American laws and mores to the accomplishments of this larger-than-life hero, but a human being he remains. Reliving the American Revolution might be inspiring, but would it provide cosmic regeneration?

Third, moderns travel back in time only in their imaginations, not in reality. Americans may feel *as if* they are present at the Revolution, but they hardly claim actually to be back there, whisked on a mythic time machine. Once the play, book, movie, or other vehicle is over, so is the myth. One may remember a stirring story long afterward, but as a memory or an inspiration only. As affecting as Eliade's effort to confer a future on myth is, it is unconvincing.

Rudolf Bultmann

The second main regrouping response to the challenge of science has come from the existentialist camp: from the New Testament scholar and theologian Rudolf Bultmann and from his one-time student, the philosopher Hans Jonas. Both were students of Martin Heidegger. For both Bultmann and Jonas, myth does not explain the world because myth is not about the world. The true subject matter of myth is the place of human beings in the world, and the function of myth is to describe that place. As Bultmann puts it, 'The real purpose of myth is not to present an objective picture of the world as it is, but to express man's understanding of himself in the world in which he lives. Myth should be interpreted not cosmologically, but anthropologically, or better still, existentially.'[12]

Bultmann acknowledges that, read literally, myth is about the world itself. But unlike Eliade and Tylor, both of whom retain a literal interpretation of myth, Bultmann, together with Jonas, offers a symbolic one. In Bultmann's celebrated, if excruciatingly confusing, phrase, one must 'demythologize' myth, by which he means not eliminating, or 'demythicizing,' the mythology but instead extricating the true, existential subject matter of the mythology.

Taken literally, myth for Bultmann is exactly as it is for Tylor: a prescientific explanation of the world, an explanation rendered not merely superfluous but plainly false by science. Were myth to harbor no other subject matter, Bultmann no less than Tylor would spurn it altogether as primitive.

Demythologized, however, myth ceases to be an explanation at all and becomes an expression, an expression not of the nature of the world but of the nature of the human experience of the world. Myth ceases to be merely primitive and becomes universal. It ceases to be false and becomes true. It becomes a statement of the human condition.

Read literally, the New Testament in particular describes a cosmic battle between good and evil anthropomorphic gods and angels for control of the physical world. These beings intervene not only in the operation of nature, as for Tylor, but also in the lives of human beings. The beneficent beings direct humans to do good; the malevolent ones compel them to do evil. Taken literally, the New Testament describes a prescientific outlook:

The world is viewed as a three-storied structure, with the earth in the centre, the heaven above, and the underworld beneath. Heaven is the abode of God and of celestial beings – the angels. The underworld is hell, the place of torment. Even the earth is more than the scene of natural, everyday events, of the trivial round and common task. It is the scene of the supernatural activity of God and his angels on the one hand, and of Satan and his daemons on the other. These supernatural forces intervene in the course of nature and in all that men think and will and do. Miracles are by no means rare. Man is not in control of his own life. Evil spirits may take possession of him. Satan may inspire him with evil thoughts. Alternatively, God may inspire his thought and guide his purposes. He may grant him heavenly visions. He may allow him to hear his word of succour or demand. He may give him the supernatural power of his Spirit.[13]

Demythologized, the New Testament still refers in part to the physical world, but now to a world ruled by a single, nonanthropomorphic, transcendent God. Because God does not act directly in the world and because no evil powers exist, human beings are free rather than controlled like puppets:

> Mythology expresses a certain understanding of human existence. It believes that the world and human life have their ground and their limits in a power which is beyond all that we can calculate or control. Mythology speaks about this power inadequately and insufficiently because it speaks about it as if it were a worldly [i.e., physical] power. It [rightly] speaks of gods who represent the power beyond the visible, comprehensible world. [But] it speaks of gods as if they were men and of their actions as human actions. ... Again, the conception of Satan as ruler over the world expresses a deep insight, namely, the insight that evil is not only to be found here and there in the world, but that all particular evils make up one single power which in the last analysis grows from the very actions of men, which form an atmosphere, a spiritual tradition, which overwhelms every man. The consequences and effects of our sins become a power dominating us, and we cannot free ourselves from them.[14]

Demythologized, God still exists, but Satan does not. Sin becomes one's own doing, and Satan symbolizes only one's own evil inclinations. Damnation refers not to a future place but to one's present state of mind, which exists as long as one rejects God. Similarly, salvation refers to one's state of mind once one accepts God. Hell symbolizes despair over the absence of God; heaven, joy in his presence. The eschatology refers not to the coming end of the physical world but to the personal acceptance or rejection of God in one's daily life.

Because a literal interpretation of the New Testament reduces human beings to the pawns of cosmic forces, a literal reading focuses on those forces themselves, which means on the world itself. Because a symbolic interpretation pronounces humanity free, it concentrates on the actions humans choose in response to the world.

Taken literally, myth, as a supernatural explanation of the physical world, is incompatible with science and is therefore unacceptable to moderns:

Man's knowledge and mastery of the world have advanced to such an extent through science and technology that it is no longer possible for anyone seriously to hold the New Testament view of the world – in fact, there is no one who does. What meaning, for instance, can we attach to such phrases in the creed as 'descended into hell' or 'ascended into heaven'? We no longer believe in the three-storied universe which the creeds take for granted. ... No one who is old enough to think for himself supposes that God lives in a local heaven. There is no longer any heaven in the traditional sense of the word. The same applies to hell in the sense of a mythical underworld beneath our feet. … Now that the forces and the laws of nature have been discovered, we can no longer believe in spirits, whether good or evil.[15]

Once demythologized, however, myth is compatible with science because it now refers both to the transcendent, nonphysical world and, even more, to humans' experience of the physical one.

Like Eliade, Bultmann urges moderns to accept myth. But where Eliade neglects to show how moderns can accept myth, Bultmann translates myth into existentialist terms in order to make it acceptable. At the same time he justifies his translation not on the pragmatic grounds that otherwise moderns could not accept it but on the grounds that its true subject matter *is* human existence: 'If the truth of the New Testament proclamation is to be preserved, the only way is to demythologize it. But our motive in so doing must not be to make the New Testament relevant to the modern world at all costs. The question is simply whether the New Testament message consists exclusively of mythology, or whether it [itself] actually demands the elimination of myth [at the literal level] if it is to be understood as it is meant to be.'[16] The incompatibility of literally read myth with science provides the opportunity to extricate the symbolic meaning of myth intended all along.

To say that myth is acceptable to scientifically minded moderns is not, however, to say why myth should be accepted. In providing a modern *subject matter* of myth, Bultmann provides no modern *function*. Perhaps for him the function is self-evident: myth serves to express the human condition. But why is it necessary to express that condition, and why is it necessary to express that condition through myth? Perhaps for Bultmann myth does not merely express but outright reveals the human condition, and perhaps for Bultmann myth alone does so. Still, what is the function served by that revelation? Why do humans need to know their condition? Bultmann never says.

Moreover, myth, even when demythologized, is acceptable to moderns only when the existence of God is. For as a religious existentialist rather than, like Jonas, a secular one, Bultmann takes myth to be preserving the reality of God, simply of a nonphysical god. Bultmann saves myth from science only insofar as moderns can accept even a sophisticated conception, not to mention a specifically Christian conception, of God. Where Eliade saves myth from science by appealing to the existence of distinctively modern myths – myths without gods in them – Bultmann retains an ancient myth with its God. Furthermore, at least Eliade tries to demonstrate that moderns, however avowedly atheistic, actually espouse myth. Bultmann merely leaves myth as something worthy of espousal. He does say that the message of myth need not be conscious: 'It goes without saying that this existential self-understanding need not be conscious.'[17] But he nowhere establishes that this message is commonly espoused.

[…]

C. G. Jung

C. G. Jung and Joseph Campbell offer the fullest reprieve to the death sentence that Tylor pronounces on myth.[18] For the two transform both the function and the subject matter of myth. Like Eliade, they make the function of myth more – indeed, other – than explanatory. Like Bultmann and Jonas, they make the subject of myth other than the physical world. Because I have discussed Campbell's theory at length elsewhere, I will focus here on Jung.[19]

For Jung, myth functions to reveal the existence of the unconscious: 'Myths are original revelations of the preconscious [i.e., collective] psyche, involuntary statements about unconscious psychic happenings. ... Modern psychology treats the products of unconscious fantasy-activity as self-portraits of what is going on in the unconscious, or as statements of the unconscious psyche about itself.'[20] Whoever takes myth literally *thinks* that it is revealing the existence of something external like the godhead and the immaterial world, but in fact it is revealing the workings of the unconscious.

Myth functions not merely to tell one about the unconscious but actually to open one up to it. Because the unconscious for Jung is inherently unconscious, one can never experience it directly but must experience it via myths and other symbolic manifestations.

Jung is entranced by ancient Gnosticism because he sees in it an uncanny parallel to the present.... for Jung the key similarity is the experience of alienation from *oneself.* The alienation is projected onto the world, so that one feels severed from the world, but one is really severed from oneself. The world is the manifestation, not the source, of that alienation.

For Jung, late antiquity and the twentieth century are the periods in Western history when human beings have most felt lost, aimless, unfulfilled, incomplete – with traditional myths and religions no longer working and humans consequently being cut off from their unconscious.

[...]

Jung, gives myth a reprieve by translating its subject matter into a contemporary idiom.... He makes sense psychologically of the state of Gnostics not merely upon receipt of the revelation but also both before and after. Jung renders into psychological lingo the course of Gnostic myths from the prefallen state of the world through the fallen one to the restored one.[21]

Understood in Jungian terms, Gnostic myths, which either present or presuppose a cosmogony, describe the development not of the world but of the human psyche. The godhead symbolizes the primordial unconscious. It is the source or agent of everything else. Prior to emanating anything, it lacks nothing. It is whole, self-sufficient, perfect. The godhead thus symbolizes the unconscious before the emergence of the ego out of it.

The emergence of matter alongside the material godhead symbolizes the beginning, but only the beginning, of the emergence of the ego out of the unconscious. Inert matter itself does not symbolize the ego, which requires a reflective entity conscious of itself as a subject distinct from the external world. The ego fully emerges not with the creation of either the Demiurge or Primal Man but only with the creation of individual human beings.

The ego is symbolized not by the spark but by the thinking part of the human world. The spark, as the link to the forgotten godhead, symbolizes the unconscious. As long as one remains unaware of the spark, one remains an unrealized self. As long as one's values are material, one is merely an ego.

Insofar as a Jungian interpretation of myth is psychological, it collapses the literal distinction between the outer world and humanity. Both matter and the body symbolize the development of the ego – raw matter symbolizing the beginning of the process and the thinking portion of the body the end. Similarly, both the immaterial godhead and the spark symbolize the unconscious, if also at opposite stages of development.

The ego in Jungian psychology develops not just alongside the unconscious but also out of it. Those Gnostic myths in which matter originates out of the godhead express the dependence of the ego on the unconscious. Those myths in which matter is preexistent and merely comes into contact with the godhead evince dissociation of the unconscious from the ego and thereby foreshadow the problems that dissociation spells.

Non-Gnostics, who for Jung's interpretation should also possess a divine spark, are not only ignorant of their origin and the origin of the world but also smugly content with the false, material nature of both. Their complacency makes them apt counterparts to nineteenth-century moderns. Gnostics have also forgotten the true nature of themselves and the world, but they are nevertheless dissatisfied with the existing nature of both. Their dissatisfaction makes them suitable counterparts to twentieth-century moderns.

If ignorance alone, according to Gnostic tenets, keeps humans tied to the material world, knowledge frees them from it. Because humans are ignorant, that knowledge must come from outside them. Because the powers of the material world are ignorant, too, that knowledge must come from beyond them as well. It can come from only the godhead. The dependence of humanity on the godhead matches the dependence of the ego on the unconscious to reveal itself.

The response of Gnostics to the revelation parallels that of twentieth-century moderns to their own discovery: gratitude. The disclosure of a heretofore unknown self and, for Gnostics, of a heretofore unknown world provides a fulfillment tantamount to salvation. As Jung says of twentieth-century moderns, 'I do not believe that I am going too far when I say that [twentieth-century] modern man, in contrast to his nineteenth-century brother, turns to the psyche with very great expectations, and does so without reference to any traditional creed but rather with a view to Gnostic experience.'[22]

The response of non-Gnostics to the revelation parallels that of nineteenth-century moderns to their own discovery: fear. The disclosure, which applies to non-Gnostics as well as to Gnostics, shatters the non-Gnostics' vaunted image of both human nature and the world.

Gnostic myths preach total identification with one's newly discovered divinity. Because that identification symbolizes the Gnostic's identification with the unconscious, Jungian psychology would consider it no less lopsided and no less dangerous than the non-Gnostic's identification with the ego – more precisely, with ego consciousness, or consciousness of the external world. Jungian psychology would consider both attitudes unbalanced. It would say that non-Gnostics, like nineteenth-century moderns, suffer from an exaggerated persona: their ego identifies itself wholly with the conscious, public personality. But Jungian psychology should equally say that Gnostics, whether or not twentieth-century moderns, suffer from an exaggerated, or inflated, ego, which, conversely, identifies itself wholly with the rediscovered unconscious. Minimally, the consequence of inflation is excessive pride in the presumed uniqueness of one's unconscious. Maximally, the consequence is outright psychosis, or the dissolution of any consciousness of the external world. The Jungian aim is no more to reject ego consciousness for the unconscious than, like the nineteenth-century aim, to reject the unconscious for ego consciousness. Rather, the aim is to balance the two.

Jung himself idiosyncratically interprets Gnosticism as seeking the equivalent of balance between ego consciousness and the unconscious rather than identification with the unconscious. Jung is so eager to find similarities between ancients and moderns that he misses the differences.[23] But Jung's misinterpretation of Gnosticism does not preclude a more accurate Jungian interpretation of Gnosticism, according to which Gnosticism espouses the equivalent of inflation rather than balance.

By interpreting the Gnostic's permanent return to the godhead as inflationary, Jungian psychology would even be able to make sense of what in Gnostic metaphysics is paradoxical: the creation by an omniscient and omnipotent godhead of a world that the godhead then seeks to destroy. Jungian psychology would make not the creation but the dissolution of the world the mistake. Though it would admittedly thereby be evaluating Gnosticism by its own world-affirming rather than world-rejecting ideal, it would at least be able to make sense of creation. The unconscious, as symbolized by the godhead, would not be erring in creating the ego, as symbolized by the material side of humanity. The unconscious would truly be both omniscient and omnipotent. It is the ego that would be neither: lacking both the knowledge and the will to resist the allure of the unconscious, it would be returning of its own accord to the unconscious, which, to be sure, would be enticing it.

… Jung would say that Gnostic mythology served not just to reveal the unconscious but actually to put Gnostics in touch with it. Jung even deems the Gnostics budding psychologists: 'it is clear beyond a doubt that many of the Gnostics were nothing other than psychologists.'[24] Jung thus accords Gnostic mythology, and mythology generally, a role as well as a viewpoint that is acceptable to moderns. Still, Jung does not go so far as Joseph Campbell, who proclaims myth outright indispensable. As valuable for Jung as myth is, religion, art, dream, and the 'active imagination' can serve as well, even if he sometimes loosely uses the term 'myth' to apply to all of them. For Jung, the functions that myth serves are themselves indispensable, but myth is not itself indispensable to serving them. And in even keener contrast to Campbell, myth for Jung can never substitute for therapy, to which it is only a most helpful adjunct.[25]

Jung grant[s] myth a future not only by providing a function as well as a subject matter that is acceptable to moderns but also, like Eliade, by uncovering modern as well as ancient myths. Jung does not claim to find modern *Gnostic* myths, but he does claim to find modern myths of other varieties. Because he psychologizes the subject matter of all myths, he circumvents Eliade's dilemma that myths acceptable to moderns lack the element necessary for their efficacy: gods. For Jung, gods are merely the symbols that ancient myths used to represent archetypes. Modern myths, using other symbols, are equally efficacious.

Whether the theories of myth discussed are correct is not at issue here. At issue is whether those theories commit themselves to a future for myth. Of the four theories that do – Eliade's, Bultmann's, Jonas's, and Jung's – Jung's theory envisions the brightest future for myth.

Notes

1   See Marcel Detienne, *The Creation of Mythology*. Translated by Margaret Cook (Chicago: University of Chicago Press, 1986), chaps. 3–5.

2   See Robert Ackerman, *The Myth and Ritual School*. Theorists of Myth Series, vol. 2 (New York: Garland Publishing, 1991), pp. 55–60.

3   See Edward Tylor, *Primitive Culture* [1871] II (Retitled *Religion in Primitive Culture*), 5th ed. (New York: Harper Torchbooks, 1958), 2:41, 85.

4   Ibid., p. 284.

5   See ibid., p. 85.

6   Ibid., p. 41.

7   See, for example, Carl G. Hempel, *Aspects of Scientific Explanation and Other Essays in the Philosophy of Science* (New York: Free Press, 1965), pp. 463–487.

8   On this interpretation of Adonis see my 'Adonis: A Greek Eternal Child', in *Myth and the Polis*, ed. Dora C. Pozzi and John M. Wickersham (Ithaca, NY: Cornell University Press, 1991), pp. 65–68.

9   See Wesley C. Salmon, 'Determinism and Indeterminism in Modern Science', in *Reason and Responsibility*, ed. Joel Fineberg, 2nd ed. (Encino, CA: Dickenson, 1971), p. 321.

10   See Tylor, *Primitive Culture*, 1:277–278, 408 ff.

11   Ibid., p. 277.

12   Mircea Eliade, *Myth and Reality*, trans. Willard R. Trask (New York: Harper Torchbooks, 1968 [1963]), p. 5.

13   Ibid., p. 11.

14 Ibid., p. 92.

15 Mircea Eliade, *The Sacred and the Profane*, trans. Willard R. Trask (New York: Harvest Books, 1968 [1959]), p. 82.

16 Gen. 3:8.

17 Eliade, *Sacred and Profane*, p. 82.

18 Hans Jonas, *The Gnostic Religion*, 2nd ed. (Boston, MA: Beacon, 1963 [1958]), p. 322.

19 Ibid., p. 324.

20 Ibid., p. 329.

21 See my *Joseph Campbell: An Introduction*, rev . ed. (New York: New American Library, 1990 [1987]).

22 C. G. Jung, 'The Psychology of the Child Archetype', in *The Archetypes and the Collective Unconscious*. Collected Works, vol. 9, pt. 1, 2nd ed., ed. Sir Herbert Read and others, trans. R. F. C. Hull and others (Princeton, NJ: Princeton University Press, 1968), pp. 154–155.

23 C. G. Jung, 'The Spiritual Problem of Modern Man', in *Civilization in Transition*. Collected Works, vol. 10, 2nd ed. (Princeton, NJ: Princeton University Press, 1970), pp. 83–84.

24 Ibid., p. 83.

25 See Jonas, *Gnostic Religion*, pp. 320–321.

References

Ackerman, Robert. (1991). *The Myth and Ritual School*. Theorists of Myth Series. Vol. 2. New York: Garland Publishing.

Detienne, Marcel. (1986). *The Creation of Mythology*. Translated by Margaret Cook. Chicago: University of Chicago Press.

Eliade, Mircea. (1968). *Myth and Reality* [1963]. Translated by Willard R. Trask. New York: Harper Torchbooks.

Eliade, Mircea. (1968). *The Sacred and the Profane* [1959]. Translated by Willard R. Trask. New York: Harvest Books.

Hempel, Carl G. (1965). *Aspects of Scientific Explanation and Other Essays in the Philosophy of Science*. New York: Free Press.

Jonas, Hans. (1954). *Gnosis und spätantiker Geist*. Vol. 2, pt. 1. Göttingen: Vandenhoeck & Ruprecht.

Jonas, Hans. (1963). *The Gnostic Religion* [1958]. 2nd ed. Boston, MA: Beacon.

Jonas, Hans. (1967). 'Delimitation of the Gnostic Phenomenon–Typological and Historical'. In *Le Origini dello Gnosticismo*. Edited by Ugo Bianchi. Supplements to *Numen*, XII, 90–108. Leiden: Brill.

Jonas, Hans. (1969). 'Myth and Mysticism: A Study of Objectification and Interiorization in Religious Thought'. *Journal of Religion* 49 (October): 315–329.

Jung, C. G. (1968). 'Gnostic Symbols of the Self'. In *Aion*, Collected Works. Vol. 9, pt. 2, 2nd ed., 184–221. Princeton, NJ: Princeton University Press.

Jung, C. G. (1968). 'The Psychology of the Child Archetype'. In *The Archetypes and the Collective Unconscious*. Collected Works. Vol. 9, pt. 1, 2nd ed. Edited by Sir Herbert

Read and others. Translated by R. F. C. Hull and others, 151–181. Princeton, NJ: Princeton University Press.

Jung, C. G. (1968). 'The Structure and Dynamics of the Self'. In *Aion*. Collected Works. Vol. 9, pt. 2, 2nd ed., 222–265. Princeton, NJ: Princeton University Press.

Jung, C. G. (1970). 'The Spiritual Problem of Modern Man'. In *Civilization in Transition*. Collected Works. Vol. 10, 2nd ed., 74–94. Princeton, NJ: Princeton University Press.

Salmon, Wesley C. (1971). 'Determinism and Indeterminism in Modern Science'. In *Reason and Responsibility*. Edited by Joel Fineberg. 2nd ed., 316–332. Encino, CA: Dickenson.

Segal, Robert A. (1990). *Joseph Campbell: An Introduction* [1987]. Rev. ed. New York: New American Library.

Segal, Robert A. (1991). 'Adonis: A Greek Eternal Child'. In *Myth and the Polis*. Edited by Dora C. Pozzi and John M. Wickersham, 64–85. Ithaca, NY: Cornell University Press.

Segal, Robert A., ed. (1992). *The Gnostic Jung*. Princeton, NJ: Princeton University Press; London: Routledge.

Tylor, Edward. (1958). *Primitive Culture* [1871] I (Retitled *The Origins of Culture*). 5th ed. New York: Harper Torchbooks.

Tylor, Edward. (1958). *Primitive Culture* [1871] II (Retitled *Religion in Primitive Culture*). 5th ed. New York: Harper Torchbooks.

Voegelin, Eric. (1952). *The New Science of Politics*. Chicago: University of Chicago Press.

Voegelin, Eric. (1968). *Science, Politics and Gnosticism*. Chicago: Regnery Gateway Editions.

Index